Building a Brand Image Through Electronic Customer Relationship Management

Arshi Naim
King Kalid University, Saudi Arabia

Sandeep Kumar Kautish
Lord Buddha Education Foundation, Asia Pacific University, India

A volume in the Advances in Marketing, Customer Relationship Management, and E-Services (AMCRMES) Book Series

IGI Global
PUBLISHER of TIMELY KNOWLEDGE

Published in the United States of America by
IGI Global
Business Science Reference (an imprint of IGI Global)
701 E. Chocolate Avenue
Hershey PA, USA 17033
Tel: 717-533-8845
Fax: 717-533-8661
E-mail: cust@igi-global.com
Web site: http://www.igi-global.com

Library of Congress Cataloging-in-Publication Data

Names: Naim, Arshi, 1976- editor.
Title: Building a brand image through electronic customer relationship management / Arshi Naim and Sandeep Kautish, editors.
Description: Hershey, PA : Business Science Reference, [2023] | Includes bibliographical references and index. | Summary: "The goal of this book is to develop electronic customer relationship management (ECRM) systems strategies for organizations to attract and retain customers over the internet, achieving customer satisfaction for fast moving customer goods allowing organizations to meet their strategic and customer loyalty objectives while building brand image"-- Provided by publisher.
Identifiers: LCCN 2022018660 (print) | LCCN 2022018661 (ebook) | ISBN 9781668453865 (hardcover) | ISBN 9781668453872 (paperback) | ISBN 9781668453889 (ebook)
Subjects: LCSH: Customer relations--Management. | Branding (Marketing) | Consumer satisfaction.
Classification: LCC HF5415.5 .B83 2023 (print) | LCC HF5415.5 (ebook) | DDC 658.8/12--dc23/eng/20220701
LC record available at https://lccn.loc.gov/2022018660
LC ebook record available at https://lccn.loc.gov/2022018661

This book is published in the IGI Global book series Advances in Marketing, Customer Relationship Management, and E-Services (AMCRMES) (ISSN: 2327-5502; eISSN: 2327-5529)

British Cataloguing in Publication Data
A Cataloguing in Publication record for this book is available from the British Library.

Advances in Marketing, Customer Relationship Management, and E-Services (AMCRMES) Book Series

ISSN:2327-5502
EISSN:2327-5529

MISSION

Business processes, services, and communications are important factors in the management of good customer relationship, which is the foundation of any well organized business. Technology continues to play a vital role in the organization and automation of business processes for marketing, sales, and customer service. These features aid in the attraction of new clients and maintaining existing relationships.

The Advances in Marketing, Customer Relationship Management, and E-Services (AMCRMES) Book Series

addresses success factors for customer relationship management, marketing, and electronic services and its performance outcomes. This collection of reference source covers aspects of consumer behavior and marketing business strategies aiming towards researchers, scholars, and practitioners in the fields of marketing management.

COVERAGE

- Cases on Electronic Services
- Web Mining and Marketing
- CRM in financial services
- B2B marketing
- Electronic Services
- Relationship Marketing
- Cases on CRM Implementation
- Ethical Considerations in E-Marketing
- Telemarketing
- CRM and customer trust

IGI Global is currently accepting manuscripts for publication within this series. To submit a proposal for a volume in this series, please contact our Acquisition Editors at Acquisitions@igi-global.com or visit: http://www.igi-global.com/publish/.

The Advances in Marketing, Customer Relationship Management, and E-Services (AMCRMES) Book Series (ISSN 2327-5502) is published by IGI Global, 701 E. Chocolate Avenue, Hershey, PA 17033-1240, USA, www.igi-global.com. This series is composed of titles available for purchase individually; each title is edited to be contextually exclusive from any other title within the series. For pricing and ordering information please visit http://www.igi-global.com/book-series/advances-marketing-customer-relationship-management/37150. Postmaster: Send all address changes to above address.

Titles in this Series

For a list of additional titles in this series, please visit:
www.igi-global.com/book-series/advances-marketing-customer-relationship-management/37150

Cases on Social Justice in China and Perspectives on Chinese Brands
Youssef El Haoussine (Beijing Normal University - Hong Kong Baptist University United International College, China) and Lulu Wang (Sinotrend Consulting, China)
Business Science Reference • © 2023 • 335pp • H/C (ISBN: 9781668449554) • US $215.00

Implementing Automation Initiatives in Companies to Create Better-Connected Experiences
Jorge Remondes (Instituto Superior de Entre Douro e Vouga, Portugal & ISCAP, Instituto Politécnico do Porto, Portugal) and Sandrina Teixeira (ISCAP, Instituto Politécnico do Porto, Portugal)
Business Science Reference • © 2022 • 320pp • H/C (ISBN: 9781668455388) • US $250.00

Social Customer Relationship Management (Social-CRM) in the Era of Web 4.0
Nedra Bahri Ammari (IHEC of Carthage, Tunisia)
Business Science Reference • © 2022 • 317pp • H/C (ISBN: 9781799895534) • US $250.00

Handbook of Research on Global Perspectives on International Advertising
Ipek Krom (Istanbul Esenyurt University, Turkey)
Business Science Reference • © 2022 • 397pp • H/C (ISBN: 9781799896722) • US $315.00

Handbook of Research on Consumer Behavior Change and Data Analytics in the Socio-Digital Era
Pantea Keikhosrokiani (School of Computer Sciences, Universiti Sains Malaysia, Malaysia)
Business Science Reference • © 2022 • 458pp • H/C (ISBN: 9781668441688) • US $315.00

Handbook of Research on Interdisciplinary Reflections of Contemporary Experiential Marketing Practices
Gökhan Akel (Antalya Akev University, Turkey)
Business Science Reference • © 2022 • 596pp • H/C (ISBN: 9781668443804) • US $315.00

Developing Relationships, Personalization, and Data Herald in Marketing 5.0
Jasmine Kaur (Chitkara Business School, Chitkara University, Punjab, India) Priya Jindal (Chitkara Business School, Chitkara University, Punjab, India) and Amandeep Singh (Chitkara Business School, Chitkara University, India)
Business Science Reference • © 2022 • 327pp • H/C (ISBN: 9781668444962) • US $250.00

IGI Global
PUBLISHER of TIMELY KNOWLEDGE

701 East Chocolate Avenue, Hershey, PA 17033, USA
Tel: 717-533-8845 x100 • Fax: 717-533-8661
E-Mail: cust@igi-global.com • www.igi-global.com

Table of Contents

Detailed Table of Contents

intention in the fast-moving consumer goods (FMCG) industry in Malaysia. Five important E-CRM elements of service quality, customisation, transaction security, online feedback, and website features will be explored as antecedents to customer satisfaction and its effect on repurchase intention. Stimulus-organism-response (S-O-R) theory offered the underpinning theoretical explanation in the development of the conceptual framework for this study. By using empirical study to prove the relationship effect, the study provides better understanding of consumers' experiences on E-CRM strategies implemented by the FMCG firms, and its roles in building customer satisfaction and repurchase intention. FMCG firms can leverage on the proposed strategies to improve their E-CRM planning, implementation, and controlling to achieve desired business performance.

Chapter 3
Development of Effective Electronic Customer Relationship Management (ECRM) Model by the Applications of Web Intelligence Analytics 44
Salma Abdulaziz Alquhtani, King Khalid University, Saudi Arabia
Anandhavalli Muniasamy, King Khalid University, Saudi Arabia

Analysis of customer relationships based on their satisfaction is a practical and motivating success factor for the growth of every company. Web intelligence describes the scientific development that uses information technology and artificial intelligence for new frameworks, services, and products provided by the web. This chapter aims to present the model of analyzing the users' sentiments from their online reviews on an e-commerce platform using machine-learning classifiers, namely naive bayes, logistic regression, support vector machine, and neural network. For data analysis, latent semantic analysis has been applied to examine the most frequent words used in online reviews. Finally, customers' interest in online shopping analysis has been performed to classify the customers' sentiments from their posted reviews on the e-commerce platform. In addition, the authors compared the performance results of these classifiers on the e-commerce dataset. The results reveal that the naive bayes classifier has performed better than all the other three classifiers.

Chapter 4
Content Marketing Framework for Building Brand Image: A Case Study of Sohar International School, Oman 64
Muhammad Saleem, University of Buraimi, Oman
Shad Ahmad Khan, University of Buraimi, Oman
Hesham Magd, Modern College of Business and Science, Oman

In an increasingly interconnected digital world, content marketing plays a pivotal role in building the brand image of contemporary organizations. For the current study, a leading international school in Oman is selected to study the effectiveness of their content marketing over the last two years and as a result to develop a framework,

which can be followed by other organizations as well. The school's content marketing efforts and active social media presence consistently had a positive impact on their audiences resulting in high enrollments even during the unprecedented times under the COVID-19 scenario. This study utilizes the tools like netnography and thematic analysis of the qualitative data. Considering the dimensions of AIDA model, an analysis is done as to how effective content marketing can grab the attention of consumers through eye-catching images and videos, making them indulge and develop interest in the content's usefulness, followed by a strong desire to avail the organization's services, and finally opting for the action to use the services.

Sara Kamal, Albarkat Institute of Management Studies, India
Arshi Naim, King Khalid University, Saudi Arabia
Hesham Magd, Faculty of Business and Economics, Modern College of Business and Science, Oman
Shad Ahmad Khan, College of Business, University of Buraimi, Oman
Farheen Mujeeb Khan, ICFAI University, Dehradun, India

The purpose of this study is to determine the relationship of e-service quality (ESQ) and ease of use (EOU) to electronic customer relationship management (E-CRM), which is referred by brand image (BI). This study presents the relevance of e-commerce (E-COM) in the business world especially in the pandemic situation and how ESQ, EOU contributes in building E-CRM. To show the relation between variables, the authors have applied scattered methods under correlation analysis. The sample was asked various closed ended questions in the domain of ESQ for E-CRM, EOU for E-CRM, ESQ for BI, EOU for BI. The results showed that there is a relationship between BI and E-CRM, ESQ and BI, ESQ and E-CRM, EOU and BI. There is no direct relation between EOU and E-CRM, but BI can facilitate in building the E-CRM. Also, the results show the direct relation between ESQ and E-CRM referred by BI.

Sadaf Fatima, Aligarh Muslim University, India
Hamed Alqahtani, King Khalid University, Saudi Arabia
Arshi Naim, King Khalid University, Saudi Arabia
Fatma Alma'alwi, King Khalid University, Saudi Arabia

The aim of the research is to examine the effect of social media marketing activities on brand awareness, brand image, and brand loyalty. In addition, it has been aimed

Preface

INTRODUCTION

Building a Brand Image Through Electronic Customer Relationship Management will apply ECRM strategies for achieving customer satisfaction for building brand image. This book will provide concepts and planning policies to the organizations and academicians to learn new trends of doing business and explain the concepts of ECRM and technologies that can be applied amid COVID:19 in the business processes to meet their strategic objectives and customer loyalty, build brand image.

Effective e-customer relationship management is imperative for increasing customer satisfaction, online sales, website patronage, loyalty, and retention. To understand exactly how this business strategy can be applied to enhance business operations, further study on its various benefits, opportunities, and challenges is required.

Building a Brand Image Through Electronic Customer Relationship Management develops electronic customer relationship management strategies for achieving customer satisfaction and explains the concepts and uses of electronic customer relationship management to meet strategic objectives, improve customer loyalty, and build brand image. Covering topics such as marketing, brand equity, customer loyalty, and social media, this reference work is ideal for business owners, managers, entrepreneurs, industry professionals, researchers, scholars, practitioners, academicians, instructors, and students.

Electronic customer relationship management (ECRM) is a comprehensive business and marketing strategy for attracting and retaining customers over the internet. ECRM involves the integration of Web channels into the overall enterprise CRM strategy with the goal of driving consistency within all channels relative to sales, customer service and support (CSS) and marketing initiatives, the benefits of E-CRM include Improved customer relations, service and support, Matching the customers' behavior with suitable offers, Increased customer satisfaction and loyalty, Greater efficiency and cost reduction, Increased business revenue.

ECRM is a blend of various components that include an e-commerce selling platform, customer communication infrastructure, and business applications. Effective E-Customer Relationship Management (ECRM) is a strategic imperative for increasing customer satisfaction and service, online sales, website patronage, loyalty, and retention.

The impact of this book will be on Academicians, Business Professionals/ Entrepreneurs, researchers, IS/IT experts. Academic and industry researchers, designers working on business information system, design and engineering for ECRM applications. They will receive the updated trends and unique aspects of ECRM for building brand image, achieving customer loyalty and customer satisfaction that eventually facilitate in their learning, profit maximization and ways to reach out to the customers, wholesalers and retailor in an online environment.

This book will provide great value to the educational sector such as to post graduate students, researchers, academicians and to the business sectors such as firms in fast moving customer goods (FMCG) categories who are willing to know the latest trends, methods, tools and techniques that can be applied by ECRM to achieve customer satisfaction.

Firms will be able to optimize profit, can use new ways of digital marketing, improve electronic supply chain management and develop new strategies for ECRM for different types of products such as consumer electronics, over the counter medicines, beverages, fashion products, etc.

This book focuses on the paradigm of customer relationship management (CRM), regarding the principles of customer value and the constructs of customer loyalty and customer satisfaction. The significance of customer relationship management is to lead to satisfied and loyal customers. From one side it is oriented to synchronize relations between the customers and the firms in businesses; from the other side it is dedicated to optimize sources of information for better comprehension of consumer behavior. The CRM outline the main directions for development of customer's oriented products, high level consumer service and long term partnership with the company audiences and it is also an instrument of the intelligent company management in the field of customers relationship, taking into consideration the personal preferences and characteristics.

CHAPTER DESCRIPTIONS

Chapter 1: E-CRM in Digital Payment Services – Its Role and Proposed Framework for Adoption

Supported by technology, digital payment expanded at a rapid pace in the last decade, constantly reducing cash transactions across the world. Across the world, the shift to digital payments witnessed a dramatic rise due to the COVID-19 pandemic. As the benefits look to surpass the shortcomings, the adoption of digital payments is still affected by barriers of different kinds for different stakeholders, mainly the customers. Customer relationship management is a strategic tool that aids in retaining and improving customers' experiences. More importantly, the developments in electronic customer relationship management like the inclusion of social media, various communication channels, and web-based tools may facilitate customer adoption and satisfaction. Therefore, the role of e-CRM in digital companies needs detailed scrutiny from theoretical and practical perspectives. This chapter provides an overview of the current state of the digital payment industry and proposes a framework for the integration of e-CRM in digital payment companies.

Chapter 2: The Role of E-CRM in Building Customer Satisfaction and Repurchase Intention – Evidence from the FMCG Industry

In this era of technology, electronic customer relationship management (E-CRM) is becoming more prominently used by businesses in various industries. This chapter aims to investigate the effect of E-CRM on customer satisfaction and repurchase intention in the fast-moving consumer goods (FMCG) industry in Malaysia. Five important E-CRM elements of service quality, customisation, transaction security, online feedback and website features will be explored as antecedents to customer satisfaction and its effect on repurchase intention. Stimulus Organism-Response (S-O-R) theory offered the underpinning theoretical explanation in the development of the conceptual framework for this study. By using empirical study to prove the relationships effect, the study provides better understanding of consumers' experiences on E-CRM strategies implemented by the FMCG firms, and its roles in building customer satisfaction and repurchase intention. FMCG firms can leverage on the proposed strategies to improve their E-CRM planning, implementation and controlling to achieve desired business performance.

Chapter 3: Development of Effective Electronic Customer Relationship Management (ECRM) Model by the Applications of Web Intelligence Analytics

Analysis of customer relationships based on their satisfaction is reaching a practical and motivating success factor for the growth of every company. Web intelligence describes the scientific development that uses information technology and artificial intelligence for new frameworks, services, and products provided by the web. This chapter aims to present the model of analyzing the users' sentiments from their online reviews on an e-commerce platform using machine-learning classifiers namely Naive Bayes, Logistic regression, Support Vector Machine, and Neural Network. For data analysis, Latent semantic analysis has been applied to examine the most frequent words used in online reviews. Finally, customers' interest in online shopping analysis has been performed to classify the customers' sentiment from their posted reviews on the e-commerce platform. In addition, we compared the performance results of these classifiers on the e-commerce dataset. The results reveal that the Naive Bayes classifier has performed better than all the other three classifiers.

Chapter 4: Content Marketing Framework for Building Brand Image – A Case Study of Sohar International School, Oman

In an increasingly interconnected digital world, content marketing plays a pivotal role in in building the brand image of contemporary organizations. For the current study, a leading international school in Oman is selected to study the effectiveness of their content marketing over the last two years and as a result, to develop a framework, which can be followed by other organizations as well. The school's content marketing efforts and active social media presence consistently had a positive impact on their audiences resulting in high enrollments even during the unprecedented times under COVID 19 scenario. This study utilizes the tools like netnography and thematic analysis of the qualitative data. Considering the dimensions of AIDA model, an analysis is done as to how effective content marketing can grab the Attention of consumers through eye-catching images and videos, making them indulge and develop Interest in the content's usefulness, followed by a strong desire to avail the organization's services, and finally opting for the Action to use the services.

Chapter 5: The Relationship Between E-Service Quality, Ease of Use, and ECRM Performance Referred by Brand Image

The purpose of this study is to determine the relationship of E-Service Quality (ESQ) and Ease of Use (EOU) to Electronic Customer Relationship Management

(E-CMR) which is referred by Brand image (BI). This study presents the relevance of e-commerce (E-Com) in the business world especially in the pandemic situation and how ESQ, EOU contributes in building ECRM.To show the relation between variable, we have applied scattered method under correlation analysis. The sample was asked various closed ended questions in the domain of ESQ for ECRM, EOU for ECRM, ESQ for BI, EOU for BI. The results showed that there is a relationship between BI and ECRM, ESQ and BI, ESQ and E- CRM, EOU and BI. There is no direct relation between EOU and ECRM but BI can facilitate in building the ECRM. Also the results show the direct relations between ESQ and ECRM referred by BI.

Chapter 6: ECRM Through Social Media Marketing Activities for Brand Awareness, Brand Image, and Brand Loyalty

The aim of the research is to examine the effect of social media marketing activities on brand awareness, brand image and brand loyalty. In addition, it has been aimed to analyze the effect of brand awareness and brand image on brand loyalty in this research. The population of the research consists of the consumers who actively follow five brands with the highest social score according to the Marketing Gulf social media brand performance data on social media communication channels such as Facebook, Twitter and Instagram. In this research, qualitative method has been used and research data has been obtained via online questionnaires shared on social media from 100 brand followers and their responses were scaled on Likert scale. As a result of the analysis, social media marketing activities have been found as effective factors on brand image and brand loyalty, besides it has been determined that the most obvious effect seen on brand awareness. Also, brand awareness and brand image have a significant effect on brand loyalty, though brand awareness has a limited effect on the brand image

Chapter 7: Critical Success Factors for Transforming CRM to SCRM for Building ECRM

In the current scenario, entire Middle East is witnessing drastic digitalization and consumer behavior is also widely affected by the technological development. This has created a platform for the growth of E-commerce (Ecom) in the Middle East through social networking. The success factors that facilitate in transforming the customer relationship management (CRM to Social Customer Relationship management (SCRM) for achieving electronic customer relationship management (ECRM) are customer values and customer loyalty. These success factors are digitally termed as electronic customer values (ECV) and Electronic Customer Loyalty (ECL). This study has involved 100 digital consumers of Ecom on various social apps and social networking in the middle- east. This study is an empirical analysis where ten critical success factors are measured to achieve the positiveness of ECV to contribute in ECL success. ECL success can transform CRM to SCRM and build strong ECRM.

Chapter 8: CRM as Antecedent of Electronic Retailing and Online Customer Satisfaction

As location-based banking continues to give way for online banking globally, this paper examines whether E-tailing practices yield customer satisfaction. The paper also examines how CRM influences E-tailing and whether E-tailing can serve as a medium through which CRM yields customer satisfaction. Data, conveniently collected from 681 bank customers, was used for this study and analysed with PLS-SEM. The study found that CRM practices lead to better customer retail buying experiences for banks. E-tailing, mostly perceived by customers as an innovation in the service delivery process of banks, improved the image perceptions of banks. The study suggests that as part of a digital channel configuration, banks must build customer relationship marketing technologies as a backbone.

Chapter 9: Brand Extension in FMCG Sector Through Social Media-Enabled CRM and Investigating Its Impact on Brand Equity

Web technologies have enabled companies to have a personalized and interactive relationship with the customers thus engaging customers in improved experience. The disruptive free tools and techniques of Social media are used to foster effective E-CRM. Companies like ITC, HUL, P&G, and many multinational companies are using the existing brand name for new product launch as a marketing strategy for brand extension and therefore exploiting Brand equity amongst loyal customers. The study is an effort to examine the effects of FMCG ITC Aashirwaad Social CRM brand extensions strategies on customer engagement behaviour and brand equity. The study further investigates the effect of Product extension perceived Fit, Brand Image, Brand Experience and Brand love on Customer Engagement Behaviour. To test and validate the proposed model of the present study has employed Structural equation modelling with a sample size of 462 respondents. The findings show that Social CRM brand extensions strategy does affect customer engagement and brand equity.

Chapter 10: Application of MIS in ECRM – A Literature Review in FMCG Supply Chain

The proliferating demands of consumers today have sparked the need for ECRM, leveraging the technological advancements in MIS and its applications. This chapter elaborates tracking and maintaining ECRM by means of Big Data Analytics tools and Artificial Intelligence algorithms. It elucidates the predictions and forecasts a business makes based on consumer behaviour, the chapter further delves into the various avenues of Artificial Intelligence (AI). The taxonomy of AI is explained and its decision making capability is applied to design and simulate effective SCM systems Various AI methods are holistically applied to the FMCG supply chain context. In this chapter the role of Big Data Analytics in aiding the enterprises to maintain ECRM by studying consumer preferences and choices is explored, further advancing into its applications in maintaining FMCG supply chain. This research report provides the various methods of AI used in supply chain and the Data Analytics tools employed in maintaining ECRM and the FMCG supply chain, as our world spins around consumer goods.

Chapter 11: Entrepreneurial Marketing of E-CRM in SMEs

Marketing in medium and small-scale enterprises (SME's) is all together very different to marketing as proposed theoretically for large organizations. This chapter is dedicated to the gathered research evidences on the effect and impact of (IBTs) on the customer relationship management (CRM) activities (i.e. e-CRM) of SMEs in Gurgaon. Design/Approach A cocktail method approach including an online in-depth interviews, online questionnaire and projective techniques was followed. On 286 respondents, factor analysis was carried out, leading to communication With customers and management of customer information being processed as the main area within the e-CRM in SMEs. Findings In order to provide better communication and information management abilities to varying customers, SMEs is following relatively simple IBTs. It is as harder to consolidate customer information into their decision making than just the communication side of it. we can say in SMEs, e-CRM tries to be ad hoc rather than strategic.

Chapter 12: Alert-Driven Customer Relationship Management in Online Travel Agencies – Event-Condition-Actions Rules and Key Performance Indicators

Currently, online travel agencies (OTA) allow their customers to make timely travel reservations anytime and anywhere through websites and mobile technologies.

Customer service is vital to the success of any tourism and hospitality business, including online travel agencies. One major challenge that online travel agencies face is continuously declining customer experience because this may result in a high customer churn rate. Customer relationship management (CRM) is a strategy used by most organizations to increase customers' lifetime value by selecting customers and maintaining their relationships. Delivering timely and consistently higher customer service levels are goal of every OTA, and they need to evolve and implement a new approach to address customer issues proactively to increase customer retention and loyalty. This study analyzes some common CRM workflows of OTAs and proposes an alert-driven approach to CRM to enhance their effectiveness in creating satisfying customer experiences and retaining customers.

CONCLUSION

This book will provide well-balanced coverage of important ECRM strategies, E-commerce practices, marketing aspects, Social CRM, Electronic supply chain management and Electronic procurement. The title is also one of the only comprehensive academic texts to focus on the broad scope of CRM solutions from a marketing management perspective. *Building a Brand Image Through Electronic Customer Relationship Management* will provide the practitioners looking to update their work with new and proven techniques developed to increase their marketing power and versatility, some of the specific topics readers will learn more about in the book include ECRM system, Ecommerce categories, Digital Marketing, role of management information systems in CRM and Electronic supply chain management.

Arshi Naim
King Kalid University, Saudi Arabia

Sandeep Kumar Kautish
Lord Buddha Education Foundation, Asia Pacific University, India

Acknowledgment

We are delighted to welcome the readers of our new book *Building a Brand Image Through Electronic Customer Relationship Management*. We congratulate all chapter authors for their valuable submissions and keeping patience during critical review process. We wish to thank all reviewers as well who spared their precious time for the review process.

We are thankful to our family members and friends for giving me eternal happiness and support during the entire process.

Last but not the least, we express our gratitude to the almighty god for blessing us with wonderful life and showing us right paths in our all ups and downs during the so far journey of life.

Chapter 1
E-CRM in Digital Payment Services:
Its Role and Proposed Framework for Adoption

Najmul Hoda
https://orcid.org/0000-0002-1772-7551
Umm Al-Qura University, Saudi Arabia

ABSTRACT

Supported by technology, digital payment expanded at a rapid pace in the last decade, constantly reducing cash transactions across the world. Across the world, the shift to digital payments witnessed a dramatic rise due to the COVID-19 pandemic. As the benefits look to surpass the shortcomings, the adoption of digital payments is still affected by barriers of different kinds for different stakeholders, mainly the customers. Customer relationship management is a strategic tool that aids in retaining and improving customers' experiences. More importantly, the developments in electronic customer relationship management like the inclusion of social media, various communication channels, and web based tools may facilitate customer adoption and satisfaction. Therefore, the role of e-CRM in digital companies needs detailed scrutiny from theoretical and practical perspectives. This chapter provides an overview of the current state of the digital payment industry and proposes a framework for the integration of e-CRM in digital payment companies.

DOI: 10.4018/978-1-6684-5386-5.ch001

INTRODUCTION

In the recent past, multiple factors have led to the adoption of online processes by organizations. One compelling factor was the emergence of the pandemic Covid-19 that forced a massive disruption in various ways, affecting human lives in totality. But even before the pandemic, other factors were resulting in the rapid adoption of electronic transactions. These factors are, "consumer behavior, emerging technologies, competition, as well as regulatory push" (Nair & Prabhu, 2018). Payment method is an extremely significant process for any business, that traditionally relied on cash but has seen a paradigm shift to digital methods. Apart from various other benefits such as speed, convenience, cost-effectiveness, and development of safe technology, digital payments proved to be a panacea during the pandemic. It allowed customers to operate without contact, minimizing the need for physical interactions. Several contactless payment methods such as e-Wallets, peer-to-peer transfers, customer-to-business payments, mobile payments, etc. gained wide acceptance when the exchange of cash was discouraged. As a result, the digital payment industry has seen a sharp rise with a projected CAGR of 15.4% from USD 88.1 billion in 2021 to USD 180.2 billion by 2026 (Markets and Markets, 2021).

The growth of digital payment services is a disruptive phenomenon as it has impacted every type of industry in varying degrees. It has been seen that the use of digital payment as an innovative strategy boosted the growth of many companies across the world. Many studies have highlighted the role of digital payments at various levels and strata of the economy and society. Such an upscaling of digital technology means more demand for improved solutions and more space for competition within the digital payments industry. The payment services have now taken the form of a "commodity" with consumers demanding higher value. FinTech companies have been mainly responsible for this dramatic upheaval in payment technology. This change was a boon to the Generation Z individuals who are more accustomed to modern technologies. It was also adopted by business firms because it brings strategic benefits in the form of, "better inventory management; improving customer satisfaction; improved cash flow; minimizing theft of cash; accuracy in recording" (Emergen Research, 2022). Further, government policies have also been favorable to the switch to cashless transactions.

Customer relationship management is, "a business approach that integrates People, Processes, and Technology to maximize the relations of organizations with all types of customers" (Hoda, 2010). The core function of CRM is to integrate data from various channels to, "sustain and enhance customer relationships" (Rostami et al., 2016). The various benefits of an effective CRM accrue in the form of revenues, profitability, and overall business growth. Industries that are characterized by "high value per client and greater availability of customer data" are said to benefit more from CRM. The banking and financial services industry has long been using CRM. It plays a significant role in the overall value creation by providing a better insight into the customer buying preferences and factors of satisfaction.

As a result of the advances in database technology and the availability of various communication media, electronic customer relationship management (e-CRM) has been adopted in different industries. Electronic customer relationship management (e-CRM) is, "a management strategy that combines marketing with information technology to gain customers' satisfaction" (Rao, 2013). While the traditional CRM used phones, distribution outlets, or fax, the e-CRM is characterized by the usage of the latest communication technologies such as e-mails, social media, etc. (Al-dmour et al., 2017). Traditional CRM is more human and based on a personal approach, whereas e-CRM is completely technical and adopts advanced ICT tools to achieve customer satisfaction and increase loyalty (Bhatnagar & Saxena, 2013). Electronic customer relationship management improves and increases the relationship between the company and its clients by creating and enhancing customer relationships through new technology.

The main aim of this chapter is to discuss the characteristics of e-CRM, the benefits of e-CRM for the digital payment industry, and the critical factors in the adoption of e-CRM in the digital payments industry. Following the introduction, the next sections include a discussion on e-CRM, the role of e-CRM in digital payment services, critical factors in the adoption of e-CRM in digital payment services, and a conclusion.

BACKGROUND

Electronic Customer Relationship Management

e-CRM is a "web-centric approach to synchronize customer relationships, business functions, and audiences" (Abu-Shanab & Anagreh, 2015). It involves the collection and categorization of customer information for delivering better value. This information may be regarding the various customer transactions with the company such as, "payment methods, purchases, and customers' interests" (Abu-Shanab & Anagreh, 2015). It offers multiple benefits to a firm in the form of, "acquisition of new customers, retention of existing customers, cross-selling, and enhancing overall customer value" (Oanh, n.d.). Further, Roh et al (Roh et al., 2005) mention that it allows both in "developing and maintain new channels as well as establish long term relationship with the customers". e-CRM is a "key component of electronic marketing" (Fjermestad & Romano, 2003). The communication channels generally used by the financial services industry are, "internet banking; telebanking; e-mail service; mobile banking" (Abu-Shanab & Anagreh, 2015).

Definitions of e-CRM

Electronic customer relationship management (e-CRM) has been defined in different ways. A simple definition of e-CRM is that it is a tool to, "develop customer relationships by utilizing internet facilities" (Adnan et al., 2021). Other notable definitions of e-CRM found in the literature are listed below.

"a marketing strategy for organizations that uses Internet and web applications and technologies to identify, categorize and serve customers for enhancing their loyalty and generating profit" (Usman et al., 2012).

"a service with a web-based application to create and increase levels of service quality satisfaction and information confidence; the results in an increase in customer interaction, potentially helping companies achieve what is called maximizing portfolio profits" (Adnan et al., 2021).

"a strategy of marketing, selling and integration of online service which plays a role of identifying, obtaining and maintaining the customers who they are the largest assets of the companies" (Al-dmour et al., 2017)

In terms of financial services, (Miremadi et al., 2012) defined e-CRM as,

"a set of activities that enable the firms to utilize the new technology of the internet to implement CRM".

Types of e-CRM

e-CRM is classified into two types – operational and analytical e-CRM (Khodakarami & Chan, 2011). These are explained below.

i. Operational e-CRM – This type of e-CRM focuses on the customers' processes. It includes facilities such as "voice reaction systems, mobile telephones, and customer established communication centers" (Maroofi et al., 2012).
ii. Analytical e-CRM – This type of e-CRM is internal to an organization and deals with the technology to handle the customer data (Sivaraks et al., 2011).

Digital Payment Services

A "digital payment", also called "electronic payment" is, "the transfer of money or digital currency from one account to another using digital payment technologies such as mobile wallets or mobile payment apps" (Insider Intelligence, 2021). Digital payment is an "umbrella term that encompasses a range of technologies used in different payment instruments that enable payments through digital modes" (Markets and Markets, 2021). The transaction requires infrastructural support such as, "point of sale (POS) machines; mobile applications; GPRS machines; Bluetooth dongles; cloud computing; data analytics technology; internet of things".

Digital payment process

Electronic payment transactions can be classified into two types – "debit pull and credit push" (CGAP, 2019). The debit pull transaction is initiated by the merchant on behalf of the customer. On the other hand, the credit push transaction starts with the customer's action, like using the mobile app. Like any other monetary transaction, digital payment also essentially needs two parties, "the payer and the payee". Further, payments are generally classified into, "few-to-many; many-to-many; and many-to-few" (PiStrategy, 2016). The process of digital payment is depicted in *Figure 1*. It starts from the service provided by the issuing bank (app/card/internet banking) to its customer. The customer initiates the process by using the service to pay for an order. This process gets authorized by the payment gateway and then reaches the acquiring bank. The information then reaches the credit card (or debit card) network where the payment is approved. Finally, the seller (merchant) receives the credit.

Players in Digital Payment

The main players in the digital payment ecosystem are explained below.

a. Issuers – These are banks or financial institutions that issue the cards authorized by the card networks.
b. Acquirer – These are banks or financial institutions that enable the merchant (seller) to accept digital payment.
c. Credit card networks – They are the providers of electronic services that facilitate payments through cards.
d. Payment processors – They are also called "merchant service providers" and mainly help the sellers in processing their digital payment transactions.

Figure 1. Payment process cycle
Source: Author

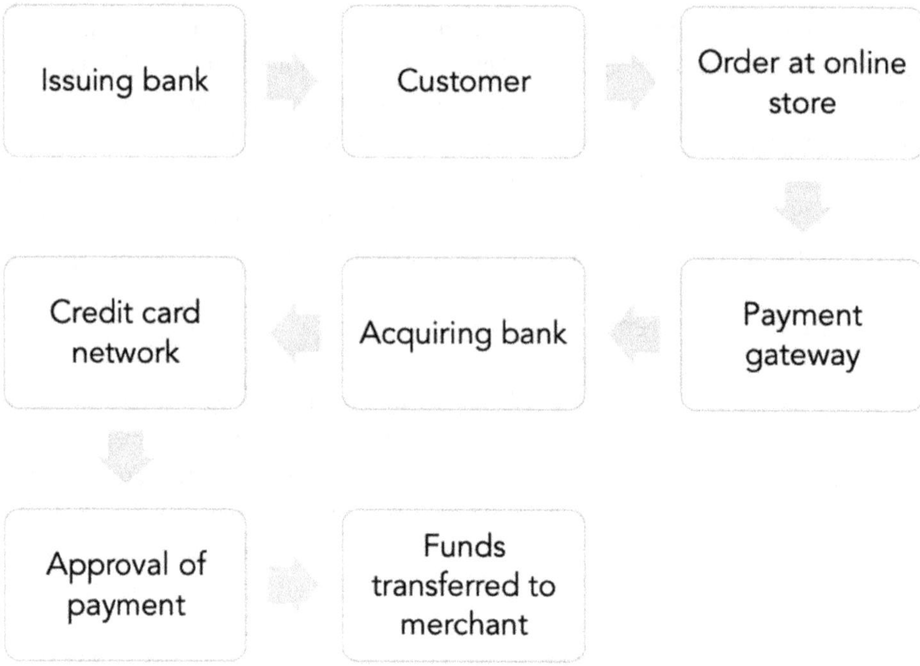

e. Payment gateways – These are mainly the "software applications" that allow digital transactions for merchants. It can be entirely or partially digital (online shopping or point of sale payment).
f. Independent Sales Organizations – These are commonly called ISOs and act as an intermediary between the sellers, payment processors, and acquirers.
g. Payment facilitators – These are similar to ISOs but it offers services to sub-merchants.

The process of digital payment includes various revenue points such as transaction discounting rate (TDR), special charges for international transactions, maintenance and support costs, setup fees, and other charges.

Role of e-CRM in Digital Payment

The fast-changing digital payments landscape has brought additional challenges to the players in the digital payments industry. A summary of the main trends in this industry is mentioned in a study by (Nair & Prabhu, 2018) are listed below.

i. New disruptions – The entry of technology companies, popularly called GAFA (Google, Apple, Facebook, and Amazon), have resulted in the obsolescence of existing methods. New technologies such as "virtual reality or voice-first solutions" are adding more value to the customers.
ii. Real-time technologies – The speed of transactions is continuously being enhanced by the innovative technologies mainly being introduced by the technology players than the banks.
iii. Standardization in the industry – Globally, the digital payments industry is witnessing efforts to unify and standardize. As a result, the industry players are being forced to adapt with banks bearing greater pressure.
iv. The emergence of a new payment ecosystem – The pressure on the industry to innovate and add value to the various stakeholders has resulted in the emergence of a new ecosystem with various collaborations or enhancements. The banks are trying to develop their technological capabilities or collaborating with technology companies; the development of open application performing interface (API); and open banking are some paradigm trends.
v. Changes in foreign remittance – With the technology bringing down the cost of the overall process, the players in the digital payment industry will have the opportunity to add more value.
vi. Changes in regulatory norms – Across the world, policymakers are trying to introduce new rules to safeguard the customers. These rules vary from transactional to technological.
vii. Changing the economics of payments – Largely due to the introduction of "mobile-based payment services", the customers (including retailers) have access to low or no-cost services.
viii. Contradiction in short-term and long-term profitability – One of the main success factors in this industry is to upscale to reach the "critical mass". This requires heavy investment. On the other hand, competing with cash adds to the problem as it is free to use. Therefore, the players in this industry struggle to align their short and long–term profitability.

Different challenges affecting the profitability and sustainability of digital payment players require not just an alteration in the price/revenue model but creating an innovative model guided by a solid strategic tool, which might well be e-CRM.

e-CRM has the capabilities to "improve customer service, retain valuable customers, and to aid in providing analytical capabilities" (Adnan et al., 2021). It has been reported that e-CRM contains features that might offer a "competitive advantage" to the players in the digital payment industry. (Miremadi et al., 2012) mentioned that the competitive advantages may be, "preparation of up-to-date technology, up to date banking systems, the proliferation of channels, marketing opportunities and fragmentation of customer segment". Further, it can "benefit both the customer and the business sides" (Al-dmour et al., 2017). Studies support the hypotheses that e-CRM can "increase customer satisfaction" (Dhingra & Dhingra, 2013); "increase profitability and revenues" (Akhlagh et al., 2014); increase relationship quality (Sivaraks et al., 2011). The industry also needs to adapt to the principle that "willingness to pay is driven by perceived value" (CGAP, 2019) again both on the business and the customer sides. e-CRM can also play a vital role in "selling value-added services (VAS) based on the data generated from payments transactions" (CGAP, 2019). It has been reported that the biggest card issuers Visa and Mastercard have plowed great commercial benefits from the "analysis and sale of their customer data" (CGAP, 2019).

A study on the Thai banking industry (Sivaraks et al., 2011) listed six benefits of e-CRM perceived by customers namely, *"timely access to accurate information, complete information, personalized information and service, up-to-date information, contacting banks from anywhere, and a one-stop service."* Another study (Dhingra & Dhingra, 2013) added to the benefits of e-CRM namely, "customer satisfaction; speed and accuracy of transactions; comfort and convenience to customers; extra benefits by better access to information; increased trust". Increased convenience has also been identified as a benefit by (Maroofi et al., 2012). Further, e-CRM can help in better understanding of future needs of customers and a better understanding of customer satisfaction (Usman et al., 2012). (Abu-Shanab & Anagreh, 2015) found that "factors of relationship quality are significantly correlated with factors of relationship outcomes". (Al-dmour et al., 2017) add that if implemented effectively, e-CRM can prove beneficial to both banks and customers. This holds tor digital payments by being a part of the same industry.

STRATEGIC FRAMEWORK FOR E-CRM IMPLEMENTATION IN DIGITAL PAYMENT COMPANIES

An essential step in the implementation of e-CRM is to understand the process. As per (Fjermestad & Romano, 2003), "e-CRM is not just about technology or software but about aligning business processes with customer strategies supported with software and technology". To effectively implement e-CRM, it is important to understand the system and its components. (Al-dmour et al., 2017) mention that the main components of e-CRM are "appropriate process, customer data quality, and e-CRM system technology". These are discussed below.

a. *appropriate process* - (Roh et al., 2005) describe the appropriate process as the "process to improve the performance of e-CRM through an appropriate level called "fitness level" of the customer relationship process, sales channels process, personalization process after-sales services process".
b. *quality* of data - The quality of data collected through the e-CRM system is critical to its success (Akoka et al., 2007). (Ballou & Tayi, 1999) list four parameters for evaluating the quality of data, namely, "data accuracy; timeliness; completeness; and consistency".
c. *system* technology - Any success of e-CRM can be achieved only if the firm has the required technology infrastructure. (Fjermestad & Romano, 2003) mention that the main e-CRM system technology is, "to support and manage the organizational and business process for a competitive advantage in the market". Past studies listed several characteristics of a good system technology namely, "reliability, response time, structure, framework, flexibility, and consistency of user interface" (Fjermestad & Romano, 2003).

To reap the strategic benefits of e-CRM, its "effective implementation" is vital (Hoda, 2010; Rostami et al., 2016). Further, (Rostami et al., 2016) mention that lacking a "framework for e-CRM implementation" result in its failure. e-CRM, like the traditional CRM, is not just the adoption of a few technologies. Rather it requires a company-wide strategic adoption. Two different frameworks for implementing e-CRM are found in the literature (Fjermestad & Romano, 2003). These are the usability framework given by (Gould & Lewis, 1985) and the resistance model (Markus, 1983). (Fjermestad & Romano, 2003) suggest that an integration of the two models would provide a holistic framework by "minimizing resistance while increasing usability". (Abu-Shanab & Anagreh, 2015) listed four factors that facilitate the implementation of e-CRM. These are, "technological factors; project-related factors; environmental factors; and organizational factors".

A proposed strategic framework for implementing e-CRM effectively in digital payment companies is explained in the following points.

Creating an Efficient e-CRM Program

To develop an e-CRM system that delivers greater value to the customer and achieves organizational overall objectives, a congenial approach is required, as presented in *Figure 2*. The digital payment companies adopting e-CRM should develop the entire

Figure 2. e-CRM Program
Source: Author

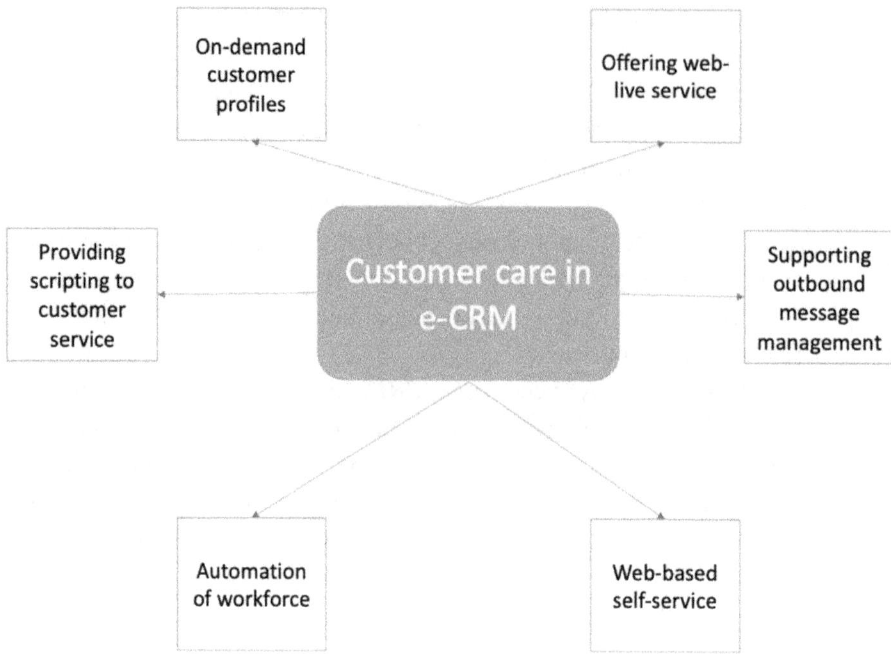

ecosystem centered on the customers. The program should be pivoted on corporate-wide customer care that would utilize the customer data to personalize contacts and encourage customer loyalty. This may be achieved by, "providing scripting to the staff; automation of workforce management; implementing web-based self-service; offering live web-chat; and supporting outbound message management" (Hoda, 2010).

Managing Customer Orientation

Being a strategic tool centered around customers, e-CRM must incorporate features that depict customer orientation. The customers in the digital payment services must be able to perceive the value they are receiving through the adoption of e-CRM. Hoda (2010) listed eight conditions to ensure that customer orientation is effectively implemented through the traditional CRM. These are equally significant even in e-CRM. These conditions are, "balancing efficiency and effectiveness; capitalizing customer insights; alignment of offerings with customers' needs; managing customer experience across touchpoints; guiding customer to the right channel; connecting the front office and back office; creating customer-driven value network; technology framework that facilitates integration and adoption" (Hoda, 2010). *Figure 3* presents the process of managing customer orientation. Balancing efficiency and effectiveness in e-CRM implementation means looking at both the processes and the outcomes. Customer insights represent the information obtained beyond the obvious and then include it in critical decision-making. Another important factor to be considered in managing customer orientation is an integrated approach at the firm level. All the departments must act in synchrony with customer value at the front. It is also required that the quality of service across the channels used by the digital payment company is uniform. It acts as a differentiator when companies manage complex customer exchanges across different channels, synchronizing effectively the online and offline exchanges. The next factor includes the optimization of channel mix to ensure customers are guided to the right channels. Only pushing the customers to "low-cost self-service channels" may harm the digital payment companies. Another factor is the integration of front-office and back-office operations of the digital payment companies. This integration should be "seamless and in real-time". Customer-driven "value network" is another requirement of e-CRM customer orientation in digital payment companies. This requires partners to be intrinsically integrated with the digital payment company. Finally, the e-CRM cannot be successful without an adequate technological infrastructure that supports adaptation and integration. It also should be agile and flexible in processing information and in mapping changes.

Managing Quality of Customer Data

The quality of e-CRM in any company, including digital payment companies, rest on the soundness of customer database management. The process of database management is depicted in *Figure 4*. This process starts with knowing the best customers, then identifying the customer preferences. The knowledge of customer preferences includes information on customers' preferences as well as what factors stimulate them. This knowledge also allows the system to predict future customer preferences. The next step in the process is to determine the factors that result in a profitable customer. This leads to mapping the results with future goals and integration of the "customer workflow automation". The workflow automation result in effective data integration, data mapping, process mapping, process analysis, and overall functional integration" (Hoda, 2010).

Managing Quality of Customer Analytics

As explained earlier, the digital payment ecosystem comprises an intricate process involving multiple players and partnerships. e-CRM in digital payments would be successful only when there is an effective inter-firm integration. This means the various players in the ecosystem are integrated. (Hoda, 2010) provided an illustration

Figure 3. Managing customer orientation in e-CRM
Source: Author

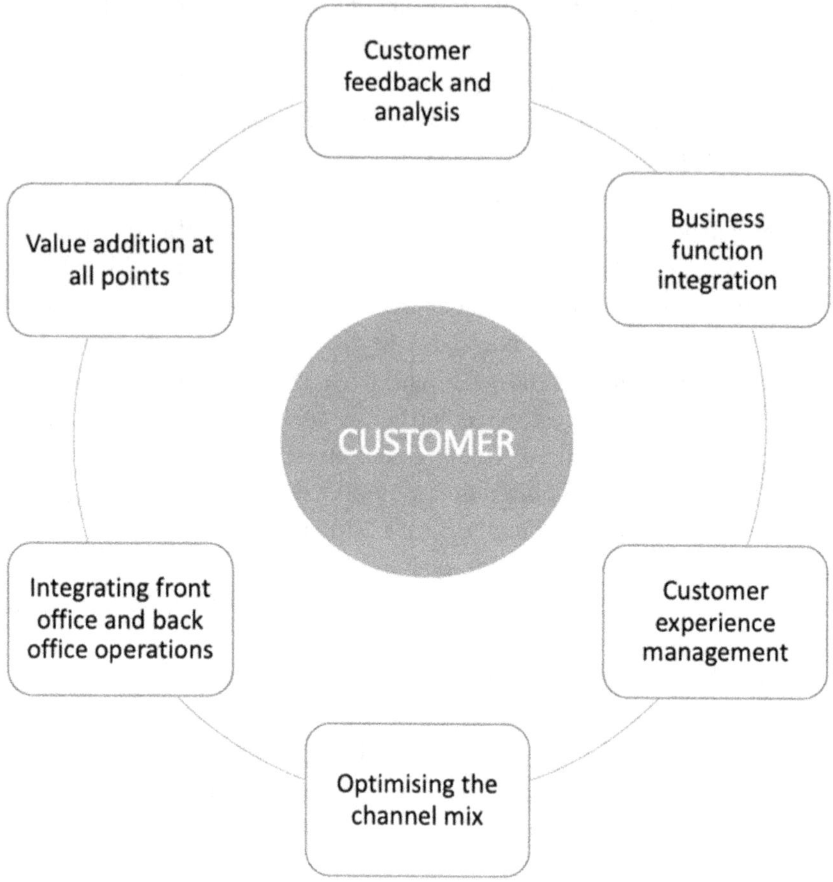

of partner integration for traditional CRM. This holds good for e-CRM too. The overall partnership integration rests on sound e-CRM infrastructure. It includes business systems that traditionally included operations like billing, provisioning, accounts payable, calls center, and sales. The information gathered through different operations is gathered in an integrated database, which is a source of business intelligence when analyzed by the firm system. Simultaneously the customer feedback is also analyzed to understand the scope of process improvement. The analysis stage results in refined business actions, that are reflected in the various customer touchpoints such as call centers, web access, e-mails, usage, direct sales, and fax. The entire process, as presented in *Figure 5,* across the various touchpoints results in the development of psychographic, firmographic, infographic, and demographic profiles of the customers.

Figure 4. Managing quality of customer data
Source: (Hoda, 2010)

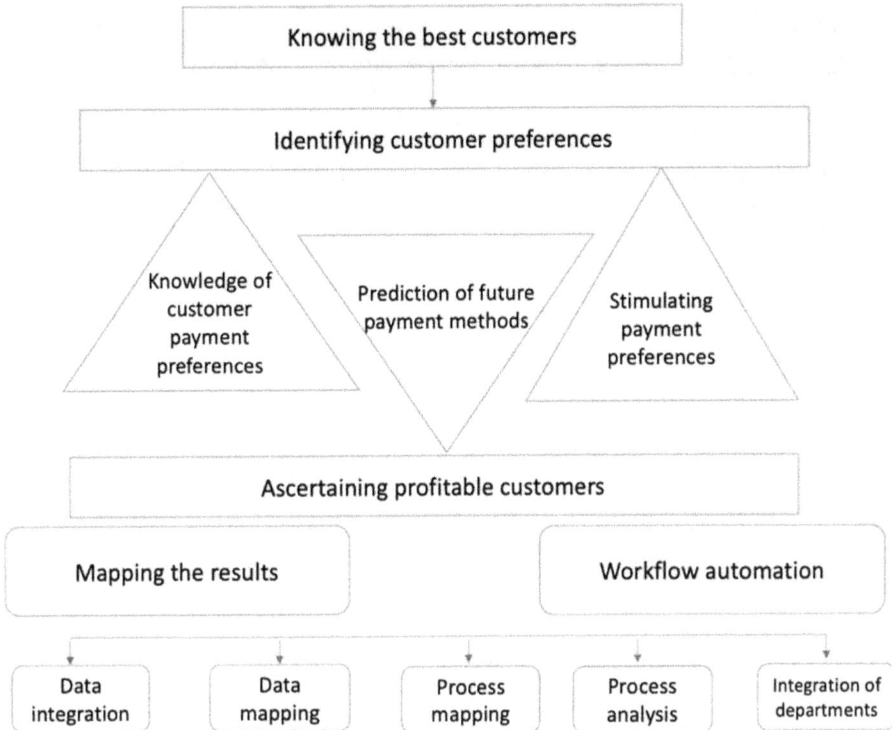

This information can help the digital payment companies in upscaling, cross-selling, increasing customer satisfaction, and providing a competitive advantage.

Post-Implementation Operations

Like any other strategic intervention, specifically that banks on technology, post-implementation operations are critical for its success. First of all, careful monitoring of the results must be done to track the benefits benchmarked against the past. Upgradation of the infrastructure is essential to maintain the competitive advantage and also avoid obsolescence. Selection of the e-CRM software that best optimizes the processes in the digital payment company is equally important. The solution provider should be ready to support the company in maintaining and upgrading the processes. Digital payment companies adopting e-CRM should always be looking out for "hybrid deployment models" as they may benefit from the customization.

Figure 5. Managing customer analytics
Source: Adapted from (Hoda, 2010)

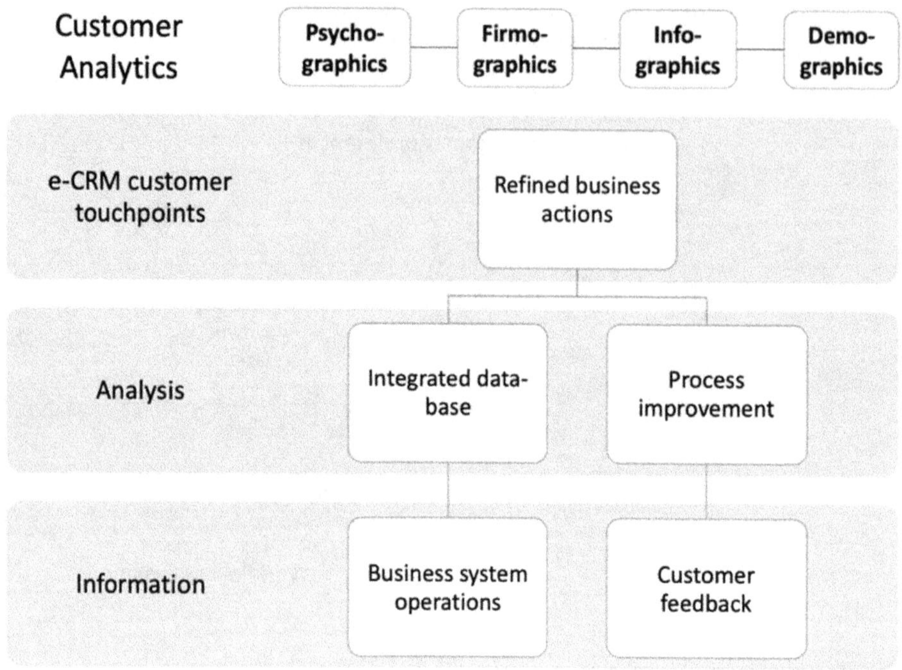

FUTURE RESEARCH DIRECTIONS

The chapter discussed the potential role of e-CRM in improving the capabilities of digital payment services. The theoretical model proposed in the chapter provides a sound basis for empirical investigations to determine its validity. Further, each aspect of e-CRM implementation also forms research questions that may be empirically examined. The outcomes of the implementation may also be investigated to ascertain the commercial benefits of the research.

CONCLUSION

The main aim of the chapter was to provide a comprehensive overview of the digital payment industry and the scope for e-CRM in bringing advantages to the various players in the digital payments ecosystem. Further, a theoretical framework is developed to help the digital payment companies at various stages of the adoption of e-CRM.

Like the traditional CRM, e-CRM is not just a technology solution supporting a particular function, but an enterprise-wide strategy. The adoption of e-CRM may offer various benefits to the digital payment companies that are facing ever-increasing pressure on their margins and profitability. An important factor critical to this industry is the competition with cash and providing a "value network" in the entire ecosystem. e-CRM would be able to play a significant role in addressing some of the critical challenges, customer management being one of them. The success of e-CRM adoption relies on careful planning and implementation. This includes a careful understanding of the program, database management, partnership management, and over all infrastructure.

The changing customer behaviors and "reimagined customer experiences" increase the importance of e-CRM in the digital payment industry. The increased usage of digital payments due to the Covid-19 pandemic is not likely to reverse. The trend shows that it is going to increase which would result in the testing of newer business models and innovative practices in the industry.

This chapter therefore would be helpful to the industry practitioners in analyzing the role e-CRM may play in facing the challenges. Further, they may also benefit from adopting the framework for implementing the e-CRM, not just as a tool but as a strategy. Researchers will also find this chapter provides new insights and future research directions. More specifically, the testing of critical success factors for adopting e-CRM by digital payment companies.

ACKNOWLEDGMENT

The author would like to thank Umm Al-Qura University especially the Dean of the College of Business and Head of the Department of Business Administration for providing a supportive environment in completing the research. The author is also grateful to the editor and the three external reviewers for their constructive feedback.

REFERENCES

Abu-Shanab, E., & Anagreh, L. (2015). Impact of electronic customer relationship management in banking sector. *International Journal of Electronic Customer Relationship Management*, *9*(4), 254–271. doi:10.1504/IJECRM.2015.074196

Adnan, A. Z., Rahayu, A., Hendrayati, H., & Yusuf, R. (2021). The Role of Electronic Customer Relationship Management (E-CRM) in Improving Service Quality. *Journal of Physics: Conference Series*, *1764*(1), 012051. Advance online publication. doi:10.1088/1742-6596/1764/1/012051

Akhlagh, E., Allahyar, D., & Somayeh, Y. (2014). The Impact of Electronic Customer Relationship Management on Improving Marketing Performance of Private Banks. *Interdisciplinary Journal of Contemporary Research in Business*, *6*(6), 134.

Akoka, J., Berti-Équille, L., Boucelma, O., Bouzeghoub, M., Comyn-Wattiau, I., Cosquer, M., Goasdoué-Thion, V., Kedad, Z., Nugier, S., Peralta, V., & Sisaid-Cherfi, S. (2007). A framework for quality evaluation in data integration systems. *ICEIS 2007 - 9th International Conference on Enterprise Information Systems, Proceedings*.

Al-dmour, H. H., Khwaja, R., & Al-dmour, R. (2017). The Impact of Electronic Customer Relationship Management (ECRM) Practices in Business Performance of Jordanian Commercial Banks. *European Journal of Economics. Finance and Administrative Sciences*, *93*, 49–70.

Ballou, D. P., & Tayi, G. K. (1999). Enhancing data quality in data warehouse environments. *Communications of the ACM*, *42*(1), 73–78. Advance online publication. doi:10.1145/291469.291471

Bhatnagar, A., & Saxena, R. (2013). CRM vs E-CRM to study and understand the impact of traditional CRM vs technological CRM. *International Conference on Technology and Business Management*, 1–6.

CGAP. (2019). *Choosing a Profit Strategy for Merchant Payments*. https://www.cgap.org/research/publication/choosing-profit-strategy-merchant-payments

Dhingra, M., & Dhingra, V. (2013). Determinants of Electronic customer relationship management (e-CRM) for customer satisfaction in banking sector in India. *African Journal of Business Management*, *7*(10), 762–768. doi:10.5897/AJBM11.712

Emergen Research. (2022). *Top 10 Leading Digital Payment Companies in the World*. https://www.emergenresearch.com/blog/top-10-leading-digital-payment-companies-in-the-world

Fjermestad, J., & Romano, N. C. Jr. (2003). Electronic customer relationship management: Revisiting the general principles of usability and resistance – an integrative implementation framework. *Business Process Management Journal*, *9*(5), 572–591. doi:10.1108/14637150310496695

Gould, J. D., & Lewis, C. (1985). Designing for usability: Key principles and what designers think. *Communications of the ACM, 28*(3), 300–311. Advance online publication. doi:10.1145/3166.3170

HodaN. (2010). *CRM Implementation: Critical Success Factors.* doi:10.2139/ssrn.2406488

Insider Intelligence. (2021). *Digital Payment Industry in 2021 : Payment methods, trends, and tech processing payments electronically.* https://www.insiderintelligence.com/insights/digital-payment-services/

Khodakarami, F., & Chan, Y. (2011). Evaluating the Success of Customer Relationship Management (CRM) Systems. *Proceedings of the European Conference on Information Management & Evaluation.*

Markets and Markets. (2021). *Digital payment market: Global forecast to 2026.* https://www.marketsandmarkets.com/Market-Reports/digital-payment-market-209834053.html?gclid=CjwKCAjw0a-SBhBkEiwApljU0lvGFZsDX_qj-wwVttzaS-UUgwvRYObnSOrK6IcJWbTkAekxDdfn5BoC2MMQAvD_BwE

Markus, M. L. (1983). Power, Politics, and MIS Implementation. *Communications of the ACM, 26*(6), 430–444. Advance online publication. doi:10.1145/358141.358148

Maroofi, F., Darabi, A., & Torabi, J. (2012). Effects of e-CRM on Customer-Bank Relationship Quality and Results. *International Journal of Academic Research in Accounting.*

Miremadi, A. R., Ghalamakri, S., & Ramezani, A. A. (2012). Challenges in trust and security by implementation of E-CRM among banks and financial institution: A case study of e-banking in iran". *International Journal of Information Science and Management, 10*, 99–118.

Nair, R. D., & Prabhu, P. (2018). *Payments in the Digital Age.* https://dokumen.tips/documents/payments-models-for-the-digital-age-accenture-transforming-the-payments-landscape.html

Oanh, N. (n.d.). *ECRM Meaning, a useful tool for your electronic customer relationship management.* Retrieved February 9, 2022, from https://www.appvizer.com/magazine/customer/client-relationship-mgt/ecrm-meaning

PiStrategy. (2016). *Payment ecosystem.* http://pistrategy.org/payment-ecosystem/

Rao, T. (2013). Impact of socio-economic characteristics of the bank customers on CRM. *Tactful Management Research Journal, 1*, 1–8.

Roh, T. H., Ahn, C. K., & Han, I. (2005). The priority factor model for customer relationship management system success. *Expert Systems with Applications*, *28*(4), 641–654. Advance online publication. doi:10.1016/j.eswa.2004.12.021

Rostami, M., Izadbin, A., Zakipour, M., & Rostami, S. (2016). Assessing electronic customer relationship management (E-CRM) readiness and its impact on banking quality of service (case study: Saderat Bank Branches-West of. *International Journal of Humanities and Cultural Studies*, *2*(4). http://www.ijhcs.com/index.php/ijhcs/article/view/537

Sivaraks, P., Krairit, D., & Tang, J. C. S. (2011). Effects of e-CRM on customer-bank relationship quality and outcomes: The case of Thailand. *The Journal of High Technology Management Research*, *22*(2), 141–157. Advance online publication. doi:10.1016/j.hitech.2011.09.006

Usman, U., Jalal, A., & Musa, M. (2012). The impact of electronic customer relationship management on consumer's behavior. *International Journal of Advances in Engineering and Technology*, *3*(1), 500–504.

KEY TERMS AND DEFINITIONS

Analytical E-CRM: The type of e-CRM internal to an organization and deals with the technology to handle the customer data.

Debit Pull: The payment transaction initiated by the merchant or the seller on behalf of the customer.

Digital Payment: The transfer of money using digital channels.

Credit Push: The payment transaction initiated by the customer himself/herself.

CRM: A business approach integrating the firm and customer for enhanced relationship.

E-CRM: The set of various operations that rely on web technology to offer CRM.

Integrative Framework: The integration of usability and resistance frameworks in implementation of a technology.

Operational E-CRM: The type of e-CRM that focuses on the customers' processes.

Chapter 2
The Role of E-CRM in Building Customer Satisfaction and Repurchase Intention:
Evidence From the FMCG Industry

Bee Lian Song
Asia Pacific University of Technology and Innovation, Malaysia

ABSTRACT

In this era of technology, electronic customer relationship management (E-CRM) is becoming more prominently used by businesses in various industries. This chapter aims to investigate the effect of E-CRM on customer satisfaction and repurchase intention in the fast-moving consumer goods (FMCG) industry in Malaysia. Five important E-CRM elements of service quality, customisation, transaction security, online feedback, and website features will be explored as antecedents to customer satisfaction and its effect on repurchase intention. Stimulus-organism-response (S-O-R) theory offered the underpinning theoretical explanation in the development of the conceptual framework for this study. By using empirical study to prove the relationship effect, the study provides better understanding of consumers' experiences on E-CRM strategies implemented by the FMCG firms, and its roles in building customer satisfaction and repurchase intention. FMCG firms can leverage on the proposed strategies to improve their E-CRM planning, implementation, and controlling to achieve desired business performance.

DOI: 10.4018/978-1-6684-5386-5.ch002

INTRODUCTION

Customer relationship management (CRM) has been widely used by businesses to acquire new customers, retain customers and grow relationship with customers (Anshari et al., 2019). CRM is focusing on creating and building long-term profitable customer relationships. The technology advancement has transformed CRM to online system, known as electronic customer relationship management (E-CRM), for better management, implementation and control. Furthermore, the changing business landscape and environment pressures have contributed to the need for organisations to have more effective communication tool, better target market segment and prioritised on personalised marketing through the utilisation of E-CRM (Pradana et al., 2017). There are significant differences between CRM and E-CRM in its approaches, tools and processes in creating and building customer satisfaction and repurchase intention in the FMCG industry (Adejumo, 2019). E-CRM has provided platforms for seamless business transactions and customer interfaces through the usage of internet, email, wireless and latest technologies, while CRM leveraged on traditional mean of telephone, fax and retail store (Eltahir et al., 2021; Pradana et al., 2017). Therefore, both CRM and E-CRM have utilised different strategies, as well as can be used as tools that complement each other to achieve customer satisfaction and repurchase intention.

The increasing competitive business environment and growing importance of E-CRM, businesses boost their global market presence by leveraging on E-CRM to influence customer behaviour to purchase the products or services. E-CRM has three core functions of contact and information (e.g., site customisation, local search engine, alternative channels, membership, site tour, mailing list, chat, forum and electronic bulletin board), e-commerce (e.g., online purchasing, preview product and external links), and post-sales support (e.g., frequent asked questions, problem solving, complaining ability and spare parts ordering) (Feinberg et al., 2002). Effective E-CRM comprises the overall process of building and maintaining customer relationships by delivering superior customer value and satisfaction through various electronic touch points (Dawn & Chowdhury, 2011). E-CRM contributes to costs savings in marketing, generation of sales, increased personalisation, enhanced customer service and improved customer loyalty (Dehghanpouri et al., 2020).

The fast-moving consumer goods (FMCG) industry is growing rapidly through the innovation of E-CRM (Adejumo, 2019). FMCG are defined as relatively inexpensive, frequent purchased and rapidly consumed items by consumers with minimal purchasing efforts (Dibb et al., 2006, pp. 298). FMCG is a product produced at relatively low cost and sold quickly to consumers (Miralam, Junnaidi & Moizuddin, 2019). Better known as consumer-packaged goods, the three main product categories under FMCG are food and beverages, personal care and household care products

(Mohan and Sequeira, 2016). FMCG firms have utilised E-CRM to gain competitive advantages over others and to thrive in the dynamic market environment. FMCG is the one of the most important industry in Malaysia with approximately one-fifth of household consumption expenditure is spent on FMCG segment (Hirschmann, 2021). FMCG industry in Malaysia is expected to achieve continuous growth due to the strong consumer demand, increasing online shopping trend, innovativeness and diverse brands presence in the market (Vasudevan & Arokiasamy, 2021).

There are various challenges faced by the FMCG firms or marketers in utilising E-CRM effectively to influence consumer purchase behaviour. E-CRM requires substantial allocation of resources, such as technology capabilities and manpower skills to manage the platforms (Anshari et al., 2019). In addition, the critical roles and management of E-CRM involves customer feedback and complaints handling, after sales services, customer following up, and maintaining customer relationship (Kakeesh et al., 2021). The increasing concerns on E-CRM are related to its ability to secure company and customer information from theft, fraud and publishing (Bujage, 2015). Furthermore, there are many FMCG brands in the market which have created more intense competition between the firms to stimulate consumers' purchases and build loyalty (Hardjono & Tan, 2017; Ebrahim et al., 2016). Transaction security issues (Pramudito et al., 2021) and poor website features (Pham & Ahammad, 2017) in E-CRM have negatively affected customer satisfaction and created challenging conditions in maintaining loyal customers for repurchase behaviour in FMCG industry (Kakesh et al., 2021). Therefore, customer satisfaction which was not being fulfilled well will affect customer loyalty and intention to repurchase, leading to FMCG businesses will lose customers, market share and profitability (Namini, 2016; Zaman et al., 2012). Khanh et al. (2021) stressed that E-CRM strategies applied by firms greatly varies according to suitability and efficiency depending on the industry. In the FMCG industry, E-CRM have contributed to positive customer satisfaction through effective service quality (Feinberg et al., 2002).

Previous studies have investigated E-CRM and customer satisfaction in hotel industry (Ibrahim et al., 2021), retailing industry (Feinberg et al., 2002), mobile industry (Alim & Ozuem, 2016), tax management services (Dehghanpouri et al., 2020), and banking industry (Kumar et al., 2022; Mang'unyi et al., 2018). Empirical studies (e.g., Yoon et al., 2008; Rhee, 2010) related to E-CRM have shown a positive association between customer satisfaction and repurchase intention. A few studies (e.g., Zatalini & Pamungkas, 2017; Oumar et al., 2017) have suggested that future research related to E-CRM and consumer purchase behaviour should extend to other industries to provide better insights on its applicability and development. In view that there is paucity of such research in the context of FMCG industry, thus have justified the need to conduct the present study.

As the problem formulation that can be drawn from this research is little understanding towards the role of E-CRM in building customer satisfaction and repurchase intention in the FMCG industry. Hence, this chapter aims to investigate the effect of E-CRM on customer satisfaction and repurchase intention in the FMCG industry in Malaysia. Five important E-CRM elements of service quality, customisation, transaction security, online feedback and website features will be examined as antecedents to customer satisfaction, and its effect on repurchase intention. The Stimulus-Organism-Response (S-O-R) theory will be applied as the theoretical foundation. S-O-R theory has been extensively applied in examining customers' behavioural process in various industries (Kim et al., 2020), but exist limitations in its application in the context of E-CRM, and consumer behavioural and purchase decision in the FMCG industry. Therefore, this study will be testing new constructs representing e-CRM for the Stimulus (environment stimuli factors) variable. Customer satisfaction reflect the Organism (inner behavioural state) variable, which intervene between the Stimuli inputs and Response output of repurchase intention.

There are two main contributions from this study. In theoretical contributions, the S-O-R theory will be developed through the application of e-CRM influence on customer satisfaction and repurchase intention in the context of FMCG industry. The proposed theoretical model that applied S-O-R theory will be useful practically in the context E-CRM in influencing customer satisfaction and repurchase intention in the FMCG industry. Therefore, this chapter is expected to build the knowledge areas related to E-CRM and consumer purchase behaviour context. In managerial contributions, the findings will assist in better understanding of consumers' experiences and perceptions on E-CRM strategies implemented by the FMCG firms or marketers, and the effectiveness of E-CRM strategies in building customer satisfaction and repurchase intention. Marketers can have better insights on the most important dimensions of e-CRM as perceived by consumers. Hence, marketers can leverage on the proposed constructive strategies to improve their E-CRM planning, implementation, management and controlling to achieve their desired business performance.

LITERATURE REVIEW

Stimulus-Organism-Response (S-O-R) Theory

S-O-R theory conceptualised that environment stimuli influence an individual's experiential and non-experiential organisms, which in turn lead to response behaviours (Jacoby, 2002). The environment stimuli consists of factors outside an individual's control, such as marketing stimuli factors. These stimuli factors affects the internal states of organisms (e.g., attitude, motivation, emotion, feeling, belief, perception, thinking and judgement) (Evans et al., 2006). Behavioural responses involves individual's physiological or psychological responses that reflects behavioural outcomes. S-O-R theory has been widely applied in research to understand consumer behaviour (Li et al., 2021). A few scholars have applied S-O- R theory in E-CRM context to explore on customer experiences and satisfaction in banking industry (Kumar et al., 2022), perceived benefits and value on customer loyalty in electronic commerce (Khoa, 2022), and customer satisfaction in shopping websites (Yang & Babapour, 2022).

Nevertheless, there is paucity of research in S-OR theory application in understanding consumer purchase behaviour in E-CRM, specifically in exploring the effect of E-CRM on customer satisfaction and repurchase intention. To add contribution to the body of knowledge in this area, the present study will be testing new constructs representing E-CRM as a Stimulus (environment stimuli factors), customer satisfaction reflect the Organism (inner behavioural state) variable, and Response output of repurchase intention. As a stimulus mechanism, E-CRM provides various characteristics or activities such as information, payment methods and post-sales support. Customer satisfaction reflects customer's affective and cognitive reactions (Palaci et al., 2019) towards the usage of E-CRM. Consumer repurchase intention is a response of behavioral intention of using E-CRM services affected through the E-CRM characteristics and consumer's experiential and non-experiential organisms. Therefore, the conceptual framework for this study was developed by using S-O-R theory as the theoretical foundation.

Customer Satisfaction

Customer satisfaction refers to the customer's pleasurable fulfillment through their consumption achieve some needs, desired, goal or so forth (Oliver, 1999). Customer satisfaction can be conceptualised as trade-off between customer expectations and customer receives from the usage of products or services (Yi & Nataraajan, 2018). The customers have certain expectations on the products or services that they experienced usage, and the favourable experience leads to the achievement of satisfaction.

Zaim et al. (2020) asserted that customer satisfaction is the important outcome for E-CRM performance. E-CRM have contributed to positive customer satisfaction (Nikou et al., 2016). Scholars have affirmed that customer satisfaction is a strong predictor for behavioural variables (Ravald & Grönroos, 1996). Customer satisfaction contributes to subsequent consumer behavioural outcomes of purchase intention, actual purchase, repurchase intention and loyalty (Kumar & Mokha, 2022; Majeed et al., 2022). A few scholars (e.g., Mustikasari et al., 2021; Rhee, 2010) have tested and confirmed the mediating role of customer satisfaction in between the relationship of E-CRM and repurchase intention. However, such relationships investigation in the context of FMCG industry are limited.

Service Quality

Service quality is defined as the ability of the organisation to meet or exceed customer expectations (Parasuraman, 1988). Service quality is measured by the difference between customers' expectations for service performance and perceived service (Lewis & Mitchell, 1990). Service quality is considered as the most important aspect in a business relationship between the firm and the customer (Helkkula & Kelleher, 2010). Accordingly to Al-Hawary and Al-Smeran (2016), the dimensions for service quality in the context of E-CRM are reliability, ease of use, effectiveness, privacy and responsiveness.

Quality of E-commerce services under E-CRM was found to have effects on customer satisfaction (Tzavlopoulos et al., 2019). Feinberg et al. (2002) affirmed that E-CRM has the effective and low cost means that enables customers to utilise the service at anytime, anywhere and anyhow. Dehghanpouri et al. (2020) asserted that customers who have experienced using the quality E-CRM systems and services, found it to be effective and responsiveness.

Hypothesis One: Service quality has a significant positive influence on customer satisfaction.

Customisation

Customisation implies empowerment for customers through the flexibility of offering personalised services by the organisations (Dehghanpouri et al., 2020). E-CRM enables users to filter the contents they see through customisation features. For example, social media marketing can provide customised information related to brands and products that fits customer needs (Rohm et al., 2013), arouse attention and generate satisfaction (Schulze et al., 2015). Khalifa and Shen (2005) asserted that E-CRM sites' customisation is important to facilitate customer decision-making process to reducing risks and attaining customer's trust that contributes to customer satisfaction. For example, customers can opt for product customisation through E-CRM platforms that meet their requirements and satisfied their needs.

Furthermore, the customisation features in E-CRM enables customers to provide personalised information for marketers to effectively segment the target market and position their products or services effectively to the targeted customers (Alim & Ozuem, 2014; Vyas & Patel, 2004). Therefore, maximisation of customer value could be achieved which leads to higher customer satisfactions (Hendriyani & Auliana, 2018). Thus, the hypothesis is stated as:

Hypothesis Two: Customisation has a significant positive influence on customer satisfaction.

Transaction Security

Transaction security refers to the security of the organisation's website for business transaction (Kumar and Kumar, 2014). Consumer's fear and concern on security in online transaction through E-CRM are the major drawbacks in promoting E-CRM usage (Rashwan et al., 2019). Dehghanpouri et al. (2020) posited that E-CRM has the element of reliable business transaction that increased consumers' trust and satisfaction. They found that consumers believed E-CRM systems were fully secured as risk-free payment platforms and protected their personal information that leads to increased customer satisfaction.

E-CRM systems that are lack of financial security and privacy will negatively affect customer satisfaction, as they will feel insecure risky and unsafe to conduct purchase transactions (Meuter et al., 2000). In the e-grocery business, online transactions are exposed to cybercrime and fraud that negatively affected consumers' trust and satisfaction (Pramudito et al., 2021; Al-dweeri et al., 2019). This study postulates the following:

Hypothesis Three: Transaction security has a significant positive influence on customer satisfaction.

Online Feedback

E-CRM enables customers to obtain valuable online feedbacks from companies or other shoppers and recommendations (Amazhanova & Huseynov, 2018). E-CRM through social media, online blogs, or customer reviews provides valuable communication platforms for consumers to obtain feedbacks on the products or services, that influenced their satisfaction level (Maecker et al., 2016). The efficacy and quality of customer service can be boost through E-CRM, as well as strengthen the relationship between firms and customers when problems are solve efficiently through speedy online feedback (Kumar & Mokha, 2020; Khalifa & Shen, 2009).

E-CRM as useful platforms for customers to easily provide feedback and share their experience on the product or service (Tariq et al., 2019). Firms obtained customer information or feedback from various touch points in E-CRM system (Kampani & Jhamb, 2020), e.g., during post-purchase of products, customers were asked to complete survey evaluation feedback form. Ahuja and Medury (2010) posited that firms used corporate blog as an e-CRM tool to solicit feedback from customers and response to controversies that built better engagement and customer satisfaction. In addition, Customer Information Management System (CIMS) served as the main platform to acquiring customer database and consolidating customer feedback. Referring to the above review, the following hypothesis is formed:

Hypothesis Four: Online feedback has a significant positive influence on customer satisfaction.

Website Features

Website features refers to the appearance, functionality, design and user-friendliness of the website system (Vila et al., 2021). Shen and Khalifa (2008) categorised E-commerce website features as hedonic and utilitarian. Utilitarian features involves physical appearance and problem solving (Bilgihan & Bujisic, 2015). Therefore, utilitarian features in E-CRM focused on accessibility, information searching and supply of information (Kim et al., 2008). While Hedonic features relates to interactive and social aspect (Bilgihan & Bujisic, 2015). Among the hedonic website functions includes animated images, colours, sounds, appealing visual layouts, gamifications, social interactions, and social engagement (Anim & Omar, 2021).

E-CRM website features are essential to provide consumers seamless online experiences throughout the process of purchasing products or services (Farmania et al., 2021). The effective usability of E-CRM which enables consumers to obtained quality information and ease of use increased customer satisfaction (Zaim et al., 2020). Zatalani and Pamungkas (2017) reported that consumers' easy access to information through E-CRM enhanced their satisfaction level. Hence, the below hypothesis is derived:

Hypothesis Five: Website features has a significant positive influence on customer satisfaction.

Repurchase intention

Repurchase intention refers to consumers' motivation to continuously buying the product or service (Hellier et al., 2003). In the context of e-grocery retailing industry, Kumar et al. (2022) reported that E-CRM in mobile application features have generated consumer satisfaction to continuous usage intention for purchase or repurchase. Shin and Lee (2018) found that service quality of online fresh food shopping mall has positive effect on e-customers' satisfaction and repurchase intention.

In e-commerce, offline-online trust transference exists which significantly influences customer satisfaction and repurchase intention (Jeon et al., 2021). Rhee (2010) found that E-CRM dimensions of service level, customer contact, benefit and advice have played important influencing factors in stimulating customer satisfaction, and subsequently repurchase intention. The following hypothesis is put forward:

Hypothesis Six: Customer satisfaction has a significant positive influence on repurchase intention.

Drawing on S-O-R theory, the conceptual framework for this study is presented in Figure 1. The dimensions of E-CRM comprising service quality, customisation, transaction security, online feedback and website features represented by hypotheses, H1 to H5, as antecedents to customer satisfaction. Customer satisfaction is correlated to repurchase intention which is represented by H6.

Figure 1. Conceptual framework

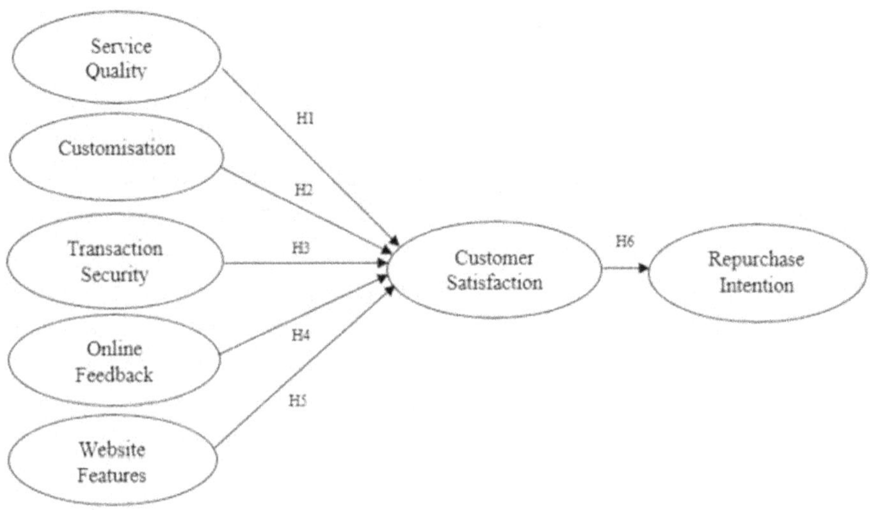

RESEARCH METHODOLOGY

Sample, Data Collection and Measurement Items

The sample size was determined based on the criteria set by Hair et al. (2017), for a structural model with seven construct, a minimum 300 samples are required. Based on this criteria, a total of 420 samples were decided to enable structural equation analysis to be conducted for the structural model. By adopting quantitative approach, data are obtained through survey questionnaire from 420 customers who have experienced purchase of FMCG product through e-CRM platforms for the past three months in Malaysia.

Convenience sampling method was chosen to select the samples which facilitate easy access to the targeted respondents. Through convenience sampling method, respondents were approached personally by the researcher when they presence at the selected FMCG outlets located in Kuala Lumpur, Selangor, Johor, Sabah, Pahang and Penang in Malaysia. Respondents were briefed on the survey process and answering the survey questionnaires. The response rate for the survey instrument was 97% with a total of 420 responses received.

As for the measurement items, a total of 29 items for seven constructs were developed from past studies' adapted sources as shown in Table 1. The closed-ended survey questionnaires and Likert scale of 6-points were adopted from the range of 1 = strongly disagree to 6 = strongly agree. In addition, respondent's demographic questions were developed, such as gender, age, monthly income and occupation.

Validity and Reliability Assessment

Validity refers to the assessment to ensure that the measurement variables are accurately used to measure that variable (Bryman & Bell, 2007). Reliability refers to the consistency of the measurement in a variable, or a set of variables (Hair et al., 2010). Pilot study was performed on 30 respondents to validate the survey questionnaires. The Exploratory Factor Analysis (EFA) was conducted to assess the validity of the measures and items with factor loading values of <0.3 was eliminated (Hair et al., 2010). By using Maximum Likelihood extraction and Promax rotation, the EFA results indicated dimensions with KMO value of 0.906, which is above the threshold value of 0.5 and values above 0.9 were categorised as excellent (Field, 2013). The Bartlett's test of Sphericity shown significant value at p=0.000 (Pallant, 2007).

The factor loading results for all the items were between the ranges of 0.684 to 0.877, which were above the cut off value of 0.3 (Field, 2013). Therefore, the assessments shown that all the 29 items have well construct validity and maintained for subsequent analysis. Cronbach's alpha (CA) is used to assess the internal reliability with all values were above the acceptance level of 0.7 (Saunders et al., 2009). The composite reliability (CR) values fall between 0.863 to 0.896, above the acceptance limit of 0.6 (Bagozzi & Yi, 1988). The convergent validity through assessment of the Average Variance Extracted (AVE) were achieved between 0.574 and 0.683, and meet the minimum acceptance value of 0.5 (Fornell & Larcker, 1981). Table 1 presents the validity and reliability assessment results.

Table 1. CFA, CA, CR and AVE results

Construct (Source)	Item	Statement	Factor Loading	CA, AVE, CR
Service quality (Tian & Wang, 2017)	SQ1	The customer relationship features available at the E-CRM has good service quality	0.701	0.860 (CA) 0.614 (AVE) 0.863 (CR)
	SQ2	The E-CRM provides complete customer service information	0.787	
	SQ3	The E-CRM is an important channel that provides information on its service quality	0.857	
	SQ4	Overall, the E-CRM online service quality provided by this organisation is excellent	0.781	
Customisation (Cheung et al., 2020; Kumar et al., 2022)	CN1	The E-CRM provides customised information	0.717	0.868 (CA) 0.574(AVE) 0.871(CR)
	CN2	The E-CRM provides customised services	0.791	
	CN3	The E-CRM allows customisation of products tailored to my need	0.779	
	CN4	The E-CRM allows me to have personalised interaction with the staff	0.811	
	CN5	Service customisation given by the E-CRM, motivates me to purchase their product	0.684	
Transaction security (Kumar et al., 2022)	TS1	The E-CRM website is secure for my information	0.789	0.901 (CA) 0.681 (AVE) 0.895 (CR)
	TS2	The E-CRM website is secure for purchase transaction	0.851	
	TS3	The E-CRM website protects my private information	0.877	
	TS4	The E-CRM provides sufficient security	0.828	
Online feedback (Kumar et al., 2022)	OF1	The E-CRM has online feedback features	0.739	0.863 (CA) 0.613 (AVE) 0.863 (CR)
	OF2	The E-CRM has online customer service representatives	0.797	
	OF3	The E-CRM provides efficient online feedback channel	0.820	
	OF4	I always use the online feedback form available at the E-CRM	0.773	
Website features (Ismail & Hussin, 2015)	WF1	The E-CRM has an attractive appearance	0.739	0.893 (CA) 0.683 (AVE) 0.896 (CR)
	WF2	The E-CRM has efficient information search system	0.839	
	WF3	The E-CRM provides valuable products information	0.871	
	WF4	The E-CRM has fast loading page	0.850	
Customer satisfaction (Tian & Wang, 2017)	CS1	I am satisfied using the E-CRM	0.774	0.870 (CA) 0.626 (AVE) 0.870 (CR)
	CS2	The E-CRM meets my expectations	0.802	
	CS3	I am satisfied with the information given by the E-CRM	0.779	
	CS4	Overall, my experience in using the E-CRM is good	0.809	
Repurchase intention (Jeon et al., 2021)	RP1	I will frequently use the E-CRM for purchase in future	0.802	0.869 (CA) 0.617 (AVE) 0.866 (CR)
	RP2	I will be loyal to the E-CRM for purchase in future	0.811	
	RP3	I will strong recommend the E-CRM for others to use for purchase	0.771	
	RP4	I have good intention to repurchase from the E-CRM	0.758	

RESULTS

Sample Characteristics

From a total of 420 respondents, the female respondents represented 55% (231) and male respondents represented 45% (189). Majority of the respondents were under age group between 36 and 45 recorded 30% (126), followed by age group between 26 and 35 with 24% (101), 46 and 55% with 20% (84), 18 and 25 with 14% (59), 56 and 65 with 10% (42), and 66 and above with 2% (8). As for the monthly income, most of the respondents belongs to category of RM5,000 to RM6,999 recorded 31% (130), followed by RM3,000 to RM4,999 recorded 21% (88), RM 1,500 to RM 2,999 with 20%, RM7,000 and above with 18% (76), and below RM1,500 recorded 10% (42). In occupation types, majority of the respondents fell under category of employed with 55% (231), followed by self-employed with 22% (92), non-employed with 15% (63) and student with 8% (34).

Model Compatibility Testing

Structural equation modeling (SEM) using SPSS AMOS version 26 was used for data analysis. The objectives of using SEM is to assess the proposed research model and enable hypotheses testing. The final structural model indices shown that overall good fit was achieved. The model p value was significant at 0.00. The chi-square value was 761.204 and ratio of x2/df was 2.109. Subsequently, RMSEA value recorded as 0.051, and this value meet the minimum requirement of 0.08 (Hooper et al., 2008). As for the incremental fit indices, IFI value was 0.946, CFI was 0.945 and TLI was 0.938. Therefore, all the incremental fit values were above 0.9 which have met the minimum requirement (Awang, 2014). Subsequently, the proposed research model proceeded to estimate the path coefficients and research hypotheses testing were performed.

Hypotheses Testing

In this study, a total of six hypotheses were tested and accepted. The results concluded that H1 was accepted ($r=0.223$, $p<0.001$), shown service quality had a significant positive influence on customer satisfaction. Customisation also had a significant positive effect on customer satisfaction with H2 was supported ($r=0.195$, $p<0.001$). In addition, H3 ($r=0.135$, $p<0.05$) and H4 ($r=0.215$, $p<0.001$) were accepted which indicated both transaction security and online feedback had a significant positive influence on customer satisfaction. Website features was found had significant influence on customer satisfaction with H5 ($r=0.317$, $p<0.001$) was supported.

Table 2. Hypothesis testing

Hypothesized relationships	Estimate	*p* Values	Result
H1 Service quality → Customer satisfaction	0.223	***	Supported
H2 Customisation → Customer satisfaction	0.195	***	Supported
H3 Transaction security → Customer satisfaction	0.135	0.002	Supported
H4 Online feedback → Customer satisfaction	0.215	***	Supported
H5 Website features → Customer satisfaction	0.317	***	Supported
H6 Customer satisfaction → Repurchase intention	0.745	***	Supported

Note: ***p < 0.001

Finally, H6 (r=0.745, p<0.001) was also accepted, proven customer satisfaction had significant positive effect on repurchase intention. Table 2 summarises the hypotheses results. Figure 2 illustrates the final structural model.

Figure 2. Structural model

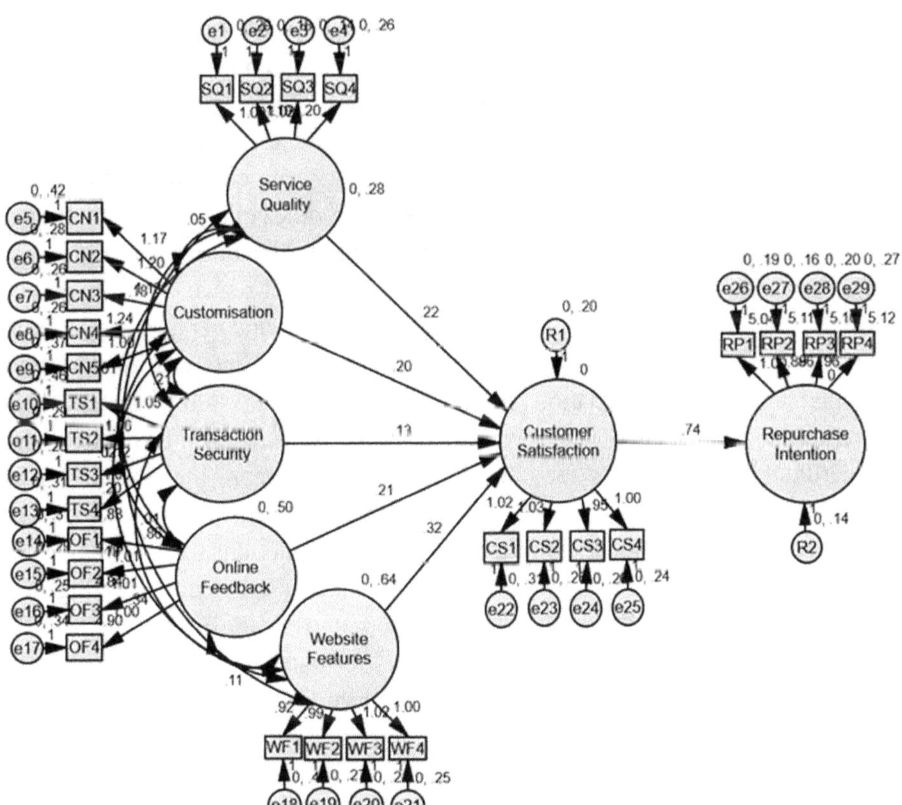

The squared multiple correlations for the customer satisfaction construct is 0.557 and repurchase intention construct is 0.636. The five E-CRM dimensions of service quality, customisation, transaction security, online feedback and website features have a proportion of the variance in customer satisfaction (55.7%).

DISCUSSION

Through service quality improvements, FMCG firms should effectively leverage on service quality offering in the E-CRM by forming various key online customer touch points, which are well connected to facilitate information sourcing, communications, purchasing transaction, problem solving and other important elements. Service quality improvements can be focused on the product information online, online purchasing, quick order ability, ease of check out, ability to track order status, member benefits, account information, customer service and engagement. FMCG firms can improve customisation focus to meet the different needs of customers and increase their satisfaction. E-CRM should serve as effective tool and platform in providing customised information on FMCG products to assist customers in their purchase decision making. The customisation of products tailored to specific customers' needs available at E-CRM will provide opportunities for customer co-creation of products and innovations can be encouraged.

Transaction security had the lowest coefficient value on its effect on customer satisfaction in this study. To overcome consumers' security concerns and enhance their satisfaction level, FMCG firms and government should collaborate to strengthen the security of E-CRM systems through appropriate tools and legal affordances. FMCG firms should focus on increasing customer confidence through proper communication and fast confirmation of secure payment and capture transaction. Effective communications by providing clear statements on data confidentiality to ensure that customers' information and transaction details are well protected. With that, customers feel secure when providing private transaction information (e.g. credit card/debit card numbers) for online purchase. Furthermore, the E-CRM should have automated functions to answer the queries of consumers instantly relating to privacy, security and payment conditions of online transactions.

The online feedback through a cohesive feedback system documenting and authenticating users' experiences should be incorporated into the E-CRM application interface. More effective engagement initiatives to foster instant value exchange between customers or users should be implemented in the E-CRM system. For example, FMCG firms can leverage on social media integration tools such as Instagram to handle the social sharing of content (e.g., ratings and reviews, community question and answer (Q&A), delivery promptness and available substitutes, visual reviews (e.g. pictures of grocery items) and checkout comments (e.g. reviews at the point of sale). Furthermore, automated online feedback can be set at the E-CRM system to provide fast, efficient and instant reply to customers. The effective online feedback system incorporated in E-CRM will be valuable to enhance customer satisfaction.

The findings indicated that website features had the highest coefficient value on its relationship to customer satisfaction. E-CRM websites could create positive shopping through innovative and attractive website designs. E-CRM websites should incorporate games, build online communities, enable co-creation possibilities, and create an engaging online experience to improve customer satisfaction. For example, the social media sites should facilitate active engagement between the users or consumers for co-creation experiential value and sharing of information. E-CRM should facilitate as efficient information search system with comprehensive FMCG products information given and quick link to other associated websites or external links for the convenience of customers. Various promotional and advertising campaigns that can induce customers to repurchase the FMCG products are recommended to be incorporated in the E-CRM systems. Therefore, the E-CRM as one-stop platform with various customer touch points focus can increase customer satisfaction and subsequently build repurchase intention.

IMPLICATIONS

The present study has contributed to the development of S-O-R theory whereby E-CRM dimensions were tested as Stimulus factors that influenced customer satisfaction (as Organism) and repurchase intention (as Response) constructs. The structural model fit indicated that E-CRM works effectively to enhanced customer satisfaction and stimulate repurchase intention. Therefore, the model can be used in practical application by the FMCG firms to utilise E-CRM effectively to enhance their market competitiveness and profitability. With the combination of important antecedents of service quality, customisation, transaction security, online feedback and website features, the FMCG firms can implement more focused E-CRM strategies to improve values for their targeted consumers to enhance satisfaction level, which in turn will help consumers to make important repurchase decision.

In practical implications, this chapter has provided valuable approach for FMCG firms to effectively plan and manage the utilisation of E-CRM to build customer satisfaction and repurchase intention. E-CRM serve as an effective platform for FMCG firms to reduce operating costs, generate sales, build relationship with customers and expand their markets globally. Thus, it is crucial for the firms to focus on the five E-CRM elements of service quality, customisation, transaction security, online feedback and website features to enhance customer satisfaction.

FMCG firms should prioritise on their resource allocations to enhance the E-CRM systems. In view that E-CRM involves a lot of work-process planning, refitting and reorganisation, thus sufficient amount of manpower allocation, trainings and developments, as well as investment on technology advancement should be given by the firms. The seamless customer experience in using the E-CRM systems will create positive word-of-mouth, enjoyment, trust and value that are beneficial to enhance customer satisfaction and repurchase intention.

CONCLUSION

This chapter has provided valuable insights on how FMCG firms can effectively utilise E-CRM to enhance customer satisfaction and repurchase intention. There are several limitations in the present study. First, the investigations on E-CRM on customer satisfaction and repurchase intention were confined to the FMCG industry. Future studies should explore other industries through comparative studies to achieve generalisation of the findings. Second, the E-CRM dimensions were confined to service quality, customisation, transaction security, online feedback and website features. Researcher proposed subsequent studies should explore on other E-CRM dimensions or characteristics such as reliability features, alternative payment methods, entertainment, trendiness and privacy. Third, the present study was conducted based on the samples obtained from Malaysia. Future studies should be conduct in other locations, as well as sample size could be extended. Forth, as the consumer behavioural outcome of repurchase intention is crucial to be investigated in the context of FMCG, subsequent studies should explore on other consumer behavioural outcomes of brand loyalty, brand image, E-CRM usage continuance and actual repurchase.

REFERENCES

Adejumo, A. A. (2019). Integrating Implementation Strategy, Challenges and Success Factors of CRM and e-CRM among Selected FMCG in Nigeria. *International Journal of Business and Risk Management*, 2(1), 27–35.

Ahuja, V., & Medury, Y. (2010). Corporate blogs as e-CRM tools: Building consumer engagement through content management. *Journal of Database Marketing and Customer Strategy Management*, *17*(2), 91–105. doi:10.1057/dbm.2010.8

Al-dweeri, R. M., Ruiz Moreno, A., Montes, F. J. L., Obeidat, Z. M., & Al-dwairi, K. M. (2019). The effect of e-service quality on Jordanian student's e-loyalty: An empirical study in online retailing. *Industrial Management & Data Systems, 119*(4), 902–923. doi:10.1108/IMDS-12-2017-0598

Al-Hawary, S. I. S., & Al-Smeran, W. F. (2016). Impact of Electronic Service Quality on Customers Satisfaction of Islamic Banks in Jordan. *International Journal of Academic Research in Accounting. Finance and Management Sciences, 7*(1), 170–188.

Alim, S., & Ozuem, W. (2014). The Influences of e-CRM on Customer Satisfaction and Loyalty in the UK Mobile Industry. *Journal of Applied Business and Finance Researches, 3*(2), 47–54.

Alim, S., & Ozuem, W. (2016). The influences of e-CRM on customer satisfaction and loyalty in the UK mobile industry. *Journal of Applied Business and Finance Researches, 3*(2), 47–54.

Amazhanova, K., & Huseynov, F. (2018). The impact of electronic customer relationship management on customer satisfaction in Turkey. *Yönetim. Ekonomi ve Pazarlama Araştırmaları Dergisi, 2*(4), 13–26.

Anim, N. A. H. M., & Omar, N. A. (2021). Does gamification work in a serious context? The influence of gamification, utilitarian, and hedonic features in the community-based crowdfunding platform. *Malaysian Journal of Society and Space, 17*(2), 79–92.

Anshari, M., Almunawar, M. N., Lim, S. A., & Al-Mudimigh, A. (2019). Customer relationship management and big data enabled: Personalization & customization of services. *Applied Computing and Informatics, 15*(2), 94–101. doi:10.1016/j.aci.2018.05.004

Awang, Z. (2014). Research Methodology and Data Analysis (2nd ed.). UiTM Press.

Bagozzi, R., & Yi, Y. (1988). On the evaluation of structural equation models. *Journal of the Academy of Marketing Science, 16*(1), 74–94. doi:10.1007/BF02723327

Bilgihan, A., & Bujisic, M. (2015). The effect of website features in online relationship marketing: A case of online hotel booking. *Electronic Commerce Research and Applications, 14*(4), 222–232. doi:10.1016/j.elerap.2014.09.001

Bryman, A., & Bell, E. (2007). *Business Research Methods.* Oxford University Press Inc.

Bugaje, I. B. (2015). Effect of Electronic-Customer Relationship Management (e-CRM) on Business Organisations. *Abuja Journal of Business and Management, 1*(1), 73–80.

Cheung, M. L., Pires, G., & Rosenberger, P. J. (2020). The influence of perceived social media marketing elements on consumer–brand engagement and brand knowledge. *Asia Pacific Journal of Marketing and Logistics, 32*(3), 695–720. doi:10.1108/APJML-04-2019-0262

Dawn, S. K., & Chowdhury, R. (2011). Electronic Customer Relationship Management (E-CRM): Conceptual Framework and Developing a Model. *International Journal of Business & Information Technology, 1*(1), 75–84.

Dehghanpouri, H., Soltani, Z., & Rostamzadeh, R. (2020). The impact of trust, privacy and quality of service on the success of E-CRM: The mediating role of customer satisfaction. *Journal of Business and Industrial Marketing, 35*(11), 1831–1847. doi:10.1108/JBIM-07-2019-0325

Dibb, S., Simkin, L., Pride, W., & Ferrell, O. (2006). *Marketing: Concepts and Strategies* (5th ed.). Houghton Mifflin.

Ebrahim, R., Ghoneim, A., Irani, Z., & Fan, Y. (2016). A brand preference and repurchase intention model: The role of consumer experience. *Journal of Marketing Management, 32*(13-14), 1230–1259. doi:10.1080/0267257X.2016.1150322

Eltahir, A. M., Ahmed, T. M., Ahmed, H., & Abdalfadil, T. A. (2021). Comparative study of customer relationship management (CRM) and electronic customer relationship management (E-CRM). *International Journal of Advanced and Applied Sciences, 8*(7), 1–6. doi:10.21833/ijaas.2021.07.001

Evans, M., Jamal, A., & Foxall, G. (2006). *Consumer Behaviour*. John Wiley & Sons Ltd.

Farmania, A., Elsyah, R. D., & Tuori, M. A. (2021). Transformation of CRM Activities into e-CRM: The Generating e-Loyalty and Open Innovation. *Journal of Open Innovation, 7*(2), 109. doi:10.3390/joitmc7020109

Feinberg, R. A., Kadam, R., Hokama, L., & Kim, I. (2002). The State of Electronic Customer Relationship Management in Retailing. *International Journal of Retail & Distribution Management, 30*(10), 470–481. doi:10.1108/09590550210445344

Field, A. (2013). *Discovering Statistics using SPSS* (4th ed.). Sage.

Fornell, C., & Larcker, D. F. (1981). Evaluating structural equation models with unobservable variables and measurement error. *JMR, Journal of Marketing Research, 18*(1), 39–50. doi:10.1177/002224378101800104

Hair, J. F., Black, W. C., Babin, B. J., & Anderson, R. E. (2010). *Multivariate Data Analysis: A Global Perspective*. Pearson Education Inc.

Hair, J. F., Hult, G. T. M., Ringle, C. M., & Sarstedt, M. (2017). *A primer on partial least squares structural equation modeling (PLS-SEM)* (2nd ed.). Sage.

Hardjono, B., & Tan, B. Y. (2017). Brand Extension of Fast Moving Consumer Goods To Customers' Perception. *Trikonomika, 16*(2), 51–62. doi:10.23969/trikonomika.v16i2.714

Helkkula, A., & Kelleher, C. (2010). Circularity of customer service experience and customer perceived value. *Journal of Customer Behaviour, 9*(1), 37–53. doi:10.1362/147539210X497611

Hellier, P. K., Geursen, G. M., Carr, R. A., & Rickard, J. A. (2003). Customer repurchase intention: A general structural equation model. *European Journal of Marketing, 37*(11), 1762–1800. doi:10.1108/03090560310495456

Hendriyani, C., & Auliana, L. (2018). Transformation from Relationship Marketing to Electronic Customer Relationship Management: A Literature Study. *Review of Integrative Business and Economics Research, 7*(2), 116–124.

Hirschmann, R. (2021, April 9). *FMCG market in Malaysia - statistics & facts*. https://www.statista.com/topics/7617/fmcg-market-in-malaysia/

Hooper, D., Coughlan, J., & Mullen, M. R. (2008). Structural equation modelling: Guidelines for determining model fit. *Electronic Journal of Business Research Methods, 6*(1), 53–60.

Ibrahim, Y., Abbas, T. M., & Kamal, M. (2021). The Use of Electronic Customer Relationship Management (E-CRM) Features through Hotel' Website to Enhance Customer Loyalty and Brand Image. *Journal of Association of Arab Universities for Tourism and Hospitality, 21*(7), 103–125. doi:10.21608/jaauth.2021.79828.1190

Ismail, N. A., & Hussin, H. (2015). Perception on E-CRM features for Airline Websites in Malaysia: Some Empirical Evidence. In *Proceedings of the International Conference of E-Commerce*. UUM.

Jacoby, J. (2002). Stimulus-organism-response reconsidered: An evolutionary step in modeling (consumer) behaviour. *Journal of Consumer Psychology, 12*(1), 51–57. doi:10.1207/S15327663JCP1201_05

Jeon, H. G., Kim, C., Lee, J., & Lee, K. C. (2021). Understanding E-Commerce Consumers' Repeat Purchase Intention: The Role of Trust Transfer and the Moderating Effect of Neuroticism. *Frontiers in Psychology, 12*, 690039. doi:10.3389/fpsyg.2021.690039 PMID:34140923

Kakeesh, D., Al-Weshah, G., & Al-Ma'aitah, N. (2021). Maintaining Customer Loyalty Using Electronic Customer Relationship Management (E-CRM): Qualitative Evidence from Small Food Businesses in Jordan. *Impact of Current Trends in Social Commerce, Economics, and Business Analytics, 39*(7), 1–18. doi:10.25115/eea.v39i7.4810

Kampani, N., & Jhamb, D. (2020). Analyzing the Role of E-CRM in Managing Customer Relations: A Critical Review of the Literature. *Journal of Critical Review, 7*(4), 221–226.

Khalifa, M., & Shen, N. (2005). Effects of electronic customer relationship management on customer satisfaction: a temporal model. In *Proceedings of the 38th Hawaii International Conference on System Sciences*. IEEE Computer Society. 10.1109/HICSS.2005.224

Khalifa, M., & Shen, N. (2009). Modeling electronic customer relationship management success: Functional and temporal considerations. *Journal of Behaviour and Information Technology, 28*(4), 373–387. doi:10.1080/01449290802030373

Khanh, C. N. T., Phong, L. T., & Cao, K. D. (2021). The impact of organizational factors on E-CRM success implementation. *VINE Journal of Information and Knowledge Management Systems*. Advance online publication. doi:10.1108/VJIKMS-05-2020-0096

Khoa, B. T. (2022). Dataset for the electronic customer relationship management based on S-O-R model in electronic commerce. *Data in Brief, 42*, 108039. doi:10.1016/j.dib.2022.108039 PMID:35313498

Kim, C., Zhao, W., & Yang, K. H. (2008). An Empirical Study on the Integrated Framework of e-CRM in Online Shopping: Evaluating the Relationships Among Perceived Value, Satisfaction, and Trust Based on Customers' Perspectives. *Journal of Electronic Commerce in Organizations, 6*(3), 1–19. doi:10.4018/jeco.2008070101

Kim, M. J., Lee, C. K., & Jung, T. (2020). Exploring Consumer Behavior in Virtual Reality Tourism Using an Extended Stimulus-Organism-Response Model. *Journal of Travel Research, 59*(1), 69–89. doi:10.1177/0047287518818915

Kumar, A., Sikdar, P., Gupta, M., Singh, P., & Sinha, N. (2022). Drivers of satisfaction and usage continuance in e-grocery retailing: a collaborative design supported perspective. *Journal of Research in Interactive Marketing*. https://doi-org.ezproxy.um.edu.my/10.1108/JRIM-02-2020-0035

Kumar, M. P., & Kumar, T. S. (2014). E-business: Pros and cons in Customer Relationship Management. *International Journal of Management and International Business Studies*, *4*(3), 349–356.

Kumar, P., & Mokha, A. K. (2022). Electronic Customer Relationship Management (E-CRM) and Customer Loyalty: The Mediating Role of Customer Satisfaction in the Banking Industry. *International Journal of E-Business Research*, *18*(1), 1–22. doi:10.4018/IJEBR.293292

Kumar, P., Mokha, A. K., & Pattnaik, S. C. (2022). Electronic customer relationship management (E-CRM), customer experience and customer satisfaction: Evidence from the banking industry. *Benchmarking*, *29*(2), 551–572. doi:10.1108/BIJ-10-2020-0528

Lewis, B. R., & Mitchell, V. W. (1990). Defining and Measuring the Quality of Customer Service. *Marketing Intelligence & Planning*, *8*(6), 11–17. doi:10.1108/EUM0000000001086

Li, X., Zhou, Y., Wong, Y. D., Wang, X., & Yuen, K. F. (2021). What influences panic buying behaviour? A model based on dual-system theory and stimulus-organism-response framework. *International Journal of Disaster Risk Reduction*, *64*, 102484. doi:10.1016/j.ijdrr.2021.102484

Maecker, O., Barrot, C., & Becker, J. U. (2016). The Effect of Social Media Interactions on Customer Relationship Management. *Business Research*, *9*(1), 133–155. doi:10.100740685-016-0027-6

Majeed, M., Asare, C., Fatawu, A., & Abubakari, A. (2022). An analysis of the effects of customer satisfaction and engagement on social media on repurchase intention in the hospitality industry. *Cogent Business & Management*, *9*(1), 2028331. doi:10.1080/23311975.2022.2028331

Mang'unyi, E. E., Khabala, O. T., & Govender, K. K. (2018). Bank customer loyalty and satisfaction: The influence of virtual e-CRM. *African Journal of Economic and Management Studies*, *9*(2), 250–265. doi:10.1108/AJEMS-08-2017-0183

Meuter, M. L., Ostrom, A. L., Roundtree, R. I., & Bitner, M. J. (2000). Self-service technologies: Understanding customer satisfaction with technology-based service encounters. *Journal of Marketing*, *64*(3), 50–64. doi:10.1509/jmkg.64.3.50.18024

Miralam, M. S., Junnaidi, M. H., & Moizuddin, S. (2019). A Study on Customer Satisfaction in FMCG Sector with Select Hypermarkets in Riyadh City Kingdom of Saudi Arabia. *International Review of Management and Business Research, 8*(2), 170–178.

Mohan, B. C., & Sequeira, A. H. (2016). The impact of customer-based brand equity on the operational performance of FMCG companies in India. *IIMB Management Review, 28*(1), 13–19. doi:10.1016/j.iimb.2015.11.002

Mustikasari, A., Krisnawati, M., & Sutrisno, E. (2021). Customer Experience and Repurchase Intention in Multi-Channel: Customer Satisfaction as Mediating Variable. *Journal of Industrial Distribution & Business, 12*(3), 7–19.

Namini, N. S. (2016). *Effective Factors on Customer Satisfaction and Customer Loyalty in FMCGs.* https://www.proquest.com/openview/c7530b55b5166341bdebf8e192013648/1?pq-origsite=gscholar&cbl=2026366&diss=y

Nikou, S. H., Selamat, H. B., Yusoff, R. C. M., & Khiabani, M. M. (2016). Electronic Customer Relationship Management, Customer Satisfaction, and Customer Loyalty: A Comprehensive Review Study. *International Journal of Management and Economics Invention, 2*(12), 1133–1144. doi:10.18535/ijmei/v2i12.02

Oliver, R. L. (1999). Whence consumer loyalty? *Journal of Marketing, 63*(4_suppl1), 33–44. doi:10.1177/00222429990634s105

Oumar, T. K., Mang'unyi, E. E., Govender, K. K., & Rajkaran, S. (2017). Exploring the e-CRM – e-customer- e-loyalty nexus: A Kenyan commercial bank case study. *Management & Marketing. Challenges for the Knowledge Society, 12*(4), 674–696. doi:10.1515/mmcks-2017-0039

Palaci, F., Salcedo, A., & Topa, G. (2019). Cognitive and Affective antecedents of Consumers' Satisfaction: A systematic Review of two research approaches. *Sustainability, 11*(2), 431. doi:10.3390u11020431

Parasuraman, A., Berry, L., & Zeithaml, V. (1988). SERVQUAL: A multiple-item scale for measuring customer perceptions of service quality. *Journal of Retailing, 64*, 26–43.

Pham, T. S. H., & Ahammad, M. F. (2017). Antecedents and consequences of online customer satisfaction: A holistic process perspective. *Technological Forecasting and Social Change, 124*, 332–342. doi:10.1016/j.techfore.2017.04.003

Pradana, H. A., Riza, B. S., Naseer, M., Soetarno, D., & Mantoro, T. (2017). The effect of e-CRM towards service quality and net benefits using structure equation modeling. In *Proceedings of the 2017 Second International Conference on Informatics and Computing*. Institute of Electrical and Electronics Engineers. 10.1109/IAC.2017.8280535

Pramudito, D., Mursitama, T. N., Abdinagoro, S. B., & Harischandra, H. (2021). The Moderation Effect of e-Trust and Big Data Quality in e-Grocery: An Empirical Research from Outside of Java Island. *Turkish Journal of Computer and Mathematics Education*, *12*(10), 6445–6459.

Rashwan, H. H. M., Mansi, A. L. M., & Hassan, H. E. (2019). The impact of the E-CRM (expected security and convenience of website design) on E- loyalty field study on commercial banks. *The Journal of Business and Retail Management Research*, *14*(1), 106–122. doi:10.24052/JBRMR/V14IS01/ART-10

Ravald, A., & Grönroos, C. (1996). The value concept and relationship marketing. *European Journal of Marketing*, *30*(2), 19–30. doi:10.1108/03090569610106626

Rhee, Y. J. (2010). The Effects of e-CRM on Consumer Satisfaction and Repurchase Intention. *Journal of Korean Society of Clothing and Textiles*, *34*(8), 1277–1289. doi:10.5850/JKSCT.2010.34.8.1277

Rohm, A., Kaltcheva, V. D., & Milne, G. R. (2013). A mixed-method approach to examining brandconsumer interactions driven by social media. *Journal of Research in Interactive Marketing*, *7*(4), 295–311. doi:10.1108/JRIM-01-2013-0009

Saunders, M., Lewis, P., & Thornhill, A. (2009). *Research Methods for Business Students* (5th ed.). Prentice Hall.

Schulze, C., Schöler, L., & Skiera, B. (2015). Customizing social media marketing. *MIT Sloan Management Review*, *56*(2), 8–10.

Shen, K., & Khalifa, M. (2008). Exploring multidimensional conceptualization of social presence in the context of online communities. *International Journal of Human-Computer Interaction*, *24*(7), 722–748. doi:10.1080/10447310802335789

Shin, J. K., & Lee, S. Y. (2018). The Effects of the Delivery Service Quality of Online Fresh Food Shopping Malls on E-Satisfaction and Repurchase Intention of Online Customers. *East Asian Journal of Business Economics*, *6*(2), 14–27. doi:10.20498/eajbe.2018.6.2.14

Tariq, M., Jamil, A., Ahmad, M. S., & Ramayah, T. (2019). Modeling the effectiveness of electronic customer relationship management (E-CRM) systems: Empirical evidence from Pakistan. *Revista Gestão & Tecnologia, 19*, 77–100. doi:10.20397/2177-6652/0.v0i0.1747

Tian, J., & Wang, S. (2017). Signaling Service Quality via Website e-CRM Features: More Gains for Smaller and Lesser Known Hotels. *Journal of Hospitality & Tourism Research (Washington, D.C.), 41*(2), 211–245. doi:10.1177/1096348014525634

Tzavlopoulos, Y. E., Gotzmani, K., Andronikidis, A., & Vassiliadis, C. A. (2019). Determining the impact of e-commerce quality on customers' perceived risk, satisfaction, value and loyalty. *International Journal of Quality and Service Sciences, 11*(4), 576–587. doi:10.1108/IJQSS-03-2019-0047

Vasudevan, P., & Arokiasamy, L. (2021). Online Shopping Among Young Generation in Malaysia. *Electronic Journal of Business and Management, 6*(1), 31–38.

Vila, T. D., González, E. A., Vila, N. A., & Brea, J. A. F. (2021). Indicators of Website Features in the User Experience of E-Tourism Search and Metasearch Engines. *Journal of Theoretical and Applied Electronic Commerce Research, 16*(1), 18–36. doi:10.4067/S0718-18762021000100103

Vyas, P. H., & Patel, A. V. (2004). Customising e-CRM Strategy in eMarketing. *Delhi Business Review, 5*(2), 67–79.

Yang, Z., & Babapour, H. (2022). Critical variables for assessing the effectiveness of electronic customer relationship management systems in online shopping. *Kybernetes*. Advance online publication. doi:10.1108/K-10-2021-0952

Yi, Y., & Nataraajan, R. (2018). Customer satisfaction in Asia. *Psychology and Marketing, 35*(6), 387–391. doi:10.1002/mar.21093

Yoon, J. H., Chung, J. B., & Kim, Y. M. (2008). A Study on the e-CRM, Customer Satisfaction, Repurchase Intention and Word of Mouth Intention in the Internet Shopping Mall. *Journal of Information Systems, 17*(1), 63–82. doi:10.5859/KAIS.2008.17.1.063

Zaim, H., Ramdani, M., & Haddi, A. (2020). E-CRM Success Factors as Determinants of Customer Satisfaction Rate in Retail Website. *International Journal of Computer Information Systems and Industrial Management Applications, 12*, 82–92.

Zaman, K., Bibi, S., Arshad, A., & Shahzad, A. (2012). Customer Loyalty in FMCG Sector of Pakistan. *Information Management and Business Review, 4*(1), 41–48. doi:10.22610/imbr.v4i1.962

Zatalini, M. A., & Pamungkas, T. N. (2017). Exploring the Success Factors of E-CRM Implementation on B2C E-Commerce: Satisfaction and Loyalty A Conceptual Framework. *Jurnal Ekonomi Bisnis*, *22*(2), 94–106.

KEY TERMS AND DEFINITIONS

Consumer Purchase Behaviour: A set of activities by consumer involving purchase and use of product or service.

Customer Satisfaction: The difference between customer expectations and customer receives from the usage of products or services.

Customer Touch Points: Any direct or indirect contact a customer has with the organisation offering product or service.

Customisation: To make or alter to individual or personal specifications.

Electronic Customer Relationship Management: The activities to manage customer relationships by using information technology.

Repurchase Intention: Consumers' motivation to continuously purchase the product or service.

Service Quality: The ability of the organisation to meet or exceed customer expectations

Chapter 3
Development of Effective Electronic Customer Relationship Management (ECRM) Model by the Applications of Web Intelligence Analytics

Salma Abdulaziz Alquhtani
King Khalid University, Saudi Arabia

Anandhavalli Muniasamy
https://orcid.org/0000-0001-8940-3954
King Khalid University, Saudi Arabia

ABSTRACT

Analysis of customer relationships based on their satisfaction is a practical and motivating success factor for the growth of every company. Web intelligence describes the scientific development that uses information technology and artificial intelligence for new frameworks, services, and products provided by the web. This chapter aims to present the model of analyzing the users' sentiments from their online reviews on an e-commerce platform using machine-learning classifiers, namely naive bayes, logistic regression, support vector machine, and neural network. For data analysis, latent semantic analysis has been applied to examine the most frequent words used in online reviews. Finally, customers' interest in online shopping analysis has been performed to classify the customers' sentiments from their posted reviews on the e-commerce platform. In addition, the authors compared the performance results of these classifiers on the e-commerce dataset. The results reveal that the naive bayes classifier has performed better than all the other three classifiers.

DOI: 10.4018/978-1-6684-5386-5.ch003

INTRODUCTION

Online shopping is a form of e-commerce and provides advantages such as avoiding store visits and travel costs, shopping at any time, increasing marketing, decreasing overhead expenses, and offering variety of products for both consumers and retailers. According to (Sam & Chatwin, 2015), it has been found that more than 85% of the world's online population supported the online shopping via internet during the recent year. This involves the technical specifications of an online store focused on the technology-centered view, which influences consumer's awareness of using that technology (Cheng, 2009). It allows the customer to buy products or services directly online by choosing products while visiting online shopping mobile applications or websites (Kütz, 2016).

The study (Mohammed & Mouhoub, 2014) sheds light on an important topic in the field of e-marketing, which is accepting online shopping by consumers. It also discussed the benefits of using online shopping in terms of saving money, time, effort, and getting rare products at competitive prices, and its impact and the results of using Internet in marketing, promotion, and sales to reduce operational costs.

The study (Moore, 2020) helps in understanding and analyzing the factors affecting individuals' behavior and decisions towards adopting or using internet shopping and ensuring their confidence in using internet-shopping technology as the human factor is the main driver of this process.

The chapter aims to apply four classifiers namely Neural Network, Support Vector Machine, Naive Bayes and Logistic Regression on e-commerce dataset, and compare the performance of the classifiers using various metrics in mining the buying interest of the customers in online shopping. The rest of the chapter has planned as follows: Section 2 focuses on background and survey related to online shopping and customer interests in e-commerce. Section 3 experimental methodology and problems on online-shopping. Section 4 covers the solutions& recommendations. Future research directions and the conclusion of the chapter is summarized in section 5 & 6 respectively.

BACKGROUND

Online Shopping

Business is the process of buying and selling products or providing services to customers. The traditional way of buying takes place when customers visit stores and search for the products or services they need. One of the obstacles to this traditional way of doing business is that the seller can obtain business from a specific geographic area where he has an organization and the buyer is restricted to accessing the products/services within the region he resides in, therefore, many companies have considered selling their products/services online.

E-commerce uses the World Wide Web for at least one part of the commercial transaction lifecycle, and it may use other technologies such as email. These technologies help in reaching a narrow market segment and increasing the percentage of sales and profits. On the other hand, the buyer can search for the products or services they want to buy all over the world, and because the market has become wider, there are many online rooms to negotiate with the product owner about the price of the service or product that he offers. E-commerce companies use online shopping sites for wholesale or retail sales directly to consumers or provide products or participate in markets via the Internet, which allows selling from the third-party to the consumer, or consumer-to-consumer sales, or buying and selling from one company to another company.

There are many benefits for the e-commerce business, starting with reducing the costs of buying and selling transactions. When offline stores calculate the costs of their transactions, they have to factor in other business expenses such as operational costs and others along with the actual number of transactions and may overwhelm the cost of employees or distributors in the event that the value of these costs increases, but by using electronic commerce, the cost of transactions is the same in almost all areas, whether one order or thousands of orders. In addition to these benefits, electronic selling almost eliminates processing errors that occur in issuing billing and order problems, which reduces the effort and wasted time in solving billing problems, so e-commerce provides employees with a focus on mainly profit-generating activities without engaging in other work. On the other hand, e-commerce can improve the buying or selling process due to the speed of communication that occurs between the seller and the buyer, which increases the buyer's desire to repeat purchases continuously, so that the volume of business will increase as for volume increases, cost decreases. Internet-based supply chain managements systems help to deliver the right product, in the right quantity, right place, on time to the customers. For this purpose, the business partners use ICT systems. These systems work together temporarily to share, exchange and process data during the whole business boundaries of the cooperating organizations. Data security and data privacy as well as compliance with laws and procedures have, of course, to be guaranteed.

Web Intelligence

The entry of the new information age, and the rapid growth of the Internet has changed almost every aspect of human life and technology, as it is considered a rich means of communication, which goes far beyond the traditional means of communication. Web technology has changed the methods of collecting, processing and storing information, which creates great opportunities and challenges for e-commerce, business, and marketing.

The term WI introduces a web-based conceptual model in which humans, machines, and things can collaborate to solve large scale intelligence-intensive problems more efficiently and. WI depends on artificial intelligence and information technology in covering various areas such as knowledge networks and network intelligence, semantics, social networking and social intelligence, web agents, web information filtering and retrieval, web mining, web security, integrity, privacy and trust, web and network services, web support systems, worldwide wisdom web, and web applications (e-learning, e-business, and evaluation) where the primary goals of WI are to understand and develop smart web-based systems, and these systems integrate all capabilities at the human level such as real-time response, power, and independent interaction with their environment, communication in natural language, logical thinking, planning, learning, discovery, and creativity.

Semantic analytics, also termed semantic relatedness, is the use of ontologies to analyze content in web resources. This field of research combines text analytics and Semantic Web technologies like Resource Description Framework (RDF). Semantic analytics measures the relatedness of different ontological concepts. Cognitive Computing in E-Commerce deals with simulation of human thought processing and analyzing it. Through analysis, Algorithms are generated by system in order to gain self-learning capabilities. E-commerce is one of the most human-interacting web intelligent applications that can track user browsing behavior for individual mouse clicks to increase targeted marketing.

Machine Learning

Machine learning (ML) is one of the areas of Artificial Intelligence, which has been a major component of solutions to technological problems that have caught major attention in the digital arena. In general, learning is the process of improving performance through experience, but in machine learning, a computer program is designed to perform some tasks after it is trained through different learning algorithms, and if its measurable performance improves, the program will learn from experience and gains more experience in implementing these tasks. The program produced by the learning algorithm contains millions of data, and if it is properly trained, then the program works with new cases with high accuracy, in addition to the cases that was trained on.

Logistic Regression

Logistic regression is selected as the employed machine learning technique in this research for performing classification of the sentiment analysis. Logistic regression is a statistical model used by machine learning in the field of statistics. It was developed by statisticians to describe the properties of a given procedure whose values rise rapidly and reach the maximum in carrying capacity, as its value forms s-shaped curve that can take any real number and map it into a value between 0 and 1, but not exactly at these limits (Swamy & Gorabal, 2020).

Naïve Bayes

The Naïve Bayesian (NB) statistical algorithms are among the most widely employed algorithms in text analysis and classification (Xu et al., 2020). The naive Algorithm is a straightforward probabilistic classifier that uses Bayes' Theorem and strong independence assumptions to classify data. Independent feature model is a more descriptive name for the basic probability model. Because of these feature independence assumptions, the sequence of features is unimportant, and the presence of one feature does not influence the presence of other features in classification tasks. These assumptions improve the efficiency of the Bayesian classification approach's calculation, but they significantly limit its application. The nave Bayes classifiers may be taught very efficiently, depending on the precise form of the probability model, by needing a relatively minimal amount of training data to estimate the parameters essential for classification. Because independent variables are assumed, just the values of the variables for each class should be calculated.

Support Vector Machine

SVM splits a data into two subsets by drawing a line, or "hyperplane" as shown in Figure 1. Vectors (tags) that falls into the category are in one subspace, whereas vectors, which do not relate to that category, are in another (Mourya & Kaur, 2020). That is one of the advantages of SVM algorithms, that they are "multi-dimensional." As a result, the more complicated the data, the more accurate the findings.

Neural Network

Traditional machine learning methods require a lot more training data than neural network algorithms (at least millions of tagged examples). Neural networks, also known as artificial neural networks (ANN) or feedforward neural networks, are computer networks based on neural networks found in the human brain.

Figure 1. Best Hyperplane in SVM

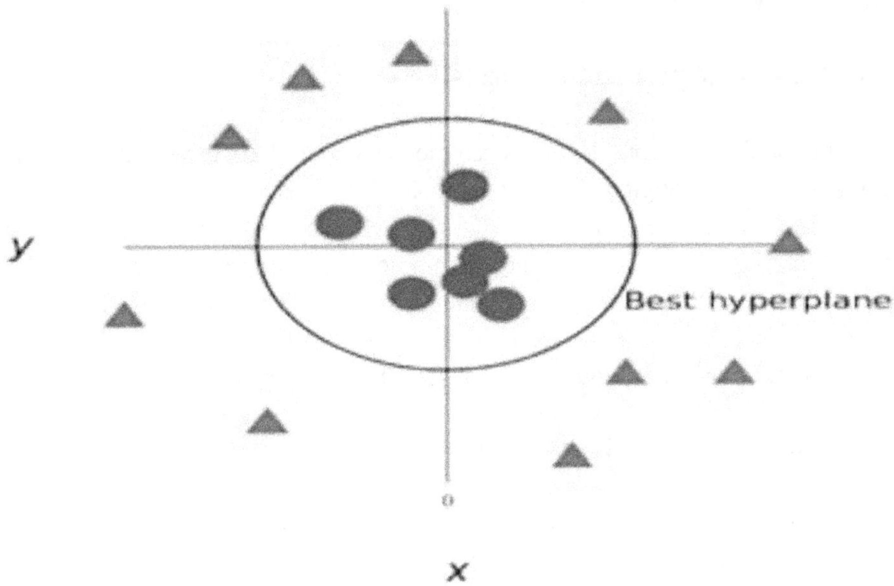

They are made up of neurons (also known as nodes) that are linked in the manner shown in Figure 2.

The feature vectors can be fed into a layer of input neurons, and the values are subsequently sent forward to a hidden layer. You feed the value forward at each connection, while the value is multiplied by a weight and a bias is applied to the

Figure 2. Model of a Neural Network

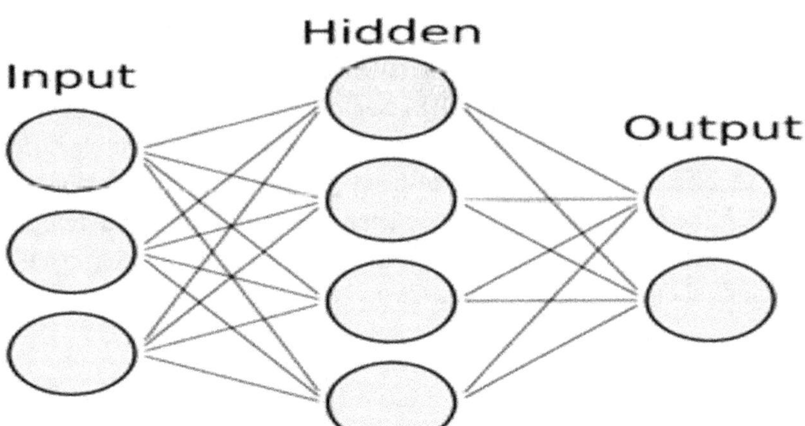

value. This occurs for each connection, and you eventually arrive at an output layer with one or more output nodes.

Natural Language Processing (NLP)

In order to achieve a strong level of customer service and effectively analyze their complaints, natural language processing technology and in-depth text mining are used. Where natural language processing (NLP) can be defined as a branch of artificial intelligence, and a subset of text mining. It is an interdisciplinary field that studies and develops algorithms and systems that enable computers to understand and carry out tasks that involve a human language. NLP may also be referred to as computational linguistics, computational speech, and language.

Latent Semantic Analysis (LSA)

Latent Semantic Analysis (LSA) is a technique in natural language processing, especially the distributional semantics. It aims to analyze the relationships between groups of terms in documents and produce a set of concepts related to these documents and terms. It is done by making some mathematical computation and analyzing the relationships between terms used in various applications, with the aim of retrieving intelligent information in search engines and news sites on the Internet, which require an accurate method to reach similarity in documents in order to carry out the tasks of classification, clustering, summarization, and research (Kherwa & Bansal, 2017).

Sentiment Analysis

Sentiment analysis is also called subjective analysis, as it classifies text according to the polarity and orientation of the opinion expressed, which helps analysts within organizations to gauge public opinion and conduct accurate market studies, study the popularity of their products, and the impact of the brand, in addition to learning about customer experiences (Zhang et al., 2018). Sentiment analysis consists of sentiment identification, feature selection, sentiment polarity and sentiment classification. With the accelerating developments in deep learning and artificial intelligence technologies, the ability of algorithms to analyze text has improved dramatically, thus making it easier for analysts to categorize incoming customer conversation and their opinions about the brand (Sam & Chatwin, 2015).

Literature Review

According to (Amiah et al., 2020), the number of online shoppers in US during 2019 has reached 93 million, as an increase of 35 million compared the year 2018. Authors in (Mourya & Kaur, 2020) reported that more than 60% of consumers shopping online at least once a month and only 1% have never shopped online. Thus, competition between online shopping sites has become intense due to the profitable marketing through the Internet. Factors like the basic way to get the product and the store's environment may affect the evaluation and selection of the product by the customer and thus environmental factors are very important to enhance the shopping behavior as the study showed (Mohan et al., 2013).

The study (Cheng & Fu, 2018) analyzed the online customer behavior, and reported that the websites social features, compatible with lifestyle. The online customer services has a significant impact on customer behavior and their intentions to adopt online purchase services, the number of visits by other consumers to the product had a positive impact on the dimensions of financial situations and compulsive buying online (Nanji, 2013).

e-commerce is the transaction channels in which people, organizations, and governments all participating for doing business transaction (Johan et al., 2020). Despite the several ad-vantages of e-commerce, the study (Huang et al., 2018) shows that there are some technical problems that e-commerce faces, such as the lack of understanding of the users' interests, due to the limited interaction between human and computer. In addition to the fact that using the same keywords in searching across different platforms may lead to unsecured results due to huge data and also lack of customization. The study (Napitupulu & Hidayat, 2020) also discussed the problem of inflexible interactive mode like text input and mouse click on ecommerce transaction rather than the voice interaction, which is more convenient.

Extracting useful information from complex big data is a hot research topic in the recent years due to the application of various classification algorithms for improving ecommerce with web data mining, feature extraction concept, text categorization and clustering, web text association analysis etc. for accurately extracting the text data in the web pages (Lin et al., 2017). In online shopping, the product page is usually the first page where the customers are directed to the product page has an important role in the success of online businesses and plays important role in the success of online shopping (Ramadhan et al., 2017).

LSA is an algebraic-statistical method (Evangelopoulos, 2001) for detecting and extracting the hidden semantic structures of words and sentences from the underlying topical structure of a document corpus. LR is a supervised learning algorithm and it extends the regression model to classify data and attain results of two or more possible values. LR is useful to perform sentiment analysis based on text classification and to examine the relationship between variables to investigate the most influencing factors on users' buying decision (Nicapotato, 2018).

NN has been successfully been used in various classification problems and recently it has been used for text mining. Neural networks techniques are used to increase the accuracy of classifiers learned with standard machine learning algorithms by obtaining better vector representations for words (Garg & Sharma, 2020). NB is a straightforward probabilistic classifier that uses Bayes' theorem and strong independence assumptions to classify the given data. Independent feature model is a more descriptive name for the basic probability model. Because of these feature independence assumptions, the sequence of features is unimportant, and the presence of one feature does not influence the presence of other features in classification tasks (Khan & Baharudin, 2010) while using NB.

SVMs are a strong text analysis machine learning method that, like Naive Bayes, requires little training data to begin producing correct results. SVM, on the other hand, requires more computing power than Naive Bayes, but the outcomes are quicker and more accurate (Burbidge, 2001). Each of the reviewed works showed different factors affecting the adoption of online shopping and the buying decision, and many studies presents the trust as an important factor for customer behavior. Therefore, this research proposed using machine learning techniques to investigate the customer's interest towards the adoption of online shopping and focuses on the impact of trust.

MAIN FOCUS OF THE CHAPTER

Problems of Online Shopping

Online shopping, whether at home, at the workplace, or in a different country, is becoming an appropriate way to make all purchases. This is particularly true for developing countries, where each store can have its own website. Promotions such as cash on delivery and exclusive discounts on online orders can be easily conveyed.

The motivation of this study appears from the low acceptance level and adoption of online shopping by consumers, and also the negative perception of individuals towards this technology even with the great benefits that it can offer for them in terms of saving time, effort and money. This negative perception is dept to two parts, one part is regarding the technology itself and one part is regarding the consumer, including the lack of confidence among consumers to use this technology.

Customer satisfaction with online shopping depends directly on a variety of factors. However, there is an ongoing consumer problem associated with the issue of the influence of the determinants of online shopping on customer approval and satisfaction.

Some researchers stated that retailers should focus on customer experiences, others found that compelling online service increases customer usage of online shopping. Several researchers showed that designing interactive systems with graphical user interfaces is an important step in developing devices and websites to improve online shopping systems and recommendations to appeal more customers. The Interface design has proven to be a great sales funnel and helps secure more sales. Some examples of design elements affecting sales are composition, color balance, navigation placement, and demonstration of the functionality of an application related to an actual case. It is important to understand and take into consideration the needs and preferences of the online shopper. In this regard, many online shopping systems rely on evoking customer preferences while others suggest products based on recommendations of other customers.

Although, many research examined online shopping behavior and drivers of online shopping such as perceived price, risk, website characteristics, and consumer reviews. One of the main problems is still not enough covered or answered by researchers, why many online users are not using online shopping especially in the developing countries and what are the most significant factors that influence their buying decisions.

PROPOSED METHODOLOGY

The experimental methodology used in this paper is shown in Figure 3. Firstly, we pre-processed the dataset before simulating the classification algorithms. All the experiments are performed in Python platform. We used the ratio of 80/20 data split for training and testing sets. For the classification of the customer recommendation for the product and their review, the four classifiers are applied to the preprocessed datasets and the performance of every classifier is analyzed using the metrics given in Figure 3.

Online customer reviews are text data, which is mainly consisting of nouns, adjectives, adverbs, verbs, and emoticons. Before applying customer's review analysis, the data should be prepared in a form that machine can understand and deal with. The e-commerce dataset is pre-processed using several NLP techniques to prepare data for analysis. Then, data has been analyzed using LR, SVM, NB, and NN classifiers to implement sentiment analysis.

Figure 3. Experimental Methodology

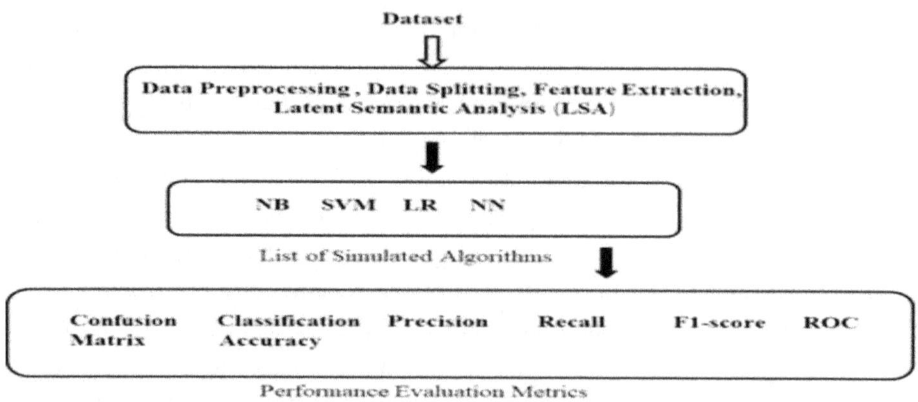

DATA PREPROCESSING AND ANALYSIS

Natural language processing (NLP) tools were imported from NLTK library. The main NLTK tools used for pre-processing For data analysis, firstly, Latent semantic analysis (LSA) is applied to examine the most frequent words used in the online reviews. Then a word cloud is created for clearer view, Finally, a sentiment analysis is performed using four main classifiers to classify the customers' sentiment from their posted reviews on the e-commerce platform. LSA has been applied to know the top 20 frequent used words and their weight are as follows Figure 4 and Figure 5.

FEATURE SELECTION

Feature selection is the method of reducing the number of input variables while creating a machine learning model. In order to reduce the the computational cost of modeling and/ or to increase the model's accuracy, the number of input variables should be reduced. We concentrated on two features for our task: the review text and the Recommended IND. The "review text" includes all the online reviews from customers, it is selected to be analyzed and mining the customer interest using text mining techniques.

Figure 4. Top 20 words in recommended reviews

	Coefficient
perfect	5.059418
little	4.332028
great	4.038365
comfortable	4.036251
love	3.983114

	Coefficient
unflattering	-4.005775
cheap	-4.324764
be	-4.384440
disappointed	-5.105635
return	-5.121882

Figure 5. Top 20 words in recommended reviews

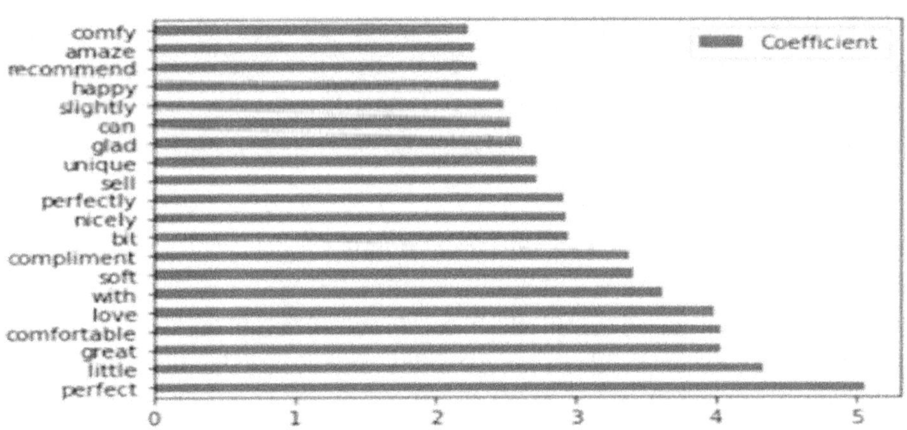

Table 1. Description of Metrics

Name of the Metrics	Formula
Confusion Matrix	Predicted Actual 0 1 0 True Negatives False Positives 1 False Negatives True Positives
Classification Accuracy	$\frac{True\,Positives + True\,Negatives}{Total}$
Precision	$\frac{True\ Positives}{True\ Positives + False\ Positives}$
Recall	$\frac{True\ Positives}{True\ Positives + False\ Negatives}$
F1-Score	$2 * \frac{Precision * Recall}{Precision + Recall}$

MACHINE LEARNING CLASSIFIERS

Four classifiers are trained using the train data, then applied on the test data to predict users' sentiments. The applied classifiers are logistic regression (LR), Support Vector Machine (SVM), Naïve Bayes (NB), and Neural Network (NN). The column (Recommended IND) is used to represents the sentiments, "Recommended IND" includes Binary variables stating where the customer recommends the product, 1 is recommended, 0 is not recommended. We consider 0 for negative sentiment and 1 for Positive sentiment. Finally, different performance metrics are used to evaluate and compare between the four classifiers.

SOLUTIONS AND RECOMMENDATIONS

We analyzed and evaluated four machine learning classifiers using six performance metrics. Table 1 depicts the description of all the metrics used in this study.

Evaluation with the receiver operating characteristic curve (ROC) are shown in Figure 6, which shows that results look appropriate for all the classifiers.

Figure 6. ROC for each classifier

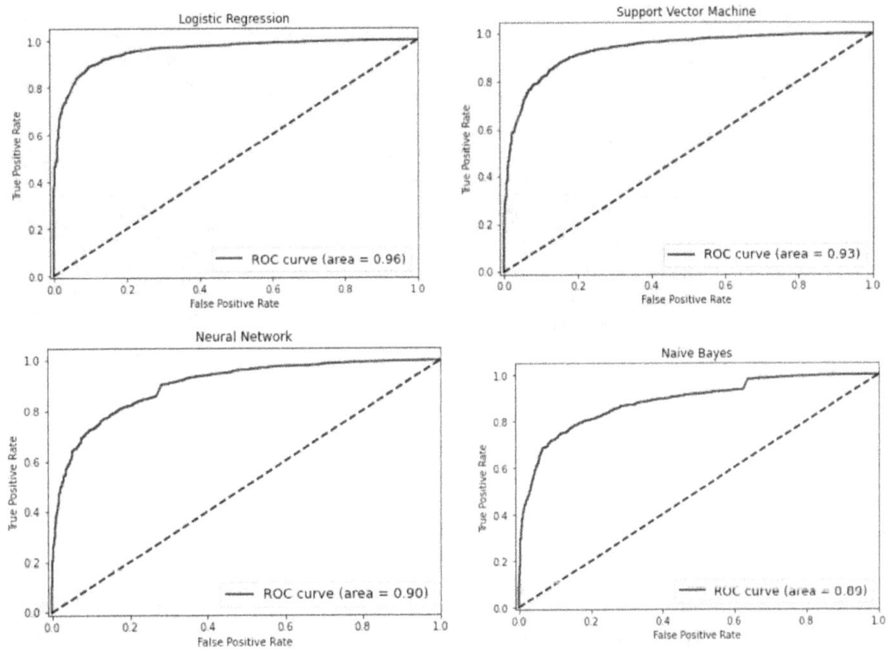

We started the evaluation with the receiver operating characteristic curve (ROC) and Area under the curve (AUC). As shown in Figure 6, Logistic regression achieves the highest AUC (0.96). However, results look good for all the classifiers. To verify this result, we examined other evaluation metrics such as confusion matrix.

Confusion matrix (CM) measure used while solving classification problems. It shows the classification measures of the given dataset in a specific table layout that allows visualization of the performance of a classifier.

To reach more information, we used confusion matrices. Four values were presented by the confusion matrix as shown in Table 1. TP, FP, FN, TN.

Figure 7 shows the resulted confusion matrices. As shown in Figure 7, the highest true positive (TP) values were achieved by LR and NN. However, the highest true negative (TN) values were achieved by SVM, but the TP for NB is not clear in the resulted matrix. Therefore, we cannot rely on the results of these confusion matrices, and we used classification report to verify the results of classification.

It has been found that SVM classifier does not give good results although it has high ROC values.

We have already examined ROC curves and confusion matrices, but this is not enough for a final decision. In this case, the classification report might be the best

Figure 7. Confusion Matrix for Each Classifier

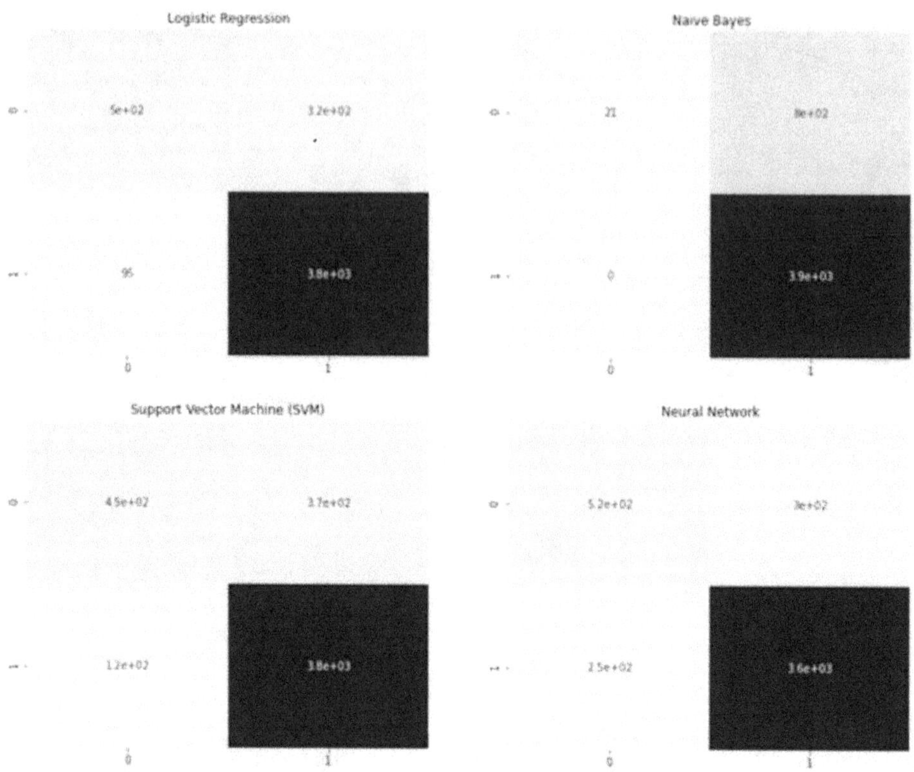

choice to evaluate our models. Table 2 shows all the four classifiers' results based on the metrics precision, recall, F1-score and accuracy.

LR and NB achieves the best F1-score values among other classifiers (0.96 and 0.97). To decide which one is the best from these two classifiers, the elapsed time in the classification process is calculated for each classifier, NB consumed the least execution time. Therefore, NB is considered as the best classifier in this research work.

Table 2. Comparison between the classifiers' results

Classifier	Precision	Recall	F1-Score	Accuracy	Execution Time
LR	0.87	0.94	0.96	0.94	0:00:01.143353
NB	0.96	0.98	0.97	0.94	0:00:00.012192
SVM	0.79	0.89	0.94	0.89	0:00:58.608685
NN	0.96	0.97	0.96	0.93	0:01:59.735018

FUTURE RESEARCH DIRECTIONS

Apply the Techniques on Different Datasets

The dataset is the key factor, when dealing with machine learning and deep learning techniques. The better the dataset, the better the results. The best dataset includes more information (big data) and involves more related variables to the research. To have more results that are correct and extract more valuable and accurate information, a larger and more appropriate dataset might be used as a future work.

FOCUS ON MORE AI TECHNIQUES

This research focuses on quantitative research to investigate the relationships between variables, to define the most influenced factors on users' attitude. For future work, one can try to depend more on AI techniques to investigate the relationships between variables and analyses the impact factors. Recent AI techniques such as deep learning algorithms, which are widely employed lately in several applications, can be utilized in analyzing and extracting more useful information from review texts.

CONCLUSION

The ecommerce domain generates massive online shopping data due to the advancement of information technologies. Finding the hidden knowledge in this data is a challenging task in machine learning. Web Intelligence techniques used in this research have succeeded to analyze the data of an online store shopping.

This chapter reports the applications of the well-known machine learning algorithms for the analysis of customer's interest on online shopping and classify the customers' sentiment from their posted reviews on the e-commerce platform. In addition, we compared the performance results of these classifiers on e-commerce dataset. Logistic regression was the most effective classifier for predicting customers' sentiments from their text reviews, while SVM is the second best classifier among other machine learning algorithms in terms of execution time and the metrics like accuracy, recall, F1-score, confusion matrix and ROC.

ACKNOWLEDGMENT

We acknowledge King Khalid University for giving the opportunity to carry out this research. This research received no specific grant from any funding agency in the public, commercial, or not-for-profit sectors.

REFERENCES

Amiah, G., Martin, M., Minard, M., Smruthi, S. T. S., Alexandrova, Y., Khokhar, A., & Trajcevski, G. (2020). TOSNOS: To Online Shop, or Not-to Online Shop-Enabling Combined Improvements. In *2020 IEEE International Conference on Pervasive Computing and Communications Workshops* (pp. 1-3). IEEE.

Burbidge, B. (2001). *An Introduction to Support Vector Machines for Data Mining. UCL.* Computer Science Dept.

Cheng, C. H. (2009). *A study on the applications of data mining techniques to enhance customer lifetime value. WSEAS Transactions on Information Science and Applications.*

Cheng, H. H., & Fu, T. J. (2018). The Determinants of Online Shopping Behavior. In *2018 International Conference on Intelligent Autonomous Systems (ICoIAS)* (pp. 97-100). 10.1109/ICoIAS.2018.8494098

Evangelopoulos, N. (2001). Tracing Taylorism's technical and sociotechnical duality through Latent Semantic Analysis. Analysis. *Journal of Business and Management*, 57–74.

Garg, N., & Sharma, K. (2020). Machine Learning in Text Analysis. In Handbook of Research on Emerging Trends and Applications of Machine Learning (pp.383-402). IGI Global. doi:10.4018/978-1-5225-9643-1.ch018

Huang, Y., Chai, Y., Liu, Y., & Shen, J. (2018). Architecture of next-generation e-commerce platform. *Tsinghua Science and Technology*, *24*(1), 18–29. doi:10.26599/TST.2018.9010067

Johan, K., Samantha, W., Tandean, M. J., & Sihombing, S. O. (2020). *The Relationships between Web Design, Reliability, Privacy, Service Quality, and Purchase Intention of Customers at E-commerce Business: An Empirical Study*. Academic Press.

Khan, A., Baharudin, B., & Lee. (2010). A review of machine learning algorithms for text-documents classification. *Journal of Advances in Information Technology, 1*(1), 4-20.

Kherwa, P., & Bansal, P. (2017). Latent Semantic Analysis: An approach to understand semantic of text. In *2017 International Conference on Current Trends in Computer, Electrical, Electronics and Communication (CTCEEC)* (pp. 870-874). IEEE. 10.1109/CTCEEC.2017.8455018

Kütz. (2016). Introduction to E-commerce. Academic Press.

Lin, W., Dongying, L., Haizhang, S., & Shengbao, D. (2017). Research on the evolution law of the semantic web structure of online shopping reviews. *2nd Advanced Information Technology, Electronic and Automation Control Conference (IAEAC)*, 395-398.

Mohammed, B., & Mouhoub, M. (2014). Evaluation of an Online Shopping System under Preferences and Constraints. In *Canadian Conference on Electrical and Computer Engineering* (pp. 1-8), IEEE. 10.1109/CCECE.2014.6900974

Mohan, G., Sivakumaran, B., & Sharma, P. (2013). Impact of store environment on impulse buying behavior. *European Journal of Marketing*, *47*(10), 1711–1732. doi:10.1108/EJM-03-2011-0110

Moore, K. (2020). *Ecommerce 101 + The History of Online Shopping: What The Past Says About Tomorrow's Retail Challenges*. Retrieved from big commerce: https://www.bigcommerce.com/blog/ecommerce/#faqs-about-ecommerce

Mourya, A. K., & Kaur, H. (2020). Performance and Evaluation of Different Kernels in Support Vector Machine for Text Mining. In *Advances in Intelligent Computing and Communication* (pp. 264–271). Springer. doi:10.1007/978-981-15-2774-6_33

Nanji, A. (2013). *Online shopping trends 2013: Most popular categories, top purchase drivers*. Academic Press.

Napitupulu, N. A., & Hidayat, Z. (2020). The Influence of Online Shopping Applications, Strategic Promotions, and Hedonist Habits on e-Shopaholic Behavior. In *2020 International Conference on Information Management and Technology (ICIMTech)* (pp. 922-927). IEEE. 10.1109/ICIMTech50083.2020.9211181

Nicapotato. (2018). *Women's E-Commerce Clothing Reviews* [Dataset]. https://www.kaggle.com/nicapotato/womens-ecommerce-clothing-reviews

Ramadhan, W. P., Novianty, S. A., & Setianingsih, S. C. (2017). Sentiment analysis using multinomial logistic regression. In *International Conference on Control, Electronics, Renewable Energy and Communications (ICCREC)* (pp. 46-49). IEEE.

Sam, K. M., & Chatwin, C. R. (2015, December). Evaluating the effectiveness of online product planning and layout tools in online apparel shopping. In *IEEE International Conference on Industrial Engineering and Engineering Management (IEEM)* (pp. 635-639). 10.1109/IEEM.2015.7385725

Swamy, L. N., & Gorabal, J. V. (2020). Logistic regression-based classification for reviews analysis on E-commerce based applications. In *Frontiers in intelligent computing: Theory and applications* (pp. 323–334). Springer. doi:10.1007/978-981-13-9920-6_34

Xu, F., Pan, Z., & Xia, R. (2020). E-commerce product review sentiment classification based on a naïve Bayes continuous learning framework. *Information Processing & Management, 57*(5), 102221. doi:10.1016/j.ipm.2020.102221

Zhang, L., Wang, S., & Liu, B. (2018). Deep learning for sentiment analysis: A survey. *Wiley Interdisciplinary Reviews. Data Mining and Knowledge Discovery, 8*(4). Advance online publication. doi:10.1002/widm.1253

ADDITIONAL READING

Agarap, A. F. (2018). Statistical analysis on E-commerce reviews, with sentiment classification using bidirectional recurrent neural network (RNN). arXiv preprint arXiv:1805.03687.

Ahmad, N. B. H., & Shamsuddin, S. M. (2010). A comparative analysis of mining techniques for automatic detection of student's learning style. In 2010 10th International Conference on Intelligent Systems Design and Applications (pp. 877-882). IEEE. 10.1109/ISDA.2010.5687150

Al Amrani, Y., Lazaar, M., & El Kadiri, K. E. (2018). Random forest and support vector machine based hybrid approach to sentiment analysis. *Procedia Computer Science, 127*, 511–520. doi:10.1016/j.procs.2018.01.150

Xu, F., Pan, Z., & Xia, R. (2020). E-commerce product review sentiment classification based on a naïve Bayes continuous learning framework. *Information Processing & Management, 57*(5), 102221. doi:10.1016/j.ipm.2020.102221

Xu, X. W., Wang, X., Li, Y., & Haghighi, M. (2017). Business intelligence in online customer textual reviews: Understanding consumer perceptions and influential factors. *International Journal of Information Management, 37*(6), 673–683. doi:10.1016/j.ijinfomgt.2017.06.004

Qureshi, M. A., Asif, M., Hassan, M. F., Abid, A., Kamal, A., Safdar, S., & Akber, R. (2022). Sentiment Analysis of Reviews in Natural Language: Roman Urdu as a Case Study. *IEEE Access: Practical Innovations, Open Solutions, 10*, 24945–24954. doi:10.1109/ACCESS.2022.3150172

Sintoris, K., & Vergidis, K. (2017). Extracting business process models using natural language processing (NLP) techniques. In 2017 IEEE 19th conference on business informatics (CBI) (Vol. 1, pp. 135-139). IEEE.

KEY TERMS AND DEFINITIONS

AI: Artificial intelligence.
ANN: Artificial neural network.
AUC: Area under the curve.
E-Commerce: Electronic commerce.
FP: False positive.
LR: Logistic regression.
LSA: Latent semantic analysis.
ML: Machine learning.
NB: Naïve Bayes.
NLP: Natural language processing.
NN: Neural network.
ROC: Receiver operating characteristic.
SVM: Support vector machine.
TP: True positive.

Chapter 4
Content Marketing Framework for Building Brand Image:
A Case Study of Sohar International School, Oman

Muhammad Saleem
University of Buraimi, Oman

Shad Ahmad Khan
https://orcid.org/0000-0001-7593-3487
University of Buraimi, Oman

Hesham Magd
Modern College of Business and Science, Oman

ABSTRACT

In an increasingly interconnected digital world, content marketing plays a pivotal role in building the brand image of contemporary organizations. For the current study, a leading international school in Oman is selected to study the effectiveness of their content marketing over the last two years and as a result to develop a framework, which can be followed by other organizations as well. The school's content marketing efforts and active social media presence consistently had a positive impact on their audiences resulting in high enrollments even during the unprecedented times under the COVID-19 scenario. This study utilizes the tools like netnography and thematic analysis of the qualitative data. Considering the dimensions of AIDA model, an analysis is done as to how effective content marketing can grab the attention of consumers through eye-catching images and videos, making them indulge and develop interest in the content's usefulness, followed by a strong desire to avail the organization's services, and finally opting for the action to use the services.

DOI: 10.4018/978-1-6684-5386-5.ch004

INTRODUCTION

Marketing as a term is very common to a business. Normally in a narrow term it is considered to be synonymous to advertising however, in the modern times, the term itself has evolved in the form of a process, and has emerged as a mega concept that influences every department of the organization. Further the tradigital approach to marketing requires a marketer to employ the best combination of tools to achieve the organizational goals (Mumtaz, 2019; Fanning, 2019). Marketing is utilised to promote product or services of the organization. However, in the modern times the way these products and services are offered to the target audience is undergoing a paradigm shift. This shift requires the marketers to become more proactive in their approach, along with the element of being creative and innovative (Mumtaz, 2019). Loyalty and satisfaction of the customer have been the main focus of the marketing process (Khan et al., 2020). With the shift towards online marketing tools and platforms, a greater level of customer exposure and interaction is made possible (Khan et al., 2020). Further with concepts like the big marketing concepts that focus on the buyer decision process; the total product concept and circle of satisfaction (Fanning, 2019). The objective of the marketing activities has even become more sophisticated and challenging. The online platforms are changing the way education sector used to function (Khan & Magd, 2021). Due to covid 19, the dependency on the online platform has undergone a boost and thus, the organizations that make a better use to the online platforms are expected to sustain better (Mumtaz, 2019). Social media, an important element of the online platform requires a different skillset to be used for the marketing purposes (Hassan et al., 2015; Mumtaz, 2019). The existing trends show that the customers trust their social media contacts and friends as compared to the advertisements by the commercial companies. The era of referring to customer reviews and feedback is getting prominence among the potential customers. The social media not only facilitates the word-of-mouth publicity but also gives the first-hand user information (Woodcock & Green, 2010). Thus, the content used in the social media and other online platform is expected to be a game changer for the brand building process of the contemporary organization (Gold et al., 2001; Mumtaz, 2019).

BACKGROUND

In an increasingly interconnected digital world, content marketing plays a pivotal role in in building the brand image of contemporary organizations (Rowley, 2008; Wang & Chan-Olmsted, 2020). Appropriately designed content can positively influence the consumer behaviour by providing today's tech-savvy consumers the needed information, which is timely, useful and easily accessible (Wang & Chan-Olmsted, 2020). The last two years have added new dimensions to the content marketing practices as the pandemic hit the world where a huge increase in the use of digital technologies was witnessed. Some organizations, taking this as an opportunity, focussed their energies on creating useful content, helping them strengthen their relationship with their consumers (Wang & Chan-Olmsted, 2020). For the current study, a leading international school in Oman is selected to study the effectiveness of their content marketing spanning over the last two years and as a result, to develop a framework, which can be followed by other organizations as well. The school's content marketing efforts and active social media presence consistently had a positive impact on their audiences resulting in high enrolments even during the unprecedented times under CoVID 19 scenario. This study utilises the tools like, Netnography and thematic analysis of the qualitative data. Considering the dimensions of AIDA model, an analysis is done as to how effective content marketing can grab the Attention of clients through eye-catching images and videos, making them indulge and develop Interest in the content's usefulness, followed by a strong desire to avail the organization's services, and finally opting for the Action to use the services (Hadiyati, 2016; Hassan et al., 2015). AIDA model is considered to be an appropriate model to be used for such studies as it covers the essential elements. It also logically covers the sequential stages influencing the target audience (Hadiyati, 2016; Hassan et al., 2015).

METHODOLOGY

For this study, a leading international school in Oman i.e. Sohar International School is selected to study the effectiveness of their content marketing activities spanning over the last two years (from August 2019), and as a result, to develop a framework and gain insights, which can be followed by other organizations as well. This study utilizes the tools like, netnography and thematic analysis of the qualitative data. The data extracted through netnography technique from the various social media platform of the school, however a major concentration was made on the data extracted from Facebook and Instagram. The due permission and access to the admin data was secured from the school's Head of Marketing.

ANALYSIS AND INTERPRETATION

Sohar International School functions under the aegis of ABQ Education Group, a leading education provider of choice in the Sultanate of Oman, characterized by world-class infrastructure, excellent results and unparalleled quality endorsed by international bodies. Their long, established and successful presence in Oman has won the confidence of the parent community. Currently they are managing three schools in Oman with two of them in Muscat and one in Sohar. This chapter focusses on analyzing the content marketing strategies used by Sohar International School for building the brand image.

Preview of Market and Marketing Activities

The school is located in a port city with multiple adjoining small cities with scanty presence of good international schooling options. Local schools with Arabic as the medium of learning abound. This region hosts a number of expatriates in white-collar jobs who mainly communicate in English. So the school's target market mainly consists of locals who prefer English as a medium of education for their children and expatriates in professional jobs, who are living with their families. In the absence of good international schooling facilities in the past, such expatriates had to send their children back to their native countries to continue their studies in their preferred academic fields. This was indeed very difficult for them as it led to split family structures along with multiple complexities. With the availability of high quality international schooling facilities which are recognized all over the world, the expatriates now much relieved as it is now possible for them to have their children living with them while studying, helping them manage their family life in a much better and effective way. Although, there are other international schools as well in the region, Sohar International School has been able to provide excellent educational facilities to the community. There are 36 nationalities represented in the school which provides a diverse and multi-cultural environment to reap the benefits of *global village* in its true sense. In order to enhance students' proficiency in multiple languages, various languages are taught in the school including English, Arabic, Urdu and French. The school has excelled in curricular and extra-curricular activities and gained the confidence of students and their parents. The school's academic performance in recent years has been rated as one of the best in Oman.

Before relocating to the brand new campus, marketing at Sohar International School was mainly based on word-of mouth and the school's social media accounts were mainly used to share photos of key events at the school. A defined marketing strategy was not outlined to connect with the target audience. There was a need to engage the target audience in a more effective way so that the school's endeavors are showcased in in the best possible ways. A well-designed and coherent marketing strategy needed to be implemented in line with the latest changes and trends particularly in the region and generally across the world.

New Marketing Strategy

When Sohar International School shifted to a state-of-the-art campus of international standards in August 2019, the top management focused on revamping the overall marketing strategy for better interaction and engagement with the target audience according to their need and aspirations. Given the changing global trends of relying more on social media platforms, the school concentrated its efforts on creating meaningful content for the existing and potential stakeholders.

Starting from an updated website featuring engaging text and high-resolution graphics, a number of creative initiatives were taken in order to improve social media interaction using the Instagram and Facebook platforms. First of all, the existing contents of the school's website were carefully analyzed including the textual material, relevant statistics, accompanying graphics and pictures. A well designed website is a primary digital contact which greatly impacts the perceptions of the audience. The updated website was more engaging with useful information for the audience. Social media platforms including Facebook and Instagram were given special attention. Effective, timely, engaging and useful content was created and disseminated through these social media platforms on a regular basis. It played a vital role in keeping all the stakeholders well-informed about the curricular and extra-curricular activities taking place at the school.

Another creative step was to launch '*The Learning Curve*', a weekly e-newsletter showcasing the activities at school in a colorful and engaging manner. At the end of every week, all curricular and extra-curricular activities are beautifully showcased in the e-newsletter with sections such as the principal's message, quote of the week, theme of the month, highlights of the week, graduate diaries, staff diaries, birthdays, upcoming events and a specially designed fun zone. The e-newsletter is sent to the parents through the parents' WhatsApp group and has been very much appreciated by all stakeholders in general and gained much popularity among parents. The school also started to share all relevant content with staff, parents, students and other stakeholders using various communication mediums.

School's Marketing Efforts and the AIDA Model

The school developed a well-balanced content marketing framework by **(a)** identifying the relevant target audience which included the parents, students (both existing and potential), staff members and the regulators, **(b)** designing and disseminating timely, consistent and comprehensive content based on the expectations and aspirations of the target audience, by highlighting the school's endeavors in curricular and extra-curricular domains **(c)** continuously improving the content marketing efforts

Figure 1. Content Marketing and Brand Image framework through AIDA

based on the learning and experience, adding more engaging and interesting ways to disseminate the useful information.

All the creative marketing content developed by the school depicts the sequential stages of the AIDA model aiming at creating the ***awareness*** first, about the unique services offered by the school, creating ***interest*** of target audience in the services offered by showing how the school develops the students through teaching and learning activities, influencing the ***desire*** among the target audience to avail the services followed by ***action*** by the target audience to patronize the school by availing the services. AIDA model depicts a logical and sequential methodology to achieve the objectives of marketing strategies in an effective way.

A balanced content marketing strategy aligned with the AIDA model plays a pivotal in building a positive brand image of Sohar International School as one of the top international schools in the Sultanate of Oman.

This study primarily focuses on the content marketing efforts of the school during the last 2 years in general and the school's content marketing on social media platforms in particular, which have had a profound impact on various stakeholders.

Stakeholders' Varied Expectations and Aspirations

Students want to learn in a conducive environment. They want to maximize their potential and excel in their curricular and extra-curricular activities. They gradually discover their strengths and weaknesses to take appropriate course of actions accordingly, to become well-rounded individuals in future. ***Parents*** want to see their children grow as well-rounded individuals. There is an emotional bond between the parents and their children and one of the greatest happiness for any parent is to see their children as successful individuals in all spheres of life. ***Regulatory bodies*** strive to ensure the effective compliance of all regulations. The ministry of education, Oman, for example, strives to supervise the implementation of various instructions and guidelines issued from time to time. Particularly during the uncertain period of COVID 19 pandemic, there were various instructions issued from time to time aimed at the health and safety of students, faculty and staff; and the strict compliance to those guidelines was expected. ***The alumni*** want to connect with their alma mater and are very much interested in its reputation and growth. At the same time, the alma mater wants to keep a close relationship with the alumni to know about their personal and professional achievements in life as it reflects positivity as far as the alma mater is concerned. The alumni can act like role models for graduating students as they can learn a lot from them in terms of expectations and realities of their personal and professional lives ahead. All over the world, notable alumni from prestigious academic institutions remain in touch with their alma mater and enjoy a mutually-beneficial relationship. ***The community at large*** wants to see today's students as responsible citizens of tomorrow. There is a dire need of talented human resource which can convert the challenges of tomorrow into opportunities. The community needs individuals who are effective communicators, have an employable skill-set, innovative mindset and leadership qualities with high ethical standards.

By focusing on these multi-faceted expectations and aspirations, Sohar International School's content marketing efforts have resulted in a positive impact on its brand image. The key to such activities lies in consistency and timeliness of all marketing activities.

Challenge of Developing Pandemic-Relevant Content

Although the detrimental effects of the pandemic seem to be fading out, the last 2 years have witnessed drastic impacts in terms of uncertainty in all walks of life. Content marketing in such a scenario has been an extremely challenging task, given the expectations and aspirations of various stakeholders – students, teachers, parents, alumni, country's regulatory bodies and the community at large. The school made excellent progress by addressing such issues by designing and disseminating well thought-out content on a regular basis to various stakeholders. The time period during pandemic was characterized by a high level of uncertainty in all walks of life as the situation unfolded a new set of expectations which were unprecedented in the past. Similar situation prevailed in the education sector where all stakeholders were expected to join hands in order to reduce the negative impact of pandemic on academic activities.

With the ministry's decided shifting to online teaching during the pandemic, the school engaged in timely and effective communication with the target audience by spelling out detailed procedures required for online teaching, and provided dedicated Chromebooks to all the students with pre-loaded software to facilitate learning. This innovative initiative known as *ABQ 1:1 Chromebook,* played a pivotal role in supporting the online learning of students during the intense period of pandemic. It facilitated the students and parents alike as a dedicated Chromebook (which could be used both as a laptop as well as a tablet), was provided to all the students on an individual basis. Therefore, even if there were three children from the same family, they got three Chromebooks separately. It helped them attend their classes and perform academic activities without any interruption or unnecessary delays.

Numerous videos were created highlighting the guidelines for students related to online learning from home. Such videos provided an interesting and fun-filled content related to guidelines and tips for an effective study routine. Likewise, when the on-campus teaching resumed, videos showing the necessary safety protocols at the school were posted on social media accounts. The health protocols (including wearing the safety masks and maintaining proper social distance) were demonstrated in these interesting videos. These videos were then widely shared via Parent Care Team with parents, which resulted in boosting their confidence to send their children to the school premises.

Salient Features of School's Content Marketing Framework

Imbibed by the school's motto 'We Care', the content marketing at Sohar International School is characterized by optimism – giving a message of hope for tomorrow. The school's endeavors are reinforced by delivering consistent content repetitively, which in turn leads to brand loyalty. The marketing content focusses on the school's distinctive features, students learning activities, school's community engagement and social responsibility activities.

The content marketing tools reflect the corporate identity in terms of integrated marketing efforts. Corporate colours and the official logos form an essential part of all the content that is shared. A few examples are outlined below:

Videos

Be it infomercials or teasers, event coverage or teaching & learning endeavours of the school, the videos are carefully produced with useful and meaningful marketing content. Special care is taken to make engaging videos with well-designed visuals and a befitting background music that keeps the audience engrossed till the end. Considering the preferences of today's time-starved audience who prefer to watch rather than read, the school decided to opt this approach as it helps in connecting well with the audience despite the fact that creating such content is a highly demanding and requires lots of efforts, time and energy.

Visuals

Visuals used on the school's social media accounts are much more than mere photographs. From event advertisements to key school activities and achievements, the thematic and eye-catching designs of the visuals always incorporate the school logo, corporate colours and creative titles. This consistency plays a critical role in building a unique brand identity for the school.

Creative descriptions

All social media posts have pertinent descriptions that always elaborate the intended purpose and value addition to the teaching and learning activities at school. Such creative writings engage the audience well and reading the descriptions followed by viewing the videos, creates a profound impact on the audience as far as the overall message is concerned. In other words, both the written and visual media are used to convey the message effectively in a coherent way.

e-Newsletter

To enhance the school's content marketing portfolio, it was decided to launch *"The Learning Curve"* - a weekly e-Newsletter from 2021-22 academic year. This initiative has been well received by the parents, students and staff members alike. Although it is highly demanding task to design and distribute the e-newsletter on a weekly basis, the school is making extra efforts to do so. This gives the parents a wonderful opportunity to know the ongoing activities at the school and have an enjoyable read during the weekend.

The school makes continued efforts to reflect the elements of the AIDA model in its marketing communications.

a. The activities primarily focused on generating the ***Attention*** of the target audience include incorporating appropriate hashtags in social media posts, tagging key associated stakeholders (staff, students and parents) and collaborations with famous personalities. For example, a renowned artist's work was put on a prominent display at the school's reception area which generated much interest in the school's offerings as the event was attended in large numbers by the parents and other stakeholders. At times, some posts are boosted as well, which leads to more awareness about the school in a particular region, as the school is catering to the needs of Sohar and adjoining areas. There are students coming from other geographical areas like Shinas, Buraimi, Liwa, Saham Khaboora, Bidaya and Swaiq. Social media posts showing the school's community engagement activities in coordination with other organizations, also helps increase the awareness. One such example is the awareness campaigns including Cancer Awareness and Blood Donation Drives in coordination with National University of Science & Technology, Oman. This collaborative venture proved to be highly successful and had a positive impact on the goodwill of school as it depicted the social responsibility endeavors of Sohar International School.

b. ***Interest*** is generated through well-designed social media posts with creative written content and engaging videos with high-quality audiovisual elements. The subject matter covers the topics of general interest showing the school's activities in a colorful and thought-provoking manner. For example, *teasers* for House Launch were able to generate curiosity and gain the interest of a huge audience before the launch. In these teasers, partial logos of different houses were shown leading to curiosity and interest by the audience. Later on when the full house logos were revealed, the audience really enjoyed the eventual house launch. It was very much enjoyed by both the students and their parents.

c. The element of ***Desire*** is addressed by showcasing parents' testimonials which are made available on the school's website as well as played on the monitors located at key places around the campus. When the parents express their positive feedback on school's performance, it has a profound impact on the potential students and new families who would like to join the school in future. Short videos and informational visuals showcasing the school's state-of-the-art facilities also boost the parents' desire to get their children admitted accordingly. Such short videos contain relevant audio visual material showing the glimpse of facilities related to curricular and extra-curricular activities, boosting the desire of prospective families to join the school.

d. Efforts targeted on the ***Action*** element of AIDA model are focused on encouraging the parents to contact the school for consultation and detailed discussion about their children educational needs. These online endeavors are reinforced by conducting open days at the school, encouraging the prospective students with their families to visit and have a guided campus tour, avail the marketing material and complete the admission formalities. This provides the interested families an excellent opportunity to have a first-hand experience of the school's facilities on their own. They can interact with the school's faculty members as well as administrative staff to get a clear idea about the school's offerings. The school's Open Day advertisement which was boosted in Sohar and all adjoining cities, created that desire in the target audience for further consultation leading to increased enrolments as a result.

Social Media Insights

Social Media of the school has more organic followers that belong to the same city and adjoining areas, majority of which are existing stakeholders of the school. Many families have been availing the school's services for their children for a number of years and have a long term association and emotional attachment with the school.

Figure 2. Social Media Followers on Facebook (in terms of likes) and Instagram
Source: https://www.facebook.com/abqsohar ; https://www.instagram.com/abqsohar/

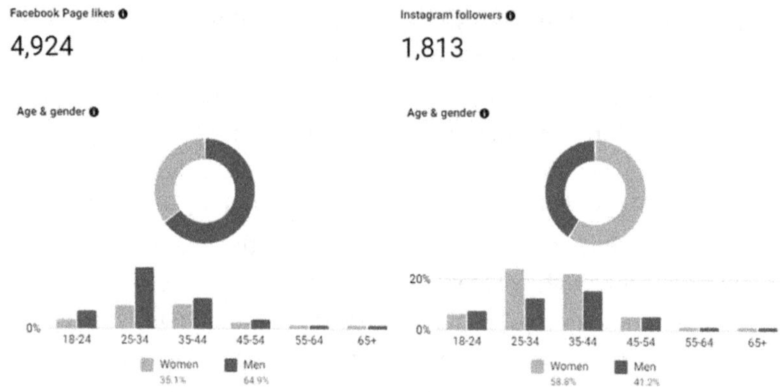

Followers

The social media accounts have seen a continuous and consistent increase in organic followers in recent years. Efforts to increase the organic follower base include tagging key people pertaining to the post, boosting the post within the region and collaborations with other organizations or important personalities belonging to the region. Majority of the Parent Community uses Facebook, whereas, Instagram is mainly used by younger audience, as characteristics of both these platforms differ. It is quite encouraging the see that both of these social media platforms are used effectively by the school's target audiences. The same is explained in Figure 2.

Increase in followers is depicted in the chart below. Instagram followers have been increasing as more young followers have been opting for Instagram as their social media platform of choice especially during the pandemic when the world switched to e-tools for teaching and learning purposes. This is presented in Figure 3.

Page and Profile Visits

Page and profile visits by target audience increases when engaging content is shared or the posts are boosted. A remarkable surge in the number of page visits was observed during the pandemic when safety-specific and learning modes content was shared. The prevailing situation at that time was characterized by uncertainty and the health-conscious students and parents eagerly looked forward to such content to be shared on a regular basis. The same can be seen in Figure 4.

Figure 3. New Social Media Followers on Facebook and Instagram
Source: https://www.facebook.com/abqsohar ; https://www.instagram.com/abqsohar/

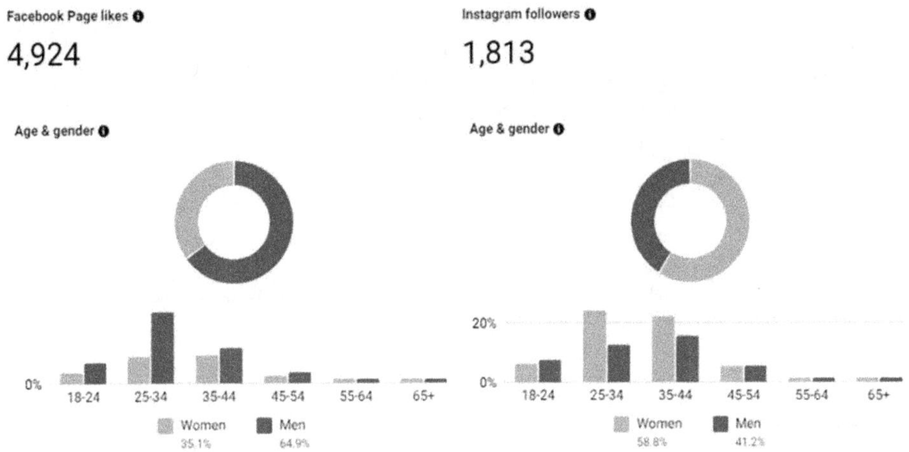

Page reach

Through boosted posts and page shares, page reach has a multiplier effect. For instance, when the achievements of exit batches are shared, the page reach extends to different countries across the world as this is an international school with a presence of students from a wide range of nationalities across the globe, and they enthusiastically share the social media content with their friends and relatives in their native countries. This has been presented in Figure 5.

Figure 4. Social Media page visits (Facebook and Instagram)
Source: https://www.facebook.com/abqsohar ; https://www.instagram.com/abqsohar/

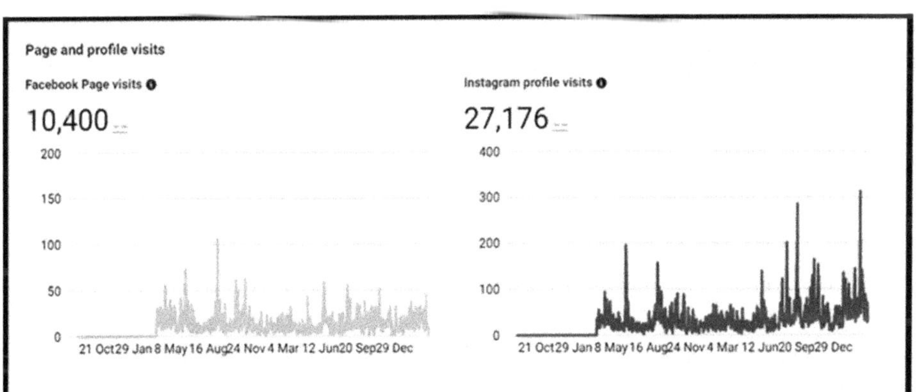

Figure 5. Social Media page reach (Facebook and Instagram)
Source: https://www.facebook.com/abqsohar ; https://www.instagram.com/abqsohar/

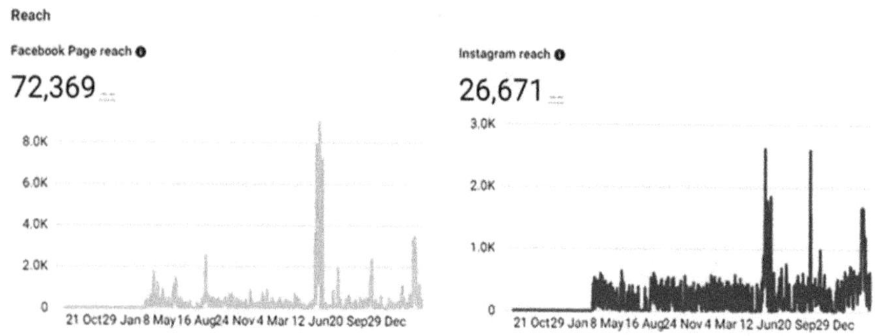

Content analysis

Content on social media accounts, as well as other mediums of communication including students' emails, school website, parent broadcast lists, an integrated Parent App with multiple features and Student Classroom Dashboards primarily pertain to the following categories:

Unique selling propositions:

The services that differentiate the school from all others are highlighted very often on the social media accounts in the form of infomercials and short videos to reinforce the school's image and brand identity in the minds of the audience.

- **Academic Brilliance:** The school ranks in top 100 Cambridge International Schools globally and boasts outstanding results in Oman's local body exit examinations. This uniqueness is showcased in social media posts on a regular basis.
- **Exceptional Educators:** The school is proud of its internationally qualified and experienced educators who receive ongoing professional development. In addition to having expertise in their academic areas of specialization, they excel in pedagogical aspects making the learning process more engaging, meaningful and effective. They enthusiastically provide the academic support to all the students to achieves their learning outcomes.
- **World class facilities:** State-of-the-art campus with interactive teaching aids for optimal student engagement. Spacious classrooms, well-equipped laboratories, high-speed fiber-optic internet availability, well-stocked library, swimming pool, play areas (both indoor and out door) are some of

the prominent facilities which the school proudly offers to its students. The unique blend of facilities ensures the intellectual and physical development of all the students.

- **Value-added educational experience:** The school has always made efforts to provide an exceptional learning experience for its students. Even during the pandemic, the school came up with unique ideas to make the online learning effective. The ABQ 1:1 Chromebook initiative included providing each student a separate Chromebook to facilitate the learning process. The ABQ 1:1 Chromebook initiative has been appreciated by all stakeholders as it provided an effective way to maximize the potential of online teaching and learning tools.
- **Well-rounded curriculum:** An array of extracurricular activities including the Discovering You Programme, along with unique personal and academic development initiatives. Critical skills necessary for success in the 21st century, are emphasized such as communication, collaboration and teamwork resulting in a high level of confidence among students to add value and make a difference in their future professional endeavors.
- **We Care Initiatives**: A dedicated Parent Care Team forms a vital link between the parents and the school. They mainly use WhatsApp messages to relay timely and comprehensive information to the Parent Community. The prompt, timely and comprehensive feedback and interaction with the parent care team plays a vital role in managing queries and concerns of parents in an effective manner.

Teaching and Learning Activities

The day-to-day learning experiences of students are showcased frequently and it has helped in strengthening the confidence of the parents that their children are receiving high quality education. The collaborative efforts of both teachers and students enhance the overall learning process.

Success stories

The posts related to achievements of graduating batches have always received the highest number of likes, comments and shares and it speaks volumes about the school's continuous quest for excellence in academia and beyond. The school makes sure to acknowledge the hard work and efforts of students and they are recognized and appreciated on a regular basis.

Testimonials

Endorsements by parents, students and teachers are a testimony of the school's high standing and its unique selling points. These are shared not only on school's social media accounts but also on the school website and through the Parent Care Team to improve its reach and effect.

Theme-based activities

For a holistic educational experience, the school strives to ensure that the teaching and learning process is made more meaningful and challenging through theme-based learning. Themes like "We Care", "Respect the differences", "Harmony – Stronger together" have helped in creating coherence across the entire school thereby enhancing the bonding between the learners of various age brackets.

Event coverage

Elaborate and well-designed advertisements announcing the events with relevant details are shared with all concerned stakeholders Teasers are often shared to arouse an element of curiosity of the concerned audience. For example, the House Launch Teasers were able to seek attention of students and parents alike and kept them actively engaged in the teasers and the countdown posts. The coverage of the actual event ensures that the event's aims and objectives are highlighted in the form of videos or visuals with the pertinent text.

Effective collaborations

The school has also been in the forefront of community engagement to create a positive synergy with various entities in the society at large. Many projects have been done in collaboration with charitable organizations, a leading University in Oman and with renowned personalities. Social Media posts depicting these socially responsible endeavours and elite events has always seen a huge increase in reach, post likes, comments, shares and increase in followers.

CONCLUSION

The school's marketing initiatives in line with the AIDA model have led to a positive impact on the target audience leading to a better brand image. The school's efforts have resulted in drawing the audience's attention, generating corresponding interest, inculcating a strong desire to be a part of it and eventually making a decision to enroll in the school. The school's endeavors for content marketing have excellently focused on these sequential stages of AIDA model leading to the desired results. These efforts have resulted in a premium brand image with the following positive outcomes:

- There has been increased level of loyalty of the parents to keep availing the school's services for their children. There are many parents who have been availing the school's services for a long period of time and their children have availed these services from primary classes, eventually graduating from the school to take admission in renowned universities around the world. The strength of this bond is a testimony of the parents' positive attitude and inclination towards the school. The smiles and pride reflected on the parents' faces during the graduation ceremonies doesn't go unnoticed.
- There has been an increase in the number of enrollments. Effective content marketing has led to a premium brand image which has resulted in many more students opting for the school's services. Many families have shifted their children from other schools keeping in view Sohar International school's better environment and facilities. Even during the uncertain times of COVID 19 pandemic, there were many families willing to join the school because of its quality. It is noteworthy that some students attending the school actually live in areas which are far away from Sohar but still they have decided to take admission because the school provides them much greater value than many other international school in the region.
- There has been an active and enthusiastic participation of the learners in various activities. It has been observed that the learners enjoy taking part in the curricular and extra-curricular activities of the school and try to add as much value as they can, to make such activities successful. It is very satisfying to observe that this enthusiasm is depicted equally by the primary and secondary sections alike, which is very encouraging.
- An excellent brand image has resulted in the feeling of pride amongst the staff, students and parents to be associated with such a prestigious institution. To be associated with a world-class academic institution gives a unique feeling of happiness and motivates them to perform better in the form of a productive community.
- There has been an increase in the commitment by all concerned stakeholders to add more value to the school's vision to become an education provider of choice. A strong brand image has influenced all the stakeholders to collaborate and nurture a mutually-beneficial relationship for effective community engagement for a better future. The school has received many

Cambridge Learners Awards, which shows the untiring efforts of both the students and teachers as compared with other schools in Oman. The school also enjoys the membership of prestigious academic bodies like Council of International Schools, Council of International British Schools; and British Schools in the Middle East.

MANAGERIAL IMPLICATIONS

Insights gained from the current study can be applied on the educational scenario in the gulf countries and beyond. Although the current study is based on analyzing a school's content marketing but the same considerations can be applied for the tertiary level institutions including universities. These insights can provide helpful hints for the educational framework at various academic levels, in order to make the appropriate decisions accordingly. There is a growing awareness and demand of high-quality education at various levels in the gulf region. There are examples of establishment of new academic institutions of repute and the content marketing practices of such institutions can lead to attracting the right audiences at the right time and at the right place.

Like other parts of the world, the gulf region is undergoing unprecedented challenges and opportunities. Countries like UAE have a majority of their population composed of expatriates who are looking for the best educational opportunities for their children. Many of these expatriates are in white-collar jobs and can afford the relatively high fee structure of the best academic institutions. The laws in the gulf countries provide the family visa facility for the accompanying children till certain age and after that the expatriates usually send their children back home to pursue their further studies in the universities across the world. This puts the entire family in a difficult situation as it leads to split families living in different countries which leads to heavy expenditures on multiple fronts. Such conditions lead to a lot of psychological and financial burden on all members of the family. If good tertiary level facilities academic facilities are available in in abundance in the gulf countries, the expatriate parents can convert their children's visas into the study visas and they can continue living with them. This will provide a great opportunity not only for the families but for the local economy as well as almost all the family expenditures will be within the gulf region.

Countries like UAE are making concrete efforts to become a knowledge hub where both the local and international population can get the benefits. It can only be possible with the presence of world-renowned institutions catering to the needs and aspirations of the target audience. Degrees from countries like UK, USA, Canada and Australia are still considered highly prestigious because of the high quality of their educational system. There is a growing need for regions like gulf, to have the facilities and support for such endeavors. It is very encouraging to note that this region has started paying more attention to this important aspect. There has been a good focus on the primary and secondary level and as a result, there is a growing presence to internationally renowned schools catering to these segments. There is a need to cater to the tertiary segment including the universities which can compete with others in the global arena in terms of academic excellence as well as research.

Dubai Knowledge Village is a good example where the government has actively made consistent efforts to invite renowned universities from all over the world in an integrated place where academic activities flourish. Well-established universities from various countries have opened their branch campus in Dubai Knowledge Village which has an exceptional infrastructural support and academic ambience. There is a huge potential for the education sector in gulf countries as the overall standard of living a very good and the law and order situation is very stable. If the proper educational facilities are available at primary, secondary and tertiary levels, people would love to keep their children with them and continue living in the same countries without thinking of sending their children to another country which will lead to a win-win situation for all stakeholders.

The content marketing practices for academic institutions in the gulf region can also be customized to cater to the needs of the target audience. For example, the content can be translated into Arabic language and sent to the target audience which prefers Arabic to be their medium of communication. Another important consideration is the cultural sensitivity as the marketing content should not include any elements which are contrary to the local norms and ethical values. Due consideration must be given to the Islamic traditions and festivals considering to the needs of local and expatriate Muslim population. Islamic occasions like Eid, Ramadan, New Islamic Year, Hajj etc. can be highlighted in the content marketing of as it will have an overall good impact on the target audience.

FUTURE DIRECTIONS

The gulf region is undergoing a number of changes and there is a growing demand of quality education of international level, both by the expatriates and locals. There is a growing awareness that the key to a better future lies in improving the intellectual capital and enhancing the intellectual and physical capabilities of the young generation. In future, such studies can be extended to other international schools in the region, to gain in-depth insights related to their content marketing practices and their impact in their brand image in the educational settings. After successfully conducting such studies at the regional level, they can be further expanded to the international level to find out the similarities and differences in the content marketing activities. This benchmarking can help to improve the way how content marketing strategies and conceived, designed, executed and perceived at the regional and international levels.

Another important area to be studied in future is to explore the academic institutions' endeavors to engage in content marketing activities based on sound footing and strategies. It has been observed that still some of the academic institutions don't have the expertise or resources to run their marketing activities in line with similar activities in the corporate sector. Some of the academic institutions still don't have a well-established department with requisite staff and facilities to run a critically important function like marketing. In such institutions, the responsibilities of marketing activities are usually assigned to existing faculty members whose primary responsibilities are different, therefore, it is not possible for them to devote a lot of time and energy to carry out these functions properly. This leads to content marketing which, at times, is not as effective as expected. The marketing function requires dedicated staff with appropriate competencies and resources to achieve its objectives in the best possible way.

No matter how well the academic institution performs, if it is not communicated properly to the target audience, it might have negative impact on the perception of the target audience. That's why it is extremely important to be very careful in designing appropriate marketing content in accordance with the social and cultural norms of the region to derive the maximum benefit. In addition to this, the content marketing by academic institutions can be analyzed to see which types, formats, and even timings are better than the other in terms of their effectiveness based on the feedback from the target audience. The insights gained as a result, can play a pivotal role in designing and executing better content marketing strategies in future.

REFERENCES

Fanning, S. (2019). The marketing concept (4th ed.). Academic Press.

Gold, A. H., Malhotra, A., & Segars, A. H. (2001). Knowledge management: An organizational capabilities perspective. *Journal of Management Information Systems, 18*(1), 185–214. Advance online publication. doi:10.1080/07421222.2001.11045669

Hadiyati, E. (2016). Study of marketing mix and aida model to purchasing on line product in indonesia. *British Journal of Marketing Studies, 4*(7).

Hassan, S., Nadzim, S. Z. A., & Shiratuddin, N. (2015). Strategic Use of Social Media for Small Business Based on the AIDA Model. *Procedia: Social and Behavioral Sciences*, *172*, 262–269. Advance online publication. doi:10.1016/j.sbspro.2015.01.363

Khan, S. A., & Magd, H. (2021). Empirical Examination of Ms Teams in Conducting Webinar: Evidence from International Online Program Conducted in Oman. *Journal Of Content Community And Communication*, *14*(8), 159–175. doi:10.31620/JCCC.12.21/13

Khan, S. A., Thoudam, P. D., Ligori, A. A., & Saleem, M. (2020). Customer Satisfaction and Customer Loyalty in Online Shopping A Study on University Students of Bhutan. *Delhi Business Review*, *21*(2), 11–22. doi:10.51768/dbr.v21i2.212202002

Mumtaz, R. (2019). Awareness and perspectives social media as new strategic marketing approach in minor industries; notion grounded on AIDA model. *Journal of Content. Community and Communication*, *10*(5). Advance online publication. doi:10.31620/JCCC.12.19/22

Rowley, J. (2008). Understanding digital content marketing. *Journal of Marketing Management*, *24*(5–6), 517–540. Advance online publication. doi:10.1362/026725708X325977

Sohar International School. (n.d.b). *Facebook page*. https://www.facebook.com/abqsohar

Sohar International School (n.d.a). *Instagram page*. https://www.abq.edu.om/sohar-international-school/

Wang, R., & Chan-Olmsted, S. (2020). Content marketing strategy of branded YouTube channels. *Journal of Media Business Studies*, *17*(3-4), 294–316. Advance online publication. doi:10.1080/16522354.2020.1783130

Woodcock, N., & Green, A. (2010). *Social CRM as a business strategy, the customer framework*. Retrieved from http://customerframework.com

Chapter 5
The Relationship Between E-Service Quality, Ease of Use, and E-CRM Performance Referred by Brand Image

Sara Kamal
Albarkat Institute of Management Studies, India

Arshi Naim
King Khalid University, Saudi Arabia

Hesham Magd
Faculty of Business and Economics, Modern College of Business and Science, Oman

Shad Ahmad Khan
https://orcid.org/0000-0001-7593-3487
College of Business, University of Buraimi, Oman

Farheen Mujeeb Khan
ICFAI University, Dehradun, India

ABSTRACT

The purpose of this study is to determine the relationship of e-service quality (ESQ) and ease of use (EOU) to electronic customer relationship management (E-CRM), which is referred by brand image (BI). This study presents the relevance of e-commerce (E-COM) in the business world especially in the pandemic situation and how ESQ, EOU contributes in building E-CRM. To show the relation between variables, the authors have applied scattered methods under correlation analysis. The sample was asked various closed ended questions in the domain of ESQ for E-CRM, EOU for E-CRM, ESQ for BI, EOU for BI. The results showed that there is a relationship between BI and E-CRM, ESQ and BI, ESQ and E-CRM, EOU and BI. There is no direct relation between EOU and E-CRM, but BI can facilitate in building the E-CRM. Also, the results show the direct relation between ESQ and E-CRM referred by BI.

DOI: 10.4018/978-1-6684-5386-5.ch005

INTRODUCTION

In the current scenario when most of the modern businesses are going virtual, it is important to build Electronic customer relationship management (ECRM) and learn the mapping and dependence of features such as E-Service Quality (ESQ), Ease of Use (EOU) and Brand Image (BI) (Al-Hawary & Alhajri, 2020).

Electronic Customer Relationship Management (ECRM)

ECRM involves the integration of Web channels into the overall enterprise CRM strategy with the goal of driving consistency within all channels relative to sales, customer service and support (CSS) and marketing initiatives (Melovic et al., 2020). There are three main types of CRM systems such as collaborative, analytical, and operational. Electronic Customer Relationship Management (ECRM) is implemented electronically using a web browser, the internet, and other electronic media such as e-mail, call centers, and personalization (Melovic et al., 2020). ECRM is a technique for companies that are carried out online to strengthen the relationship between the company and its customers (Naim, Hussain, Naveed et al, 2019). This aims to increase customer satisfaction and gain loyalty from its customers (Kumar et al., 2021). The use of the Internet as a channel for commerce and information provides an opportunity for businesses to use the Internet as a tool for customer relationship management. This study reveals the relationship between ECRM and customer satisfaction by determining the ECRM feature on the website (Khan et al., 2019). There are three types of ECRM and figure 1 shows the types of ECRM and their applications.

There are many benefits of ECRM like it improves the customer relations, service and support, provide suitable offers matching with the customers' behavior and needs, increased customer satisfaction and loyalty, improve efficiency and reduce cost and finally increase revenue for the businesses (Seify et al., 2020). Some of the benefits of ECRM are shown in figure 2.

The success factors of ECRM include operational and strategic benefits, top management support, technological readiness, and knowledge management capabilities. These factors are important for the firms to consider while building the strategies for achieving ECRM for their web app or Ecom activities (Naim, Khan, Hussain et al, 2019). Figure 3 shows the ECRM success factors with their inclusive.

ECRM performance measurement in organizations is very important to help companies increase revenue and increase customer loyalty. ECRM technology must be more advanced and sophisticated to meet the evolving and knowledgeable needs of customers. The use of CRM technology consistently has a strong impact on CRM performance (Hanif et al., 2020). The more comprehensive CRM technology, and the

Figure 1. ECRM types and their applications (Anaam, Abu Bakar, Mohd Satar et al, 2020)

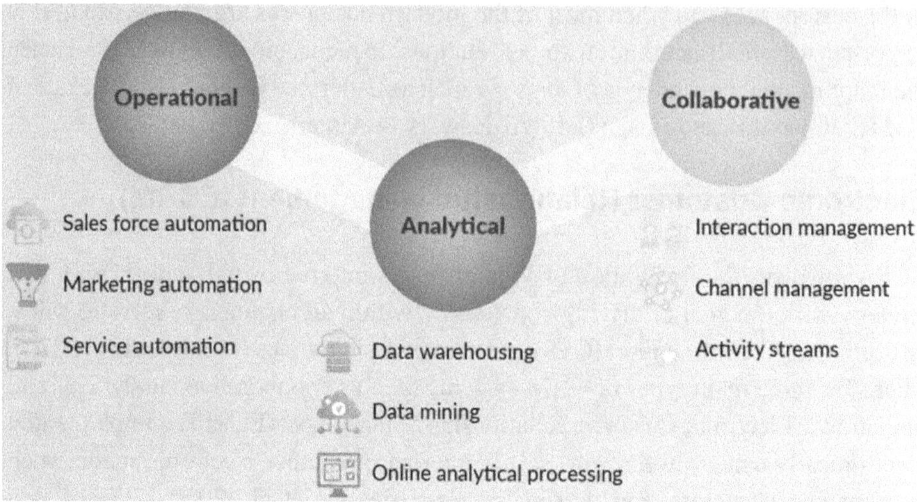

use of higher / advanced CRM technology, CRM performance is better throughout the customer lifecycle phases. However, CRM technology shows an important impact on customer relationship performance. There are 3 dimensions to ECRM such as the quality of information, ease of navigation and efficiency of customer service (Hanif et al., 2020).

Figure 2. Benefits of ECRM (Seify et al., 2020)

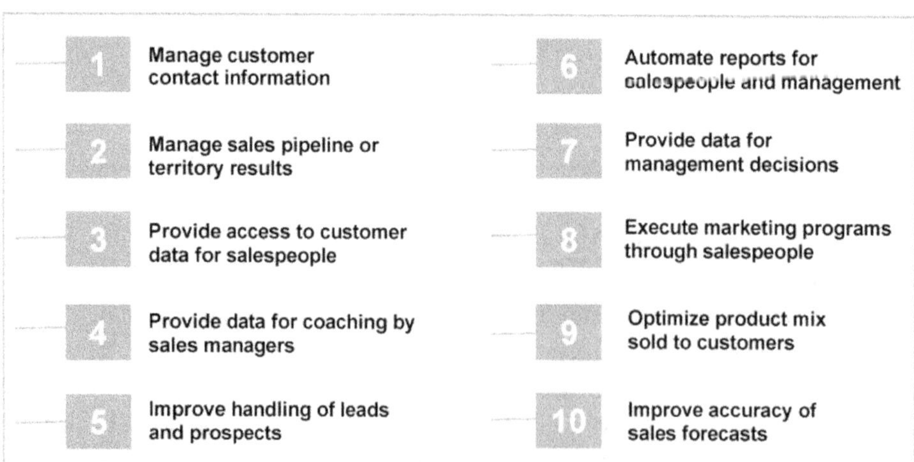

Figure 3. ECRM strategic success factors (Naim, Khan, Hussain et al, 2019)

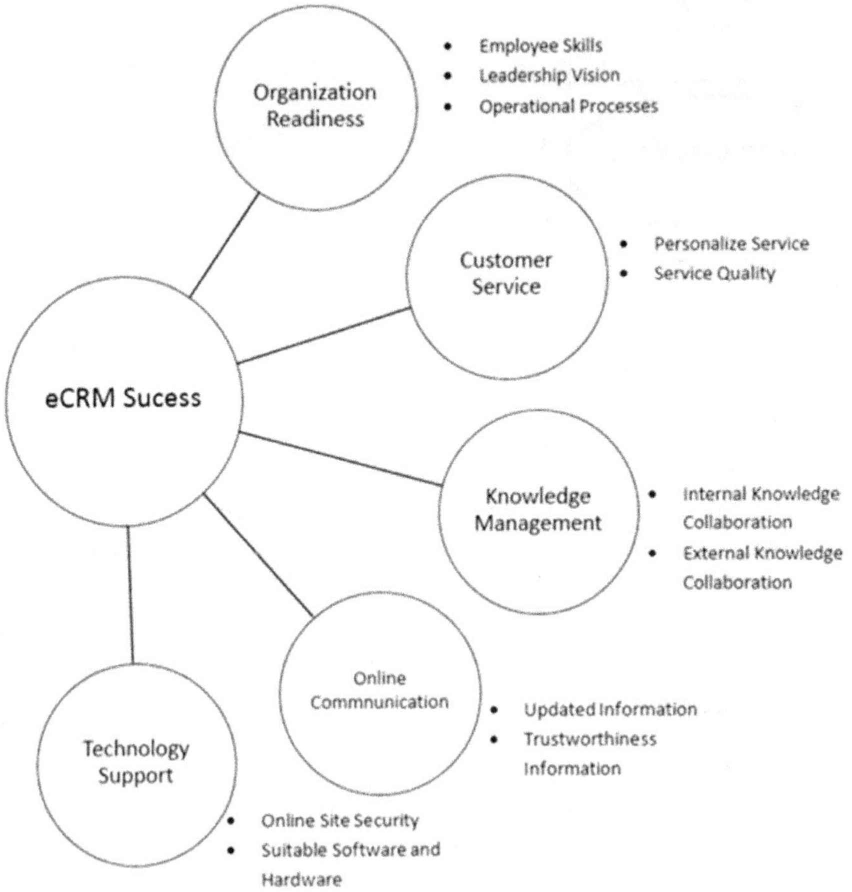

E-Service Quality (ESQ)

ESQ is one model of Service Quality. ESQ can be defined as the quality of service based on electronic media (Naim, 2021) and it is meant by online service quality in the interaction with the website is the level of website facilities such as shopping, purchasing and delivery that are effective and efficient. Figure 4 shows the ESQ perceived attributes by the customers. These attributes are defined based on consumer's experiences and rating/reviews on web blogs (Rashwan et al., 2020).

There are 4 dimensions in ESQ that are indicators for the success of ESQ. Figure 5 shows these dimensions.

Figure 4. Perceived ESQ attributes by customers (Rashwan et al., 2020)

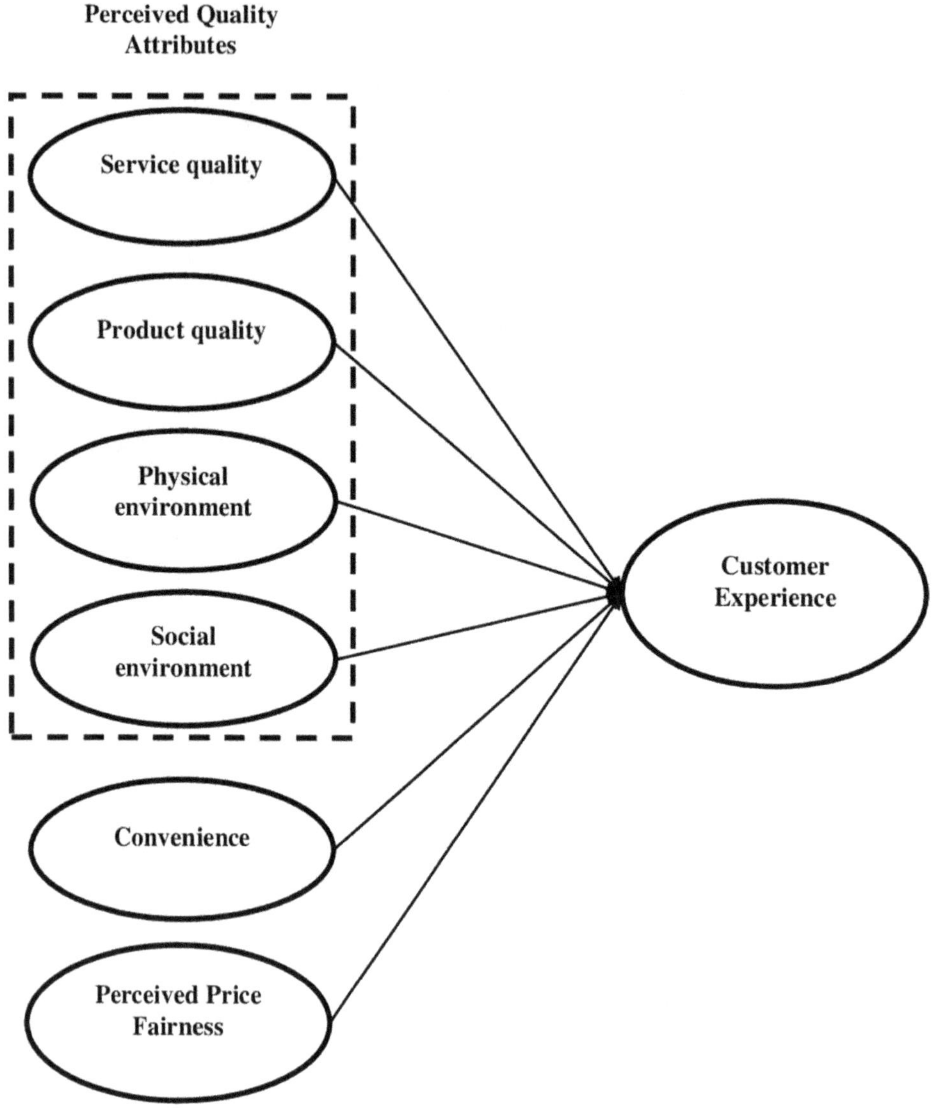

Ease of Use (EOU)

The dimension of perceived ease is an important element in the use of technology (Chatterjee et al., 2020). EOU is a level of one's belief that computers can be easily understood. Intensity of use and interaction between users and the system can also indicate EOU (Rashwan et al., 2020). The more frequently used systems indicate that they are easier to understand, easier to operate and easier to use. Based on this

Figure 5. ESQ dimensions (Lubis et al., 2020)

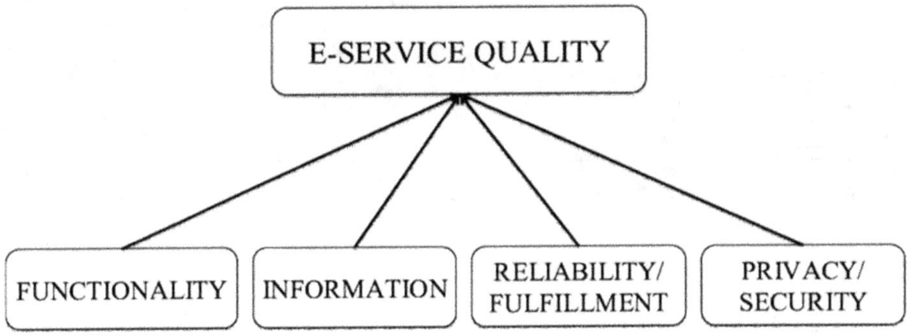

definition, it can be concluded that the EOU of a technology depends on a person's level of confidence that the technology can be easily understood and the system used can be easily understood, operated and used efficiently (Lubis et al., 2020). Figure 6 shows the dimensions of EOU that are considered as indicators in the measurement of EOU.

Figure 6. EOU performance indicators (Naim, 2021)

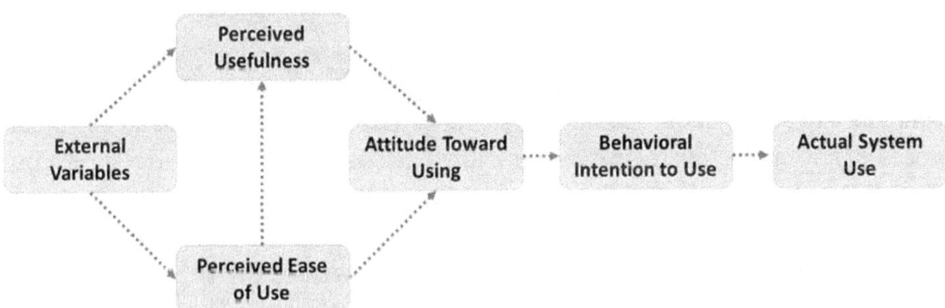

EOU is a technology that is defined as making it easy for users to carry out activities in the company (Naim, 2021).

Brand Image

BI is a set of customer beliefs about a particular brand (Adnan et al., 2021). The positive benefit of a brand image is that it provides an opportunity for companies to create new product lines by utilizing the positive image that has been formed

Figure 7. ECRM and BI indicators and their relations (Utomo et al., 2021)

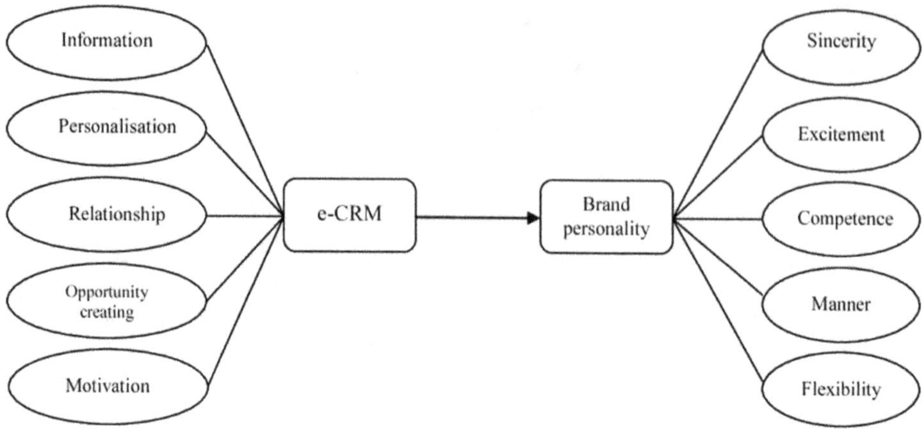

producers or companies. The company continues to introduce its brands from time to time, especially consumers who are its target market (Naim, 2021).

There are 5 indicators contained in the ECRM that affect the BI and BI also has 5 indicators to build its framework (Utomo et al., 2021). Figure 6 shows the indicators of ECRM and BI and their relation.

Significant technological developments make changes in various aspects. The use of online communication and information media through electronic media is spreading rapidly.

ECRM is a business strategy that uses information technology that gives the company a broad, reliable and integrated view of its customers so that all customer processes and interactions help maintain and expand mutually beneficial relationships (Andah, 2020). It is revealed that using the Internet as a channel for commerce and information provides an opportunity for businesses to use the Internet as a tool for customer relationship management (Kaldeen & Thowfeek, 2020).

ECRM use methods to make customers feel more understood by the company or business unit. CRM in the current scenario has developed and enhanced its features into ECRM and answers the several questions for consumers for building BI (Liu et al., 2020). The scenario is shown in figure 8.

There is a relationship between ECRM and ESQ, which can be simply defined as the quality of electronic media services (Naim, 2021). ESQ is an electronic-based service that is used to facilitate customers to carry out service activities or product sales effectively and efficiently ESQ is an assessment and provides an evaluation of the quality of service in a virtual market and was developed to evaluate and assess the services contained in the internet network. ESQ is defined as an extension of

Figure 8. Role of ECRM in responding to the queries of consumers for BI (Liu et al., 2020)

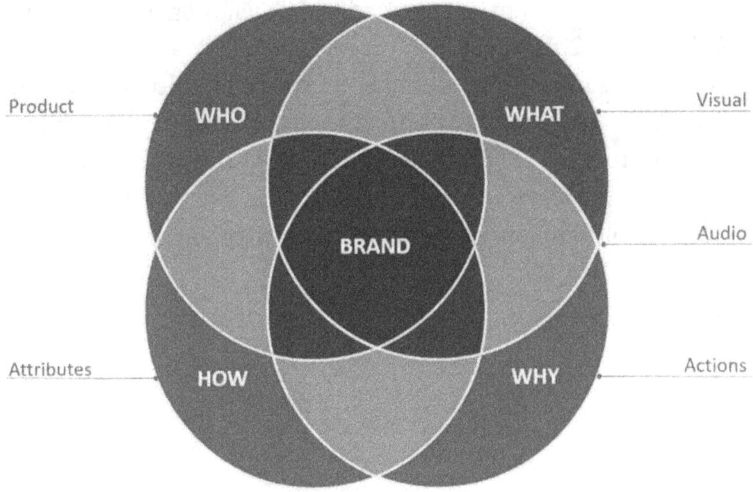

the ability of a site to provide facilities for shopping, purchasing, and distribution activities effectively and efficiently (Shahnavazi et al., 2020)

The E- CRM has a significant positive effect on ESQ because service quality has a positive influence on customer loyalty and customer satisfaction as variables that mediate the relationship between service quality and customer loyalty (Baashar et al., 2020). This study reveals the relationship between ESQ and ECRM.

Factor that has a relationship with ECRM and EOU is based on the perception of convenience as the extent to which individuals believe that using technology will be free from effort (Naim & Khan, 2021). If the individual considers the information media is still easy to use, then he will use it. On the other hand, if the individual considers the information media not easy to use, then he will not use it (Naim & Khan, 2021).

When customers who are loyal to the company can also are used by the company to add or attract new customers to relatives or close people. In this case, companies need to embed a good brand image for their products or services to loyal customers (Chatterjee et al., 2020). So the ethics of prospective customers who don't know about the company's products ask about the company's products or services, loyal customers will be able to easily tell about things about the company's products (Chatterjee et al., 2020).

BI of a product is a condition that makes customers trust to buy the product. BI is formed because of a customer's trust in a product. It is an obligation for companies to form a good and strong BI in the midst of intense competition (Koçoğlu & Kalem,

2020). BI is often affects a customer's expectations and results from satisfaction with a product or service. As a customer-oriented concept, BI reflects the customer's perspective what he receives from the brand and depends on his experience with it (Koçoğlu & Kalem, 2020).

ECRM allows consumers to get information on brand in real time or continuously in their daily life. ECRM has a significant effect on customer loyalty regarding a product which is achieved from ESQ. The dimensions of ESQ are security, responsiveness, reliability and EOU to define loyalty for the long run (Naim, 2021).

This study will show empirical evidence for the hypothesis given below.

Hypothesis of the Study

1. ESQ for ECRM
2. EOU for ECRM
3. ESQ for BI
4. EOU for BI
5. BI for ECRM

Organization of Chapter

This chapter has six parts where in first part introduction is covered for concepts and applications of ECRM, ESQ, EOU and BI.

Second part gives a background study of the concepts used in this study and also explains the competitive advantages of this study and what are the research gaps.

Third part explains the research methodology and its framework for this study.

Fourth part gives detailed information on results and their discussions.

Fifth part provides a brief analysis for the study

Sixth part gives the conclusion and scope of future work.

LITERATURE REVIEW

Relationship marketing gave birth to CRM. Since the inception of the concept of business CRM has been there. According to (Tusell-Rey et al., 2020) CRM means practical application of relationship marketing principles. Many researchers believe traditional concepts of marketing like 4Ps of marketing mix is not valid in the present scenario; rather relationship marketing is more applicable (Ahmed et al., 2020). In order to execute the concept of RM throughout the organization with desired results CRM has to be applied. The concept of CRM gained popularity only in past 6 to 10 years though the concept is as old as 1956 (Naim, 2021).

Figure 9. History and growth ECRM

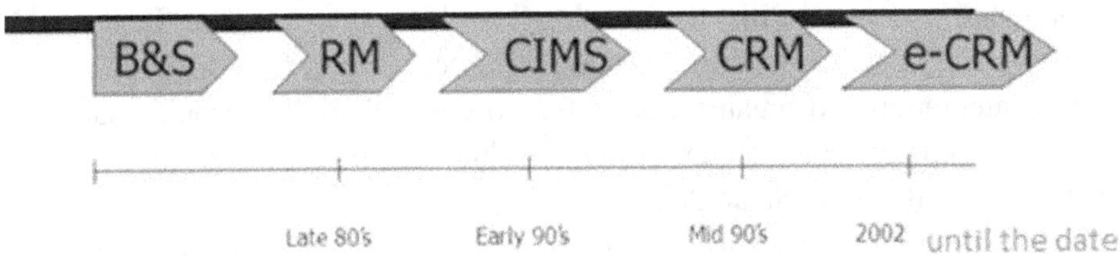

B&S – Buying & Selling
RM – Relationship Marketing
CIMS – Customer Information Management Systems
CRM – Customer Relationship Management
e-CRM- A subset of CRM that focuses on enabling customer interactions via e-channels

According to (Alshurideh, 2022) "CRM is a combination of hardware, software, process, applications and management commitment to improve customer service, retain customer, and provide analytical capabilities". Mining customer data from customer touch points is done for CRM to form extensive view of a customer (Mahafzah et al., 2020). In order to forecast purchasing patterns and uncover profiles of important consumers CRM plays an essential role. CRM facilitates finding out potential and repeat customers so that the marketing efforts can be focused on them. Companies communicate more effectively by using this knowledge (Siaw & Gitau, 2020). ECRM is not a new study it was started as buying and selling concepts as early as in 70s and gradually developed to ECRM. Figure 9 shows the history and growth of ECRM from various conceptual phases.

Being a recent concept, CRM is based on web-based or internet interaction between service provider as well as consumers (Naim & Alqahtani, 2021). In near future CRM is expected to expand its applicability in businesses and other operations to meet ROI and to retain customers (Herman et al., 2021). CRM has two approaches, management approach and information technology approach. According to management approach of CRM, it is integration of identifying, acquiring and retaining customer (Naim & Alqahtani, 2021) which is the most challenging area of ECRM because it focuses more on qualitative application of the concepts.

There are little differences between CRM and ECRM it's just that internet is used as a medium to identify, acquire and retain customer (Herman et al., 2021).

To ensure long-term customer relationship and customer loyalty, CRM concepts are applied to businesses utilizing technology to achieve this task. The "E" in CRM indicates many features not just "electronic". According to Suresh (2002) cross channel integration and organization is the core of CRM. "Electronic channels, enterprise, empowerment, economics and evaluation" are remaining five 'E's of CRM (Anaam, Bakar, & Satar, 2020).

CRM uses different tools to deal directly with customers through mobile phone, e-mail and website. Other techniques are wireless, chatting and web, wireless application protocol and technical ATM (González-Serrano et al., 2020). Advantages of utilizing CRM approach are such as quick service/response time, two-way interactive service relationships, and the ability to supply service for customers from anywhere at any time (Bashir & Naim, n.d.). As relationship between service providers and customers is essential for business success, CRM is getting a lot of attention. In order to gain customer satisfaction and loyalty it focuses on customer needs and wants rather than products or services (Adiyanto & Febrianto, 2020). Enhancing profit and customer participation is the major aim of CRM (Fiansyah, 2020). Hence, to improve profitability and loyalty of the customers, CRM plays an important role.

Organizations tend to improve CRM practices to achieve their business goals. CRM performance is affected by consistency in CRM technology (Naim, 2022). Better the CRM technology and more is its usage, superior is the CRM performance during the different stages of the customer lifecycle (Hendriyani & Auliana, 2018).

Marketing as well as information technology research gives a lot of importance to CRM performance. Relationship between e- service quality, ease of use, enjoyment and usability with CRM performance is not well researched and the exact relationship status amongst these variables are not well established hence it calls for more research in this area. CRM performance is affected by a number of factors which needs further probing and investigation (Mohammad Shafiee et al., 2020). Thus, in the course of this research study we try to explore the relationship amongst e- service quality, ease of use, enjoyment and usability as antecedents of CRM performance.

Ease of Use [EOU]

Ease of use is defined as the degree to which a person believes that using an information system would be free of effort. It is one of the "classical" concepts in information systems research (Kakeesh et al., 2021). A significant body of research in information systems has accumulated evidence for the existence of an effect of ease of use on initial user acceptance and sustained usage of systems (Krueger et al., 2020).

Some previous researchers have noted perceived ease of use as the extent the person accepts using services with no additional cost (Tahar et al., 2020). The researches have perceived EOU as the extent to which a person believes that using a particular system will be free of effort (Naim, 2022).

Past research have proposed the significance of perceived EOU that will vary with the type of task being addressed. They hypothesize that ease of use will not have a important influence on usage for something that is task oriented, such as making a purchase online, but will be significant in a task that is more essential, such as gathering information.

The two constructs, perceived ease of use and perceived usefulness proposed in TAM, have been analyzed exclusively and used to link with other external variables such as system attributes and social norms, and are proved as effectively predict the individual's actual behavior from his/her behavioral intention (Naim, 2022).

Furthermore, a study in 20s found that systems or technologies, which appeared to be easy to use and easy to understand, would be more useful from the user's perspective (Boshoff, 2007). The hypothesis of EOU will be positively related to the individual impact of CRM systems. The success of the system used depends on the level of ease of use of the system. In conclusion, it can be concluded that ease of use is one of the technology factor that plays significant role in CRM performance. Therefore, this study proposes ease of use as one of the antecedents that influence CRM performance.

E-Service Quality [ESQ]

Improving market share and revenue, service quality was regarded as a major strategic factor for product differentiation (Boshoff, 2007). E service quality affects CRM performance; hence this research tries to appraise process in which consumers evaluate service quality (Boshoff, 2007).

In 2002 new concept namely ESQ emerged (Boshoff, 2007) defined E-service quality as "the extent to which a website facilitates efficient and effective shopping, purchasing and delivery of products and services". Another definition states it as "the difference between customer expectation for service performance prior to the service encounter and their perceptions of the service received" (Barrutia & Gilsanz, 2013).

In the year 2002, the concept of ESQ explained the importance of service quality delivery with respect to customers. Their definition states service quality as "the extent to which a website facilitates efficient and effective shopping, purchasing and delivery of products and services". Details about a company and its products or services and contact information are available on informational websites. In present times, commercial websites facilitate buying products and making payment online as well. These websites allure potential customers and facilitate better engagement (Barrutia & Gilsanz, 2013).

Customer satisfaction, retention and loyalty are key indicators of quality. Same plays an essential role in online shopping (Noviana, 2021). Importance of Service quality in the telecommunication industry was studies by (Naim, 2021) in South African in order to improve customer service delivery. According to them telecommunications industry in South Africa can be evaluated on the parameters stated by porters five forces model; which are tangibles, reliability, responsiveness, assurance and empathy (Kumar & Mokha, 2022).

Shopping behavior is affected by perceived web site usability and new technological scenario which in turn influences corporate image. These days, web sites are considered essential tool to build better communication channel with customers (Naim et al., 2021).

Customer satisfaction, purchase intentions, and companies' performance can be used to determine perceived ESQ (Naim et al., 2021). A lot of researchers have explored the relationship between service quality and customer satisfaction. Findings of (Chu, 2020) study shows; ESQ has a positive effect on customer satisfaction and company's profit generation. Customer purchase intention is affected by customer satisfaction. Improvement in service quality facilitates an improvement in perceived quality and further enhances consumer satisfaction as well as loyalty (Khoa, 2022)

According to past research ESQ act as antecedent of customer satisfaction and further affects customer loyalty to help firms to build their ECRM and BI. Customer satisfaction heavily influences CRM performance (Tsou & Hsu, 2017). Hence, factors influencing customer satisfaction will further affect CRM performance as well.

Fewer literatures are available in the field of CRM hence it's a potential area for research. This paper will discuss the ESQ, EOU, and BI and cross relation between these concepts and why this dependence and relationship is important to be studied. The competitive advantage of our research is to help firms to build BI and ECRM based on the relationship these factors have with ESQ and EOU.

RESEARCH METHODOLOGY

This study is based on hypothesis if (*ESQ for ECRM, EOU for ECRM, ESQ for BI, EOU for BI and BI for ECRM)* and the results show that there is a relationship between BI and ECRM, ESQ and BI, ESQ and E- CRM, EOU and BI. There is no direct relation between EOU and ECRM but BI can facilitate in building the ECRM. Also the results show the direct relations between ESQ and ECRM referred by BI.

In this study we have used Correlation analysis by applying the scattered method.

Figure 10. Hypothesis framework

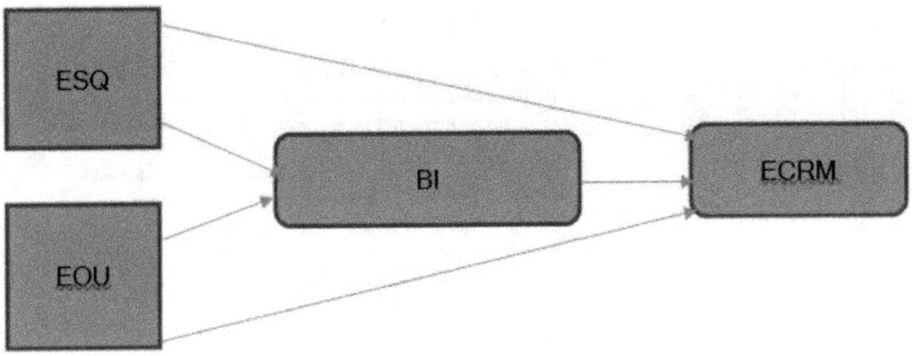

Survey questions were close ended and data was collected from 100 online consumers. We did not restrict the data collection for their demographic and geographic profile because the study focuses to cover the response from different types of users.

Correlation analysis is a method of statistical evaluation used to study the strength of a relationship between two, numerically measured, continuous variables (e.g. height and weight) (Gogtay & Thatte, 2017). This particular type of analysis is useful when a researcher wants to establish if there are possible connections between variables. Researchers have used this method to show the positive and negative dependence between variables/indicators of ESQ, EOU, ECRM and BI.

If correlation is found between two variables it means that when there is a systematic change in one variable, there is also a systematic change in the other; the variables alter together over a certain period of time. If there is correlation found, depending upon the numerical values measured, this can be either positive or negative (Hardoon et al., 2004).

The Assumption of research method is for the following conditions (Hardoon et al., 2004).

1. Positive correlation exists if one variable increases simultaneously with the other, i.e. the high numerical values of one variable relate to the high numerical values of the other.
2. Negative correlation exists if one variable decreases when the other increases, i.e. the high numerical values of one variable relate to the low numerical values of the other.
3. Zero Correlation if both variables do not affect the changes. A zero correlation suggests that the correlation statistic does not indicate a relationship between the two variables.

Table 1. Indicators of Electronic Customer Relationship Management (ECRM)

Indicators of ECRM	
Dimension	Indicator
Information Quality	The information presented on the website should be easy to understand and update
Ease of Navigation(Easy of Navigation)	The information presented on the website should be easy tounderstand and update
Customer Service Efficiency Indicator	The information presented on the website should be easy tounderstand and update
Indicators of ESQ	
Efficiency	Customer ability to access the website looking for the desired product and information related to that product
Fulfillment	Providing service guarantees in accordance with company procedures The company's actual performance contrasts with what is promised through the website
System Availability	The engineering functionality of the site is concerned Security assurance and the company's ability to maintain
Privacy (Privacy)	data integrity from customers keep personal information safe
Indicators of EOU	
Flexible	Can be accessed anywhere and anytime Quick response Flexible in operation
User Interface	The interface is good and appropriate Easy navigation Ease of operation Ease of remembering operation According to user wishes Easy to be skilled
Indicators of BI	
Mystery	Positive Experiences, Future, Aspiration Self- Congruity
Sensuality	Visual smell

RESULTS/ DISCUSSION

To show the relation between ESQ for ECRM, EOU for ECRM, ESQ for BI, EOU for BI and BI for ECRM, first we have identified the indicators to be measured for each concepts used in this study. Consumers were asked questions referring to these indicators and compared to identify the relationship applying correlation analysis. Table 1 shows the dimensions and indicators for ECRM, ESQ, EOU and BI and Table 2 represents the values for all indicators and relative measure for each indicator for the explanation of results. Four indicators are identified for ESQ, three for ECRM, two for EOU and two for BI. Each indicators are measured though various closed ended questionnaire and values are presented here as an average for each indicator. Values for EOU differ for average for ECRM and BI but BI is found to be referring both ECRM and EO that could explain the indirect relation of ECRM and EOU by the reference of BI.

H1: To show the relation between ESQ for ECRM

The results show positive relationship between the indicators for both and a slight fall for one indicator.

H2: To show the relation between EOU for ECRM

Table 2. Values for Indicators ECRM, ESQ, EOU, BI and relative representation

ECRM	values	ESQ	values	EOU	values	BI	values
Indicator 1	.8	Indicator 2	.79	Indicator 1	.7	Indicator 1	.9
Indicator 2	.9	Indicator 2	.85	Indicator 2	.7	Indicator 2	.85
Indicator 3	.75	Indicator 3	.79				
		Indicator 4	.9				
BI	values	ESQ	values	EOU	values	ECRM	values
Indicator 2	.9	Indicator 2	.79	Indicator 1	.85	Indicator 1	.8
Indicator 2	.85	Indicator 2	.85	Indicator 2	.78	Indicator 2	.9
		Indicator 3	.79			Indicator 3	.75
		Indicator 4	.9				

The results do not show any direct relationship between the indicators for both, ECRM has an incremental trended where as EOU has a linear trend.

H3: To show the relation between ESQ for BI

The results show positive relationship between the indicators for both and a slight fall for one indicator.

H4: To show the relation between EOU for BI

The results show positive relationship between the indicators for both BI and EOU.

Figure 11. Relationship between ECRM and ESQ

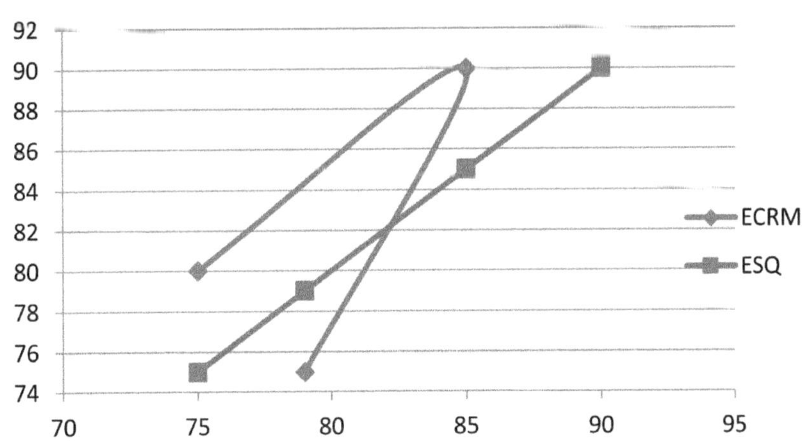

Figure 12. Relationship between ECRM and EOU

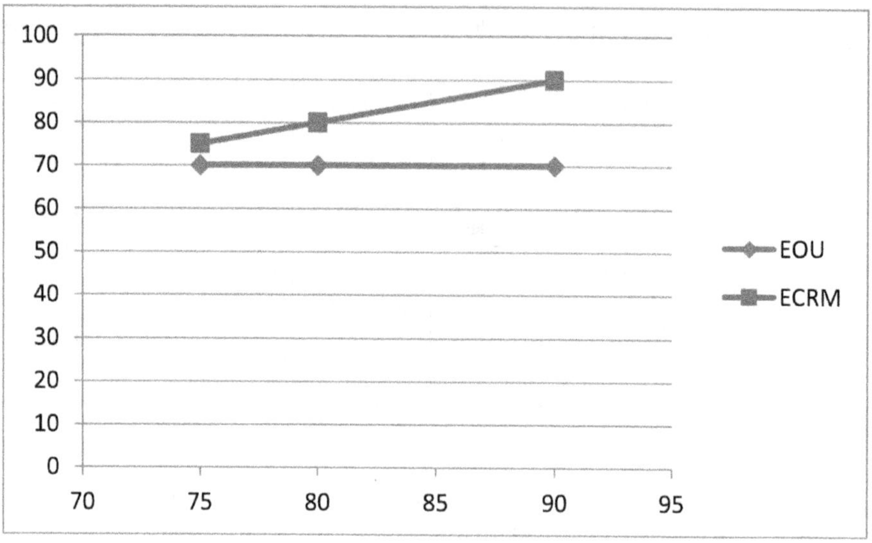

H5: To show the relation between BI for ECRM

The results show positive relationship between the indicators for both BI and ECRM.

There is no direct relation between EOU and ECRM but BI can facilitate in building the ECRM because when EOU's indicators are compared with BI's indicators

Figure 13. Relationship between ESQ and BI

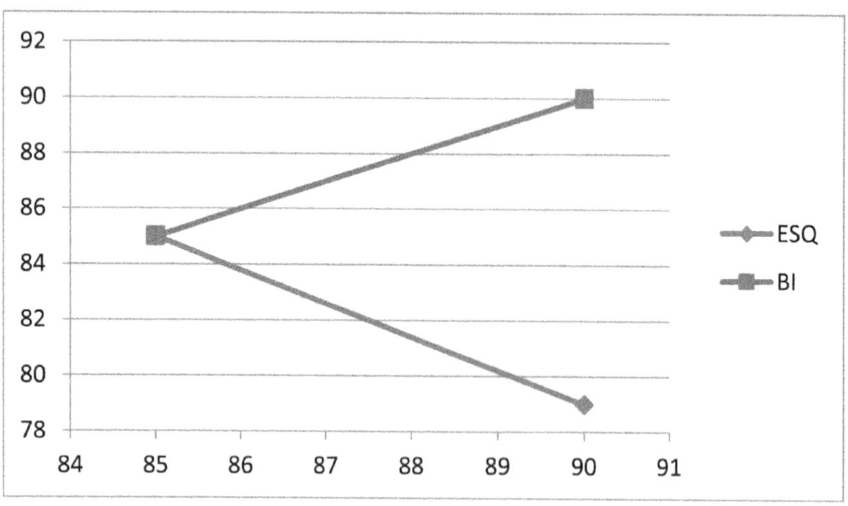

Figure 14. Relationship between EOU and BI

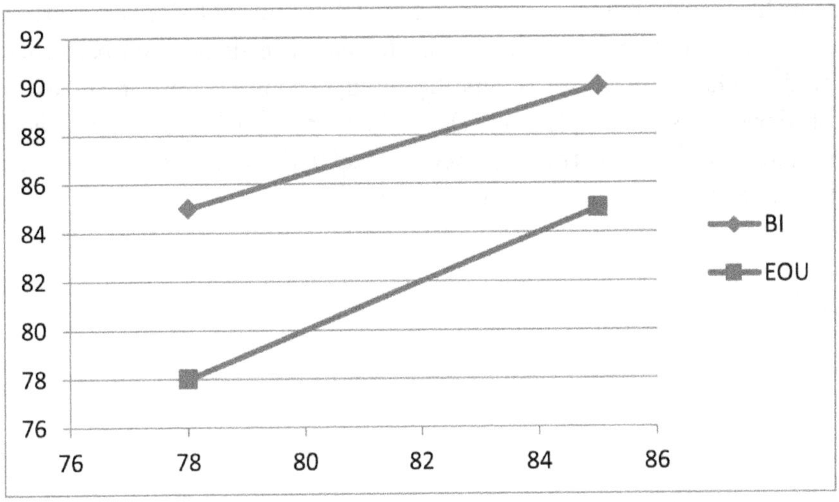

there is a clear relationship and similarly when BI's indicators are compared with ECRM's indicators also clear relationship is formulated but EOU and ECRM do not have a clear relation. However considering the separate relations, researchers can conclude for indirect relation between EOU and ECRM though BI.

Figure 15. Relationship between ECRM and BI

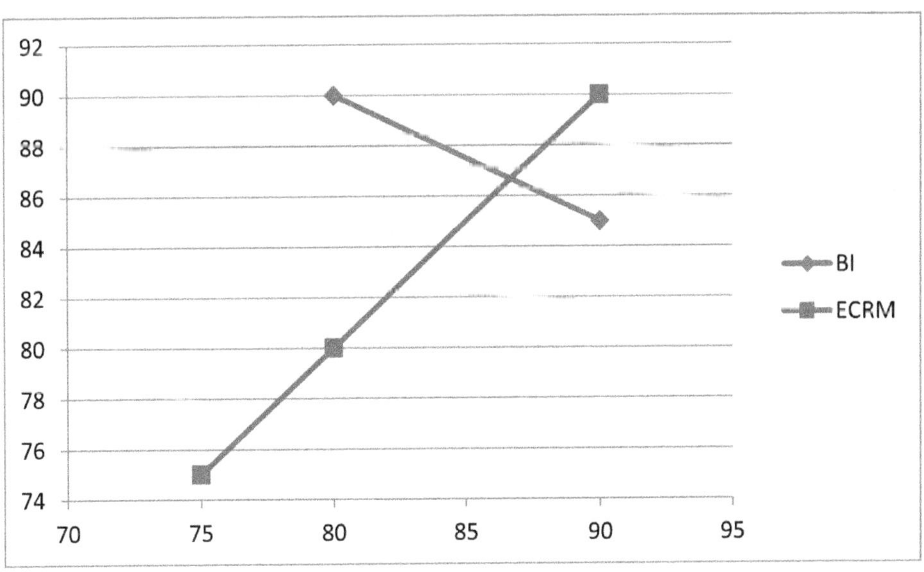

BI has a relationship with ECRM that aids in building the business strategy that builds influence or preference for an organization with individuals, distribution channels and customers, which ends with increased resilience and performance. This study explains that ECRM is important in supporting business processes where almost all operators have implemented E- CRM. Organized ECRM is able to provide opportunities for companies to create new product lines by utilizing positive images that have been formed from previous products.

ANALYSIS

ESQ and ECRM

ESQ and ECRM share a positive trend which make the inference that if the firms have strong ESQ they can build good relations with the consumers and retail them for long term. They can also measure the customer satisfaction level as well as enhance ECRM.

EOU and ECRM

The results show no direct relation between the indicators of EOU and ECRM and therefore cannot conclude any impact of EOU to ECRM but BI and EOU share a relationship and strong BI helps in building ECRM. The results conclude the indirect relation between these two factors.

ESQ and BI

ESQ and BI have positive relation that explains the relevance of ESQ in building image of the firms by providing quality of services for products, services and all the activities in BPM.

EOU and BI

The results show relation between EOU and BI and therefore firms should focus on the working of products too for enhancing their BI.

ECRM and BI

The results show relation between ECRM and BI and therefore firms should focus on the working of building strong ECRM too for enhancing their BI and vice versa.

CONCLUSION/ FUTURE WORKS

Correlation analysis shows that there is a positive relationship between BI and ECRM and high ESQ relation with BI. High rate of relation is between ESQ and ECRM and linear trend between EOU and ECRM which concludes on direct relation between their indicators. BI is a mediator or it aided in building the indirect relation between EOU and ECRM. The purpose of the study is to show the relationship between ESQ, EOU, nECRM and BI so that firms can build up their strategies to achieve good return on investment, develop products and services focusing on consumers' requirements and eventually consumer expected requirements are fulfilled.

REFERENCES

Adiyanto, A., & Febrianto, R. (2020). Authentication Of Transaction Process In E-marketplace Based On Blockchain technology. *Aptisi Transactions On Technopreneurship*, *2*(1), 68–74. doi:10.34306/att.v2i1.71

Adnan, A. Z., Rahayu, A., Hendrayati, H., & Yusuf, R. (2021, February). The role of electronic customer relationship management (E-CRM) in improving service quality. *Journal of Physics: Conference Series*, *1764*(1), 012051. doi:10.1088/1742-6596/1764/1/012051

Ahmed, B. S., Maâti, M. L. B., & Al-Sarem, M. (2020). Predictive Data Mining Model for Electronic Customer Relationship Management Intelligence. *International Journal of Business Intelligence Research*, *11*(2), 1–10. doi:10.4018/IJBIR.2020070101

Al-Hawary, S. I. S., & Alhajri, T. M. S. (2020). Effect of Electronic Customer Relationship Management on Customers' Electronic Satisfaction of Communication Companies in Kuwait. *Calitatea*, *21*(175), 97–102.

Alshurideh, M. (2022). Does electronic customer relationship management (E-CRM) affect service quality at private hospitals in Jordan? *Uncertain Supply Chain Management*, *10*(2), 325–332. doi:10.5267/j.uscm.2022.1.006

Anaam, E. A., Abu Bakar, K. A., Mohd Satar, N. S., & Ma'arif, M. Y. (2020). Investigating the Electronic Customer Relationship Management Success Key Factors in the Telecommunication Companies: A Pilot Study. *Journal of Computational and Theoretical Nanoscience*, *17*(2-3), 1460–1463. doi:10.1166/jctn.2020.8825

Anaam, E. A., Bakar, K. A. A., & Satar, N. S. M. (2020). A Model of Electronic Customer Relationship Management System Adoption In Telecommunication Companies. *Amazonia Investiga*, *9*(35), 61–73. doi:10.34069/AI/2020.35.11.5

Andah, B. D. (2020). Penerapan Electronic Customer Relationship Management (E-CRM) dalam Upaya Meningkatkan Pendapatan Penjualan pada PT. Cipta Aneka Buah. *IDEALIS: InDonEsiA JournaL. Information Systems*, *3*(1), 20–25.

Baashar, Y., Alhussian, H., Patel, A., Alkawsi, G., Alzahrani, A. I., Alfarraj, O., & Hayder, G. (2020). Customer relationship management systems (CRMS) in the healthcare environment: A systematic literature review. *Computer Standards & Interfaces*, *71*, 103442. doi:10.1016/j.csi.2020.103442 PMID:34170994

Barrutia, J. M., & Gilsanz, A. (2013). Electronic service quality and value: Do consumer knowledge-related resources matter? *Journal of Service Research*, *16*(2), 231–246. doi:10.1177/1094670512468294

Bashir, M. A., & Naim, A. (n.d.). *ICT Adoption Analysis for Innovation in Higher Education Sector*. Academic Press.

Boshoff, C. (2007). A psychometric assessment of ES-QUAL: A scale to measure electronic service quality. *Journal of Electronic Commerce Research*, *8*(1), 101.

Chatterjee, S., Chaudhuri, R., Vrontis, D., Thrassou, A., Ghosh, S. K., & Chaudhuri, S. (2020). Social customer relationship management factors and business benefits. *The International Journal of Organizational Analysis*.

Chu, K. M. (2020). The Relationships between Online Customer Engagement Value and Electronic Customer Relationship Management Effectiveness of Mobile Games. *Innovative Journal of Business and Management*, *9*(8), 238–245.

Fiansyah, E. (2020, November). Post Implementation Review of Electronic Customer Relationship Management (E-CRM) Implementation in Port Services Company, Indonesia. In *2020 International Conference on Informatics, Multimedia, Cyber and Information System (ICIMCIS)* (pp. 301-306). IEEE. 10.1109/ICIMCIS51567.2020.9354300

Gogtay, N. J., & Thatte, U. M. (2017). Principles of correlation analysis. *The Journal of the Association of Physicians of India*, *65*(3), 78–81. PMID:28462548

González-Serrano, L., Talón-Ballestero, P., Muñoz-Romero, S., Soguero-Ruiz, C., & Rojo-Álvarez, J. L. (2020). A big data approach to customer relationship management strategy in hospitality using multiple correspondence domain description. *Applied Sciences (Basel, Switzerland)*, *11*(1), 256. doi:10.3390/app11010256

Hanif, M. I., Ahsan, M., Bhatti, M. K., & Loghari, M. S. (2020). The Effect of Electronic Customer Relationship Management on Organizational Performance with Mediating Role of Customer Satisfaction. *International Review of Management and Marketing*, *10*(5), 138–147. doi:10.32479/irmm.9934

Hardoon, D. R., Szedmak, S., & Shawe-Taylor, J. (2004). Canonical correlation analysis: An overview with application to learning methods. *Neural Computation*, *16*(12), 2639–2664. doi:10.1162/0899766042321814 PMID:15516276

Hendriyani, C., & Auliana, L. (2018). Transformation from relationship marketing to electronic customer relationship management: A literature study. *Review of Integrative Business and Economics Research*, *7*, 116–124.

Herman, L. E., Sulhaini, S., & Farida, N. (2021). Electronic customer relationship management and company performance: Exploring the product innovativeness development. *Journal of Relationship Marketing*, *20*(1), 1–19. doi:10.1080/15332667.2019.1688600

Kakeesh, D., Al-Weshah, G., & Al-Ma'aitah, N. (2021). Maintaining Customer Loyalty Using Electronic Customer Relationship Management (E-CRM): Qualitative Evidence from Small Food Businesses in Jordan. *Studies of Applied Economics*, *39*(7). Advance online publication. doi:10.25115/eea.v39i7.4810

Kaldeen, M., & Thowfeek, M. H. (2020). *Factors favoring electronic customer relationship management*. E-CRM.

Khan, N., Naim, A., Hussain, M. R., Naveed, Q. N., Ahmad, N., & Qamar, S. (2019, May). The 51 v's of big data: survey, technologies, characteristics, opportunities, issues and challenges. In *Proceedings of the international conference on omni-layer intelligent systems* (pp. 19-24). 10.1145/3312614.3312623

Khoa, B. T. (2022). Dataset for the electronic customer relationship management based on SOR model in electronic commerce. *Data in Brief*, *42*, 108039. doi:10.1016/j.dib.2022.108039 PMID:35313498

Koçoğlu, C. M., & Kalem, M. Y. (2020). Electronic Customer Relationship Management in Tourism. In Handbook of Research on Smart Technology Applications in the Tourism Industry (pp. 273-294). IGI Global.

Krueger, L. J., Gaeddert, M., Koeppel, L., Brümmer, L. E., Gottschalk, C., Miranda, I. B., . . . Denkinger, C. M. (2020). Evaluation of the accuracy, ease of use and limit of detection of novel, rapid, antigen-detecting point-of-care diagnostics for SARS-CoV-2. medRxiv. doi:10.1101/2020.10.01.20203836

Kumar, P., & Mokha, A. K. (2022). Electronic Customer Relationship Management (E-CRM) and Customer Loyalty: The Mediating Role of Customer Satisfaction in the Banking Industry. *International Journal of E-Business Research, 18*(1), 1–22. doi:10.4018/IJEBR.293292

Kumar, P., Mokha, A. K., & Pattnaik, S. C. (2021). Electronic customer relationship management (E-CRM), customer experience and customer satisfaction: Evidence from the banking industry. *Benchmarking*.

Liu, W., Wang, Z., & Zhao, H. (2020). Comparative study of customer relationship management research from East Asia, North America and Europe: A bibliometric overview. *Electronic Markets, 30*(4), 735–757. doi:10.100712525-020-00395-7

Lubis, A., Dalimunthe, R., Absah, Y., & Fawzeea, B. K. (2020). The influence of customer relationship management (CRM) indicators on customer loyalty of sharia based banking system. *Lubis, A*, 84-92.

Mahafzah, A. G., Aljawarneh, N. M., Alomari, K. A. K., Altahat, S., & Alomari, Z. S. (2020). Impact of customer relationship management on food and beverage service quality: The mediating role of employees satisfaction. *Humanities & Social Sciences Reviews, 8*(2), 222–230. doi:10.18510/hssr.2020.8226

Melovic, B., Rondovic, B., Mitrovic-Veljkovic, S., Ocovaj, S. B., & Dabic, M. (2020). Electronic Customer Relationship Management Assimilation in Southeastern European Companies—Cluster Analysis. *IEEE Transactions on Engineering Management*.

Mohammad Shafiee, M., Seify, M., & Yazdi, A. (2020). Antecedents and Consequences of Implementing Electronic Customer Relationship Management in Small and Medium Enterprises. *New Marketing Research Journal, 10*(1), 129–146.

Naim, A. (2022). Economies of Scale for Antenna's Applications in Interior Regions. *International Journal of Innovative Analyses and Emerging Technology, 2*(2), 77–82. http://openaccessjournals.eu/index.php/ijiaet/article/view/1058

Naim, A. (2022). Neuro-Marketing Techniques for Proposing Information Driven Framework for Decision Making. *International Journal of Innovative Analyses and Emerging Technology, 2*(2), 87–94. http://openaccessjournals.eu/index.php/ijiaet/article/view/1060

Naim, A. (2021). Applications of E-Learning tools for Achieving Students Learning Outcomes. *Journal of Pedagogical Inventions and Practices, 2*(2), 75–82. https://zienjournals.com/index.php/jpip/article/view/320

Naim, A. (2021). Applications of Marketing Framework in Business Practices. *Journal of Marketing and Emerging Economics, 1*(6), 55–70.

Naim, A. (2021). Applications of MIS in building Electronic Relationship with customers: A case-based study. *Periodica Journal of Modern Philosophy. Social Sciences and Humanities, 1*, 1–8.

Naim, A. (2021). Green Business Process Management. *International Journal of Innovative Analyses and Emerging Technology, 1*(6), 125–134. http://openaccessjournals.eu/index.php/ijiaet/article/view/651

Naim, A. (2021). Green Information Technologies in Business Operations. *Periodica Journal of Modern Philosophy. Social Sciences and Humanities, 1*, 36–49.

Naim, A. (2021). New Trends in Business Process Management: Applications of Green Information Technologies. *British Journal of Environmental Studies, 1*(1), 12–23.

Naim, A., Alahmari, F., & Rahim, A. (2021). Role of Artificial Intelligence in Market Development and Vehicular communication. *Smart Antennas: Recent Trends in Design and Applications, 2*(28).

Naim, A., & Alqahtani, K. (2021). Role of Information Systems in Customer Relationship Management. *Pulse, 2*(2).

Naim, A., Hussain, M. R., Naveed, Q. N., Ahmad, N., Qamar, S., Khan, N., & Hweij, T. A. (2019, April). Ensuring interoperability of e-learning and quality development in education. In *2019 IEEE Jordan International Joint Conference on Electrical Engineering and Information Technology (JEEIT)* (pp. 736-741). IEEE 10.1109/JEEIT.2019.8717431

Naim, A., & Khan, M. F. (2021). Measuring the Psychological Behavior of Consumers for Medical Services. *Zien Journal of Social Sciences and Humanities, 2*, 119–131. Retrieved from https://zienjournals.com/index.php/zjssh/article/view/316

Naim, A., Khan, M. F., Hussain, M. R., & Khan, N. (2019). "Virtual Doctor" Management Technique in the Diagnosis of ENT Diseases. *JOE, 15*(9), 88. doi:10.3991/ijoe.v15i09.10665

Noviana, G. (2021, September). An Analysis of the Implementation of Electronic Customer Relationship Management (E-CRM) Towards Customer Loyalty. In *5th Global Conference on Business, Management and Entrepreneurship (GCBME 2020)* (pp. 434-438). Atlantis Press. 10.2991/aebmr.k.210831.086

Rashwan, H. H. M., Mansi, A. L., & Hassan, H. E. (2020). Exploring electronic-loyalty antecedents in Egyptian commercial banks; Electronic customer relationship management and banking electronic satisfaction. *The Journal of Business and Retail Management Research, 14*(2). Advance online publication. doi:10.24052/JBRMR/V14IS02/ART-06

Seify, M., Tabaeeian, R. A., & Khoshfetrat, A. (2020). Investigating factors in implementation of electronic customer relationship management and its consequences in private hospitals in Isfahan city. *International Journal of Electronic Customer Relationship Management, 12*(3), 225–245. doi:10.1504/IJECRM.2020.110040

Shahnavazi, A., Nemati Gonbaghi, M., Teymouri, S. F., & Ghasemi Dakdare, B. (2020). Determining the Key Indicators affecting Electronic Customer Relationship Management (e-CRM) Using an integration of balanced scorecard and fuzzy screening techniques (Case Study: Companies Covered by Parsian Data-Processors Group). *Iranian Journal of Optimization, 12*(1), 21–32.

Siaw, G. A., & Gitau, J. K. (2020). *Aspects of Electronic Customer Relationship Management and Guest Satisfaction: A Perspective of 4-Star Hotels in Nairobi County, Kenya.* Academic Press.

Tahar, A., Riyadh, H. A., Sofyani, H., & Purnomo, W. E. (2020). Perceived ease of use, perceived usefulness, perceived security and intention to use e-filing: The role of technology readiness. *The Journal of Asian Finance, Economics, and Business, 7*(9), 537–547. doi:10.13106/jafeb.2020.vol7.no9.537

Tsou, H. T., & Hsu, H. Y. (2017). Self-Service technology investment, electronic customer relationship management practices, and service innovation capability. In *Marketing at the Confluence between Entertainment and Analytics* (pp. 477–481). Springer. doi:10.1007/978-3-319-47331-4_92

Tusell-Rey, C. C., Nieto, Ó. C., & Padilla, R. T. (2020). Application of data engineering in automatic information analysis for electronic customer relationship management: A survey. *International Journal of Emerging Trends in Engineering Research, 8*(9), 5939–5946. doi:10.30534/ijeter/2020/167892020

Utomo, S. M., Sandjaja, J. R., Yustiawan, W. S., & Alamsyah, D. P. (2021, September). Consumer Behavior and Sustainable Performance: Perceived of E-Service Quality on Online Shopping. In *2021 9th International Conference on Cyber and IT Service Management (CITSM)* (pp. 1-4). IEEE.

Chapter 6
E-CRM Through Social Media Marketing Activities for Brand Awareness, Brand Image, and Brand Loyalty

Sadaf Fatima
https://orcid.org/0000-0002-5614-4383
Aligarh Muslim University, India

Hamed Alqahtani
King Khalid University, Saudi Arabia

Arshi Naim
King Khalid University, Saudi Arabia

Fatma Alma'alwi
King Khalid University, Saudi Arabia

ABSTRACT

The aim of the research is to examine the effect of social media marketing activities on brand awareness, brand image, and brand loyalty. In addition, it has been aimed to analyze the effect of brand awareness and brand image on brand loyalty in this research. The population of the research consists of the consumers who actively follow five brands with the highest social score according to the Marketing Gulf social media brand performance data on social media communication channels such as Facebook, Twitter, and Instagram. In this research, qualitative method has been used, and research data has been obtained via online questionnaires shared on social media from 100 brand followers, and their responses were scaled on Likert scale. As a result of the analysis, social media marketing activities have been found as effective factors on brand image and brand loyalty. It has been determined as the most obvious effect seen on brand awareness. Also, brand awareness and brand image have a significant effect on brand loyalty, though brand awareness has a limited effect on the brand image.

DOI: 10.4018/978-1-6684-5386-5.ch006

INTRODUCTION

Branding is a crucial aspect of today's competitive economy since it distinguishes comparable goods and services supplied by various enterprises in customers' eyes and makes them preferred over one another. While representing authenticity, value, and devotion to the products and services given to customers by companies, the brand serves various functions, including decreasing consumer risks associated with goods and services and developing social relationships without revealing their identity. Firms that have gained brand status have been classified differently from other businesses regarding the product and services (Haudi et al., 2022). They have a unique position in customers' minds that help establish a brand identity. Communication between consumers and brands is directly related to brand identity formation. The stronger the brand preference and brand loyalty marketers can confirm, the stronger the communication strength between the brand and the customer. The most important aspect of branding is that a good relationship with customers may influence their purchasing decisions and commitment (Haudi et al., 2022). As a result, firms are doing research to catch customers' attention, stay in their thoughts, build a favorable brand image, and enhance brand loyalty by utilizing all available communication channels in brand communications to develop or defend brand value (Kakeesh et al., 2021).

Social media is one of the most prevalent avenues of communication that businesses have recently used in their marketing efforts. Social media is an online application program, mass media tool, or platform that allows users to communicate, collaborate or share material (Kakeesh et al., 2021). The impact of social media on consumer behavior spans a wide range of activities, including educating, sharing ideas and attitudes, gaining knowledge and understanding, and visualizing post-purchase behavior without actually making a purchase (Taylor & Hunter, 2002). As a result, businesses are becoming more engaged in their marketing communications and developing new apps to make items and brands cheaper through online marketing efforts via social media communication channels. The social media marketing practices encourage the customers to select brands and their products, sending messages to other online customers.

Businesses may use social media marketing to create their brand profiles and provide online customer support, product information, and special offers that are simple, inexpensive, and consistent (Taylor & Hunter, 2002). Furthermore, alerting clients about goods and brands of companies that appear on social networks where millions of people sign in is highly effective in terms of familiarity and brand recognition (Taylor & Hunter, 2002). Marketers are aware of the potential and appeal that social media has offered as part of the marketing plan for their organizations (Naim, 2021). According to a study, social media marketing activities are important

Figure 1. Strategies to build brand awareness (Milović,2012)

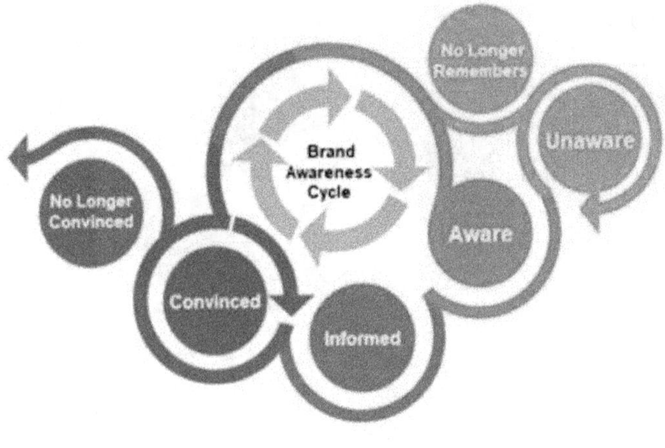

aspects of firms' branding efforts (Naim, 2021). However, it has been discovered in this research that social media marketing operations are mostly focused on customer satisfaction and the consequences on consumers' behavioral intentions (Šerić & Gil-Saura,2012). Organizations use a brand awareness strategy for their various products, and figure 1 shows the cycle of components included in building the brand awareness strategies.

The brand names need to be selected strategically as it gives a sense of positive associations. Also, it should be easy to pronounce and easy to remember. The brand name should be unique, indicating the benefits and USP of the product. Last but not least, it should not be similar to any existing registered brand names (Khanlari, 2015).

Brand awareness strategy is the marketing tactic through which a company communicates with its target audience and gets recognized within the target market. The four brand awareness strategy includes (i) line extension, (ii) brand extension, (iii) new brand strategy, and (iv) flanker/flight brand strategy (Khanlari, 2015).

To build brand awareness, firms focus on components of the brand awareness cycle (BAC) (Han et al., 2019). These components include Market Places, Aware, Trust, Attract More, and Sell More that move the brand from unaware level to awareness (Naim, 2021). Figure 2 shows the components of the brand awareness cycle.

After defining the components of BAC, if firms plan to take their brand to social media, they have to focus on social media marketing strategies (SMMS) that include various social networking platforms. Figure 3 shows some examples of the social media platform for social media marketing strategies for building brand image.

The firms use social networking sites to build SMMS. Usually, firms do not focus on one social site but compare and analyze to develop their SMMS.

Figure 2. Components of Brand awareness cycle (Naim, 2021)

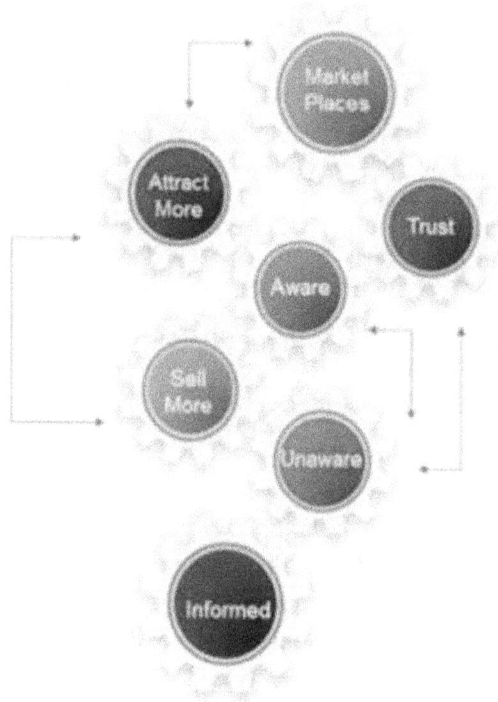

Building SMMS on social media is implementing, measuring, analyzing, and

Figure 3. Examples of Social Media Marketing Strategies (Kumar & Mokha, 2021)

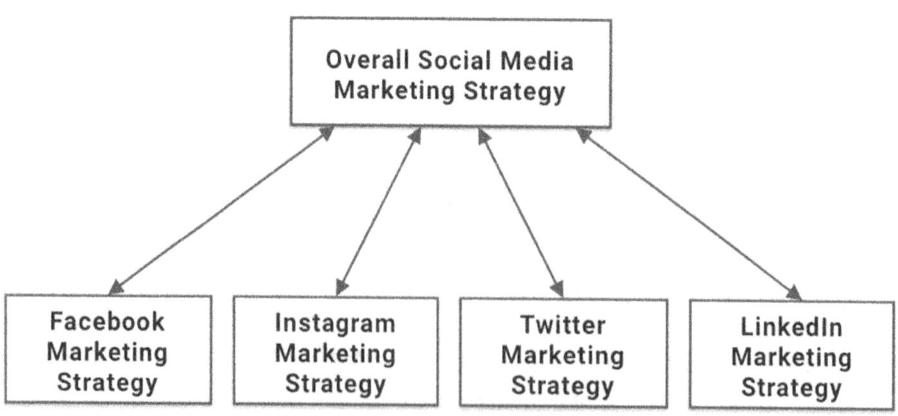

Figure 4. Steps of Social Media Marketing Strategies (Putra et al., 2021)

adjusting marketing strategies and content development. Figure 4 shows the steps of SMMS.

SMMS is based on four factors Audience participation, Managing Social Presence, Customer feedback, and viral campaigns. Firms have the choice to consider all four factors or any one or two or three. Figure 5 shows the loop of SMMS factors.

The he three basic sub-forms of SMMS are (i) Community Management, (ii) Content Creation, and (iii) Growth (Naim & Khan, 2021).

SMM (Social Media Marketing) is the marketing practice that uses social media channels to sell or promote a brand, product, or service.

SMM helps businesses to meet the following benefits: (i) Increase brand awareness, (ii) Build engaged communities (iii) **S**ell products and services, (iv) Measure brand sentiment, (v) Provide social customer service, (vi) Advertise products and services

Figure 5. Factors that influence SMMS (Naim, 2021)

to target audiences, (vii) Track performance and (viii) adjust larger marketing strategies accordingly.

SMMS is a document outlining social media goals, the tactics used to achieve the goals, and the metrics tracked to measure the progress (Ibrahim et al., 2021). SMMS should also list all existing and planned social media accounts, and goals specific to each platform customer is active. These goals should align with the business's larger digital marketing strategy (Sigala, 2011). Moreover, a good social media plan defines roles & responsibilities within-firm a team and outlines the reporting cadence (Sigala, 2011).

This chapter is divided into five parts; the first covers the Introduction, the second part covers the related studies in Literature Review, the third part explains the development of the hypothesis, the fourth part is about Research Methodology, Fifth part shows a detailed explanation of results and discusses the outcomes of the research and sixth part gives the conclusion and future work for this study.

The goals of this study are (1) assessing the impact of SMMS on brand awareness, brand image, and brand loyalty, (2) measuring the impact of brand awareness (BAE) on the brand image (BIA) and how they contribute to building the brand loyalty (BLY).

LITERATURE REVIEW

Social Media Marketing Activities

The online setting where individuals with shared interests join together to exchange their thoughts, comments, and ideas is known as social media (Ekanayake, 2016). In two ways, using these online communication platforms based on the Internet and mobile-based technologies in corporate marketing operations is crucial. The first is the impact customers have on their goods and brands and the market share they produce. According to studies, social media increases customer trust and purchase intentions and facilitates knowledge and experience exchange (Naim, 2021). Many companies leverage online interactions to encourage consumers to share their purchases (Hilal, 2019). with a few easy clicks on their preferred social media platform. Second, businesses use social media to conduct direct marketing campaigns. In this way, social media extends the boundaries of time and location in commercial contact with potential customers, encouraging a sense of intimacy (Naim, 2021). Businesses may use social media technologies to offer low-cost product and brand marketing, promotions, and adverts to their consumers and gain feedback (Purwanto, 2022). It was discovered that social media is at the heart of today's corporate strategy. Its popularity, cost-cutting measures, and rivals' social media activities inspire marketers to engage in social media marketing activities.

Researchers have defined social media marketing activities in the airline industry as entertainment, interaction, trendiness, customization, and perceived risk (Vila & González, 2022). They have identified social media marketing components in insurance services as interaction, trendiness, customization, and perceived risk (Naim, 2021).

The researcher has referred to mar.keting activities like events, information, and advertisement on social networks (Shahin et al., 2013). They have categorized social-media marketing activities as interaction, trendiness, information, customization, and word of mouth communication (Naim & Alqahtani, 2021). In this research, social media marketing activities have been considered entertainment, interaction, trendiness, advertisement, and customization. Only through structuring, defining, and effectively implementing marketing activities on social media can social media play a functional part in organizations marketing efforts. They created one of the most widely used social media marketing activity categories. Entertainment, interactivity, trendiness, personalization, and word of mouth communication are among the social media marketing activities for luxury businesses identified by them. The buying intention was added to these components in 2017 and explained the methods to increase the BAE through SMMS (Ahuja & Medury, 2010). Figure 6 shows the ways to increase BAE through SMMS.

Figure 6. Increase brand awareness through SMMS

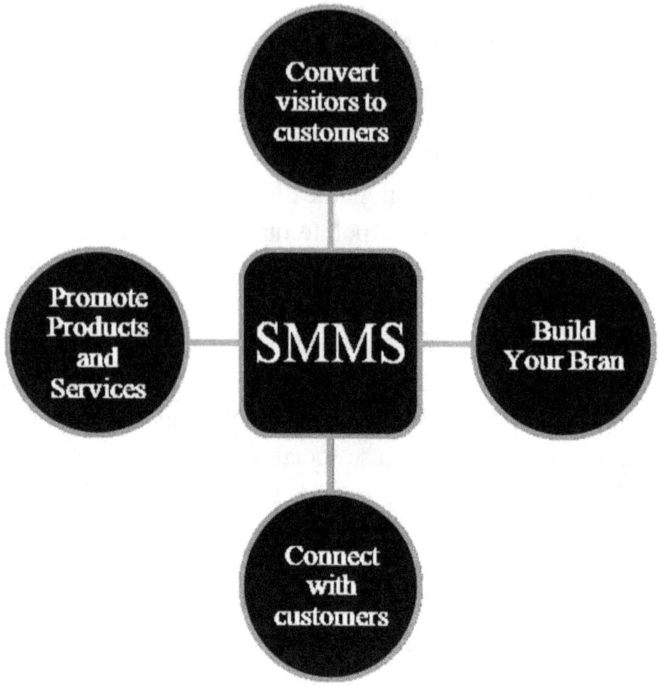

Organizations use media channels for brand awareness campaigns by sharing easy to the easy creation of content which includes (i) infographics, (ii) short videos, (iii) ads, and (iv) links to more detailed, high-quality content that answers customer's questions or addresses trending topics (Savitri et al., 2022). Social media is used to build or enhance brand awareness, increasing sales revenue. Brand awareness is important when launching new services & products; it drives consumers' decisions by differentiating competing companies. SMMS encourages repeat purchases, leading to an increment in sales and market share (Naim, 2022).

Entertainment is an important component that drives participant behavior and follow-up, resulting in favorable emotions/feelings about the brand among social media followers. The researchers stress that the information that arouses their attention finds the content humorous and attractive, even if the reasons for using social media vary (Rahimiparvar, 2014). In this regard, companies should promote the like and sharing of a large number of people and be able to profit from it by offering engaging shares. Because information is disseminated in real-time on social media, it is quickly becoming the newest and most up-to-date source of information for customers. Unlike traditional mass communication methods, social media allows businesses to communicate with their consumers, share information, and collaborate

(Zailskaitė-Jakštė, 2018). Customers' demands and requirements and their thoughts and ideas on the product and brand may be obtained in real-time by using social media as an interactive communication channel between company and consumer (Naim et al., 2022). Another aspect of social media marketing operations is to provide clients with the most up-to-date information about items. Advertising as a component refers to advertising and promotional initiatives run by businesses on social media to boost sales and expand their consumer base (Hutagalung & Situmorang, 2018). According to researchers' findings on the impact of social media advertising on consumer perceptions and awareness, advertising is an important aspect of social media marketing operations. According to some, establishing client happiness based on the business's relationship with specific consumers is known as customization (Naim, 2022). Through peer-to-peer contact, companies on social media may communicate the distinctiveness of their product and brand to their customers.

Brand Awareness

In any instance, scientists refer to brand awareness as the amount of customer identification, acceptability, and recall. Brand awareness is "the capacity of a potential consumer to recognize or recall that a brand belongs to a certain product category" (Misy, 2015). . Brand awareness is to track or crowd power in consumers' memory, reflecting their capacity to recall or recognize a brand in various situations. Consumers will spend less time and risk searching for the goods they will buy if they know the brand (Naim, 2022). Consumers are supposed to pick the brand about which they know. There are four stages of brand awareness: brand recognition, brand recall, top-of-mind brand, and dominating brand. There are five categories to measure the SMMS on social media. These five categories are shown in figure 7.

Brand awareness has two dimensions of brand knowledge, (i) an associative network and (ii) a memory model. Brand awareness is the first step to driving performance-marketing goals, like leads and sales. Figure 8 shows the factors that enhance the BAE. These factors contribute to building the BAE and lead to building BIE. Social media plays a great role in expanding the BAE effectively and promptly.

The brand awareness campaign is a marketing tactic that is designed for the creation of recognition of the brand, products, services, as well as values. Brand awareness is important as the company doesn't want to confuse the target audience on social media pages (Lam et al., 2013).

That's why the brand theme should always be consistent across all content on social media platforms so that the audience can recognize it. When a new product line is presented, brand recognition is related to customer familiarity with the brand. Still, brand recall is associated with the consumer's initial thought about the brand. Being the first brand that comes to mind in a product category means becoming the

Figure 7. Categories of SMMS on Social media (Nandya & Permana, 2021)

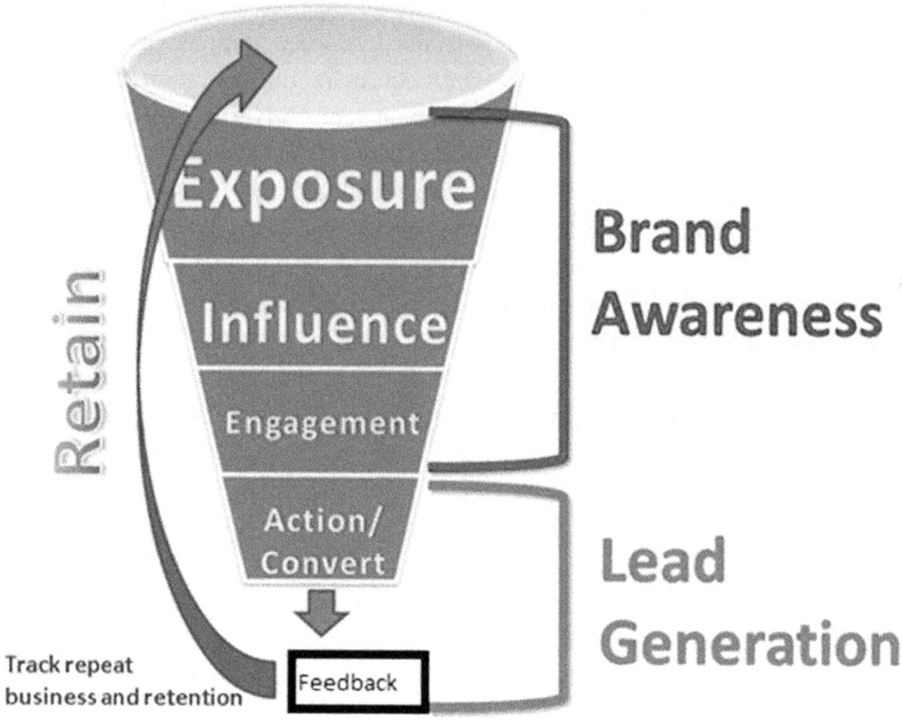

most well-known. The degree to which a brand replaces a product category is brand dominance. Consumers have up and down a continuum for their BAE, BIA, and BLY. There are points of interactions that affect this continuum for the consumers; these are shown in figure 9

SMMS is defined by the effective CCM based on customer care, success, and experience.

Customer service relates to a company's ability to respond appropriately to customer inquiries. Customer success relates to life-cycle product adoption. It includes customer care and consists of a more holistic view of customers. People in this role are tasked with ensuring that customers attain their goals related to product usage.

Customer experience is the broadest of functions and spans the entire organization. The customer experience includes product definitions, sales readiness, professional services execution, post-sales support such as customer care, and customer success. It also has other functions like billing & advertising. People filling this role understand how a product or service works and how customers accomplish their objectives (Sánchez-Casado et al., 2015).

Figure 8. Factors for improving the BAE (Anduku, 2020)

Brand Image

Brand awareness reflects a brand's concrete indications such as its name, sign, symbol, and slogan, but company image demonstrates its place beyond these indicators in the consumer's mind (Zephaniah, 2020). According to some researchers, the brand image embodies customers' symbolism, including all of the brand's definitions and assessments (Singagerda, 2020). "Consumer views of and preferences for a brand, as represented in numerous sorts of brand associations maintained in consumers' memory." The brand image incorporates information and concepts that a consumer has about the brand's many goods and their qualities. Marketing communication, consumption experience, and societal consequences contribute to customers' mental picture of a brand. These elements impact customers' attitudes toward brands and trust and the impact of brand messaging on consumers' thoughts (Noviana, 2021).

Brand image is the mental feedback of consumers when they purchase a product. A positive brand image is the customers' expectations of the brand. A positive brand image enhances the goodwill and brand value of an organization. To sum up, "Brand image" is the customer's net extract from the brand (Rana et al., 2015).

SMMS also depends on strong BIE, and firms have realized that branding has advantages that increase sales in the short term and facilitate reaping profits in a

Figure 9. Customer Continuum for BAI, BIE and BLY (Naim, 2022)

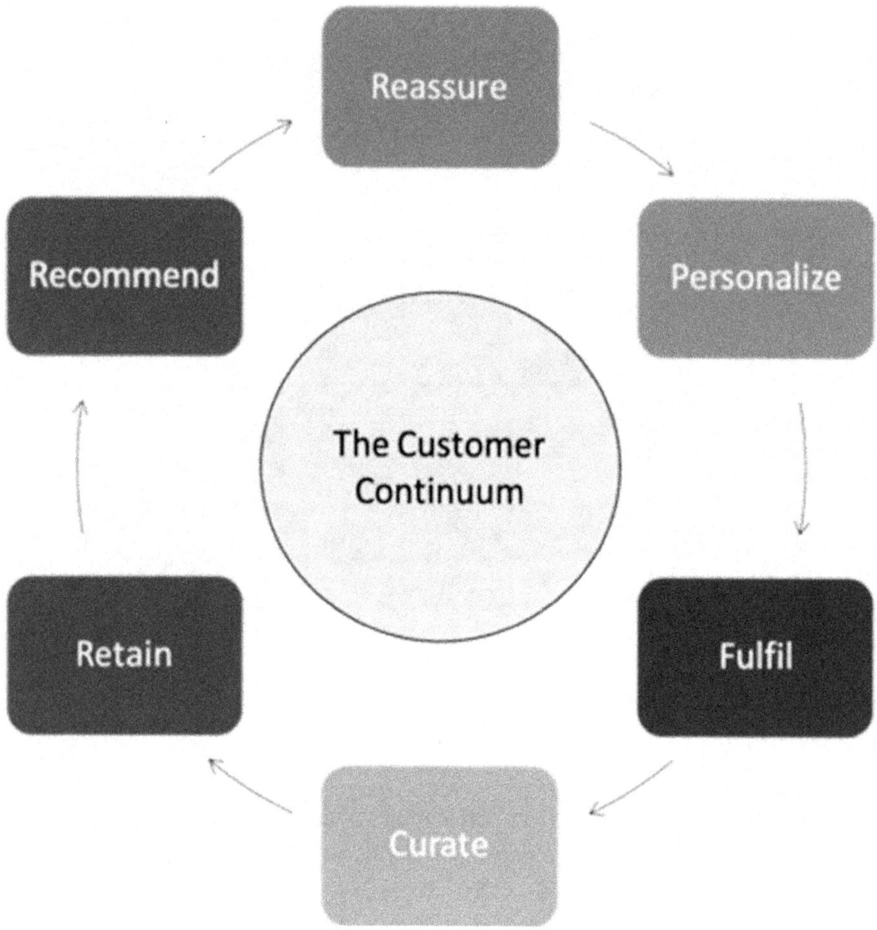

long time as consumers retain the brand name and make repurchases. Figure 9 shows the benefits of branding in SMMS.

Branding is the means that differentiate products from one another (competitor). Branding has importance for customers, organizations, and society in the competitive world. Branding is important for product identification, differentiation, advertising, demand creation, and publicity. Branding increases trust, and trust is a pillar of customer loyalty. A firm's identity attracts customers because they can tell what it stands for. When customers feel connected to a business, they're more likely to be loyal (Ibrahim et al., 2021).

There are four brand benefits (i) Functional, (ii) Emotional, (iii) Self-expressive, and (iv) Consumer benefits (Ibrahim et al., 2021).

Figure 10. Branding Benefits for SMMS (Naim, 2022)

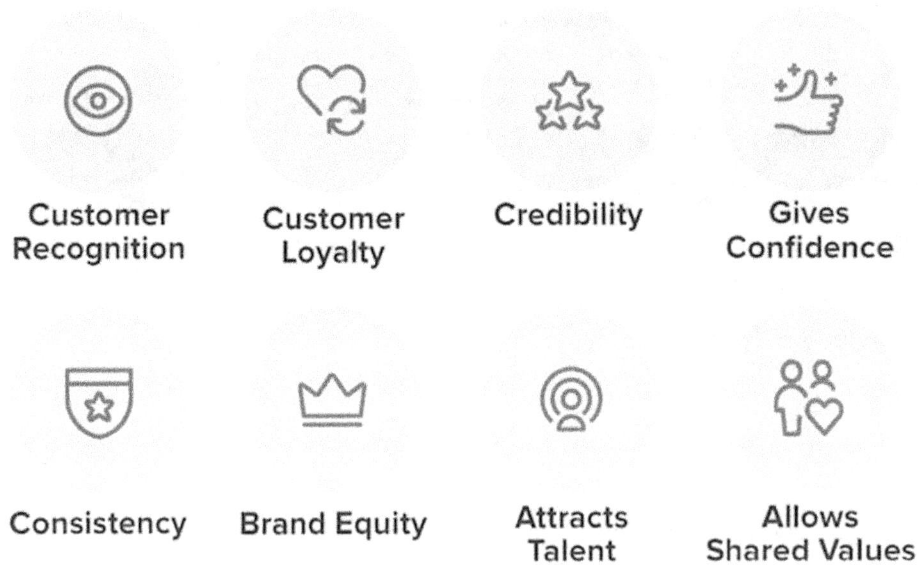

Brand Loyalty

The positive impact of loyal customers on business performance in today's competitive markets and in situations where the cost of acquiring new customers is higher than retaining current customers is gradually increasing the importance of customer loyalty (Zailskaite-Jakštė et al., 2018). Customer loyalty refers to a customer's promise to buy a company's products and services again, despite the activities of competitors, and to commit to being a customer of that company regularly in the future. The sequence of building BLY starts from awareness and moves to advocacy; figure 10 shows the flow diagram along with the factors affecting this flow to achieve BLY.

Brand loyalty is a customer's positive attitude towards a specific brand. If brand loyalty is strong, customers consistently purchase the same brand when they need a product in the product category. The three degrees of brand loyalty are (i) brand recognition, (ii) brand preference, and (iii) brand insistence (Safari & Safahani, 2015).

Various factors can positively or negatively affect building BLY, some of which are shown in figure 11.

Loyal customers remain committed to the brand. They pay a higher price for that brand and promote the same brand always (Nderitu, 2018). A company having brand loyal customers will have greater sales, less marketing and advertising costs, and the best pricing.

Figure 11. Flow diagram of BLY (Safari & Safahani, 2015)

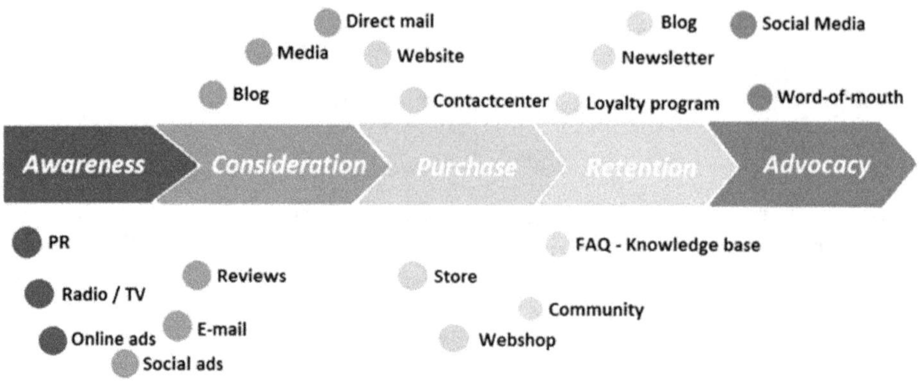

Figure 12. Factors affecting BLY (Ardyan & Sugiyarti, 2018)

Figure 13. Pyramid of BLY for SMMS (Tadayon et al., 2021)

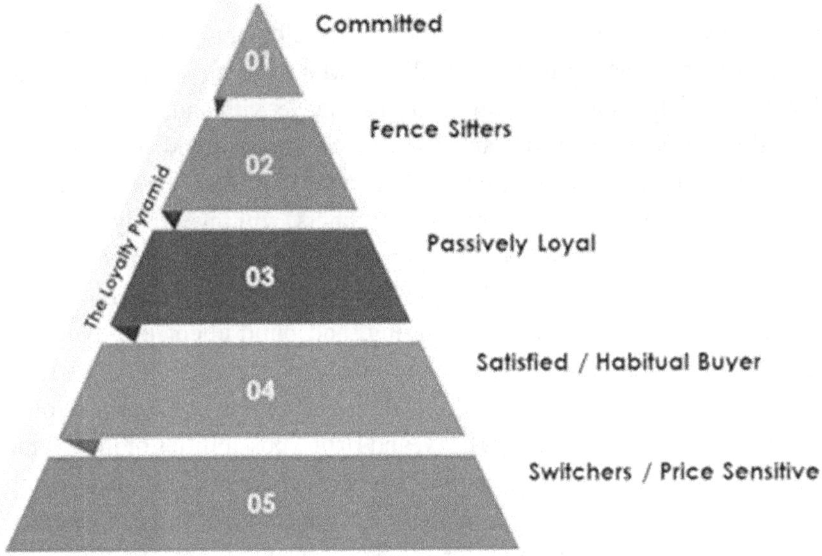

Dependability, emotional connection, superiority, and social media presence impact customer loyalty. Brands need to demonstrate consistency and excellence in the minds of the customer. This leads to an emotional attachment, and figure 12 shows how the pyramid of loyalty can be built and what is inclusive in developing BLY.

A brand pyramid is a symbolic framework that explains fundamental questions about a brand and market positioning. The framework is particularly useful for new brands to enter a market first (Tadayon et al., 2021).

Customers' purchase of the same brand demonstrates the behavioral part of loyalty. Consumers who display a behavioral commitment to a company are competent to gain new customers since they have low price sensitivity and spend more. Consumers' positive brand sharing, suggesting the brand to potential customers, and persuading them to buy it may be considered attitudinal aspects of loyalty (Chen & Chen, 2004). Loyalty has a cognitive component and is the first to spring to mind as price tolerance. Behavioral loyalty to the brand generates immediate revenue for the company. In contrast, altitudinal and cognitive loyalty increases the likelihood of making trustworthy recommendations to others in their surroundings and is critical in attracting new consumers. Brand loyalty is a crucial non-material asset for firms in this regard.

DEVELOPMENT OF HYPOTHESES

As Social networks provide several chances to develop brand-customer interactions as a marketing tool (Mang'unyi, et al., 2018). Many businesses have viewed social media as one of the most successful tools to engage with and empower customers to build distinct brand identities and improve consumer-brand communications in recent years. Interactive marketing methods that use social media linkages such as Facebook and Twitter, according to researchers, will favourably enhance brand image and generate a leveraging effect between brand and customer.

The ultimate purpose of social media marketing is to get new consumers, raise sales, strengthen word-of-mouth marketing, and build client loyalty. In contrast to the traditional branding paradigm (consecutive investments and controlled communication to guide the image), social media communications take place on a platform where the boundaries are hazy, and firms' possibilities of involvement are slim. These conversations that occur without the firm's participation have improved customer trust. Sharing information about a product or a brand can be dangerous, yet customer-created content and peer-to-peer contact can impact other consumers' purchase decisions. Furthermore, businesses aggressively use customer-generated content and information in social media marketing campaigns. Beyond facilitating consumer interactions, researchers discovered that social media impacts customers' trust feelings and purchase intent. Social media is an effective means for businesses to communicate with existing and future consumers while building a favourable brand image. According to a scientist, social media marketing messages impact customer perceptions (Kumar, 2020). According to him, social media marketing efforts move brand recognition and loyalty. According to them, social media marketing efforts favourably affect customers' repurchasing behaviour (Miremadi & Ghanadiof, 2021). According to them, customers' brand awareness, purchase intentions, and brand loyalty are all affected by social media marketing efforts in the hospitality industry. The following hypothesis will be tested in this chapter:

H1: SMM activities affect brand awareness, brand image, and brand loyalty

Individuals have used brand awareness as a strategy to become aware of, familiar with, and recall a brand. Even in the recognition phase, brand awareness may elicit a sense of familiarity and provide information about the brand as a symbol of devotion to the brand. Businesses may use social media marketing to increase brand awareness and establish a good brand image by facilitating contact with new and current consumers. The amount of money spent on advertising enhances the breadth and repetition of the advertising message, increasing brand recognition. As a result, a company's presence on social media is extremely useful in informing customers, familiarity, and brand recognition, as it overcomes time and space constraints. Increased brand awareness and image level will substantially affect following purchase behaviours once the brand has been evaluated and satisfied consumers' expectations. Consumers who are already familiar with and familiar with the brand are likely to prefer it again. According to a few researchers, strong brand awareness influences other brand aspects, such as brand image and brand loyalty, and the brand's market share.

To put it another way, brand awareness and brand recognition. Their study of international cosmetics brands in South East Asia discovered a strong positive association between brand awareness and brand loyalty (Kumar, 2020). Researchers found that brand image had a considerable impact on brand loyalty in banking services. The relationships between brand awareness, brand image, and brand loyalty have been documented in various studies. Also, this chapter measures the below-given hypothesis:

H2: Brand awareness affects the brand image and vice versa to achieve brand loyalty

METHODOLOGY

Research Model

In this study, three goals have been defined—the first looks at how social media marketing efforts affect brand recognition, image, and loyalty. The second objective is to assess the impact of brand awareness on brand image. The third step looks at how brand awareness and image affect brand loyalty. Figure 1 depicts the study variables, correlations, and the proposed research model for evaluating hypotheses. A quantitative technique was used to examine the connection between the variables in the research and meet the set objectives.

Population and Sampling

According to Marketing in Gulf social media brand performance statistics, the population of this study consists of individuals who actively follow the top five companies with the highest social score on social media communication channels such as Facebook, Twitter, and Instagram. Famous brand of category management were considered for the measurement. We have applied the convenience sampling approach, which is one of the sampling methods that are not dependent on probability and is used in the study to account for users' information limitations.

Figure 14. Proposed Research Model (PRM)

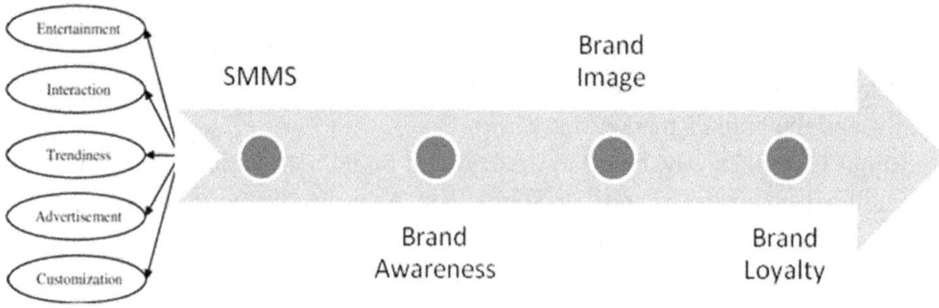

Measurement

The questionnaire approach was used to collect study data. The research questionnaire is divided into two sections. The first section provides the participants' views on the business's social media marketing operations (BSMMO). The BSMMO was evaluated across five dimensions: entertainment, engagement, trendiness, advertising, and personalization. The second section shows the relationship between brand awareness and brand image that eventually contributes to building brand loyalty. The first section of the results used the 5-point Likert scale to gauge respondents' feelings about the phrases in the measuring model (5 = strongly agree, 1 = strongly disagree). Closed-ended questions were used to assess the demographic features of the participants. The empirical qualitative method is applied to show the relationship and dependence between brand awareness and brand image for brand loyalty. There are many methods in qualitative analysis, and for measuring the second section, we have used correlation analysis to find the relation between two sets of variables. The trend shows the outcomes information as of positive, negative or neutral correlation.

Data Collection and Analysis

The data-gathering phase has begun following the formation of the data collection tool. A preliminary test was used to determine the study scale's dependability during the data-gathering stage. The created questionnaire form was given to 100 people (the study's population) who follow five different brands on social networking sites.

Figure 15. Results for dimension Entertainment for SMMS affecting BAE, BIE and BLY

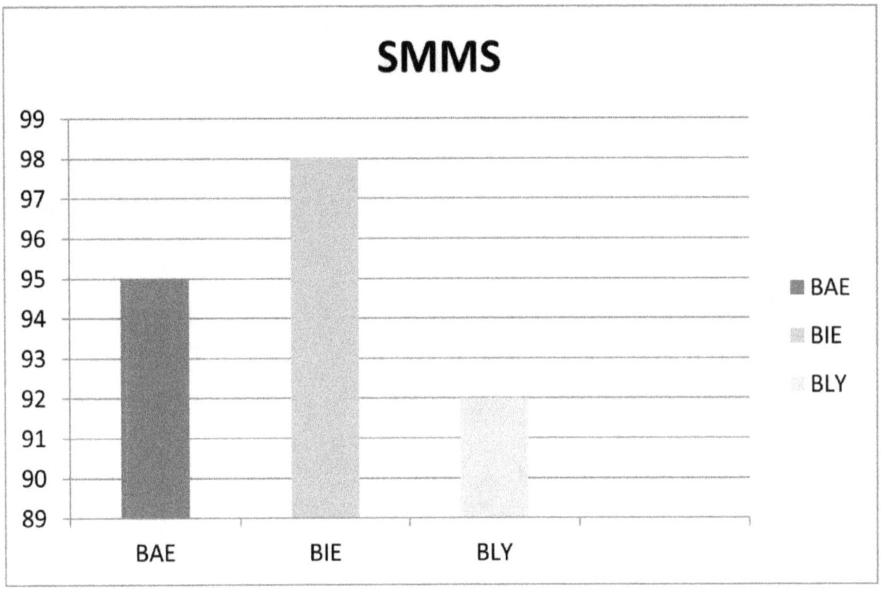

RESULTS/DISCUSSIONS

Social media marketing activities affect brand awareness (BAE). Brand image (BIE) and Brand loyalty (BLY). To show the results and analysis, we measured BAE, BIE, and BLY for social media networking sites such as Facebook, Twitter, and Instagram for five dimensions of SMMS.

Entertainment for SMMS

Social media is the connective tissue that enables consumers to multitask during their entertainment experiences by connecting with others and sharing their opinions. Results show that all three social media entertainment has contributed, on average, 95% of SMMS through BAE, BIE, and BLY.

The results show that BAE is 95% on social media, BIE is 98% and BLY is 92% that concludes a positive impact of SMMS through entertainment.

Engagement for SMMS

A social media engagement strategy is the plan that connects social media tactics to goals on social networks. The approach summarizes what you plan to do and how the firms expect to achieve its SMMS.

Figure 16. Results for dimension Engagement for SMMS affecting BAE, BIE and BLY

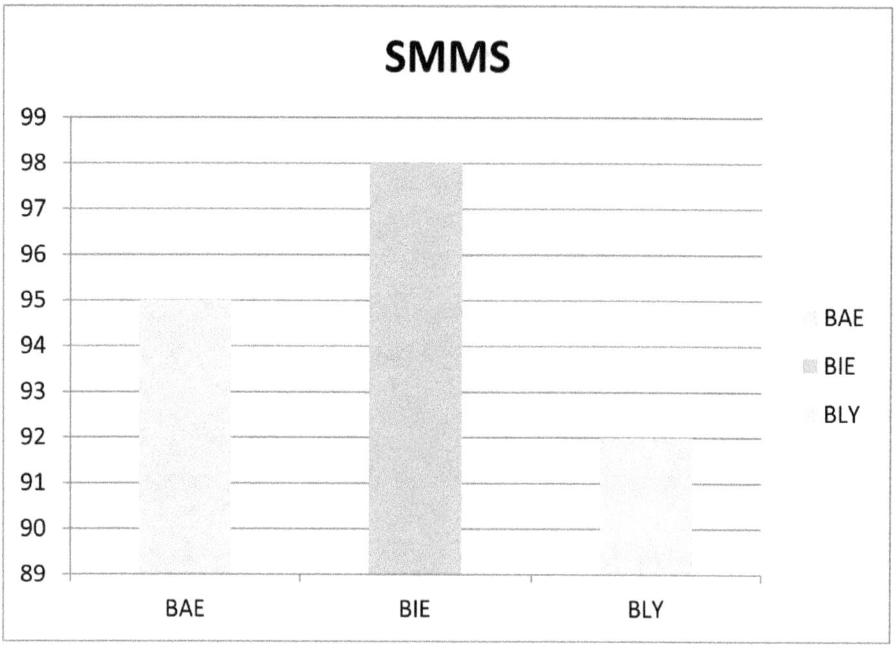

The results show that BAE is 95% on social media, BIE is 98% and BLY is 92% that concludes a positive impact of SMMS through engagement.

Trendiness for SMMA

A social media strategy is a document outlining your social media goals, the tactics that firms will use to achieve them and the metrics will track to measure the progress.

The results show that BAE is 88% on social media, BIE is 92% and BLY is 98% that concludes a positive impact of SMMS through trendiness.

Advertising for SMMS

A social media marketing strategy is a summary of everything that a firm plans to do and hope to achieve on social media. It guides the advertising plans and results of success and failure. This also explains the SMMS effectiveness on social media networking site.

The results show that BAE is 95% on social media, BIE is 90% and BLY is 93% that concludes a positive impact of SMMS through advertising on social media sites.

Figure 17. Results for dimension Trendiness for SMMS affecting BAE, BIE and BLY

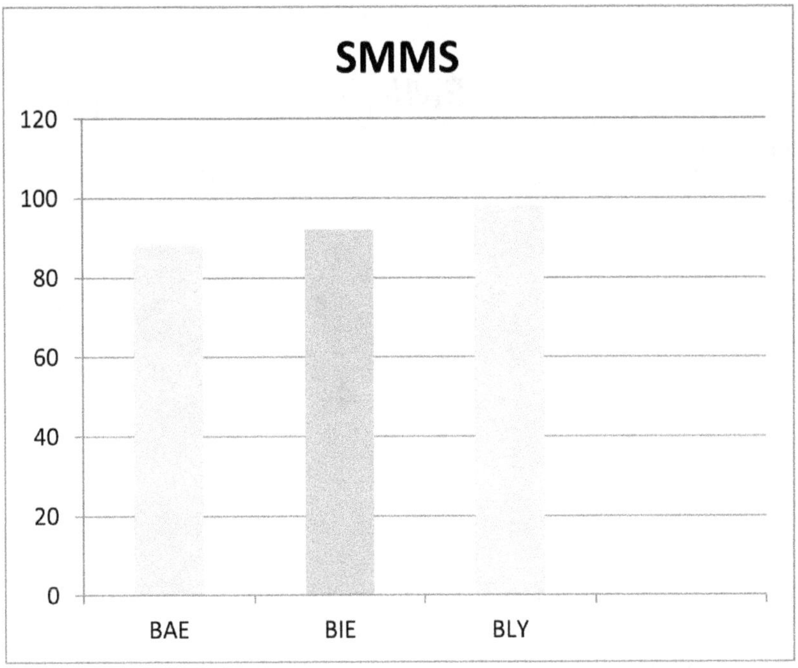

Figure 18. Results for dimension advertising for SMMS affecting BAE, BIE and BLY

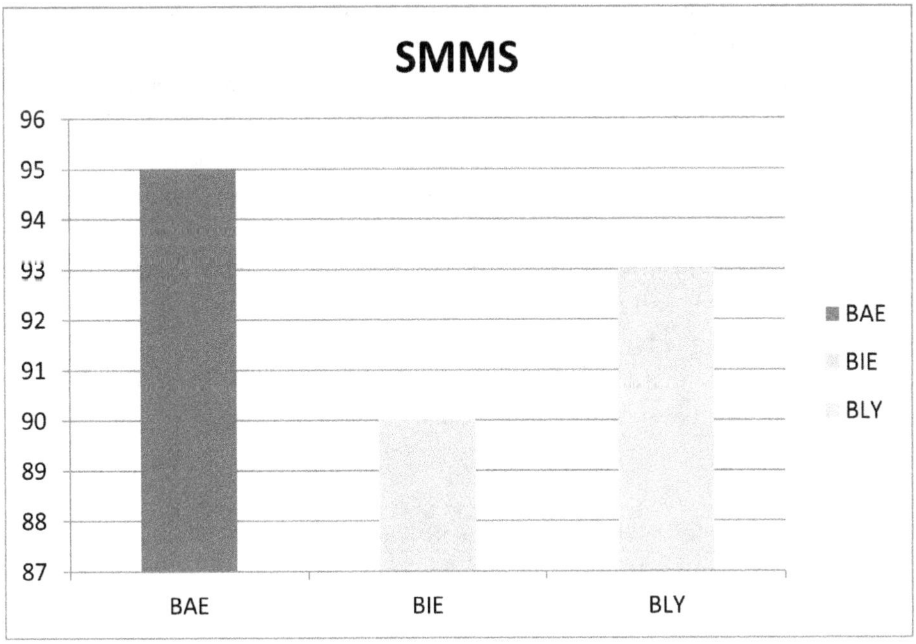

Figure 19. Results for dimension Personalization for SMMS affecting BAE, BIE and BLY

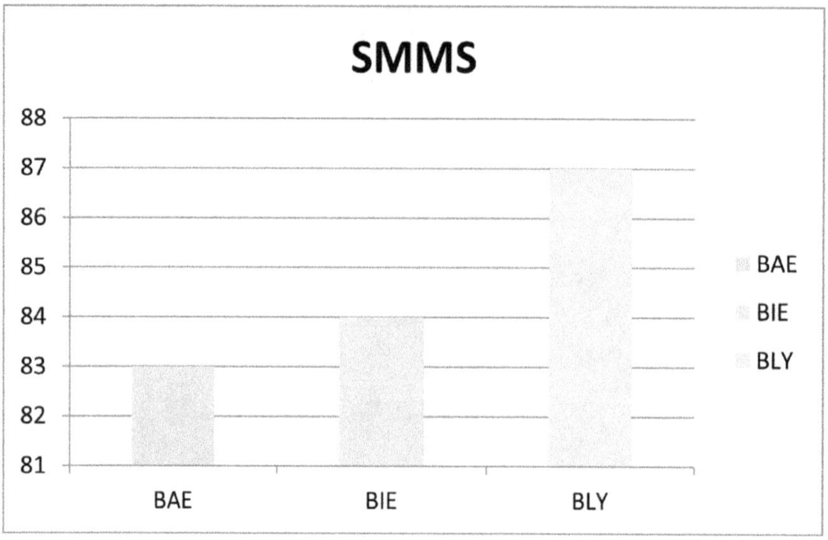

Personalization for SMMS

A personalization strategy lets the firms to identify segments of visitors with distinct preferences or needs, and then create targeted experiences for them. This provides a high level of overview of the strategic decisions that a firm can make when using Personalization for SMMS for BAE, BIE and BLY.

The results show that BAE is 83% on social media, BIE is 84% and BLY is 87% that concludes a positive impact of SMMS through personalization. The results reveal that BLY can be achieved with the personalization approach.

The second part of results and discussion shows the testing of Brand awareness for brand image and vice versa to achieve brand loyalty.

The results show positive correlation between all three on social media networking site. Increase in BAE will result in increase in BIE and increase in BIE will result in Increase in BAE and both affects the trend of BLY.

The results show that the incremental trend of BAE and BIE on Social media networking sites and eventually causing the increment in BLY.

Figure 20. Results for Correlation between BAE, BIE and BLY

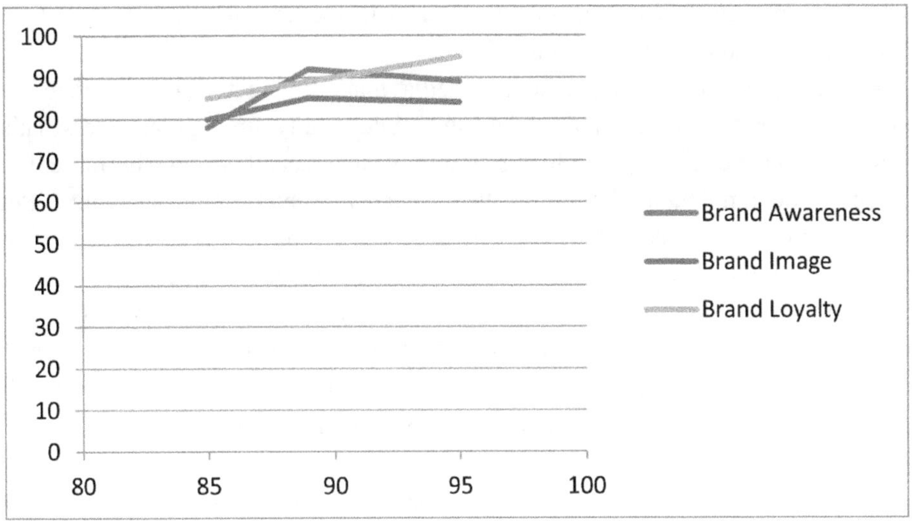

CONCLUSION AND FUTURE WORK

Social media has become a vital element of daily life in today's digital age as a communication medium. Consumers reflect their consumption patterns, tastes, views, likes, and experiences in their own eyes and communicate with other users. This vast communication space, in which users communicate with one another and with other users, provides many chances for product and brand communication activities, such as cost, time, and convenience of reaching huge customer groups. Many firms construct their brand profiles on social media communication channels and activities that engage consumers with content sharing, such as online product information, discounts, adverts, and promotions. This study was carried out to see if marketing initiatives on social media effectively create clients' brand awareness, image, and loyalty.

According to the components that make up social media marketing activities, personalization and entertainment are the most important social media marketing activities. Consumers place the least importance on trendiness and interactivity in social media marketing. Customers may place a low value on features like trendiness and interactivity, despite these features being deemed necessary for social media communication. These findings show that businesses that want to build and maintain successful brand communication on social media prioritize individual communication with customers and pay close attention to content sharing about the interesting and entertaining brand rather than correctness, advertisement, and promotion content. According to a study undertaken by these researchers, entertainment is a crucial component of social media marketing efforts. However, while they say that trendiness is the most important factor for consumers in social media marketing, the results of this study contradict this assumption.

According to the findings, social media marketing activities considerably impact brand recognition, brand image, and brand loyalty among consumers. This conclusion has been compared to the results of the researchers. Furthermore, the impact of social media marketing on clients is mostly seen in brand awareness. Put another way; social media marketing activities are important awareness tools in recalling customers and keeping them in mind. Nonetheless, data reveal that brand knowledge has no impact on a brand image or loyalty as assessed by customers with similar levels of awareness. This finding is demonstrated by the limited influence of brand awareness on brand image. Beyond that, the amount of effect in the research has been smaller, even though brand awareness and brand image are important for consumers' brand loyalty.

It's an intriguing and noteworthy finding that the significant impact of social media marketing efforts on brand awareness does not influence brand image or loyalty. This is because customers are more likely to follow businesses they are already familiar with on social media. In other words, when customers follow a company on social media, they generate brand-related material or share their experience, which implies they are thinking about brand image and loyalty. Furthermore, because consumers have a mental picture of a brand or follow brands to which they are loyal, social media marketing activities may not be effective enough to instill in consumers a favorable brand image and brand loyalty. In this regard, it has been suggested that social media marketing activities be seen as activities that promote the brand value and that social media marketing activities be integrated into traditional brand communication studies by enterprises planning to begin social media marketing activities.

According to Marketing Gulf's social media brand performance statistics, the findings of this study were acquired from customers who follow five companies from five different industries with the highest social score as of January 2020 on Facebook, Twitter, and Instagram. Future studies might focus on reflections on brands' social media marketing efforts that belong to comparable product groupings on consumers. Additionally, the impact of consumer interactions on social media on a product group or a brand that exists (independent of the company) on brand awareness, image, and loyalty may be investigated. Furthermore, the investigations that will be undertaken may comprise social media channels such as WhatsApp, Google+, YouTube, and LinkedIn; as a result, the research will be conducted on a wider scale.

REFERENCES

Ahuja, V., & Medury, Y. (2010). Corporate blogs as e-CRM tools–Building consumer engagement through content management. *Journal of Database Marketing & Customer Strategy Management, 17*(2), 91–105. doi:10.1057/dbm.2010.8

Anduku, Y. F. (2020). *Analysis Of The Relationship Between Social Bonding Strategies And Customer Loyalty Among Supermarkets In Western Region, Kenya; A Focus On The Role Of Brand Identity* (Doctoral Dissertation). Kisii University.

Ardyan, E., & Sugiyarti, G. (2018). The influence of e-CRM capability and co-information sharing activity on product competitiveness and marketing performance of small and medium-sized enterprises. *International Journal of Electronic Customer Relationship Management, 11*(2), 158–178. doi:10.1504/IJECRM.2018.090208

Chen, Q., & Chen, H. M. (2004). Exploring the success factors of eCRM strategies in practice. *Journal of Database Marketing & Customer Strategy Management, 11*(4), 333–343. doi:10.1057/palgrave.dbm.3240232

Ekanayake, C. S. (2016). *Consumer engagement with social media, brand equity and intention to purchase* (Doctoral dissertation).

Han, H., Nguyen, H. N., Song, H. J., Chua, B. L., Lee, S., & Kim, W. (2019). Role of social network services (SNS) sales promotions in generating brand loyalty for chain steakhouses. *Journal of Quality Assurance in Hospitality & Tourism, 20*(5), 617–645. doi:10.1080/1528008X.2019.1579078

Haudi, H., Handayani, W., Musnaini, M., Suyoto, Y., Prasetio, T., Pitaloka, E., & Cahyon, Y. (2022). The effect of social media marketing on brand trust, brand equity and brand loyalty. *International Journal of Data and Network Science*, *6*(3), 961–972. doi:10.5267/j.ijdns.2022.1.015

Hilal, M. I. M. (2019). *The effects of services marketing mix elements on brand equity and customer response to tourist's hotels in the east coast of Sri Lanka.* Academic Press.

Hutagalung, B., & Situmorang, S. H. (2018, January). The Effect Of Social Media Marketing On Value Equity, Brand Equity And Relationship Equity On Young Entrepreneurs In Medan City. In *1st Economics and Business International Conference 2017 (EBIC 2017)* (pp. 534-540). Atlantis Press. 10.2991/ebic-17.2018.84

Ibrahim, Y., Abbas, T., & Kamal, M. (2021). The Use of Electronic Customer Relationship Management (E-CRM) Features through Hotel'Website to Enhance Customer Loyalty and Brand Image. *Journal of Association of Arab Universities for Tourism and Hospitality*, *21*(1), 106–128.

Ibrahim, Y., Abbas, T. M., & Kamal, M. A. (2021). The Impact of Online Communities-based Social Customer Relationship Management (S-CRM) on Customer Loyalty and Brand Image on Hotels. *Journal of Association of Arab Universities for Tourism and Hospitality*, *21*(2), 206–232. doi:10.21608/jaauth.2021.84867.1202

Kakeesh, D., Al-Weshah, G., & Al-Ma'aitah, N. (2021). Maintaining Customer Loyalty Using Electronic Customer Relationship Management (E-CRM): Qualitative Evidence from Small Food Businesses in Jordan. *Studies of Applied Economics*, *39*(7). Advance online publication. doi:10.25115/eea.v39i7.4810

Khanlari, A. (Ed.). (2015). *Strategic customer relationship management in the age of social media*. IGI Global. doi:10.4018/978-1-4666-8586-4

Kumar, M. (2020). Effective Usage of E-CRM and Social Media Tools by Akshay Kumar: Most Prolific Bollywood Actor of Last Decade. *International Journal of Management*, *11*(2).

Kumar, P., & Mokha, A. K. (2021). Relationship between E-CRM, Customer Experience, Customer Satisfaction and Customer Loyalty in Banking Industry: A Review of Literature. *International Journal of Multidisciplinary*, *6*(2), 127–137.

Lam, A. Y., Cheung, R., & Lau, M. M. (2013). The influence of internet-based customer relationship management on customer loyalty. *Contemporary Management Research*, *9*(4), 419–440. doi:10.7903/cmr.11095

Mang'unyi, E. E., Khabala, O. T., & Govender, K. K. (2018). Bank customer loyalty and satisfaction: The influence of virtual e-CRM. *African Journal of Economic and Management Studies*, *9*(2), 250–265. doi:10.1108/AJEMS-08-2017-0183

Maskuroh, N., Fahlevi, M., Irma, D., Rita, R., & Rabiah, A. (2022). Social media as a bridge to e-commerce adoption in Indonesia: A research framework for repurchase intention. *International Journal of Data and Network Science*, *6*(1), 107–114. doi:10.5267/j.ijdns.2021.9.017

Milović, B. (2012). *Social media and eCRM as a prerequisite for hotel success*. Academic Press.

Miremadi, A., & Ghanadiof, O. (2021). The Ultimate Influences of Brand Equity Dimensions on Consumer Decision in Hi-Tech Market. *Academic Journal of Research and Scientific Publishing*. doi. org/. e doi:10.52132/Ajrsp

Misy, P. (2015). *The Influence of e-CRM (Electronic Customer Relationship Management) on Customer Loyalty Case Study: Customers of The Body Shop* (Doctoral dissertation). Universitas Andalas.

Naim, A. (2021a). Applications of Marketing Framework in Business Practices. *Journal of Marketing and Emerging Economics*, *1*(6), 55–70.

Naim, A. (2021b). Applications of MIS in building Electronic Relationship with customers: A case-based study. *Periodica Journal of Modern Philosophy. Social Sciences and Humanities*, *1*, 1–8.

Naim, A. (2021c). Green Business Process Management. *International Journal of Innovative Analyses and Emerging Technology*, *1*(6), 125–134. http://openaccessjournals.eu/index.php/ijiaet/article/view/651

Naim, A. (2021d). Green Information Technologies in Business Operations. *Periodica Journal of Modern Philosophy. Social Sciences and Humanities*, *1*, 36–49.

Naim, A. (2021e). New Trends in Business Process Management: Applications of Green Information Technologies. *British Journal of Environmental Studies*, *1*(1), 12–23.

Naim, A. (2022). Mapping of social customer relationship management with electronic customer relationship management. *European Journal of Interdisciplinary Research and Development*, *2*, 14–25. https://ejird.journalspark.org/index.php/ejird/article/view/10

Naim, A. (2022a). Measurement Consumer Mood and Emotions for Fast Moving Consumer Goods. *International Journal of Innovative Analyses and Emerging Technology*, *2*(2), 83 86.

Naim, A. (2022b). Neuro-Marketing Techniques for Proposing Information Driven Framework for Decision Making. *International Journal of Innovative Analyses and Emerging Technology*, *2*(2), 87–94. http://openaccessjournals.eu/index.php/ijiaet/article/view/1060

Naim, A., & Alqahtani, K. (2021). Role of Information Systems in Customer Relationship Management. *Pulse*, *2*(2).

Naim, A., & Khan, M. F. (2021). Measuring the Psychological Behavior of Consumers for Medical Services. *Zien Journal of Social Sciences and Humanities, 2*, 119–131. Retrieved from https://zienjournals.com/index.php/zjssh/article/view/316

Naim, A., Muniasamy, A., Clementking, A., & Rajkumar, R. (2022). Relevance of Green Manufacturing and IoT in Industrial Transformation and Marketing Management. In M. Lahby, A. Al-Fuqaha, & Y. Maleh (Eds.), *Computational Intelligence Techniques for Green Smart Cities. Green Energy and Technology*. Springer. doi:10.1007/978-3-030-96429-0_19

Nandya, T., & Permana, D. (2021). Analysis of the effect of electronic customer relationship management (E-CRM) and brand trust on customer satisfaction and loyalty in pixy cosmetic products. *Dinasti International Journal of Management Science*, *2*(3), 467–483. doi:10.31933/dijms.v2i3.708

Nderitu, S. W. (2018). *Influence Of E-Marketing Strategies On Brand Equity Of Parastatals In Kenya* (Doctoral dissertation). University of Nairobi.

Noviana, G. (2021, September). An Analysis of the Implementation of Electronic Customer Relationship Management (E-CRM) Towards Customer Loyalty. In *5th Global Conference on Business, Management and Entrepreneurship (GCBME 2020)* (pp. 434-438). Atlantis Press. 10.2991/aebmr.k.210831.086

Purwanto, A. (2022). How The Role of Digital Marketing and Brand Image on Food Product Purchase Decisions? An Empirical Study on Indonesian SMEs in the Digital Era. *Journal of Industrial Engineering & Management Research*, *3*(6), 34–41.

Putra, A. H. P. K., Nurani, N., Ilyas, G. B., Samiha, Y. T., & Lestari, S. D. (2021). Configure the Symmetrical and Asymmetrical Paths of Brand Equity and Relationship of Firm Created Content and User Generated Content as Antecedent. *Jurnal Manajemen Bisnis*, *8*(1), 90–103. doi:10.33096/jmb.v1i1.704

Rahimiparvar, N. (2014). eCRM Features that Affect Customer Attitude to Loyalty: A Case Study of a Sample of 402 University Students Enrolled in International Programs in Thailand. *AU-GSB e-Journal, 7*(2).

Rana, A., Bhat, A., & Rani, L. (2015). A classificatory scheme for antecedents of the sources of "online brand equity". *Journal of Research in Interactive Marketing*, *9*(4), 262–298. doi:10.1108/JRIM-02-2014-0008

Safari, M., & Safahani, N. (2015). An empirical model to explain the effects of electronic customer relationship management on customer e-satisfaction and e-loyalty: Evidence from Iranian service shopping websites. *Journal of Internet Banking and Commerce*.

Sánchez-Casado, N., Cegarra-Navarro, J. G., & Tomaseti-Solano, E. (2015, April). The use of Social Networking Sites to create customer knowledge. In *European Conference on Intangibles and Intellectual Capital* (p. 441). Academic Conferences International Limited.

Savitri, C., Hurriyati, R., Wibowo, L., & Hendrayati, H. (2022). The role of social media marketing and brand image on smartphone purchase intention. *International Journal of Data and Network Science*, *6*(1), 185–192. doi:10.5267/j.ijdns.2021.9.009

Šerić, M., & Gil-Saura, I. (2012). ICT, IMC, and brand equity in high-quality hotels of Dalmatia: An analysis from guest perceptions. *Journal of Hospitality Marketing & Management*, *21*(8), 821–851. doi:10.1080/19368623.2012.633211

Shahin, A., Gharibpoor, M., Teymouri, S., & Iraj, E. B. (2013). Studying the influence of e-CRM on web-based brand personality–the case of Mellat Bank. *International Journal of Business Information Systems*, *13*(4), 453–470. doi:10.1504/IJBIS.2013.055301

Sigala, M. (2011). eCRM 2.0 applications and trends: The use and perceptions of Greek tourism firms of social networks and intelligence. *Computers in Human Behavior*, *27*(2), 655–661. doi:10.1016/j.chb.2010.03.007

Singagerda, F. (2020). How much media marketing and brand image reinforce ecommerce consumer loyalty? *International Journal of Data and Network Science*, *4*(4), 389–396.

Tadayon, M. A., Ebrahimzadc Dastgcrdi, R., Gheitani, A., & Sadeghi, M. (2021). Determining the Dimensions of Electronic Customer Relationship Management (E-CRM) in Gharzolhasaneh Mehr Iran Bank. *Journal of System Management*, *7*(4), 93–112.

Taylor, S. A., & Hunter, G. L. (2002). The impact of loyalty with e-CRM software and e-services. *International Journal of Service Industry Management*, *13*(5), 452–474. doi:10.1108/09564230210447931

Vila, T. D., & González, E. A. (2022). eCRM. In Encyclopedia of Tourism Management and Marketing. Edward Elgar Publishing.

Zailskaitė-Jakštė, L. (2018). *Consumer engagement behaviour in social media communication impact on brand equity* (Doctoral dissertation). Kauno Technologijos Universitetas.

Zailskaite-Jakštė, L., Damaševičius, R., Ostreika, A., & Anubhav, K. (2018, July). Consumers Engagement Behaviour in Social Media: Do Different Brand Categories Matter? In *ECRM 2018 17th European Conference on Research Methods in Business and Management* (p. 444). Academic Conferences and Publishing Limited.

Zephaniah, C. O., Ogba, I. E., & Izogo, E. E. (2020). Examining the effect of customers' perception of bank marketing communication on customer loyalty. *Scientific American*, *8*, e00383.

Chapter 7
Critical Success Factors for Transforming CRM to SCRM for building E-CRM

Hamed Alqahtani
King Khalid University, Saudi Arabia

Arshi Naim
King Khalid University, Saudi Arabia

ABSTRACT

In the current scenario, the entire Middle East is witnessing drastic digitalization, and consumer behavior is also widely affected by the technological development. This has created a platform for the growth of e-commerce (Ecom) in the Middle East through social networking. The success factors that facilitate in transforming the customer relationship management (CRM) to social customer relationship management (SCRM) for achieving electronic customer relationship management (ECRM) are customer values and customer loyalty. These success factors are digitally termed as electronic customer values (ECV) and electronic customer loyalty (ECL). This study has involved 100 digital consumers of Ecom on various social apps and social networking in the Middle East. This study is an empirical analysis where 10 critical success factors are measured to achieve the positiveness of ECV to contribute in ECL success. ECL success can transform CRM to SCRM and build strong ECRM.

DOI: 10.4018/978-1-6684-5386-5.ch007

INTRODUCTION

The use of electronic gadgets in Middle East is rapidly growing. Average users are engaged for 6 to 8 hours on digital devices and the duration is increasing every year. The number is estimated to continue to rapidly increase by the end of 2022. The internet has inherent to human's lives then impose them to successfully adapt to changes (Anaam, E. A., Abu Bakar, K. A., Mohd Satar, N. S., & Ma'arif, M. Y. (2020). Gradually, the internet has replaced traditional mass media in communication (Al-Hawary, S. I. S., & Alhajri, T. M. S. (2020) and also created another way to improve psychological well-being and the quality of life (Melovic, B., Rondovic, B., Mitrovic-Veljkovic, S., Ocovaj, S. B., & Dabic, M. (2020) by fulfilling human's needs. Internet usage has evolved from mainly being used for seeking information (Anaam, E. A., Abu Bakar, K. A., Mohd Satar, N. S., & Ma'arif, M. Y. (2020) to also include activities such as product purchases, management of finances, social networking, and other activities (Anaam, E. A., Abu Bakar, K. A., Mohd Satar, N. S., & Ma'arif, M. Y. (2020). Companies must be able to adapt to the changes in digitized consumer behavior. This requires industries to enter the digital era for the development of business operational systems (BPS). In Middle East, digital start-ups are continuously being developed. Based on data from the Ministry of Communication and Information of the Middle East (Naim, A., Hussain, M. R., Naveed, Q. N., Ahmad, N., Qamar, S., Khan, N., & Hweij, T. A. (2019), there are overwhelming users who are engaged in online shopping, and this number is increasing every year. This is due to the increasing use of gadgets and the internet in Middle East. The high number of smartphone users have also caused the retail value of Ecom to increase significantly. Therefore, digital businesses in Middle East should continuously improve their BPS to ease consumers in shopping and to increase their confidence and loyalty in digital businesses such as electronic commerce (Kumar, P., Mokha, A. K., & Pattnaik, S. C. (2021).

Electronic commerce, commonly known as e-commerce (Ecom), is a type of business that emerged due to technological advances in regard to carrying out buying and selling of products, services, or even information through the internet [6]. Middle East is a country with rapid Ecom growth. This is proven by data from the Ministry of Communication and Information of the Middle East (Naim, A., Hussain, M. R., Naveed, Q. N., Ahmad, N., Qamar, S., Khan, N., & Hweij, T. A. (2019) that Middle East has the fastest-growing Ecom industry, especially amid Covid 19 outbreak.

The hasten business growth of Ecom in the marketplace is a consequence of the relevant advantages experienced by both consumers and suppliers. For firms, Ecom can be a tool to expand the marketplace quickly and easily, save costs, improve supply chain processes, and facilitate the access of product information to customers (Khan, N., Naim, A., Hussain, M. R., Naveed, Q. N., Ahmad, N., & Qamar, S. (2019). For consumers, the benefits of Ecom transactions include a wider range of options for products and services, increased convenience in conducting transactions anytime and anywhere, availability of detailed product information and reviews, and the possibility to obtain a greater number of products at a lower price (Khan, N., Naim, A., Hussain, M. R., Naveed, Q. N., Ahmad, N., & Qamar, S. (2019).

The Ecom has provided high benefits to online business owners and web apps developers. In Middle East, various Ecom companies are available to consumers as a Business to customer's category. However, despite many benefits and conveniences offered by Ecom businesses, they also have some limitations. One of many obstacles is to maintain consumer trust and loyalty (Seify, M., Tabaeeian, R. A., & Khoshfetrat, A. (2020). As they mainly use technology systems, like the internet and websites, there is no direct interaction with the firms. This physical connection and the lack of social interaction results in difficulties to build good relationships with consumers, especially in building loyalty (Naim, A., Khan, M. F., Hussain, M. R., & Khan, N. (2019). To overcome these limitations online firms are taking other measures to build relationship with consumer and retail ECRM. In this scenario, Ecom business focuses on consumers' loyalty that is called e-loyalty (ECL) (Hanif, M. I., Ahsan, M., Bhatti, M. K., & Loghari, M. S. (2020). It is defined as a strong psychological desire from a customer to use e-commerce or an online store (Hanif, M. I., Ahsan, M., Bhatti, M. K., & Loghari, M. S. (2020). A loyal customer visits the website continuously and this leads to company profitability (Naim, A. (2021). Therefore, CRM in digital businesses needs to build a website's service to attract and strengthen the relationships with their consumers both directly and indirectly (Rashwan, H. H. M., Mansi, A. L., & Hassan, H. E. (2020). CRM has been discussed in various industries as a critical strategy to increase the revenue, customer satisfaction, and intangible assets (Lubis, A., Dalimunthe, R., Absah, Y., & Fawzeea, B. K. (2020). CRM by Ecom companies is digitally regulated through the website's services, to provide the best shopping experience and fulfill customer satisfaction and customer retention (Naim, A. (2021)

The quality of a company's CRM was previously determined by the ability of employees to identify and fulfill customer needs and to communicate, negotiate, and establish good relationships directly with customers (Adnan, A. Z., Rahayu, A., Hendrayati, H., & Yusuf, R. (2021). However, the operational system of Ecom businesses needs a more comprehensive CRM approach to improve the relationship with customers through the appearance of the website's services (Naim, A. (2021). Changing the quality of a CRM into an online system is also known as ECRM. Overall, ECRM is digitally regulated through the website, to provide the best shopping experience; it is important in building a long-term relationship with consumers by fulfilling customer satisfaction and customer retention (Andah, B. D. (2020) Moreover, ECRM has an advantage as a strategy to increase intangible assets of a company with a lot of cost savings involved (Kaldeen, M., & Thowfeek, M. H. (2020), because mainly this strategy operated virtually by website or apps development. Therefore, it is important for companies to evaluate the application of the technology from the consumers' perspective (Liu, W., Wang, Z., & Zhao, H. (2020). This means that companies should develop their digital operational appearance by putting attention on consumer behavior and interests, to build a good ECRM. Middle East consumers do not hesitate to spend their time on product reviews with several online stores, before they decide to make a purchase. Additionally, consumers also consider the digital operational processes, such as the application features and the website appearance (Naim, A. (2021). The quality of the digital operational display does not only attract the customers, but it also attracts them to purchase products (Shahnavazi, A., Nemati Gonbaghi, M., Teymouri, S. F., & Ghasemi Dakdare, B. (2020). Understanding consumer behavior in the Middle East market is the first step for Ecom to develop ECRM practices so that consumer loyalty can be created. In this paper, we limit our study to the number one Ecom site in Middle East from the wide range of Ecom Company, to conduct the consumer's objectivity, rational, and precisely assess about its ECRM values to achieve its ECL. The study of ECRM in Ecom website is still very limited despite Middle East's Ecom growth. Indeed, research on how ECRM values affect ECL has not been conducted. This paper is the first to observe how the 10 factors (customization, care, cultivation, choice, online community, convenience, site security, personalization values, rewards, and interactivity) contribute to ECV that affect ECL in the best companies in Middle East and how ECRM is transformed to SCRM in Ecom.

LITERATURE REVIEW

Customer Relationship Management (CRM) emerged in the 1990s, as an extension of relationship marketing (Baashar, Y., Alhussian, H., Patel, A., Alkawsi, G., Alzahrani, A. I., Alfarraj, O., & Hayder, G. (2020). However, it has been noted that CRM exceeds the boundaries of marketing to include human resource management, sales, customer service, and other functions dealing directly with the customer (Baashar, Y., Alhussian, H., Patel, A., Alkawsi, G., Alzahrani, A. I., Alfarraj, O., & Hayder, G. (2020). In spite of that, CRM depends on the convergence of strategy and technology. From a strategic perspective, CRM is about creating and maintaining profitable customer relationships in the long-term (Arshi Naim, & Mohammad Faiz Khan. (2021) and attempts to understand the needs and desires of consumers through the integration of strategy, people, technology, and BPS (Arshi Naim, & Mohammad Faiz Khan. (2021). The main concept of CRM involves the differentiation of individual customers, in order to provide personalized treatment and deliver customized value

Figure 1. Advantages of ECRM for firms and consumers (Chatterjee, S., Chaudhuri, R., Vrontis, D., Thrassou, A., Ghosh, S. K., & Chaudhuri, S. (2020)

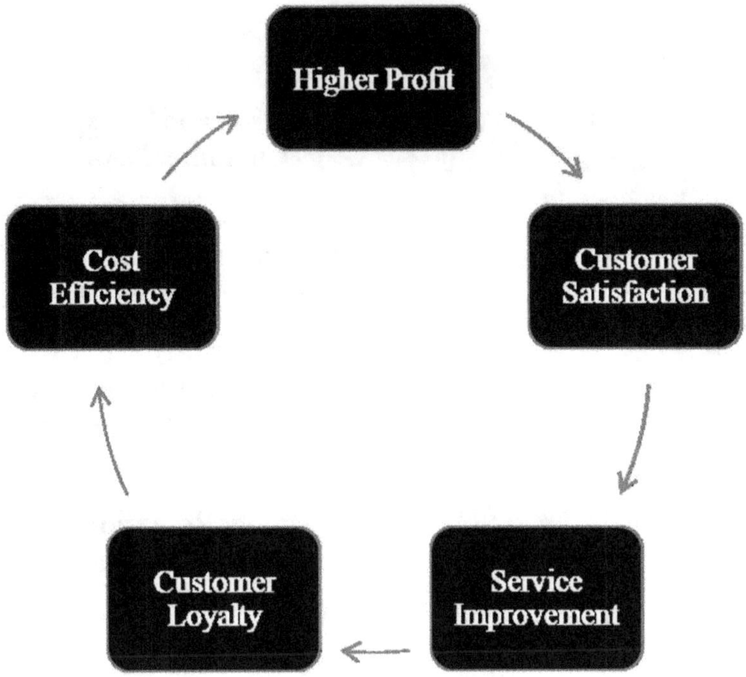

based on their specific needs (Chatterjee, S., Chaudhuri, R., Vrontis, D., Thrassou, A., Ghosh, S. K., & Chaudhuri, S. (2020). Figure 1 shows the advantages of CRM in the Ecom for both firms and consumers.

CRM has psychological as well as technical outlook for managing the consumers. Figure 2 presents the features of technical aspect of CRM.

The CRM initiatives are high risk (Koçoğlu, C. M., & Kalem, M. Y. (2020) and frequently fail to deliver the expected results (Koçoğlu, C. M., & Kalem, M. Y. (2020) because of lack of involvement from the strategic management. The success of CRM depend on support from top management, IT system integrations, employee training, and substantial customer data (Koçoğlu, C. M., & Kalem, M. Y. (2020). It also requires the adequate allocation of human, organizational, and technological resources for CRM projects (Koçoğlu, C. M., & Kalem, M. Y. (2020). It is very important to collect customer data from all online transactions, to improve the customer relationship (Naim A. (2021).

It is argued that CRM systems enable two-way communication with the customer that can be used to further enhance the relationship (Tusell-Rey, C. C., Nieto, Ó. C., & Padilla, R. T. (2020). Moreover, the proliferation of the internet has greatly

Figure 2. Technical features of CRM (Chatterjee, S., Chaudhuri, R., Vrontis, D., Thrassou, A., Ghosh, S. K., & Chaudhuri, S. (2020)

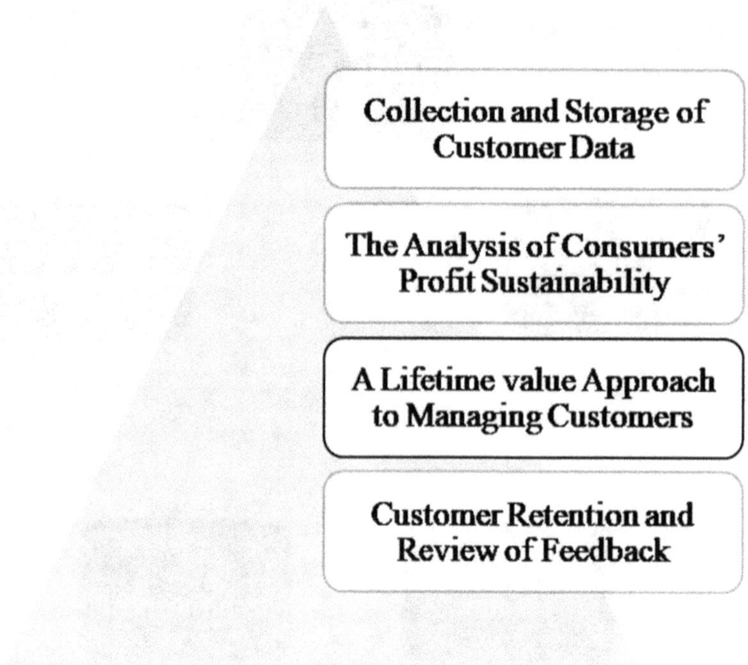

enabled the evolution of CRM and the utilization of big data and artificial intelligence as promising avenues for the future development of CRM Ahmed, B. S., Maâti, M. L. B., & Al-Sarem, M. (2020).

ECRM has the same general meaning and concept as CRM and CRM is a part of company's strategy to strengthen the relationship between consumers and companies through interaction that benefits both parties and increases their in-value or value-added (Naim A. (2021). CRM is the entire process of building and maintaining profitable customer relationships that can deliver value and satisfaction for customers (Naim A. (2021). It is stated that CRM is a business approach in understanding and influencing consumer behavior through meaningful communication to increase customer acquisition, retention, loyalty, and profitability (Alshurideh, M. (2022). The urgency of CRM is based on the needs of employees or internal companies to communicate or make direct contact with consumers in meeting consumer needs and desires (Alshurideh, M. (2022).

As the technology grows at the fast pace, digital business continues to grow rapidly resulting in changes in a company's BPS, including in the process of building relationships with consumers. The change in relationship management refers to the transformation of CRM to ECRM to adapt to digital consumer behavior in the current era. Moreover, ECRM is a company strategy to build relationships with customers online (Mahafzah, A. G., Aljawarneh, N. M., Alomari, K. A. K., Altahat, S., & Alomari, Z. S. (2020). ECRM is a comprehensive business and marketing strategy that relies on the use of the internet. Furthermore, ECRM emerged as a customer management process due to changes in consumer behavior in making online purchases (Mahafzah, A. G., Aljawarneh, N. M., Alomari, K. A. K., Altahat, S., & Alomari, Z. S. (2020). ECRM is a combination of corporate management commitments to consumer-related software, hardware, processes, and applications (Siaw, G. A., & Gitau, J. K. (2020). It can be concluded that ECRM has the same framework and ideology of working like CRM but ECRM is monitored and progressed through Ecom.

The ease of use the features and purchasing on the internet and websites can increase consumer expectations from the online-based services, which is influenced by perceived ease of use (Naim, A., & Alqahtani, K. (2021). The ease of consumers' views on the technologies induce an ECRM to pay attention to designing the features on a website. An e-commerce platform must be able to manage the website design and its features to build an ECRM experience for its consumers. The change in company activities from CRM to ECRM brings advantages for both companies and consumers Naim, A., & Alqahtani, K. (2021) and is discussed in the above figure 1 and these advantages generate value for ECRM activity, which is called ECV.

Many studies stated that there is a lot of value obtained by companies and consumers from the quality improvement of ECRM calling it as ECV. The shift from CRM to ECRM is led by the need for a company's strategies to win the ECRM value. For companies, ECRM can eliminate the cost burden needed for direct interaction with consumers. Besides that, it can save time and effort, and reduce administrative and operational costs that directly impact sales performance, by offering a lower price and improving the quality of consumers' interaction, which is not limited to time and space, since the interaction can be carried out 24 h a day without the need for direct company involvement (Herman, L. E., Sulhaini, S., & Farida, N. (2021). Moreover, ECV refers to the satisfaction of consumers for the service provided by a company.

In the field of marketing many studies have discussed the factors and causes of the formation of consumer loyalty to the company. ECL can be indicated by repeated product purchases (Anaam, E. A., Bakar, K. A. A., & Satar, N. S. M. (2020). An organization or a company obtains customer loyalty by building a good communication between vendors and consumers through direct contact. However, along with the development of online businesses such Ecom, creating customer loyalty is more difficult and complex since all the interactions and relationships between consumers and companies are mediated by technology (Anaam, E. A., Bakar, K. A. A., & Satar, N. S. M. (2020). In online-based transactions, loyalty is called ECL, which refers to the desire of virtual consumers to intensely or continuously visit certain online shopping websites due to several beneficial factors (González-Serrano, L., Talón-Ballestero, P., Muñoz-Romero, S., Soguero-Ruiz, C., & Rojo-Álvarez, J. L. (2020). ECL is the consumer's commitment to using a website, Ecom, or a particular brand when there are many alternative options available. Moreover, ECL is shown by the consistency of consumers using the website features (González-Serrano, L., Talón-Ballestero, P., Muñoz-Romero, S., Soguero-Ruiz, C., & Rojo-Álvarez, J. L. (2020). ECL refers to the desire of consumers to buy something on a certain website without wanting to turn to another website. ECL can be an indicator of achieving ECRM value for the company and consumers (González-Serrano, L., Talón-Ballestero, P., Muñoz-Romero, S., Soguero-Ruiz, C., & Rojo-Álvarez, J. L. (2020). Innovation is the process of generating new solutions based on the new knowledge that taking the form of product or process innovation (González-Serrano, L., Talón-Ballestero, P., Muñoz-Romero, S., Soguero-Ruiz, C., & Rojo-Álvarez, J. L. (2020). The open innovation surpasses the internal boundaries of a company to include all the collaborations with people and external organizations to the company (González-Serrano, L., Talón-Ballestero, P., Muñoz-Romero, S., Soguero-Ruiz, C., & Rojo-Álvarez, J. L. (2020). The open innovation is conducive to the creation of higher-value products and services and increases the competitiveness for a company (González-Serrano, L., Talón-Ballestero, P., Muñoz-Romero, S., Soguero-Ruiz, C., & Rojo-Álvarez, J. L. (2020).

There are many research in ECV that have discusses the factors related to increasing ECRM value which we have analyzed in this study. These factors are security and consistency and there are nine additional factors such as consisting of customization, interactivity, cultivation, care, community, choice, convenience, security, and market response for ECV. Past studies have focused on six factors such as site/mobile customization, alternative offers, local search engines, membership, chat, and mailing lists (Arshi Naim. (2022). Other research focus on the factors such as information quality, customer service quality, fulfillment, online community, integrated marketing channels, ease of navigation, rewards, personalization value, perceived trust, site security, value-added services, and price attractiveness. Our study fills the gap by choosing the ten most relevant factors /variables to measure the ECV.

The past research on ECL has shown that firms enhanced ECL because it is an indicator of profitability and sales performance (Arshi Naim. (2022) and ECRM can increase consumer loyalty to the company. Also past studies show the importance of ECRM to build relationship strategically Arshi Naim. (2022). The results of these studies encouraged the companies maximize their efforts in building ECRM strategy by understanding ECL that can be achieved by the increasing of ECV. In our study we have focused the same hypothesis while using ten factors but in the past only eight factors were applied to show the working of this hypothesis. In this study we suggested Ecom firms to analyze and measure the ECV to transform ECRM to SCRM by applying ten factors such as customization, cultivation, rewards, care, online community, choice, convenience, site security, interactivity and personalization values) to achieve the ECL. This study analyzed the relationship between ECV and ECL and how CRM can be transformed to SCRM through Ecom to build ECRM.

RESEARCH MODEL AND HYPOTHESIS

This study is an empirical analysis where many variables are measured to achieve the success factors of ECV and ECL. These variables are customization, care, cultivation, choice; online community, convenience, site security, personalization values and rewards.

Empirical research is research using empirical evidence (Kim, C., Zhao, W., & Yang, K. H. (2008). It is also a way of gaining knowledge by means of direct and indirect observation or experience. Empiricism values some research more than other kinds. Empirical evidence can be analyzed quantitatively or qualitatively but for or study we have applied qualitative analysis. Figure 3 shows the process of empirical analysis for the general scenario (Adiyanto, A., & Febrianto, R. (2020).

Figure 3. Process of Empirical Study (Adiyanto, A., & Febrianto, R. (2020)

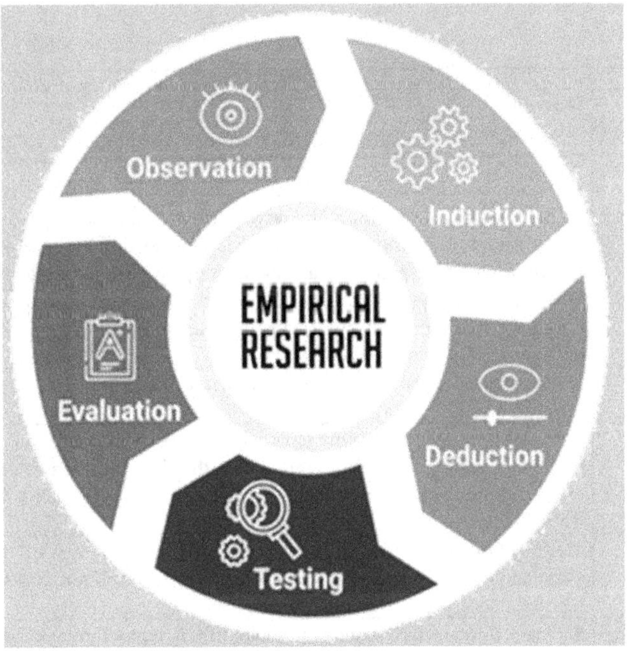

The empirical study focuses on the application of the concepts therefore for this study we have applied this study. Figure 4shows the empirical research design for this study.

Figure 4. Empirical Research Design (Adiyanto, A., & Febrianto, R. (2020)

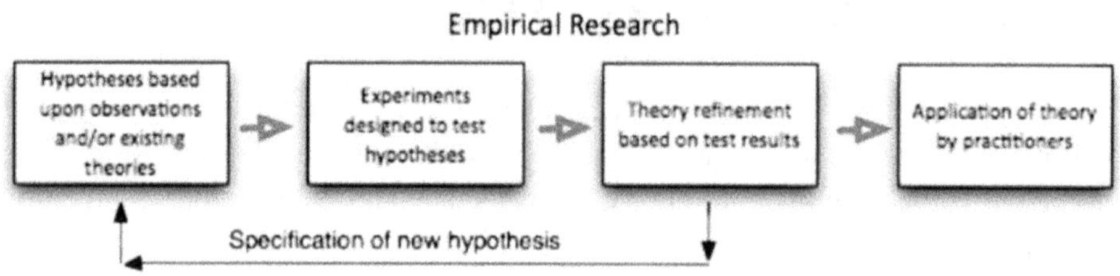

Empirical research is defined as any research where conclusions of the study are strictly drawn from concretely empirical evidence, and therefore "verifiable" evidence. The evidences can be collected by qualitative or qualitative methods and

Table 1. Empirical Research Types and Description (Adiyanto, A., & Febrianto, R. (2020)

Qualitative Types	Description
Case study	Case study method is used to find more information through carefully analyzing existing cases. It is very often used for business research or to gather empirical evidence for investigation purpose. It is a method to investigate a problem within its real life context through existing cases. The researcher has to carefully analyses making sure the parameter and variables in the existing case are the same as to the case that is being investigated. Using the findings from the case study, conclusions can be drawn regarding the topic that is being studied.
Observational Method	It is a process to observe and gather data from its target.
One-on-one interview	It is qualitative and one of the most widely used. The reason being it enables a researcher get precise meaningful data if the right questions are asked. It is a conversational method where in-depth data can be gathered depending on where the conversation leads.
Focus groups	This type of method helps researcher to find answers to why, what and how questions. A small group is generally chosen for such a method and it is not necessary to interact with the group in person.
Text analysis	Such a method is used to analyze social life by going through images or words used by the individual.

we have applied qualitative method by the application of interviews. Table1 shows the types of empirical research for qualitative methods for general studies.

The study followed the following five steps to conduct the empirical study to evaluate the research hypothesis.

1. Define the purpose of the research
2. Supporting theories and relevant literature
3. Creation of Hypothesis and measurement
4. Methodology, research design and data collection
5. Data Analysis and result

This study seeks to improve research on the factors of ECV for Ecom website in Middle East by analyzing 10 factors: customization, cultivation, rewards, care, online community, choice, convenience, website security, and interactivity and personalization values. The research framework used on this study is shown in the Figure 5.

Figure 5. Research Framework

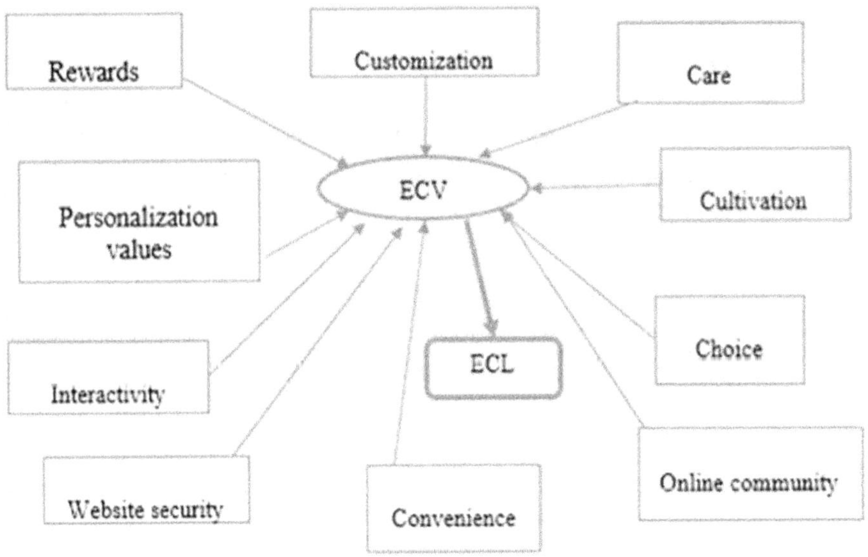

The 10 factors of ECRM value investigated in this study are defined as follows: The first factor, customization, is related to the design and layout of the features available on the website and the ease to access the website (Fiansyah, E. (2020). Interactivity, as the second factor, is related to the active response of website service providers to consumers' inquiries causing easy access to communication (Fiansyah, E. (2020). Cultivation refers to the company's efforts in building cross-selling with customers through campaigns or notification so that consumers can stay updated with the information provided by the website (Naim, A. (2022). Care is the fourth factor of ECRM and focuses on researching the needs of customers and providing relevant information in meeting their needs and desires, to reduce any potential disruption in providing services (Hendriyani, C., & Auliana, L. (2018). The online community is a discussion forum that facilitates consumers to interact and to share their experiences of online shopping (Mohammad Shafiee, M., Seify, M., & Yazdi, A. (2020). Choice refers to the number and variants of products and services available on the website, so that consumers can be more precise in selecting goods or services according to their needs (Mohammad Shafiee, M., Seify, M., & Yazdi, A. (2020). Convenience refers to the easy and fast access to the website, supported by well-designed features. Rewards can be in the form of promotions, points, coupons, or other programs that can attract consumer interest to return to the website (Kakeesh, D., Al-Weshah, G., & Al-Ma'aitah, N. (2021). Security deals with the privacy of data inputted by consumers, in their accounts, on the website, for doing online shopping. Finally, the last factor is personalization values, which relate to the strategy the website implements to invite consumers back to the website that can be monitored from the consumer account as a sign of membership in the e-commerce platform (Arshi Naim. (2022). Personalization values allow consumers to choose and design their account on the e-commerce site and determine the most needed and desired products (Noviana, G. (2021). This study analyzed those factors of ECRM value with the following hypothesis:

1. The 10 factors positively contribute to ECV.
2. ECV contributes to ECL on Ecom platform that transforms the CRM to SCRM to build ECRM

DISCUSSION AND RESULT

The analysis of this study is from the closed ended interview questions given to the focused group through online surveys on social media. 100 respondents were interviewed for 10 factors / variables of ECV. Their responses were rated on seven scale ranging from (1 = strongly disagree to 7 = strongly disagree.

Table 2. Questions for 10 factors for measuring ECV

Factors	Questions based on the description
Customization	1. The advertisement and promotion on website and application is suitable. 2. The Placement of advertisement for the location is suitable 3. The promotion is for individual requirements
Cultivation	1. Website and application send regular notifications 2. Notifications are relevant and save time 3. Notifications are related to my search query
Rewards	1. The website and application give values for my purchase 2. My values can be traded for gifts or vouchers
Care	1. The website and application are very welcoming and friendly to each visitor with any digital divide 2. Help feature is 24/7 available 3. Online customer service is prompt and helpful
Online Community	1. The website and application support me to express my personal opinion and comments 2. Feedback is publically available 3. Reviews are not altered 4. Recommendations and blogs are publically available
Choice	1. As an online customer I am satisfied with the choices of products and services provided on the website and application. 2. Policy of return in case of wrong choice
Convenience	1. Easy payment methods are available 2. Secured payment methods 3. Multichannel option to use any Ecom website and application
Site Security	1. Option for opt in and opt out in available 2. Maintaining the privacy of my personal and financial information 3. Informed consent is followed 4. Secondary use of data is not done
Interactivity	1. Chat feature is available with the experts 2. The search features of the website and application enabled to find needed product
Personalization Values	1. Registrations and making profile is available 2. Update of profile and delete feature is available 3. Control on sharing of information is available

Table 3. ECV's positive feedback for ECL determinant

Positive results from ten factors/ variable	ECL determinant
ECV	Preference to SCRM to build ECRM than focusing only on Ecom platform. Firm's transformation from CRM to SCRM to build ECRM.

Above mentioned 10 factor's results measure the ECV. The results are discussed later in the chapter. Based on the positive rating by 100 respondents ECV, values are provided for ECL which helps in transforming the CRM to SCRM and building the ECRM. Table 3 shows the determinant of ECL achieved by positive feedback received for ECV.

1. Customization

This factor helps in measuring ECV for design and virtual layout to provide easiness to consumers to access the contents and webpage. Figures 5 to 7 show the result on customization as a factor for ECV

Figure 6. Advertisement and Promotion on website and application is suitable

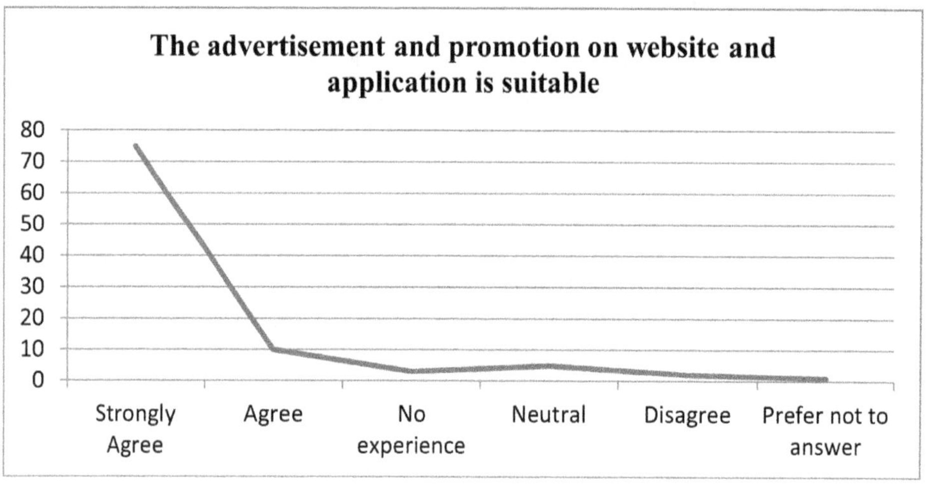

Figure 7. The Placement of advertisement for the location is suitable

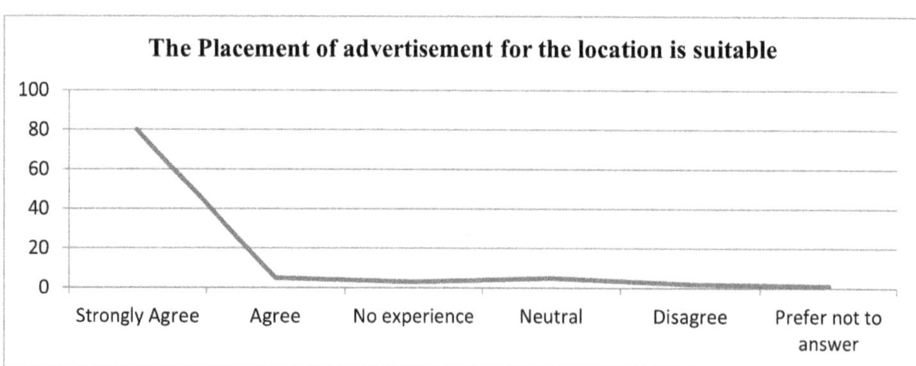

Figure 8. The promotion is for individual requirements

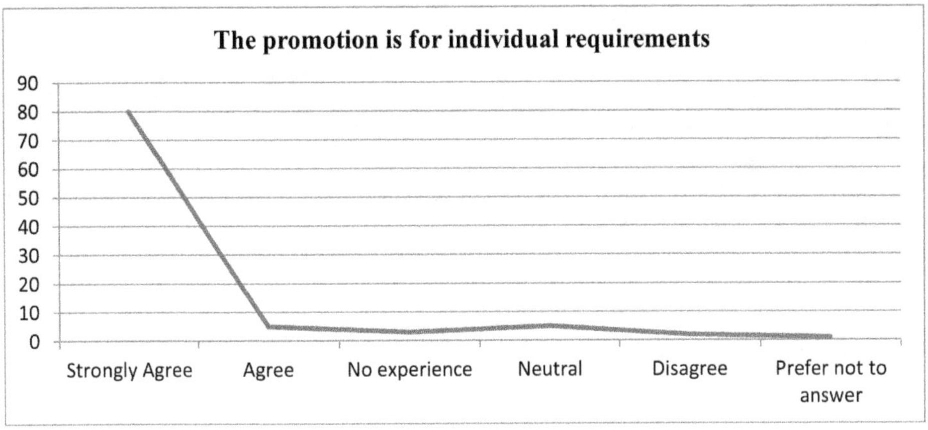

75% of the respondents strongly agree adding to the positive feedback to the ECV.

80% strongly agree responses are recorded for ECV.

80% strongly agree responses are recorded for ECV.

To measure the customization, we analyzed the responses for easy access, design of web app, layout and ease in content access, as an average 78. % of consumers share their positive experience this added positivity to the ECV.

2. Cultivation

Web apps and firms on SCRM or even Ecom work to build their site and app focusing on giving updated information and continue to update as per the new trends. Authentic

Figure 9. Website and application send regular notifications

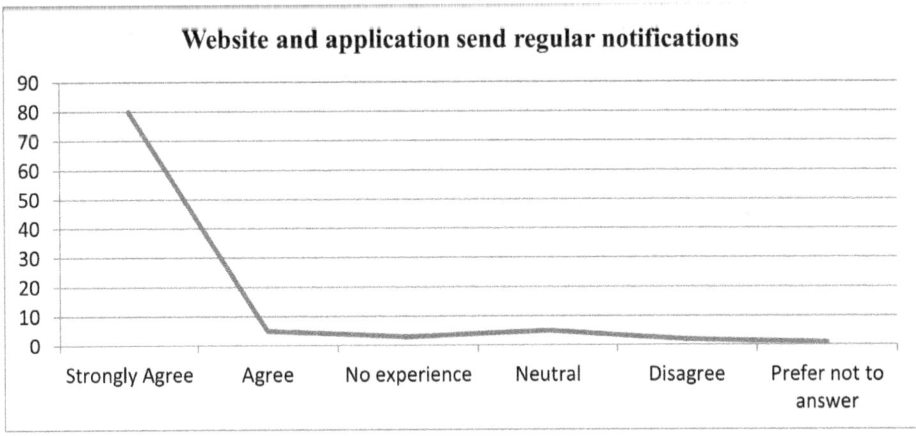

Figure 10. Notifications are relevant and save time

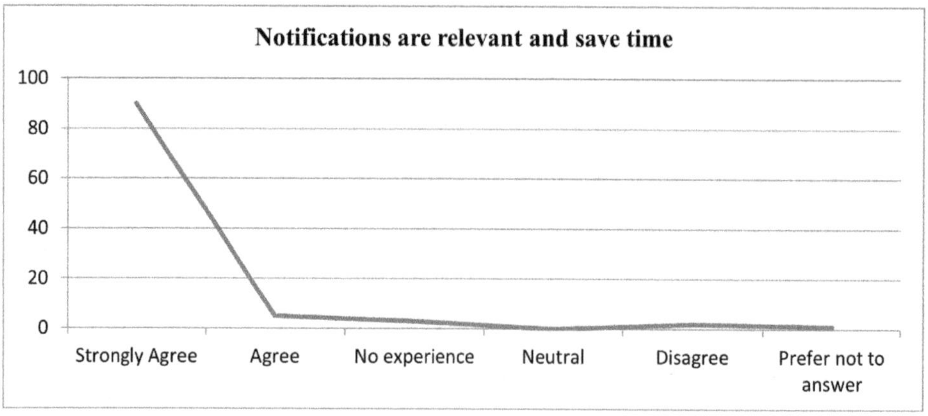

Figure 11. Notifications are related to my search query

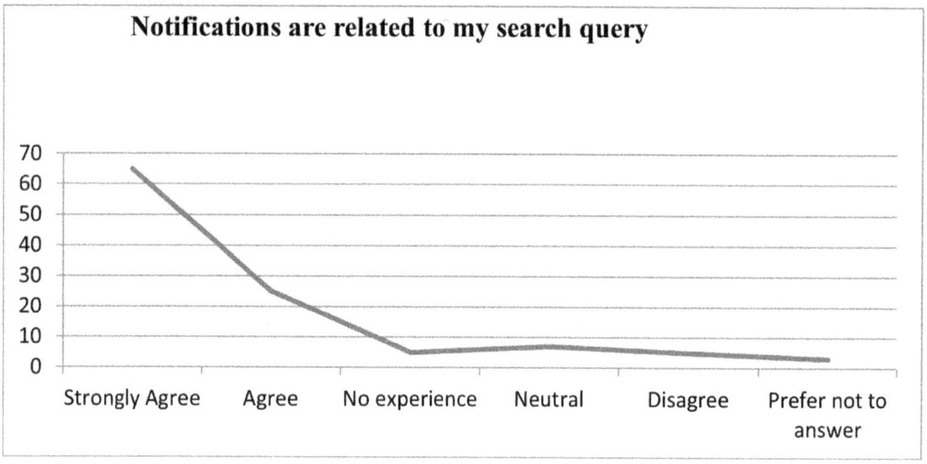

and latest information should be accessible to the consumers for positive building. Figures from 8 to 10 show the results of factor cultivation for ECV.

80% strongly agree responses are recorded for ECV.

90% strongly agree responses are recorded for ECV.

65% strongly agree responses are recorded for ECV.

To measure the cultivation, we analyzed the responses for save time, receiving updates and notification and access to updated contents. The average of 78.33% strongly agree responses are recorded which added to ECV.

3. Reward

Consumers enjoy online activities and involve in online buying and selling process if they find more values, rewards and points for their activities. Rewards from firms encourage consumers to participate in the process and they are motivated to contribute in giving feedback and review too. Figures 11 and 12 show the results of reward as one of the factors to achieve ECV.

80% strongly agree responses are recorded for ECV.

79% strongly agree responses are recorded for ECV.

Figure 12. The website and application give values for my purchase

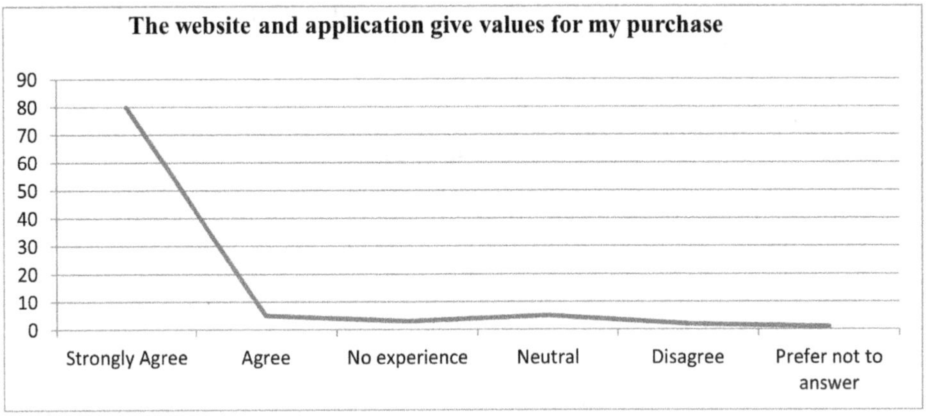

Figure 13. My values can be traded for gifts or vouchers

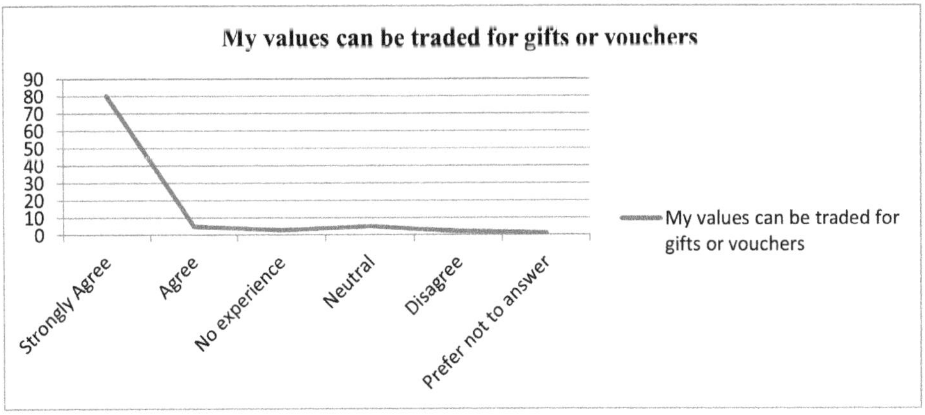

To measure the reward, we analyzed the responses for value receiving, achieving points or gifts in return to their purchase or participation. The average of 79.9% strongly agree responses are recorded which added to ECV.

4. Care

Consumers turn loyal and firms can retain them showing that their services are customer centric and they care and value the opinion and satisfaction of the consumers. This is usually a challenge on web app and SCRM but with potential

Figure 14. Website and application are very welcoming and friendly to each visitor with any digital divide

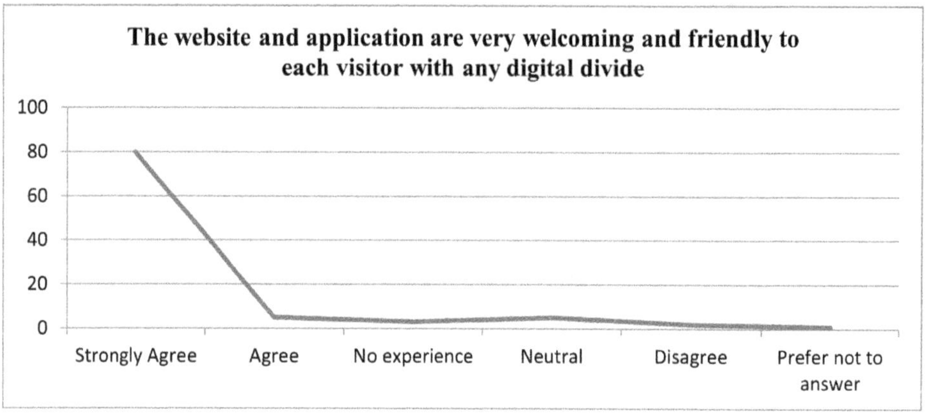

Figure 15. Help feature is 24/7 available

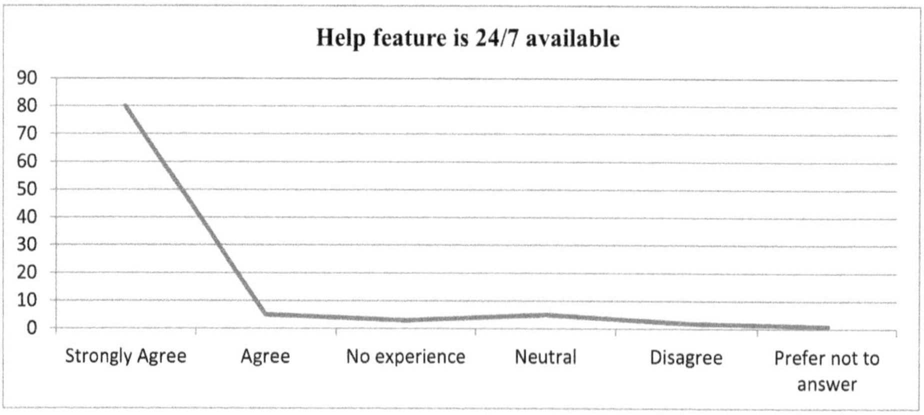

Figure 16. Online customer service is prompt and helpful

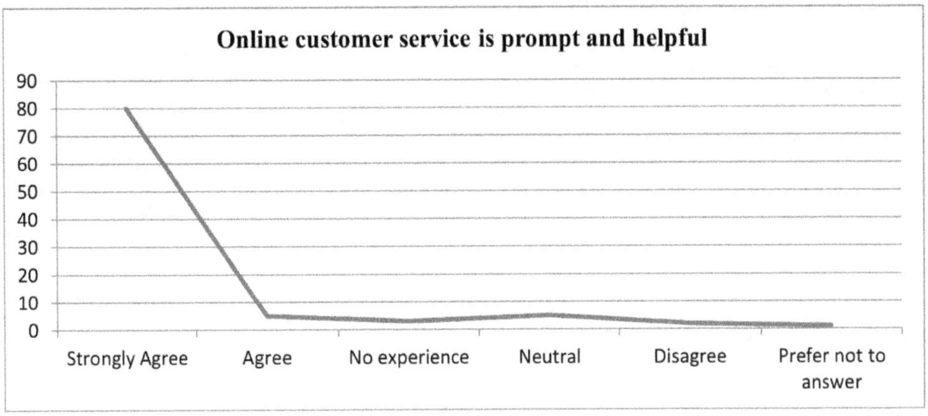

online techniques firms are able to make it as a positive factor for ECV. Figures 13, 14 and 15 present the results on care for ECV.

80% strongly agree responses are recorded for ECV.

80% strongly agree responses are recorded for ECV.

80% strongly agree responses are recorded for ECV.

To measure the care, we analyzed the responses for equality, reduction of digital divide, help features and prompt reply from the web apps, SCRM or ECom. The average of 80% strongly agree responses are recorded which added to ECV.

5. Online Community

This factor is mostly prevalent on social media or in chat functions in Web app or ECom. This factor adds group participation for ECV, where people with same interests and affinity contributes and take values from the SCRM. This factor provides group positivity to ECV and figure 16 shows the result for this factor. (Figure 17)

To measure the online community, we analyzed the responses for their reviews authentication, availability of their recommendations on public domain, firms support to welcome ideas and opinions and feedbacks. The average of 80% strongly agree responses are recorded which added to ECV.

6. Choice

Consumers are always attracted when they receive options in products and services, ways of accessing the services, options to payment methods and flexible return policies. Figure 18 shows the result on choice for ECV.

Figure 17. Online Community as critical success factors for ECV

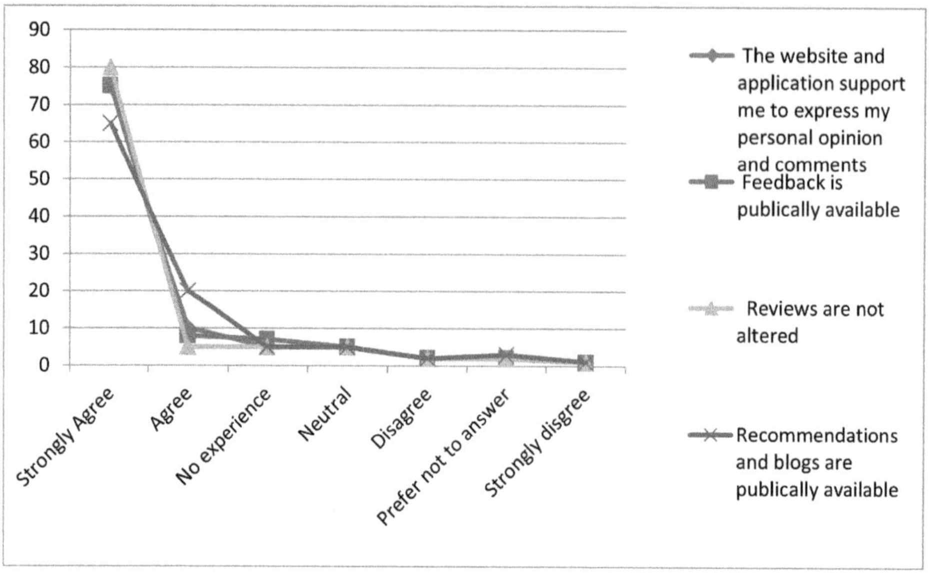

Figure 18. Choice as critical success factors for ECV

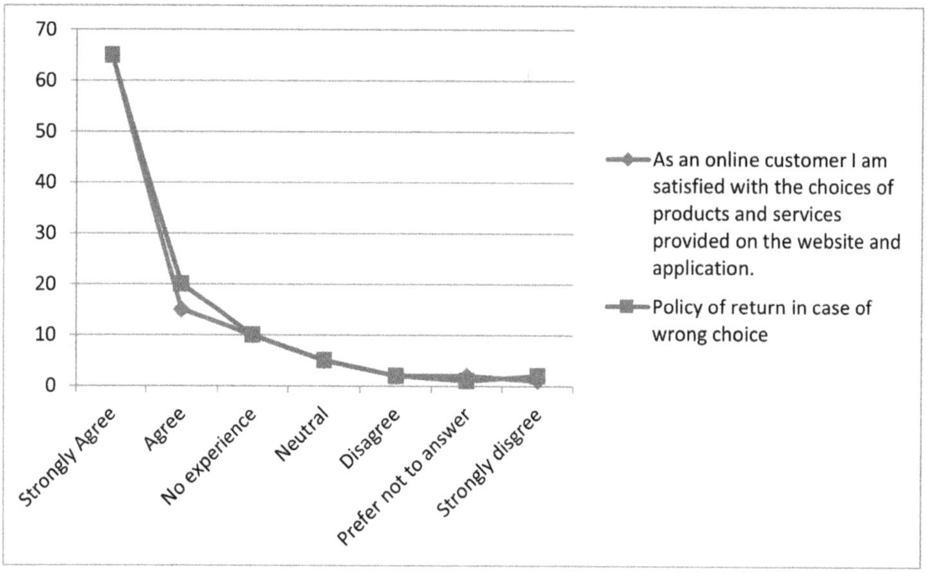

To measure the choice, we analyzed the responses for the options and choices for product mix, product line, availability of multichannel to access and flexible return policies because these features are very important to encourage the consumers to use web app and SCRM. The average of 68% strongly agree responses are recorded which added to ECV. This factor did not receive very high positivity because some consumers were unaware of benefits of choices available for them. Research recommends the web app, SCRM or Ecom to clearly define this feature or through personal chat these benefits should be communicated to the consumers.

7. Convenience

All consumers prefer simple process and easy to use that not only save time but also effective in applications. This includes many aspects from looks, design, and access to working. Figure 19 shows the results of this factor for ECV.

Figure 19. Convenience as critical success factors for ECV

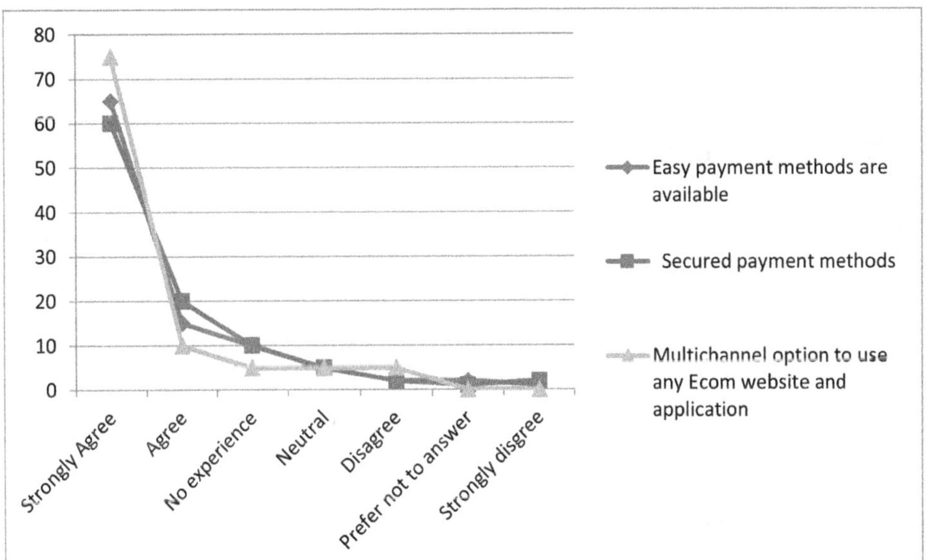

To measure the convenience, we analyzed the responses for the easy payent methods and gateways availability, security and privacy of personal and financial information, secured payment methods and possibilities of multichannel approach. The average of 78% strongly agree responses are recorded which added to ECV.

Figure 20. Website Security as critical success factors for ECV

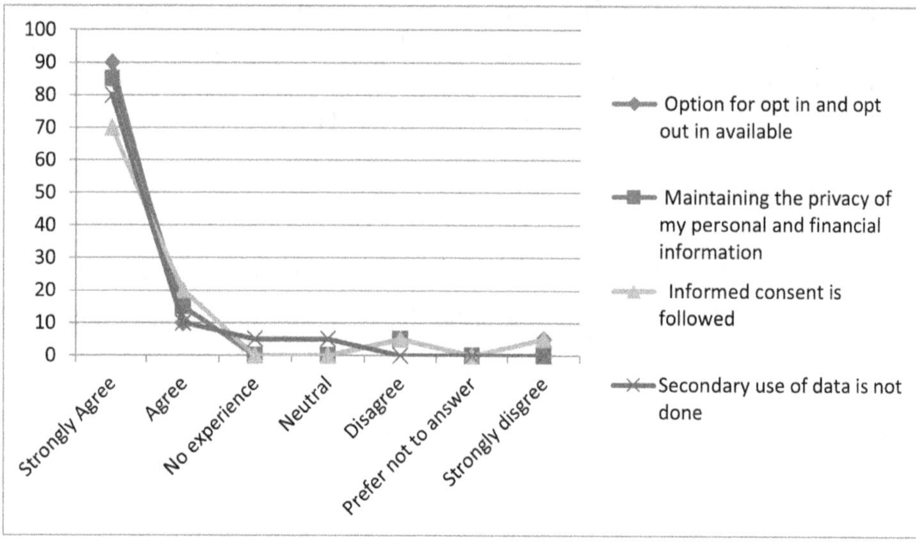

8. Website Security

This is the vital factor and all other factors are also dependent on the success of this factor. It explains and monitors the privacy, confidentiality, security and validity of data. Figure 20 shows the results for ECV.

To measure the security, we analyzed the responses for opt-in and opt-out, concept of informed consent and secondary use of data and also one securing personal and financial data. The average of 85% strongly agree responses are recorded which added to ECV.

9. Personalization

This feature of web app or ECom gives consumer to express their desire, specific needs and can receive the values as they prefer. Figure 21 shows the results on this factor for ECV.

To measure the personalization, we analyzed the responses for registration options, profile creating, and update and delete option and control on sharing the information. All the sub-factors receive very high positive response except for the sub-factor "control on sharing of information", but overall results were positive for ECV. The average of 75.33% strongly agree responses are recorded which added to ECV.

Figure 21. Personalization as critical success factors for ECV

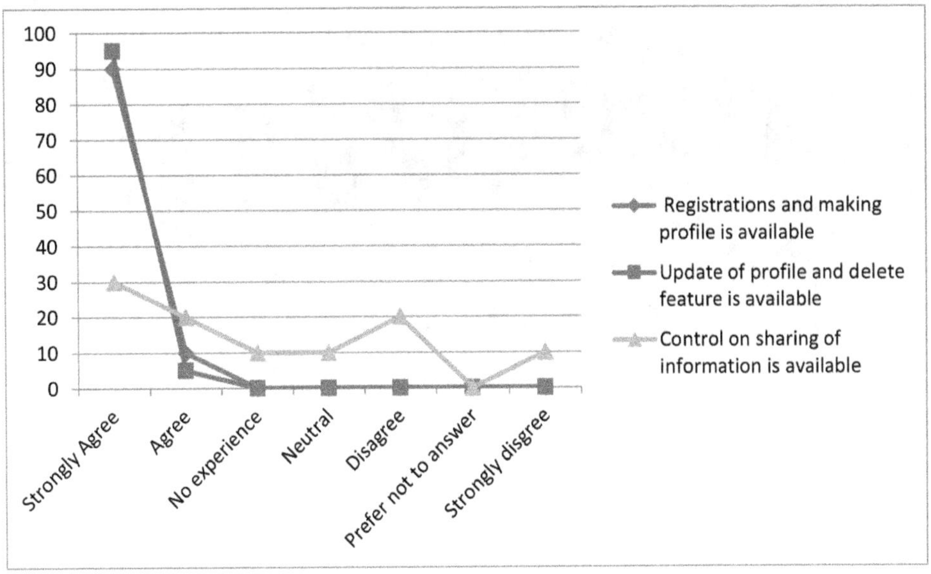

10. Interactivity

This factor provides the two ways communication between consumers and webapp, ECom or on Social media. Prompt response from service providers aids in building

Figure 22. Interactivity as critical success factors for ECV

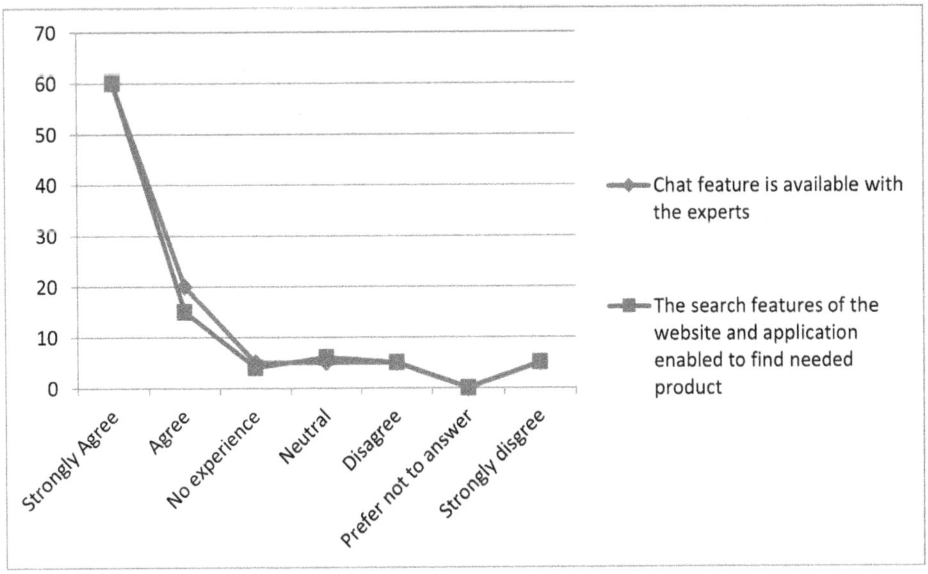

Figure 23. ECV positively contributing to ECL

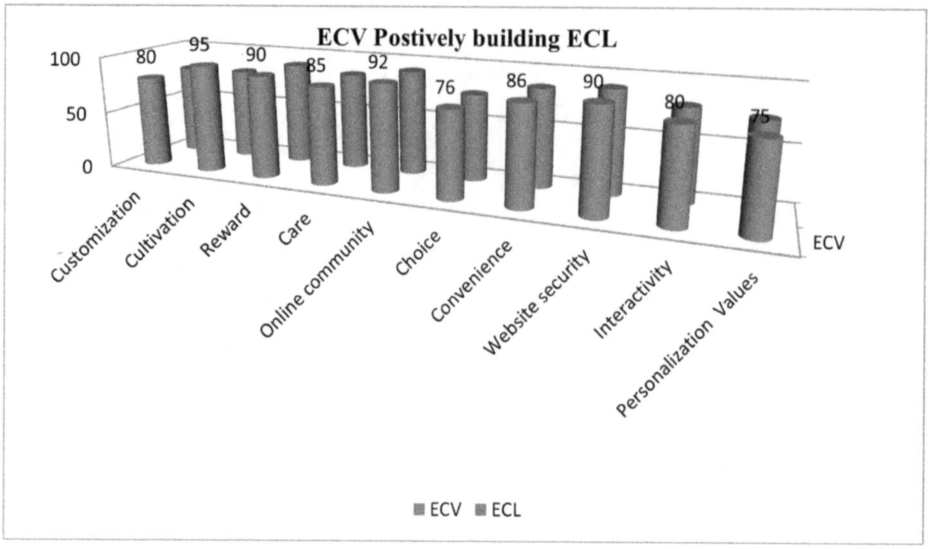

ECRM therefore focusing on this factor is also very important for ECV. Figure 22 shows the results of this factor for ECV.

To measure the interactivity, we analyzed the responses for chat features, discussion with the sales personnel or expert, search option within the app or ECom site. The average of 60.33% strongly agree responses are recorded which added to ECV. The results show slight positivity for this factor for ECV because the interaction sometimes did not add value to the purchase or did not provide solution to the issue. But overall the response was positive. The results show that all ten factors have positively contributed to the ECV.

To prove our second hypothesis we aligned the results of ECV for ECL to observe its contribution to ECL on Ecom platform and the transformation of CRM to SCRM to build ECRM. Figure 23 shows the cross dependence of all ten factors to ECV and ECV to ECL. The figure shows the results in average terms.

The results show exceeding average for all factors of ECV for ECL which concludes the positive contribution. The success of ECL helps the firms to make a shift from CRM to SCRM to build ECRM and online platforms such as web app, Ecom or social media can be applied.

ANALYSIS

Based on the results it can be concluded that the condition of the ECom in Middle East is strongly influenced by the performance of ECV. The ten critical success factors have positively contributed to ECV in middle- east and the web app or Ecom were able to achieve ECV that eventually aid in success of ECL. By the positive contribution of ECL the ECom and web app were successfully transform the CRM to SCRM and build strong ECRM. The ECV that builds from the critical success factors are reflections from the innovation of the technology based firms and their customer behavior and customer's interest. The higher ECV is the higher ECL as shown in the figure 22 which clearly present ECL contribution to ECRM and its role in transformation of CRM to SCRM.

CONCLUSION AND FUTURE WORK

This research was an empirical study based on qualitative analysis of focus group active on social media and web apps. The study aimed to present the relationship between ECV and ECL for building ECRM and transforming the CRM to SCRM on Ecom or on web app. The results showed that the middle- east consumers are technological savvy and prefer ECom, using Web apps and other social media for accomplishing their general requirements. The Ecom in Middle East has a strong influence by ECV. The ten critical success factors have positively contributed to ECV in middle- east and the web app or Ecom were able to achieve ECV that eventually aid in success of ECL. By the positive contribution of ECL the ECom and web app were successfully transform the CRM to SCRM and build strong ECRM.

This study comprehensively analyzes ECV from critical success factors (customization, interactivity, rewards, care, choice, online community, convenience, and personalization) in Middle East for their Web app and Ecom sites.

REFERENCES

Adiyanto, A., & Febrianto, R. (2020). Authentication Of Transaction Process In E-marketplace Based On Blockchain?? technology. *Aptisi Transactions On Technopreneurship*, 2(1), 68–74. doi:10.34306/att.v2i1.71

Adnan, A. Z., Rahayu, A., Hendrayati, H., & Yusuf, R. (2021, February). The role of electronic customer relationship management (E-CRM) in improving service quality. *Journal of Physics: Conference Series*, *1764*(1), 012051. doi:10.1088/1742-6596/1764/1/012051

Ahmed, B. S., Maâti, M. L. B., & Al-Sarem, M. (2020). Predictive Data Mining Model for Electronic Customer Relationship Management Intelligence. *International Journal of Business Intelligence Research*, *11*(2), 1–10. doi:10.4018/IJBIR.2020070101

Al-Hawary, S. I. S., & Alhajri, T. M. S. (2020). Effect of Electronic Customer Relationship Management on Customers' Electronic Satisfaction of Communication Companies in Kuwait. *Calitatea*, *21*(175), 97–102.

Alshurideh, M. (2022). Does electronic customer relationship management (E-CRM) affect service quality at private hospitals in Jordan? *Uncertain Supply Chain Management*, *10*(2), 325–332. doi:10.5267/j.uscm.2022.1.006

Anaam, E. A., Abu Bakar, K. A., Mohd Satar, N. S., & Ma'arif, M. Y. (2020). Investigating the Electronic Customer Relationship Management Success Key Factors in the Telecommunication Companies: A Pilot Study. *Journal of Computational and Theoretical Nanoscience*, *17*(2-3), 1460–1463. doi:10.1166/jctn.2020.8825

Anaam, E. A., Bakar, K. A. A., & Satar, N. S. M. (2020). A Model of Electronic Customer Relationship Management System Adoption In Telecommunication Companies. *Amazonia Investiga*, *9*(35), 61–73. doi:10.34069/AI/2020.35.11.5

Andah, B. D. (2020). Penerapan Electronic Customer Relationship Management (E-CRM) dalam Upaya Meningkatkan Pendapatan Penjualan pada PT. Cipta Aneka Buah. *IDEALIS: InDonEsiA JournaL. Information Systems*, *3*(1), 20–25.

Baashar, Y., Alhussian, H., Patel, A., Alkawsi, G., Alzahrani, A. I., Alfarraj, O., & Hayder, G. (2020). Customer relationship management systems (CRMS) in the healthcare environment: A systematic literature review. *Computer Standards & Interfaces*, *71*, 103442. doi:10.1016/j.csi.2020.103442 PMID:34170994

Chatterjee, S., Chaudhuri, R., Vrontis, D., Thrassou, A., Ghosh, S. K., & Chaudhuri, S. (2020). Social customer relationship management factors and business benefits. *The International Journal of Organizational Analysis*.

Chu, K. M. (2020). The Relationships between Online Customer Engagement Value and Electronic Customer Relationship Management Effectiveness of Mobile Games. *Innovative Journal of Business and Management*, *9*(8), 238–245.

Ericsson, K. A., & Smith, J. (1991). Prospects and limits of the empirical study of. *Toward a general theory of expertise: Prospects and limits*, *1*(1).

Fiansyah, E. (2020, November). Post Implementation Review of Electronic Customer Relationship Management (E-CRM) Implementation in Port Services Company, Indonesia. In *2020 International Conference on Informatics, Multimedia, Cyber and Information System* (ICIMCIS) (pp. 301-306). IEEE. 10.1109/ICIMCIS51567.2020.9354300

González-Serrano, L., Talón-Ballestero, P., Muñoz-Romero, S., Soguero-Ruiz, C., & Rojo-Álvarez, J. L. (2020). A big data approach to customer relationship management strategy in hospitality using multiple correspondence domain description. *Applied Sciences (Basel, Switzerland)*, *11*(1), 256. doi:10.3390/app11010256

Hanif, M. I., Ahsan, M., Bhatti, M. K., & Loghari, M. S. (2020). The Effect of Electronic Customer Relationship Management on Organizational Performance with Mediating Role of Customer Satisfaction. *International Review of Management and Marketing*, *10*(5), 138–147. doi:10.32479/irmm.9934

Hendriyani, C., & Auliana, L. (2018). Transformation from relationship marketing to electronic customer relationship management: A literature study. *Review of Integrative Business and Economics Research*, *7*, 116–124.

Herman, L. E., Sulhaini, S., & Farida, N. (2021). Electronic customer relationship management and company performance: Exploring the product innovativeness development. *Journal of Relationship Marketing*, *20*(1), 1–19. doi:10.1080/15332667.2019.1688600

Kakeesh, D., Al-Weshah, G., & Al-Ma'aitah, N. (2021). Maintaining Customer Loyalty Using Electronic Customer Relationship Management (E-CRM): Qualitative Evidence from Small Food Businesses in Jordan. *Studies of Applied Economics*, *39*(7). Advance online publication. doi:10.25115/eea.v39i7.4810

Kaldeen, M., & Thowfeek, M. H. (2020). Factors favoring electronic customer relationship management. *E-CRM*.

Khan, N., Naim, A., Hussain, M. R., Naveed, Q. N., Ahmad, N., & Qamar, S. (2019, May). The 51 v's of big data: survey, technologies, characteristics, opportunities, issues and challenges. In *Proceedings of the international conference on omni-layer intelligent systems* (pp. 19-24). 10.1145/3312614.3312623

Khoa, B. T. (2022). Dataset for the electronic customer relationship management based on SOR model in electronic commerce. *Data in Brief*, *42*, 108039. doi:10.1016/j.dib.2022.108039 PMID:35313498

Kim, C., Zhao, W., & Yang, K. H. (2008). An empirical study on the integrated framework of e-CRM in online shopping: Evaluating the relationships among perceived value, satisfaction, and trust based on customers' perspectives. *Journal of Electronic Commerce in Organizations*, *6*(3), 1–19. doi:10.4018/jeco.2008070101

Koçoğlu, C. M., & Kalem, M. Y. (2020). Electronic Customer Relationship Management in Tourism. In *Handbook of Research on Smart Technology Applications in the Tourism Industry* (pp. 273-294). IGI Global.

Kumar, P., & Mokha, A. K. (2022). Electronic Customer Relationship Management (E-CRM) and Customer Loyalty: The Mediating Role of Customer Satisfaction in the Banking Industry. *International Journal of E-Business Research*, *18*(1), 1–22. doi:10.4018/IJEBR.293292

Kumar, P., Mokha, A. K., & Pattnaik, S. C. (2021). Electronic customer relationship management (E-CRM), customer experience and customer satisfaction: Evidence from the banking industry. *Benchmarking*.

Liu, W., Wang, Z., & Zhao, H. (2020). Comparative study of customer relationship management research from East Asia, North America and Europe: A bibliometric overview. *Electronic Markets*, *30*(4), 735–757. doi:10.100712525-020-00395-7

Lubis, A., Dalimunthe, R., Absah, Y., & Fawzeea, B. K. (2020). *The influence of customer relationship management (CRM) indicators on customer loyalty of sharia based banking system*. Lubis, A, 84-92.

Mahafzah, A. G., Aljawarneh, N. M., Alomari, K. A. K., Altahat, S., & Alomari, Z. S. (2020). Impact of customer relationship management on food and beverage service quality: The mediating role of employees satisfaction. *Humanities & Social Sciences Reviews*, *8*(2), 222–230. doi:10.18510/hssr.2020.8226

Melovic, B., Rondovic, B., Mitrovic-Veljkovic, S., Ocovaj, S. B., & Dabic, M. (2020). Electronic Customer Relationship Management Assimilation in Southeastern European Companies—Cluster Analysis. *IEEE Transactions on Engineering Management*.

Mohammad Shafiee, M., Seify, M., & Yazdi, A. (2020). Antecedents and Consequences of Implementing Electronic Customer Relationship Management in Small and Medium Enterprises. *New Marketing Research Journal*, *10*(1), 129–146.

Naim, A. (2021). Applications of E-Learning tools for Achieving Students Learning Outcomes. *Journal of Pedagogical Inventions and Practices*, *2*(2), 75–82. https://zienjournals.com/index.php/jpip/article/view/320

Naim, A. (2021). Applications of Marketing Framework in Business Practices. *Journal of Marketing and Emerging Economics*, *1*(6), 55–70.

Naim, A. (2021). Applications of MIS in building Electronic Relationship with customers: A case-based study. *Periodica Journal of Modern Philosophy. Social Sciences and Humanities*, *1*, 1–8.

Naim, A. (2021). Green Business Process Management. *International Journal of Innovative Analyses and Emerging Technology*, *1*(6), 125–134. http://openaccessjournals.eu/index.php/ijiaet/article/view/651

Naim, A. (2021). Green Information Technologies in Business Operations. *Periodica Journal of Modern Philosophy. Social Sciences and Humanities*, *1*, 36–49.

Naim, A. (2021). New Trends in Business Process Management: Applications of Green Information Technologies. *British Journal of Environmental Studies*, *1*(1), 12–23.

Naim, A. (2022). Economies of Scale for Antenna's Applications in Interior Regions. *International Journal of Innovative Analyses and Emerging Technology*, *2*(2), 77–82. http://openaccessjournals.eu/index.php/ijiaet/article/view/1058

Naim, A. (2022). Factors of Consumer Behaviour of youth from Middle East when purchasing Organic Food. *Global Scientific Review*, *3*, 1–7. Retrieved from http://www.scienticreview.com/index.php/gsr/article/view/13

Naim, A. (2022). Neuro- Marketing Techniques for Proposing Information Driven Framework for Decision Making. *International Journal of Innovative Analyses and Emerging Technology*, *2*(2), 87–94. http://openaccessjournals.eu/index.php/ijiaet/article/view/1060

Naim, A. (2022). Understanding the customer centric approach to add value to social ECRM (SECRM). *British Journal of Global Ecology and Sustainable Development*, *4*, 1–17. https://journalzone.org/index.php/bjgesd/article/view/45

Naim, A., & Alqahtani, K. (2021). Role of Information Systems in Customer Relationship Management. *Pulse*, *2*(2).

Naim, A., & Khan, M. F. (2021). Measuring the Psychological Behavior of Consumers for Medical Services. *Zien Journal of Social Sciences and Humanities*, *2*, 119–131. Retrieved from https://zienjournals.com/index.php/zjssh/article/view/316

Naim, A., Hussain, M. R., Naveed, Q. N., Ahmad, N., Qamar, S., Khan, N., & Hweij, T. A. (2019, April). Ensuring interoperability of e-learning and quality development in education. In *2019 IEEE Jordan International Joint Conference on Electrical Engineering and Information Technology* (JEEIT) (pp. 736-741). IEEE 10.1109/JEEIT.2019.8717431

Naim, A., Khan, M. F., Hussain, M. R., & Khan, N. (2019). "Virtual Doctor" Management Technique in the Diagnosis of ENT Diseases. *JOE, 15*(9), 88. doi:10.3991/ijoe.v15i09.10665

Noviana, G. (2021, September). An Analysis of the Implementation of Electronic Customer Relationship Management (E-CRM) Towards Customer Loyalty. In *5th Global Conference on Business, Management and Entrepreneurship* (GCBME 2020) (pp. 434-438). Atlantis Press. 10.2991/aebmr.k.210831.086

Rashwan, H. H. M., Mansi, A. L., & Hassan, H. E. (2020). Exploring electronic-loyalty antecedents in Egyptian commercial banks; Electronic customer relationship management and banking electronic satisfaction. The *Journal of Business and Retail Management Research, 14*(2). Advance online publication. doi:10.24052/JBRMR/V14IS02/ART-06

Seify, M., Tabaeeian, R. A., & Khoshfetrat, A. (2020). Investigating factors in implementation of electronic customer relationship management and its consequences in private hospitals in Isfahan city. *International Journal of Electronic Customer Relationship Management, 12*(3), 225–245. doi:10.1504/IJECRM.2020.110040

Shahnavazi, A., Nemati Gonbaghi, M., Teymouri, S. F., & Ghasemi Dakdare, B. (2020). Determining the Key Indicators affecting Electronic Customer Relationship Management (e-CRM) Using an integration of balanced scorecard and fuzzy screening techniques (Case Study: Companies Covered by Parsian Data-Processors Group). *Iranian Journal of Optimization, 12*(1), 21–32.

Siaw, G. A., & Gitau, J. K. (2020). *Aspects of Electronic Customer Relationship Management and Guest Satisfaction: A Perspective of 4-Star Hotels in Nairobi County, Kenya*. Academic Press.

Tsou, H. T., & Hsu, H. Y. (2017). Self-Service technology investment, electronic customer relationship management practices, and service innovation capability. In *Marketing at the Confluence between Entertainment and Analytics* (pp. 477–481). Springer. doi:10.1007/978-3-319-47331-4_92

Tusell-Rey, C. C., Nieto, Ó. C., & Padilla, R. T. (2020). Application of data engineering in automatic information analysis for electronic customer relationship management: A survey. *International Journal of Emerging Trends in Engineering Research, 8*(9), 5939–5946. doi:10.30534/ijeter/2020/167892020

Chapter 8
CRM as Antecedent of Electronic Retailing and Online Customer Satisfaction

Joshua Kofi Doe
Ghana Institute of Journalism, Ghana

George Kofi Asamoah
Ghana Institute of Journalism, Ghana

ABSTRACT

As location-based banking continues to give way for online banking globally, this chapter examines whether e-tailing practices yield customer satisfaction. The chapter also examines how CRM influences e-tailing and whether e-tailing can serve as a medium through which CRM yields customer satisfaction. Data, conveniently collected from 681 bank customers, were used for this study and analysed with PLS-SEM. The study found that CRM practices lead to better customer retail buying experiences for banks. E-tailing, mostly perceived by customers as an innovation in the service delivery process of banks, improved the image perceptions of banks. The study suggests that as part of a digital channel configuration, banks must build customer relationship marketing technologies as a backbone.

INTRODUCTION

Location-based customer engagements continue to become less relevant, particularly in the current COVID-19 pandemic. Banks have to invest more in digital sales channels to drive performance significantly. This investment is necessary because it is clear

DOI: 10.4018/978-1-6684-5386-5.ch008

that digital sales channels have become key drivers of overall sales (Narayanaswamy & Heiens, 2021). Therefore, innovative strategic tools such as customer relationship management, electronic retailing (E-tailing) of banking services and loyal customer relationship management have become popular in most banks and insurance firms (Saxena, Gera, Nagdev & Fatta, 2021). Banks provide most of their retail services via E-tailing channels in order to reduce the cost associated with banking. For instance, customer relationship marketing is one of the banking services that has been moved to E-tailing channels as a self-service. What is unclear, however, is whether the shift of relationship management (relationship marketing activities) to E-tailing channels has been effective or not. No study has examined the connection between relationship marketing and E-tailing in the Ghanaian context. This study aims to close this knowledge gap. While CRM technologies aim to promote interpersonal relationships between banks and their customers, E-tailing technologies seek to promote self-service banking activities, which can invariably hinder interpersonal relationships. However, it is uncertain how this trend of relationship marketing activity is affected by E-tailing channels. Some studies (Amoako, Arthur, Bandoh & Katah, 2012; Anabila & Awunyo-Vitor, 2013; Asante & Achiaa, 2018; Klutse, 2016) have examined relationship marketing in Ghana. However, none of these studies has discussed the E-tailing channel or its effect on CRM. This creates a knowledge gap about the effect E-tailing technologies has on CRM technologies in the banking sector for academics as well as industry practitioners. Therefore, this study aims to close this knowledge gap by assessing the effect of E-tailing on relationship marketing and, therefore, customer satisfaction. In doing so, we examine whether E-tailing practices yield customer satisfaction. We also seek to examine how CRM influences E-tailing and whether E-tailing can serve as a medium through which CRM can yield customer satisfaction.

In general terms, this study provides an insight into how E-tailing affects relationship marketing. Specifically, it clarifies whether customers are more satisfied with the relational benefits of E-tailing channels or not. The output of this study highlights the need for organisations to invest resources in innovative E-tailing technologies.

LITERATURE REVIEW

1. Ghana's Banking Industry

Ghana's banking industry has seen some major reforms between the 1980s and 1990s with the aim of mitigating the country's ailing economy through the Structural Adjustment Programme (SAP) (Sowa, 2003; Nartey, 2013), Financial Sector

Adjustment Programme (FINSAP) and Financial Sector Strategic Plan (FINSSP). These reforms, together with the Banking Act (Amendment) 2007, Act 738, gave rise to three forms of banking licenses. These are the general banking license that includes universal and off-shore banking; class one banking license, which is limited to universal banking only; and class two banking license, which is limited to off-shore banking and has generated intense competition among banks in Ghana. By 2014, Ghana had 29 banks (15 foreign and 14 local banks) (Banking Survey, 2014), 140 rural and community banks, 66 savings and loans, 11 financial non-governmental organisations (FNGOs), 67 money lenders, 478 microfinance institutions (MFIs), and hundreds of co-operative susu collectors and credit unions scatted across the country (Bank of Ghana, 2016).

The 1999 Deregulation Law, which led to banking reforms in Ghana, generated intense competition among the banks (Adu-Asare et al., 2014). This resulted in the use of several innovative strategies that include relationship marketing, E-tailing, mobile banking, and other innovative technologies. Relationship marketing, for instance, has been offered through E-tailing channels. Banks' drive to bring banking closer to their customers has informed their consistent investment into technology geared towards safe and secure banking as well as improved customer experiences. Some of these technologies, such as electronic retailing technologies, are utilised to provide electronic services to their customers, including internet banking and mobile banking.

In 2017, the Bank of Ghana (BOG) undertook an audit of the country's whole financial sector. The audit found several irregularities in the sector. Among other things, the audit found that the capital held by some financial institutions were below the minimum requirement, some financial institutions took excessive risks without a risk management department to mitigate their risk exposure, others used depositors' money to fund non-profitable private ventures or businesses, while others lied about their actual financial situation to the Central Bank and other stakeholders. The report also found that most financial institutions had weak business governance systems, particularly with regard to board oversight, accountability, and internal controls. Most financial institutions consistently violated Bank of Ghana regulations, primarily prudential rules, and failed to carry out on-site assessment directives imposed by the Central Bank of Ghana (Affum, 2020). The minimum capital for the various kinds of financial institutions was also raised. Consequently, several institutions could not raise the new minimum capital. Subsequently, the Government of Ghana decided to clean up the financial sector. In the end, nine universal banks, 347 microfinance institutions, 39 microcredit institutions, 15 savings and loans companies, eight finance companies and two non-bank financial institutions had their licenses withdrawn (BoG, 2019).

Studying earlier reforms in the Ghanaian banking industry and its effects, Adu-Asare, Idun and Aboagye (2014) observed that the resultant competition in the banking sector has decreased the profitability of banks but motivates banks to serve their clients better through the adoption of innovative customer relationship-oriented business strategies. Such financial innovations allow firms to develop and implement new financial instruments leveraging technology and market knowledge to serve their clients (Adu-Asare Idun & Aboagye, 2014). Thus, success in Ghana's banking sector can be attributed to, among others, the advancement of information communication technology, globalisation, deregulation, legislation and intense competition. Competition in the sector results in the heightened need to promote innovative strategies to fight competition (Owusu-Frimpong, 2008; Blankson, Omar & Cheng, 2009; Nartey, 2013).

2. Conceptualisation of Relationship Marketing

The marketing mix had earlier been proposed as the foundation of marketing strategy (Grönroos, 2007). This approach to marketing strategy proposed a transactional marketing view of customer acquisition rather than customer maintenance. However, this approach has been criticised in the service marketing literature (Ashnai, Smirnova, Henneberg & Naudé, 2019). The relationship marketing approach subsequently became a more appealing approach after Berry's (1995) study, which brought back the notion into the limelight. Berry (1995) posited that customer retention is a better or more beneficial approach to marketing strategy than customer acquisition, although customer acquisition is important at the beginning of a relationship.

Furthermore, Berry (1995) and Dwyer et al. (1987) proposed a model that depicts relationship marketing as a process that begins with the establishment of benefits-triggered relationships, trust-building through ongoing communication and familiarity, interdependence, loyalty and commitment. Dwyer et al. (1987) and Zhang et al. (2016) argued that a relationship might end at its initial stage. However, trust and commitment from both parties of the business-to-customer relationship may reduce customer churn by increasing customer happiness and friendship. Trust and commitment in relationship marketing are the foundations of Dwyer et al.'s (1987) approach. Morgan and Hunt (1994) similarly proposed a model where they contended that trust and commitment are essential for healthy relationships, fostering reciprocal collaboration among partners and supporting profitable long-term outcomes of the relationship rather than short-term advantages.

3. Theoretical Base of Relationship Marketing

a. *Trust – Commitment Theory*

The Trust-Commitment Theory (Morgan & Hunt, 1994) notes that commitment and trust are essential to building successful relationships, rather than the ability to condition others into a relationship as suggested by the political economy perspective of maintaining relationships. Per the trust-commitment theory, investments in trust and commitment encourage companies to consistently invest in relationships, pursue long-term advantages and prevent appealing short-term aims.

b. *The Social Exchange Theory*

The Social Exchange Theory (Homans, 1958) suggests that human relationships are constructed using a cost-benefit analysis. The theory suggests a link between relationship marketing activity, perceived value to customer, customer satisfaction and, subsequently, customer loyalty. It further contends that as individuals give, they expect to get more in return; and the more they receive from others, the more they are pressurised to also give back to others. Therefore, the theory demonstrates how customers will maintain their relationship with a firm if the relationship is value rewarding.

c. *Theory of Technology Adoption*

Theories that seek to explain consumer adoption of E-tailing (innovation) includes the Theory of Reasoned Action (Fishbein & Ajzen, 1975), Theory of Planned Behaviour (Ajzen, 1991), Value-Based Adoption Model (Dodds & Monroe, 1985), Motivational Model (Davis, Bagozzi & Warshaw, 1992), Decomposed Theory of Planned Behaviour (Taylor & Todd, 1995), the Integrated Model of Technology Acceptance (Venkatesh, Speier & Morris, 2002), the Technology Adoption Model (Venkatesh & Bala, 2008), and the Unified Theory of Acceptance and Use of Technology (Venkatesh, Thong & Xu, 2012). A major assertion of all these theories and models is that perceived ease of use and perceived usefulness, among other factors, will lead to intention to adopt and use technology. Therefore, customers' perception that E-tailing is useful and easy to use will lead to the adoption of E-tailing technologies introduced by banks.

4. Electronic Retailing (E-tailing)

Retailing is the sale of goods in small quantities, usually directly to consumers (McGoldrick, 2012; Hagberg, Sundström & Nicklas, 2016). Digitalisation (Alba et al., 1997; Hagberg et al., 2016) is an important ongoing transformation in contemporary society and business operations. Transformation is essential for the retail industry, which impacts and is impacted by development. This promotes the digital economy (Sturiale & Scuderi, 2016). In the past, retailing had been delivered completely through physical stores and locations. However, retailers now offer consumers different digital products and services using digital technologies. It is also influenced by the new types of consumption linked to digital technology advancement.

While digitalisation has an extensive history with retailing (Salkin, 1964; Watson, 2011), digital transformation is growing rapidly. Currently, purchasing, selling, transmitting or trading of products, services or information using the Internet (Turban et al., 2006; Hagberg et al., 2016) have taken over other forms of business activities. This promotes the digital economy (Sturiale & Scuderi, 2016). This phenomenon, mostly referred to as Electronic Commerce (E-commerce) (Ducombe & Heeks, 2005; Chaffey, Hemphill & Edmundson-Bird, 2019), employs new and emerging Information and Communication Technologies (ICTs) to transact business. E-commerce may comprise selling (retailing) directly from Businesses to Consumers (B2C E-commerce) (also referred to as E-tailing), selling from a Business to others Businesses (B2B E-commerce), and selling from Business to Government (B2G E-commerce). Factors that drive digital change in business include competition (that is, competing efficiently in both local and international markets), globalisation of the production and supply of goods and services, and the 'me too' attitude that is the enticement of the newest technological devices or gadgets (Ducombe & Heeks, 2005; Chaffey et al., 2019), among others. At the same time, anxieties experienced by users of these E-tailing and other digital channels include financial, social and convenience risks (Nawi, Mamun, Nasir & Hamsani, 2021). Turban et al. (2006) describe E-tailing as retailing performed online. A broader definition of E-tailing provided by Wang, Head and Archer (2002) is that it is "the selling of goods and services to the consumer market via the internet". A comprehensive E-tailing system provides easy access, helps to resolve time, location and language differences in business, boosts the promotion of products and services through direct interactions with customers (promotional changes), produces new distribution channels for products (place changes), saves cost in communication and distribution of digitised products, and reduces the delivery time of some purchased digitised products (Block & Segev, 1996; Chaffey et al., 2019). In addition, E-tailing enhances customer service by providing detailed information about products and online help desks, supports marketing intelligence in obtaining data to assess alternatives and supports decision-making. Saxena et al. (2021) reported how consumers/customers had preference for online channel when they engage is what seems to be mostly purchases of services and physical channels for other categories of purchases such as product purchases. Using Guttman, Moukas and Maes's (1998) stages of product and merchant brokering, electronic commerce directly impacts the following aspects of retailing.

a. ***Purchasing*** - E-tailing enables automated purchasing through intelligence and valuable information focused on an individual's computer system. The availability of payment options or delivery options might affect product purchases. Direct selling provides the opportunity for a disintermediation utility.
b. ***Design*** - The internet can empower strategies like quality function deployment (QFD) and online data gathering and mining to enhance design quality; thus, improving competition in the international market. Product design engineers located in different places globally can likewise share information through the internet. The ease of sharing information can decrease design time, enhance the precision of product design and facilitate the creation of products that have the ability to gain a big market share.
c. ***Production*** - Many digitally powered supply chain processes and Enterprise Resource Planning (ERP) protocols are accessible to organisations. Outsourcing of service functions has, subsequently, become popular due to available software. This provides organisations with the choice of acquiring many of the skills needed to operate business-to-consumer E-tailing.
d. ***Sales and Distribution*** – E-tailing has become part of mainstream marketing, and retailers understand its major role in customer service. Alternative web-based, interactive cable and satellite-based teleshopping are presently said to have the potential of altering the landscape of modern retailing (Sarkis, Meade & Talluri, 2004; Chaffey et al., 2019). Hence, the competition between retailers is shaped by new technologies that offer new channels utilised by organisations to reach consumers globally, including previously difficult to penetrate markets (Gunasekarana, Marri, McGaughey & Nebhwani, 2002; Chaffey et al., 2019).
e. ***Warehousing*** – Technologies such as Electronic Data Interchange (EDI) helps firms to minimise warehousing costs by enabling minimal inventory to be placed in any particular warehousing unit (Unitt & Jones 1999). This leads to reduced costs of storage, insurance, warehousing and security. EDI, thus, results in small stock storage by all stakeholders, which decreases supply chain operation costs (Chaffey et al., 2019).
f. ***Supplier Development*** - E-tailing systems empower retailers by providing them with access to a huge variety of products; and allows many vendors to reach customers, connect and transact business with a wide range of trading partners.

Likewise, retailers are able to collaborate and transact business internationally because of the removal or lessening of the barriers linked to time and distance.

g. ***Packaging and Order Management*** - Product marketing has seen modifications owing to the advancement of e-commerce technologies. Product packaging as a functional communication tool has become less important (Sarkis et al., 2004; Chaffey et al., 2019). E-commerce encourages producers and manufacturers to decrease the size and weight of product packaging, which contributes to the shipping costs of products purchased online. Companies have found it beneficial to decrease the number of materials utilised to package their products (Sarkis et al., 2004; Chaffey et al., 2019).

E-tailing can be described as an innovation. In this regard, innovation is the application of new or considerably better artefact, procedure, marketing approach or organisational method by a company in its operations or external interactions (OECD, 2005). Thus, there are diverse kinds of innovation. These includes innovations on products, process, marketing, or even the organisational operational structures itself (Schmidt & Rammer, 2006). Digital innovation (E-tailing) is an innovation powered by digital technologies leading to the development of new kinds of digitalisation (Yoo et al., 2010). Digital innovation is generally viewed as disruptive (Christensen & Raynor, 2003; Lyytinen & Rose, 2003). It is disruptive because it generates new market structures and customer value thereby disrupting current industry structures and overthrowing recognised market leaders, products and services, as well as forming partnerships with new businesses (Christensen & Raynor, 2003). In effect, the adoption of an innovation (E-tailing) is a competition game-changer in the marketplace.

Theories or models that seek to explain firm-level adoption and usage of E-tailing (innovation) includes the Technology, Organisation and Environment Framework (TOE) (Tornatzky, Fleischer & Chakrabarti, 1990) and the Firm Technology Adoption Model (F-TAM) (Doe et al., 2017).

5. Consumer Behaviour and E-tailing

In 1972, consumer shopping behaviour gained attention in the marketing literature due to Tauber's (1972) study, which sought to find answers to the question "Why do people shop?". According to existing marketing literature, several factors influence shoppers' purchase decisions, such as individual and psychological characteristics, cultural, social and environmental variables and marketing strategies. Tauber (1972) identified three distinct activities that constitute consumer behaviour, namely shopping, buying and consuming.

Contemporary models based on the cognitive views of consumer behaviour posits that consumer buying behaviour involves problem recognition, information search for possible alternatives, assessment of alternatives, purchase action and post-purchase assessment (Nguyen, de Leeuw & Dullaert, 2018). For shopping activity (information search and evaluation of alternatives), a customer could go online and shop for a wide range of goods and services that are far cheaper than buying from a physical store. Hence, the internet and E-tailing have the potential of completely replacing physical stores, rendering physical store locations redundant (Danquah & lin Dong, 2018). For digitised products, however, the whole process can be completed online if payment options are made available online and are convenient (Wang & Head, 2007; Danquah & lin Dong, 2018).

6. Customer Relationship Marketing/ Management (CRM)

Customer relationship marketing (management) has become the focus of most businesses or organisations. This is because the general marketing orientation has been viewed as insufficient for keeping retail customers and making them loyal. The words "marketing" and "management" are usually interchangeably used because marketing is a management function (Kotler & Keller, 2006). Picton and Broderick (2005) posit that CRM emphasises the significance of the relationship organisations develop with their customers. It comprises strategic and tactical management activities that focus on establishing positive communication and lasting customer relationships. Similarly, Berkowitz (2006) postulates that customer relationship management (CRM) is "the organization's attempt to develop a long term, cost effective link with the customer for the benefit of both the customer and the organization". CRM emphasises an appreciation of the configuration of the interaction between the customer and the retailer, and managing this interaction effectively (Peel, 2002). This interaction comprises financial considerations between retailers and customers as well as communication considerations (Peel, 2002) that ensure beneficial long-term relationships. Most organisations focus on CRM as they move away from customer acquisition orientation to customer retention orientation. In this process, churn reduction strategies dictate a necessity for the best CRM procedures available.

Furthermore, customer relationship management is believed to go beyond the mere management of customers and observing the behaviour or attitude exhibited (Amoako et al., 2012; Quaye, Mensah & Amoah-Mensah, 2018). This is because CRM can potentially change a customer-firm relationship, boost revenue in the long term and help to understand customers better in order to determine those customers to stick with and those who can be lost. CRM allows businesses to deliver real-time customer care by making efficient use of customer information (Kotler & Keller, 2006). Hence, organisations have to assess the needs of their customers, and build relationships with both their present and prospective customers by meeting these needs (Quaye, Mensah & Amoah-Mensah, 2018).

Studies (Lemon, Rust & Zeithaml, 2001) indicate that CRM benefits vary from industry to industry. The difference is because the processes and technologies linked to CRM are built for specific industry structures. On the contrary, the outcomes of a cross-cultural, multi-industry study of CRM conducted by Thomas and Kumar (2004) suggest that the benefits of CRM in one industry are largely relevant across industries. Later findings on their assertion link it to three elements: value creation, relationship nurturing and brand equity improvement (Richard & Jones, 2008; Amegavie, Mensah & Kwame, 2019). CRM is associated with a list of desired benefits that are linked to the creation of customer equity. In this regard, seven core benefits have been known to serve as the value drivers of CRM. These values are enhanced capacity to focus on profitable customers; integrated offerings across channels; enhanced sales force efficiency and effectiveness; individualised marketing content; customised products and services; enhanced customer service efficiency and effectiveness; and enhanced pricing. Swift (2001) categorised these CRM benefits under the low cost of acquiring customers; not necessary to recruit a lot of customers to maintain a fixed volume of business; decreased sale costs; greater customer profitability; and improved customer retention and loyalty.

7. Customer satisfaction

The business literature offers numerous definitions of customer satisfaction. Nevertheless, customer satisfaction can be described as the customer fulfilment attitude. This means that a product or service gratifies the customer's consumption-related fulfilment expectation (Oliver, 1997). Halstead, Hartman and Schmidt (1994) view customer satisfaction as an emotional response to the tri-component process associated with a specific transaction process. The three components of satisfaction are cognitive, affective and conative. The outcome of this tri-component purchase decision making, however, results in a cognitive satisfaction that leads to repurchase intention, or a cognitive dissatisfaction, and subsequent rejection of the product (Shiffman & Kanuk, 2010; Tweneboah-Koduah & Farley, 2016). The cognitive component has been asserted in various consumer satisfaction models as an antecedent to loyalty. This is supported by Kotler (1994), who opines that the key to customer retention and repurchase intention (Hennig-Thurau & Klee, 1997; Tweneboah-Koduah & Farley, 2016) is customer satisfaction. As a result, the initial patronage or usage experience will either lead to repurchase behaviour or discontinued patronage.

Customer satisfaction has been discussed based on two viewpoints, the transaction-specific viewpoint and the cumulative experience viewpoint (Boulding et al., 1993; Tweneboah-Koduah & Farley, 2016). The transaction-specific perspective measures satisfaction in relation to a particular transaction in a specific situation. The cumulative perceptive measures customer satisfaction per a customer's complete assessment of their experiences with a particular service provider like a bank (Yu, Jacobs, Salisbury & Enns, 2013). This cumulative satisfaction was hinted at by Oliva, Oliver and MacMillan (1992). They opine that it leads to positive brand loyalty. Evidence shows that loyalty is significantly associated with volitional user behaviour (Khalifa & Liu, 2007), which leads researchers to emphasise the importance of understanding loyalty behaviour as a consequence of user satisfaction (Bhattacherjee & Lin, 2015; Lin, Wu, Hsu & Chou, 2012).

8. Relationship Marketing, E-tailing and Customer Satisfaction

Some studies have found causal links between some constructs being investigated in this study. In Asante and Achiaa's (2018) study of E-tailing, they found that trust, attitude, perceived risk and internet knowledge were significant variables that attracted customers to E-tailing. In addition, they found that customer satisfaction in E-tailing can be measured with trust, internet knowledge, perceived risk and attitude. With regard to how these factors associated with innovation impact customers of the banking industry, Saleem and Rashid (2011) reported that as higher the levels of technological innovation is associated with a bank product consumption, higher level of satisfaction is perceived by the customer. Therefore, E-tailing leads to higher satisfaction and, consequently, an increased tendency to repurchase. In support of these views, this study hypothesis that

Hypothesis One (H1): E-Tailing Experience Leads To Higher Customer Satisfaction

Amoako et al. (2012) confirm that CRM impacts customer satisfaction. Even though Amoako et al. (2012) did not cover E-tailing, they provided a pointer to the possible impact of E-tailing innovation on the connection between CRM and customer satisfaction and, subsequently, loyalty. In a related study of CRM effects on customer service experience in the retail industry, O'Reilly and Paper (2012) discovered that CRM affects perceived customer experiences. In light of these views, this study hypothesises that

Hypothesis Two (H2): CRM Leads To Higher Levels Of E-Tailing Experience

Bojei, Julian, Wel and Ahmed (2013) focused on major relationship marketing tools utilised by customer service, loyalty/reward programmes, brand/store communities, personalisation and customisation, and their connection to customer retention. From the implications of their findings, customer satisfaction is confirmed as an antecedent of customer loyalty. Moreover, CRM is expected to lead to high total customer satisfaction (Bojei et al., 2013). Other authors, such as Anabila and Awunyo-Vitor (2013), affirm that there is a substantial association between CRM practices and customer loyalty. Thus, if customer satisfaction is discovered to be an antecedent to customer loyalty, then customer satisfaction could very possibly mediate the relation between CRM and customer loyalty. Hence, this study hypothesises that

Hypothesis Three (H3): CRM Leads To High Customer Satisfaction

Studies of adoption of technological innovations, such as Venkatesh et al. (2002), Venkatesh and Bala (2008) and Venkatesh et al. (2012), posit that Perceived Usefulness and Perceived Ease of Use are very important antecedents of adoption. Perceived usefulness is defined as outcome expectancy (Doe et al., 2017). Thus, where the use of innovation (CRM) is the desired factor, consumers are likely to adopt the innovation (E-tailing). Meanwhile, the relational component of transactions, including E-tailing innovation transactions, is expected to enhance the transaction experience (Hassan, Nawaz, Lashari & Zafar, 2015). The relational component of the E-tailing innovation is what CRM ensures. Therefore, if the relational component of E-tailing powered by CRM is enhanced, it should lead to higher customer satisfaction. Thus, in this study, it is expected that CRM will moderate the link between E-tailing and customer satisfaction. Consequently, this study hypothesises that

Hypothesis Four (H4): CRM Moderates The Relationship Between E-Tailing Experience And Customer Satisfaction.

These proposed hypotheses are summarised in a conceptual model in Figure.1.

In the conceptual model (Figure 1), this study proposes that customer satisfaction (endogenous variable) is the ultimate effect created by firms and is desired by customers. Banks have introduced E-tailing as an innovation that enhances speed, ease of use and convenient banking. This is supported by CRM back-office technologies. In the framework, this study expects that CRM will positively influence customer E-tailing experiences and lead to customer satisfaction. It is also expected that E-tailing will positively influence customer satisfaction with the firm as a whole.

Figure 1. Conceptual Framework

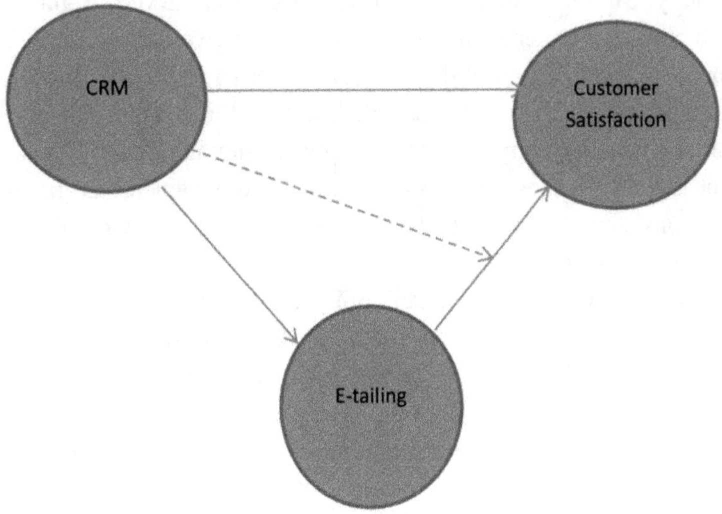

Finally, it is expected that CRM will influence the relationship between E-tailing and customer satisfaction.

RESEARCH METHODS

1. Data Collection

Data was collected from 900 customers of banks in Accra through a questionnaire using the convenient sampling method. Six hundred eighty-one (681) useable responses (76%) were used for analysis. Convenient sampling is used in this study because the sample frame was not accessible; respondents were scattered at different locations, making it nearly impossible for the researcher to use the random sampling technique (Mitchell & Education, 2018). SPSS and structural equations modelling (SEM) in SmartPLS software (Hair et al., 2016) were utilised for the analysis of data.

2. Reliability and Validity of Data Instrument

a. Reliability

The need for a reliable instrument and statistical means of computing it has been a critical issue in quantitative studies for a long time (Nunnally, 1978). The reliability of an instrument requires that it is able to measure attributes or attitudes regularly and dependably (Straits & Singleton, 2011; Leeux et al., 2008). Reliability is the extent to which measurements can be repeated under divergent settings. Common methods used to evaluate reliability in behavioural research include test-retest reliability measure, alternative forms reliability measure, split-halves reliability measure, inter-rater reliability and internal consistency measures. These methods deal with the three key issues in reliability testing of equivalence, stability over time, and internal consistency (Drost, 2011). The internal consistency reliability method was employed in this study.

Internal consistency entails the reliability of the test elements or factors. It measures consistency within an instrument and queries how well a unit of items measure a specific attribute within the test. Internal consistency is achieved when estimates of reliability are dependent on the average intercorrelations in all items of the instrument. The most common technique for evaluating internal consistency in the behavioural sciences is using the coefficient alpha, popularly referred to as Cronbach's alpha (Cronbach, 1951). If the Cronbach's alpha is extremely low, then the test is too short or the items do not have much in common. Generally, a higher coefficient than or equivalent to 0.7 is deemed adequate and a great indication of construct reliability (Nunnally, 1978). Nonetheless, values less than 0.7 might be accepted for exploratory studies. Hair et al. (1998) suggest 0.6 as the lowest acceptable value. In this study, all variables were above the recommended limit of 0.7 Cronbach alpha values.

b. Validity

The validity is the congruence of fit, also referred to as goodness of fit (Straits & Singleton, 2011), among the instrument items that attempt to measure a construct. Validity checks whether the functional definition of a construct, and items under a construct scale, measure the construct correctly (Combach & Meehl, 1995). In this light, an inaccurate instrument is usually invalid (Davis, 1971). The four kinds of validity that should be considered by researchers are: statistical conclusion validity, internal validity, construct validity and external validity (Drost, 2011).

i. **Construct Validity** - Construct validity addresses how accurately a notion, idea, or behaviour was interpreted or transformed into an instrument to measure functional and operational reality (Trochim, 2006). To verify construct validity, accumulative confirmation is performed in two categories of validity: translation validity (face validity and content validity) and criterion validity (predictive validity and convergent validity; convergent and discriminant validity) (Trochim, 2006). Translation validity and external validity were utilised in this study.

ii. **Translation Validity** - It addresses whether operationalisation reveals the precise meaning of the construct being measured, utilising the subjective judgment of face validity and assessing content validity.

iii. **Face Validity**- It is a subjective judgment of the operationalisation of a construct, which is done by mentally judging whether the question items can measure the construct.

iv. **Content Validity**- Most concepts in social sciences do not have an agreed theoretical definition; therefore, researchers need to provide a theoretical definition (of concepts) recognised by their peers and validated by indicators that thoroughly cover its dimensions (Bollen, 1989). This approach was followed in this study to ensure content validity. The data instrument used in this study comprises items adopted from other studies with slight changes to fit the context of this study (Leeux et al., 2008).

v. **External Validity** -External validity examines the ability to generalise the findings of a study to other persons, settings and times. A generalisation can be made to a target population or across populations (Cook & Campbell, 1979).

3. Administration of Instruments

The questionnaire was given to respondents at banking halls. The researcher spent time explaining the questions to participants carefully after they had consented to take part in the study. The goal was to make it easier for them to understand the purpose of the research and assure them that any information provided would be utilised exclusively for academic purposes. This was to ensure that participants provided their opinions without fear. To obtain valid and reliable data, the researcher made sure that all questions were well-framed, reducing possible errors.

4. Analysis of Data

The following stages were followed to analyse the data gathered. The data was reviewed to identify and correct mistakes and omissions that were probably present to ensure the consistency of the instrument.

The data was analysed quantitatively utilising both descriptive statistics in SPSS and Structural Equations Modelling (SEM) in SmartPLS (Hair et al., 2016). This is essential for identifying and establishing the predictability and causal associations among the main variables (or constructs) examined in the study. The outcomes of the analysis are given in the next sections.

5. Ethical Considerations

Ethical considerations constitute a major aspect of research. Following Bryman and Bell's (2007) recommendations of the key principles related to ethical considerations in research, the following were ensured in this study.

The participants of the study were not harmed in any way whatsoever. The items on the questionnaire did not contain any foul, discriminatory or other disrespectful language, while the dignity of participants was prioritised and respected (Saunders, Lewis & Thornhill, 2016).

Informed consent was attained from all participants before data collection. The participation of respondents in the study was voluntary. Moreover, participants were told they may opt out of the research at any time, if they wished (Saunders et al., 2016). The privacy of participants was ensured because the questionnaire did not ask them to provide their names. Likewise, the confidentiality of data was ensured by ensuring that data collected is used only for its intended purpose and avoid (Saunders et al., 2016).

RESULTS AND DISCUSSIONS

The demographic details of respondents are shown in Appendix A (See Table 1 of the Appendix).

1. Relationship between CRM, E-tailing and Customer Satisfaction (SEM Analysis)

The study received 681 responses out of the 900 that was targeted. Due to the high response rate (76%), testing for non-response bias was not performed (Leden et al., 2011). Exploratory factor analysis (EPA) was performed with the extraction of one factor, and the results demonstrated that the factor accounted for 26.7% (See Appendix A figure 1) of variance (less than 50%). This indicates the nonexistence of common method variance bias (Podsakoff et al., 2003). Partial least squares (PLS) in SmartPLS Release: 3.2.7 (Ringle et al., 2015) was used to analyse the data. PLS is not influenced by sample size nor data distribution (Hair et al., 2011). The significance of all paths was measured utilising bootstrap t-values (5000 sub-samples) (Tortosa et al., 2009), a procedure available in PLS.

2. Measurement model analysis

Table 1 shows the findings of reliability and convergent validity after using PLS-SEM. Cronbach's coefficient alpha, composite reliability, and average variance estimations obtained satisfy the minimum requirements of 0.7, 0.7, and 0.5, as recommended by Hair et al. (2016) for exploratory investigations. Likewise, all remaining item loadings following purification of the model were statistically significant utilising bootstrap t-values (5000 sub-samples). The results show that convergent validity has been satisfactorily fulfilled.

In Table 2, the square root of the average variance obtained for all three constructs was higher than the inter-construct associations between them (Fornell & Larcker, 1981; Barclay et al., 1995). Furthermore, the heterotrait-monotrait ratio (HTMT) of associations performed showed that all correlations were below 0.85; therefore, the three-construct model shows discriminant validity. Hence, discriminant validity has been met. See Table 3 for details.

Table 1. Reliability and Convergent Validity

Codes	Item	Loading	Bootstrap t-values	α	C.R	AVE
CRM	CRM1	0.838	32.552	0.846	0.897	0.685
	CRM2	0.889	62.950			
	CRM3	0.789	20.190			
	CRM4	0.791	29.549			
E-tailing	ER1	0.741	0.730	0.713	0.812	0.524
	ER2	0.809	0.792			
	ER3	0.781	0.767			
	ER5	0.532	0.503			
Customer Satisfaction	CS1	0.819	28.101	0.808	0.872	0.631
	CS2	0.841	38.541			
	CS3	0.799	22.312			
	CS4	0.714	13.397			
Note: All t-values are significant at p<0.01						

Furthermore, some variables scored an initial loading of Cronbach's alpha values below 0.6 (see Appendix A figure 1). Specifically, three variables under CRM and another three under E-tailing scored between 0.295 and 0.551. All items with loadings less than the minimum threshold (that is less than the minimum threshold

Table 2. Discriminant Validity (Square root of AVEs in bold diagonal)

Factor	Fornell-Larcker Criterion			Heterotrait-Monotrait Ratio (HTMT)		
	1	2	3	1	2	3
1.CRM	**0.828**					
2. E-tailing	0.221	**0.724**		0.276		
3. Customer Satisfaction	0.520	0.250	**0.795**	0.612	0.291	

of 0.6) were removed (Hair et al., 2016), after which the model was re-tested to get satisfactory loadings. Hence, based on Hair et al. (2016) and Chin's (2010) recommendations, convergence validity has been attained.

3. Structural model

An assessment of the predictive accuracy (R2) of the structural model demonstrated that an explained variance of about 5% and 29% in E-tailing and customer satisfaction, respectively, both of which are satisfactory. Q2 – values of 0.02 and 0.164 were gained for E-tailing and customer satisfaction; both values are higher than 0, demonstrating predictive relevance (Chin, 2010). Lastly, the effect sizes (f2) obtained for the exogenous variables indicated that CRM had a small effect size on E-tailing but a medium effect size on customer satisfaction. The outcomes of predictive accuracy (R2), predictive relevance (Q2) test and effect sizes (f2) are given in Table 3.

Table 3. Predictive Accuracy (R^2), Predictive Relevance (Q^2) and Effect Sizes (f^2)

Constructs	R^2	Q^2	f^2(E-tailing)	f^2(Customer Satisfaction)
CRM	–	–	0.05(Small)	0.32(Medium)
E-tailing	0.050	0.021		0.03(Small)
Customer Satisfaction	0.290	0.164	–	–

4. Testing of Study Hypotheses

Results of the structural model are shown in Table 4, as well as Figure 1. The data indicated that all the paths that were tested in the model were statistically significant. Therefore data from this study context supports hypotheses **H1, H2** and **H3**. Specifically, a significantly positive connection exists between CRM and customer satisfaction ($p<0.01$); and a significantly positive connection exists between CRM and E-tailing ($p<0.01$). Finally, a positive and significant relationship exists between E-tailing and customer satisfaction ($p<0.05$).

Figure 2. Structural paths showing regression weights and t-values

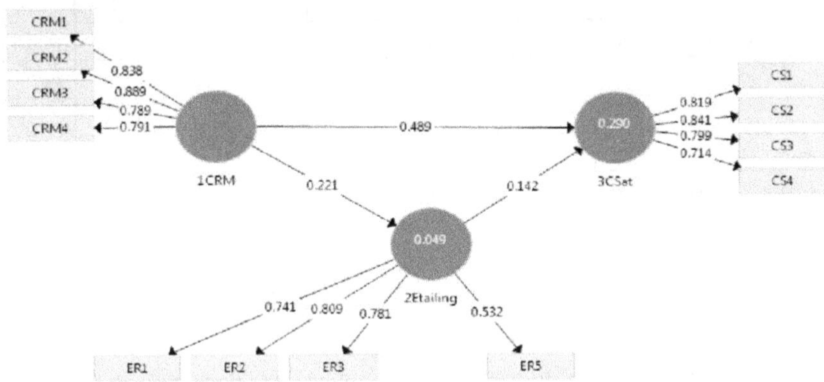

Table 4. Structural path results

Hypothesis	Structural path	Path coefficient	t-value (Bootstrap)	Hypothesis results
H1	CRM Customer Satisfaction	0.489**	10.127	Supported
H2	CRM E-tailing	0.221**	3.517	Supported
H3	E-tailing Customer Satisfaction	0.142*	2.072	Supported
Note: **Significant at p<0.01; *Significant at p<0.05				

5. Moderating Effect of CRM

This study tests the possible moderation effect CRM has on the connection between E-tailing and customer satisfaction, as depicted in Table 5. The R-square increased from an initial 0.271 (Model 1) to 0.290 (Model 2) (a moderated model involving both CRM and E-tailing). However, the inclusion of the interaction effect between CRM and E-tailing on customer satisfaction did not increase the R-square further, as shown in Table 5. Specifically, the interaction between CRM and E-tailing did not significantly influence customer satisfaction ($p>0.05$). Consequently, hypothesis **H4** is not supported in this context.

Table 5. Moderation Test Results for CRM

Rival Models	Direct Effects: Model 1	Direct Effects: Model 2	Moderated Effects: Model 3
CRM Customer Satisfaction	0.521**	0.489**	0.102**
E-tailing Customer Satisfaction		0.142*	0.144***
CRM*E-tailing Customer Satisfaction			0.01
R^2	0.271	0.290	0.290
ΔR^2		0.019	0
Note: **t-values are significant at p<0.01;*t-values are significant at p<0.05			

SUMMARY OF FINDINGS AND DISCUSSIONS

The study discovered a positive and significant association between CRM and customer satisfaction, demonstrating that customer relationship marketing results in customer satisfaction. This finding partly supports those of Amoako et al. (2012). The tri-component benefit of CRM, relationship, value and brand equity (Richard & Jones, 2008) appears to have worked in the present context. Saleem and Rashid (2011) suggested that as service organisation user higher levels of technological innovation, higher levels of customer satisfaction are perceived by the customer. This assertion is supported by the findings in the present context. Thus, higher customer satisfaction is the outcome of an enhanced CRM, which will eventually lead to customer loyalty, and subsequently, increased profitability.

The study also found a positive and significant association between CRM and E-tailing. This means that CRM practices lead to better customer retail buying experiences and perceptions of banks. This finding supports the report of O'Reilly and Paper (2012), who suggested that CRM affects perceived customer experience, which in this context is the E-tailing experience. This finding also supports the view of Hassan et al. (2015), asserting that the relational component of transactions, in this case CRM practices, enhances the transaction experience (E-tailing innovation transactions).

Finally, a significantly positive association exists between E-tailing and customer satisfaction. This implies that E-tailing, mostly perceived by customers as an innovation in the service delivery process of banks, also leads to customer satisfaction. According to Anabila and Awunyo-Vitor (2013), there is a strong correlation between CRM practices and customer loyalty, mainly precipitated by customer satisfaction. Bojei et al. (2013) have used key relationship marketing tools of customer service, loyalty/rewards programmes, brand/store community, personalisation and customisation to show how CRM leads to customer retention through customer satisfaction. CRM is also expected to lead to higher total customer satisfaction (Bojei et al., 2013). The findings of this study support these assertions and affirm that CRM leads to greater customer satisfaction. Therefore, in order to achieve greater loyalty, innovative CRM practices can be very beneficial.

This study tested the possible moderation effect CRM has on the connection between E-tailing and customer satisfaction. However, the data indicated that CRM has no moderating effect on E-tailing leading to customer satisfaction. Therefore, CRM practices will not necessarily improve bank customers' perceived level of satisfaction in relation to E-tailing practices. Thus, the relational components (Hassan et al., 2015) of E-tailing activated by CRM practices neither enhances nor diminishes customer satisfaction. It appears in this context that customers focus on the deliverables of E-tailing transactions. This result raises several questions that are discussed under recommendations.

The data showed that CRM impacts E-tailing, while E-tailing impacts customer satisfaction. This suggests, therefore, that E-tailing could be a mediator between CRM and customer satisfaction. Hence, while CRM leads directly to customer satisfaction, it can also influence other transactional practices, such as E-tailing, to indirectly lead to customer satisfaction.

CONTRIBUTION TO THEORY AND PRACTICE

Theoretically, three of the findings support those of earlier studies. The outcome of the expected moderating effect CRM has on how E-tailing influences customer satisfaction is contrary to reports of other studies such as Hassan et al. (2015). Even though E-tailing activities are reinforced by CRM processes and activities, it appears that its effect is not apparent with regard to E-tailing activities from customers' perception. Perhaps the contextual argument raised by researchers like Data (2011) may apply here. The moderating effect implied by researchers like Hassan et al. (2015) does not apply in the present context. Several questions arise as a result of this particular finding. Could this outcome simply be because of the sample size, the context of the study or perhaps the inability of customers to appreciate the back-office role of CRM in their E-tailing experiences?

For industry practitioners, the findings of this study highlight some useful insight for practice. The findings emphasise the need to strengthen CRM practices to ensure greater customer satisfaction. The findings also demonstrate that apart from CRM, other transactional innovations such as E-tailing can also be used by marketing organisations to achieve customer loyalty. Therefore, organisations should not only focus on CRM.

LIMITATIONS AND FUTURE RESEARCH DIRECTIONS

This study had some limitations. It used a sample of 681 respondents who are customers of different banks in Accra. Further studies are, therefore, recommended across banks in the country. The study was conducted within the banking sector; however, the financial sector includes other industries such as microfinance, savings and loans and insurance companies. Whether these findings will be similar in other service industries in the financial sector is worth examining. Further studies are recommended in other industries as well such as the manufacturing and academic sectors.

The model used in this study appears to be limited due to the short time used in conducting the whole study. For instance, customer satisfaction is expected to lead to customer loyalty, an assertion that has been reported by several researchers in Ghana and other contexts; therefore, it would be interesting to examine how CRM, E-tailing and customer satisfaction all influence customer loyalty and other brand equity variables like brand associations, and brand values, among others. This study, however, did not examine such relationships. Further studies that utilise an extended model are recommended.

In the present context, the moderating effect implied by researchers like Hassan et al. (2015) was not supported by the data. Contextual issues such as a possible inability of customers to appreciate the back-office role of CRM in their E-tailing experiences could explain why this was the case. Further study of the topic with a broader sample size is recommended to explain the negative results obtained. A possible mediation effect is observed between CRM and customer satisfaction. This needs further investigation to ascertain whether this mediation effect is a partial or full mediation. As suggested earlier, further studies could add more construct variables to the model and test for further moderation and mediation effects.

ACKNOWLEDGMENT

This research received no specific grant from any funding agency in the public, commercial, or not-for-profit sectors.

REFERENCES

Adu-Asare Idun, A., & Aboagye, Q. A. (2014). Bank competition, financial innovations and economic growth in Ghana. *African Journal of Economic and Management Studies*, *5*(1), 30–51. doi:10.1108/AJEMS-09-2012-0057

Affum, F. (2020). The Unintended Effects of Bank of Ghana's Clean-Up Exercise on Unaffected Financial Institutions: Evidence from Yilo Krobo Municipality, Ghana. *Asian Journal of Economics, Business and Accounting*, 1-12.

Ajzen, I. (1991). The theory of planned behaviour. *Organizational Behavior and Human Decision Processes*, *50*(2), 179–211. doi:10.1016/0749-5978(91)90020-T

Alba, J., Lynch, J., Weitz, B., Janiszewski, C., Lutz, R., Sawyer, A., & Wood, S. (1997). Interactive home shopping: Consumer, retailer, and manufacturer incentives to participate in electronic marketplaces. *Journal of Marketing*, *61*(3), 38–53. doi:10.1177/002224299706100303

Amegavie, L. O., Mensah, N. M. D., & Kwame, A. J. (2019). Consumer Relationship Management and Its Effect on Organizational Performance Within the Telecommunication Industry of Ghana. *European Journal of Business and Management Research*, *4*(6). Advance online publication. doi:10.24018/ejbmr.2019.4.6.166

Amoako, G. K., Arthur, E., Christiana, B., & Katah, R. K. (2012). The impact of effective customer relationship management (CRM) on repurchases: A case study of Golden Tulip hotel Accra –Ghana. *African Journal of Marketing Management*, *4*(1), 17–29.

Anabila, P., & Awunyo-Vitor, D. (2013). Customer relationship management: A key to organisational survival and customer loyalty in Ghana's banking industry. *International Journal of Marketing Studies*, *5*(1).

Asante, K., & Achiaa, A. (2018). Determinants of consumer adoption of online air ticketing in Ghana. *Management Science Letters*, *8*(11), 1215–1222. doi:10.5267/j.msl.2018.8.003

Ashnai, B., Smirnova, M., Henneberg, S. C., & Naudé, P. (2019). Dyadic Operationalization in Business Relationships: The Empirical Example of Marketing-Purchasing Collaboration. *Journal of Business-To-Business Marketing*, *26*(1), 19–42. Advance online publication. doi:10.1080/1051712X.2019.1565134

Bank of Ghana. (2016). *Banking sector stability report July 2016.* Retrieved from: https://www.bog.gov.gh/ privatecontent/MPC_Press_Releases/Banking%20Sector%20Report%20%20-%20July%202017.pdf

Bank of Ghana. (2019). *List of banks in Ghana*. available at: https://www.bog.gov.gh/ supervision-regulation/registered-institutions/banks/

Berkowitz. (2006). Customer Relationship Management. 8 Common goals for a CRM Program. *What are Key Drivers of Customer Satisfaction?* Available at: http:// onlinesuccesscentre.com

Berry, L. L. (1995). Relationship marketing. In L. L. Berry, G. L. Shostack, & G. D. Upah (Eds.), *Emerging Perspective on Services Marketing* (pp. 25–38). American Marketing Association.

Bhattacherjee, A., & Lin, C. P. (2015). A unified model of IT continuance: Three complementary perspectives and crossover effects. *European Journal of Information Systems*, *24*(4), 364–373. doi:10.1057/ejis.2013.36

Blankson, C., Omar, O. E., & Cheng, J. M. S. (2009). Retail bank selection in developed and developing countries: A cross-national study of students' bank-selection criteria. *Thunderbird International Business Review*, *51*(2), 183–198. doi:10.1002/tie.20257

Block, A., & Segev, A. (1996). *Leveraging e-commerce for competitive advantage: A business value framework.* In Anais da 9Th International Conference on EDI-IOS, Bled, Slovenia.

Bojei, J., Julian, C. C., Wel, C. A. B. C., & Ahmed, Z. U. (2013). The empirical link between relationship marketing tools and consumer retention in retail marketing. *Journal of Consumer Behaviour*, *12*(3), 171–181. doi:10.1002/cb.1408

Bollen, K. A. (1989). *Structural Equations with Latent Variables*. Wiley. doi:10.1002/9781118619179

Boulding, W., Kalra, A., Staelin, R., & Zeithaml, V. A. (1993). A dynamic process model of service quality: From expectations to behavioral intentions. *JMR, Journal of Marketing Research*, *30*(1), 7–27. doi:10.1177/002224379303000102

Bryman, A., & Bell, E. (2007). *Business Research Methods* (2nd ed.). Oxford University Press.

Chaffey, D., Hemphill, T., & Edmundson-Bird, D. (2019). *Digital business and e-commerce management*. Pearson.

Chin, W. W. (2010). How to write up and report PLS analyses. In Handbook of Partial Least Squares: Concepts, Methods and Application. Springer. doi:10.1007/978-3-540-32827-8_29

Christensen, C., & Raynor, M. (2003). *The Innovator's Solution*. Harvard Business School Press.

Cook, T. D., & Campbell, D. T. (1979). *Quasi-Experimentation: Design and Analysis Issues for Field Settings*. Houghton Muffin Company.

Danquah, B. A., & lin Dong, C. (2018). Empirical Evidence on Sources of Consumer Trust on E-Commerce of Ghana. In *Third International Conference on Economic and Business Management (FEBM 2018)*. Atlantis Press. 10.2991/febm-18.2018.41

Davis, F. D., Bagozzi, R. P., & Warshaw, P. R. (1992). Extrinsic and intrinsic motivation to use computers in the workplace. *Journal of Applied Social Psychology*, *22*(14), 1111–1132. doi:10.1111/j.1559-1816.1992.tb00945.x

Davis, J. A. (1971). *Elementary Survey Analysis*. Prentice Hall.

Dodds, W. B., & Monroe, K. B. (1985). The effect of brand and price information on subjective product evaluations. *Advances in Consumer Research. Association for Consumer Research (U. S.)*, *12*(1).

Doe, J. K., Van de Wetering, R., Honyenuga, B., & Versendaal, J. (2017). Toward a firm technology adoption model (F-TAM) in a developing country context. *MCIS 2017 Proceedings, 23*.

Drost, E. A. (2011). Validity and reliability in social science research. *Education Research and Perspectives*, *38*(1), 105.

Dwyer, F. R., Schurr, P. H., & Oh, S. (1987). Developing buyer-seller relationships. *Journal of Marketing*, *51*(2), 11–27. doi:10.1177/002224298705100202

Fishbein, M., & Ajzen, I. (1975). *Belief, attitude, intention and behavior: An introduction to theory and research reading*. Addison-Wesley.

Fornell, C., & Larcker, D. F. (1981). Evaluating structural equation models with unobservable variables and measurement error. *JMR, Journal of Marketing Research*, *18*(1), 39–50. doi:10.1177/002224378101800104

Grönroos, C. (2007). *In search of a new logic for marketing: Foundations of contemporary theory*. John Wiley and Sons Incorporated.

Gunasekaran, A., Marri, H. B., McGaughey, R. E., & Nebhwani, M. D. (2002). E-commerce and its impact on operations management. *International Journal of Production Economics*, *75*(1-2), 185–197. doi:10.1016/S0925-5273(01)00191-8

Guttman, R. H., Moukas, A. G., & Maes, P. (1998). Agent-mediated electronic commerce: A survey. *The Knowledge Engineering Review*, *13*(2), 147–159. doi:10.1017/S0269888998002082

Hagberg, J., Sundström, M., & Nicklas, E. Z. (2016). The digitalisation of retailing: An exploratory framework. *International Journal of Retail & Distribution Management, 44*(7), 694–712. doi:10.1108/IJRDM-09-2015-0140

Hair, J. F. Jr, Hult, G. T. M., Ringle, C., & Sarstedt, M. (2016). *A primer on partial least squares structural equation modeling (PLS-SEM)*. Sage Publications.

Hair, J. F., Anderson, R. E., Tatham, R. L., & Black, W. C. (1998). *Multivariate data analysis*.

Hair, J. F. J., Ringle, C. M., & Sarstedt, M. (2011). PLS-SEM: Indeed, a silver bullet. *Journal of Marketing Theory and Practice, 19*(2), 139–152. doi:10.2753/MTP1069-6679190202

Halstead, D., Hartman, D., & Schmidt, S. L. (1994). Multisource effects on the satisfaction formation process. *Journal of the Academy of Marketing Science, 22*(2), 114–129. doi:10.1177/0092070394222002

Hassan, R. S., Nawaz, A., Lashari, M. N., & Zafar, F. (2015). Effect of customer relationship management on customer satisfaction. *Procedia Economics and Finance, 23*, 563–567. doi:10.1016/S2212-5671(15)00513-4

Homans, G. C. (1958). Social behavior as exchange. *American Journal of Sociology, 63*(6), 597–606. doi:10.1086/222355

Khalifa, M., & Liu, V. (2007). Online consumer retention: Contingent effects of online shopping habit and online shopping experience. *European Journal of Information Systems, 16*(6), 780–792. doi:10.1057/palgrave.ejis.3000711

Klutse, C. M. (2016). Relationship Management in Hospitality Industry: The case of Hotels in Ghana. *Global Journal of Commerce and Management Perspective, 5*(1), 12–15.

Kotler, P., & Keller, K. L. (2006). *Marketing management* (12th ed.). Academic Press.

Lemon, K. N., Rust, R. T., & Zeithaml, V. A. (2001). What drives customer equity? *Marketing Management, 10*(1), 20-25.

Lin, T. C., Wu, S., Hsu, J. S. C., & Chou, Y. C. (2012). The integration of value-based adoption and expectation–confirmation models: An example of IPTV continuance intention. *Decision Support Systems, 54*(1), 63–75. doi:10.1016/j.dss.2012.04.004

Lyytinen, K., & Rose, G. M. (2003). The disruptive nature of information technology innovations: The case of internet computing in systems development organisations. *Management Information Systems Quarterly, 27*(4), 557–596. doi:10.2307/30036549

McGoldrick, P. J. (2012). Retailing. In The Marketing Book (pp. 806-835). Routledge.

Mitchell, A., & Education, A. E. (2018). A review of mixed methods, pragmatism and abduction techniques. In *ECRM 2018 17th European Conference on Research Methods in Business and Management* (p. 269). Academic Conferences and Publishing Limited.

Morgan, R. M., & Hunt, S. (1994). The Commitment-Trust Theory of Relationship Marketing. *Journal of Marketing*, *58*(07), 20–38. doi:10.1177/002224299405800302

Narayanaswamy, R., & Heiens, R. A. (2021). The impact of digital sales channels on web sales: Evidence from the USA's largest online retailers. *Int. J. Electronic Marketing and Retailing*, *12*(3), 306–322. doi:10.1504/IJEMR.2021.116505

Nawi, N. B. C., Mamun, A. A., Nasir, N. A. M., & Hamsani, N. H. B. (2021). Examining the risk factors affecting the image of online stores in Malaysia. *International Journal of Electronic Marketing and Retailing*, *12*(2), 156–170. doi:10.1504/IJEMR.2021.114244

Nguyen, D. H., de Leeuw, S., & Dullaert, W. E. (2018). Consumer behaviour and order fulfilment in online retailing: A systematic review. *International Journal of Management Reviews*, *20*(2), 255–276. doi:10.1111/ijmr.12129

Nunnally, J. C. (1978). *Psychometric theory* (2nd ed.). McGraw-Hill.

O'Reilly, K., & Paper, D. (2012). CRM and retail service quality: Front-line employee perspectives. *International Journal of Retail & Distribution Management*, *40*(11), 865–881. doi:10.1108/09590551211267610

OECD. (2005). Guidelines for Collecting and Interpreting Innovation Data. In *The Oslo Manual* (3rd ed.). OECD.

Oliva, T. A., Oliver, R. L., & MacMillan, I. C. (1992). A catastrophe model for developing service satisfaction strategies. *Journal of Marketing*, *56*(3), 83–95.

Owusu-Frimpong, N. (2008). An evaluation of customers' perception and usage of rural community banks (RCBs) in Ghana. *Journal of Emerging Markets*, *3*(2), 181–196. doi:10.1108/17468800810862632

Peel, J. (2002). *CRM: Redefining Customer Relationship Management* (1st ed.). Digital Press.

Picton, D., & Broderick, A. (2005). *Integrated Marketing Communications* (2nd ed.). Financial Times.

Quaye, D. M., Mensah, I., & Amoah-Mensah, A. (2018). Customer relationship management practices affecting customer loyalty supporting small airline carriers in Ghana. *International Journal of Electronic Customer Relationship Management, 11*(4), 411–435. doi:10.1504/IJECRM.2018.096249

Ringle, C. M., Wende, S., & Becker, J.-M. (2015). *SmartPLS 3*. Boenningstedt: SmartPLS GmbH. http://www.smartpls.com

Saleem, Z., & Rashid, K. (2011). Relationship between customer satisfaction and mobile banking adoption in Pakistan. *International Journal of Trade, Economics and Finance, 2*(6), 537.

Sarkis, J., Meade, L. M., & Talluri, S. (2004). E-logistics and the natural environment. *Supply Chain Management, 9*(4), 303–312. doi:10.1108/13598540410550055

Saunders, M., Lewis, P., & Thornhill, A. (2016). *Research Methods for Business Students* (7th ed.). Pearson Education.

Saxena, N., Gera, N., Nagdev, K., & Fatta, D. D. (2021). A conjoint analysis of customers' preferences for e-banking channels. *International Journal of Electronic Marketing and Retailing, 12*(1), 52–68. doi:10.1504/IJEMR.2021.112254

Straits, B. C., & Singleton, R. A. (2011). *Social Research: Approaches and fundamentals* (5th ed.). Oxford University Press Inc.

Sturiale, L., & Scuderi, A. (2016). The digital economy: New e-business strategies for food Italian system. *International Journal of Electronic Marketing and Retailing, 7*(4), 287–310. doi:10.1504/IJEMR.2016.080806

Swift, R. (2001). Accelerating Customer Relationship using CRM and Relationship Technologies. Prentice Hall Inc.

Tauber, E. M. (1972). Why do people shop? *Journal of Marketing*, 46–49.

Taylor, S., & Todd, P. (1995). Decomposition and crossover effects in the theory of planned behavior: A study of consumer adoption intentions. *International Journal of Research in Marketing, 12*(2), 137–155. doi:10.1016/0167-8116(94)00019-K

Thomas, J. S., & Kumar, R. (2004). Getting the most out of all of your customers. *Harvard Business Review*, 116–123. PMID:15241958

Tornatzky, L. G., Fleischer, M., & Chakrabarti, A. K. (1990). *Processes of technological innovation*. Lexington Books.

Tortosa, V., Moliner, M. A., & Sanchez, J. (2009). Internal market orientation and its influence on organisational performance. *European Journal of Marketing, 43*(11/12), 1435–1456. doi:10.1108/03090560910989975

Trochim, W. M. (2006). *Research Methods: Knowledge Base*. http.//www. social research methods. Net/kb

Tweneboah-Koduah, E. Y., & Farley, A. Y. D. (2016). Relationship between customer satisfaction and customer loyalty in the retail banking sector of Ghana. *International Journal of Business and Management*, *11*(1), 249. doi:10.5539/ijbm.v11n1p249

Unitt, M., & Jones, I. C. (1999). EDI—The granddaddy of electronic commerce. *BT Technology Journal*, *17*(3), 17–23. doi:10.1023/A:1009664017258

Venkatesh, V., & Bala, H. (2008). Technology acceptance model 3 and a research agenda on interventions. *Decision Sciences*, *39*(2), 273–315. doi:10.1111/j.1540-5915.2008.00192.x

Venkatesh, V., Speier, C., & Morris, M. G. (2002). User acceptance enablers in individual decision making about technology: Toward an integrated model. *Decision Sciences*, *33*(2), 297–316. doi:10.1111/j.1540-5915.2002.tb01646.x

Venkatesh, V., Thong, J. Y., & Xu, X. (2012). Consumer acceptance and use of information technology: Extending the unified theory of acceptance and use of technology. *Management Information Systems Quarterly*, *36*(1), 157–178. doi:10.2307/41410412

Wang, F., & Head, M. (2007). How can the Web Help Build Customer Relationships? An Empirical Study on E-Tailing. *Information & Management*, *44*(2), 115–129. doi:10.1016/j.im.2006.10.008

Wang, F., Head, M., & Archer, N. (2002). E-tailing: An analysis of web impacts on the retail market. *The Journal of Business Strategy*, *19*(1), 73–93. doi:10.54155/jbs.19.1.73-93

Watson, B. C. (2011). Barcode empires: Politics, digital technology, and comparative retail firm strategies. *Journal of Industry, Competition and Trade*, *11*(3), 309–324. doi:10.100710842-011-0109-2

YooY.LyytinenK.BolandR.BerenteN.GaskinJ.SchutzD.SrinivasanN. (2010). The Next Wave of Digital Innovation: Opportunities and Challenges: A Report on the Research Workshop' Digital Challenges in Innovation Research. *Available at* SSRN 1622170. doi:10.2139/ssrn.1622170

Yu, W., Jacobs, M. A., Salisbury, W. D., & Enns, H. (2013). The effects of supply chain integration on customer satisfaction and financial performance: An organisational learning perspective. *International Journal of Production Economics*, *146*(1), 346–358. doi:10.1016/j.ijpe.2013.07.023

APPENDIX 1

Table 6. Background Information of Respondents

Variable	Frequency	Percent
Gender		
Male	456	67
Female	225	33
Age		
15 -25	69	10.1
26 – 35	501	73.6
36 – 45	96	14.1
46 – 55	15	2.2
Educational Level		
Basic certificate	111	16.3
Undergraduate	441	64.8
Professional cert	105	15.4
Graduate	21	3.1
M.A./MSc	3	0.4
Marital Status		
Single	543	79.7
Married	138	20.3
Income		
Below GHc1500	522	76.7
Ghc 1501 -3000	111	16.3
Ghc 3001-4,500	21	3.1
4,500 - 6,000	3	0.4
Above Ghc 6,000	3	0.4
NR	21	3.1
Total	**681**	**100**

Table 7. Total Variance Explained (Following EFA with the extraction of only one factor)

Component	Initial Eigenvalues			Extraction Sums of Squared Loadings		
	Total	% of Variance	Cumulative %	Total	% of Variance	Cumulative %
1	4.800	26.664	26.664	4.800	26.664	26.664
2	2.892	16.066	42.730			
3	1.683	9.347	52.077			
4	1.251	6.952	59.030			
5	.998	5.547	64.576			
6	.831	4.618	69.194			
7	.792	4.400	73.594			
8	.694	3.858	77.452			
9	.573	3.183	80.635			
10	.513	2.852	83.487			
11	.498	2.769	86.256			
12	.443	2.460	88.716			
13	.431	2.392	91.108			
14	.417	2.315	93.423			
15	.339	1.884	95.307			
16	.333	1.850	97.157			
17	.295	1.640	98.796			
18	.217	1.204	100.000			
Extraction Method: Principal Component Analysis.						

Figure 3. Original loadings of variables

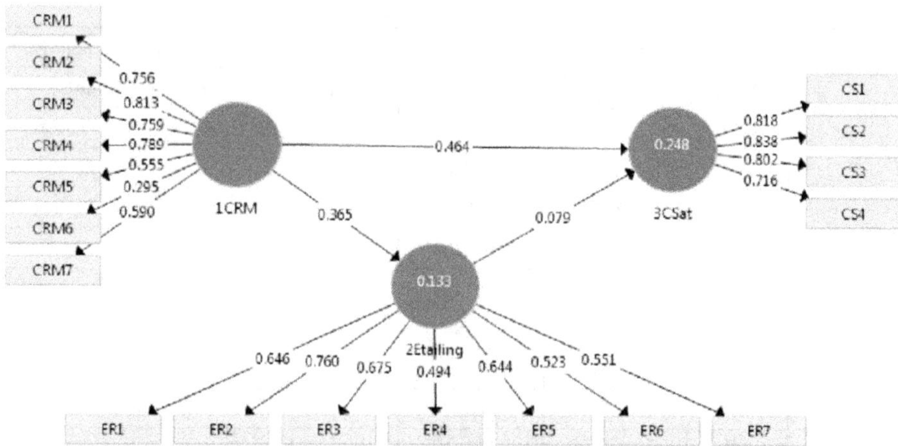

Chapter 9
Brand Extension in FMCG Sector Through Social Media Enabled CRM and Investigating Its Impact on Brand Equity

Rinki Verma
Babu Banarasi Das University, Lucknow, India

Manoj Kumar
Shri Ramswaroop Memorial University, Barabanki, India

ABSTRACT

Web technologies have enabled companies to have a personalized and interactive relationship with the customers, thus engaging customers in improved experience. The disruptive free tools and techniques of social media are used to foster effective E-CRM. Companies like ITC, HUL, P&G, and many multinational companies are using the existing brand name for new product launch as a marketing strategy for brand extension and therefore exploiting brand equity amongst loyal customers. The study is an effort to examine the effects of FMCG ITC Aashirwaad Social CRM brand extensions strategies on customer engagement behaviour and brand equity. The study further investigates the effect of product extension perceived fit, brand image, brand experience, and brand love on customer engagement behaviour. To test and validate the proposed model, the present study has employed structural equation modelling with a sample size of 462 respondents. The findings show that Social CRM brand extensions strategy does affect customer engagement and brand equity.

DOI: 10.4018/978-1-6684-5386-5.ch009

INTRODUCTION

Companies try to make strong brands which provide customers the distinguishing benefits in comparison to other brands. Brands are capable of creating value for the consumers (Zollo, et.al, 2020). Brand equity is the value added to a product by a brand name. Current and potential benefits provided by a brand as compared to the other competitive brands could be measured by Brand equity. Brand advantages and its value derived by a product brand is considered by a customers while purchasing and consuming the product. Brand equity has been widely discussed and explored in different facets of marketing (Farquhar,1989). The brand equity increases the probability of brand preference which results to customer loyalty and safeguards from competitive intimidations (Hansen, et.al, 2018). For making the brands more effective and capable of generating more value for consumers, firms have to consider the needs and requirements of customers (Saqib, & Shah, 2021). Brand equity is also capable of enhancing the brand value, which can be used for line extension or for the purpose of co-branding mainly in case of FMCG sector. Brand association is a determining factor of brand equity which constructs brand equity by differentiation (Sharma, 2016). Customers which are associated with brand provide information to the companies and help them in creating brands which also fulfils the individual customer's requirements (Jiménez & Sánchez, 2019). Customer brand engagement behaviour is capable of creating emotional value for the customers and they are elated by the brand value which fulfils their needs. The higher level of favourable connotations created by brand for customers reflects the higher level of brand loyalty, which is reflected in the form of positive word of mouth communication due to positive brands experiences, results into increased brand loyalty (Ebrahim, 2020).

The FMCG sector is one of the prevailing sectors worldwide and these goods are used by most of the population, which provides ample of opportunities to perform research in this sector. The environment of the FMCG sector cannot be predicted appropriately and is categorized as one of the challenging sector to succeed as the goods here are almost similar without any competitive advantage (Nierobisch et al., 2017). The products in the FMCG sector are of low price and frequency of purchase is large with lower level of involvement ((Menidjel et.al 2017). The lower level of involvement displays that how much a consumer is concerned while purchasing a product and the quantity of information required for making the decision (Tanner & Raymond, 2015). The usage of FMCG products is at all places whether it's urban or rural area. The distinctive promotional activities, apprising about the products and constructing an exclusive selling composition which is capable of differentiating the goods from its rivals are required for making customers committed to a brand. Manufacturing and selling are important for the FMCG brand to persist in the market, but branding is crucial for any brand to enter the minds of customers and make acquaintance with the competitors (Lakshmi & Suresh, 2021). The actual branding is capable of making positive customer valuations and is an important contributor for the brand success (Ansary & Nik 2018). The organisations have realized the importance of branding and are focusing more on the retention of consumers rather than finding the new ones (Moolla & Bisschoff, 2013). The dominant FMCG sector companies successful in achieving branding among the Indian customers are Nestle, Godrej, HUL, Glaxo, ITC etc. (Venkatesha, 2021).

Growth and expansion of a company depends mostly on the product. The vehicle for growth of any brand is directly dependent upon the extension strategies (Springen and Miller 1990). On the other hand new product launch activities incur huge cost and risks for a company and doesn't confirm its success in future (Taylor and Bearden, 2003).Therefore companies usually route these product launch with brand extension strategies. Brand extension strategies use the existing name of a brand to familiarize customer with new product offering (Aaker and Keller, 1990). These strategies mostly depend upon liking and evaluation of the original brand in that product category and how much perceived fit and association extended product has with the original product in the extended category. This way brand equity has already been established by the parent or corporate brand in existing markets (Balachander and Ghose, 2003) and may stimulate demand under the flagship of parent brand. Consequently fewer efforts are needed by the companies to transfer equity from parent brand to newly extended brand in less cost and efforts (Aaker and Keller, 1990; Milewicz and Herbig, 1994). Advantages of brand and product extensions are one of the common strategies used by marketing experts (Völckner and Sattler, 2006) amid in COVID crisis companies are bound to extend their brand from traditional to e-product/services (Ke & Wagner, 2022).

The influence of advertising on purchase decision has been long-established by Theory of hierarchy. Advertising have always been in mainstream to increase brand loyalty and brand equity amongst customers. Theory claims the effect of advertising in enlarging brand equity and brand loyalty (Martinez, Montaner, & Pina, 2009). These advertising ways strengthens the brand image and supports brand and product extension (Taylor & Bearden, 2003; Volckner et al., 2008). In the same way, Social media marketing has become a significant constituent of promotion mix. Marketers use it as a tool for promoting their products and reaching to customers. As more than 3.4 billion people use social media and spend around 2.5 hours on daily basis on social networking sites. These social media sites can be used to as a platform to reach substantial number of persons who have interest in their brands (Lim et. al 2020, Newberry, 2019, Tafesse, 2016). The companies can augment their scope and further expand customer engagement by using social media by concentrating on observing and handling the outcome of specific activities like comments from the users of their likes etc. (Newberry, 2019, Chahal and Rani, 2017). Social media is being used by companies due to convenience to use in customer management, external promotions and marketing. It is being successfully used by the firms as rates of recalling social media advertisements is much higher than 55% in comparison to traditional advertisements channels (Seo & Park, 2018).

FMCG companies attempts to strive these benefits through customer relationships these days. CRM are using various channels like social media expertise that are freely accessible and reachable to all. Thus social media could be used as a platform to increase advertisement bases and increase interactions over relationship marketing. This Social CRM could be promoted by conjoining social media technologies with CRM techniques to extract its competencies and capabilities. By means of Social CRM a company can enhance its everyday CRM by engaging customers in real time and interactive ways (Chen, Chiang and Storey, 2012; Lee & Park, 2022). These social media methods are readily and freely available to companies and used and followed commonly by consumers. Few researches have tried to methodically investigate the effects of Social CRM in Brand extension and its impact on customer Engagement is yet to researched. Identifying associated effects of other construct like perceived Fit, Brand Image, Brand Love, and Brand Experience is essential, as it will empower scholars to comprehend whether differential associations occur according to selected sample. The role of Customer engagement behaviour and its impact on the relationship on brand equity has yet to be investigated in FMCG sector.

The studies conducted during the recent years have used qualitative network approach in the brand management literature (Tasci et al., 2017, Wang and Horng, 2016). Few studies have been being conducted with Associative Network Memory Theory (ANMT) especially with the objective of studying brand equity in relation to FMCG products. ANM Theory shows how the memory functions (Srull & Wyer 1989). The theory presumes that memory consists of fragments of information know as nodes (Chang, Y., et.al, 2014, Smith 2004). A Node plays role of activator for other nodes. The principles of memory stimulate the understanding and acquaintance regarding a brand and finally impacts brand equity (Ansary & Nik Hashim, 2018, Keller 1993). ANMT specifies that semantic memory comprises of set of nodes which are linked with each other by associations (Kenett, & Thompson-Schill, 2020, Keller 1993). How Brand extensions are leveraged to stimulate demand, perceived image, and avoid the cost of promotion. This research paper describes how social media CRM tools are used by FMCG companies to endorse brand extension. Further, the paper will explore the level of impact of brand extension based social media CRM (sCRM) campaigns towards customer engagement behaviour. It will also explore its further effect on brand equity. The role of Social CRM in influencing Brand equity has been recognized in literature though it has not been explored sufficiently in the context of FMCG. Knowing the rising importance of brand in consumers purchase, an understanding of how consumers evaluate social CRM based brand extension, image, love, experience and its effect on usage and brand equity is needed. As brand extension being an important issue for CRM execution. We aim to investigate the critical role played by Social CRM initiatives as determining factors of CRM success. Previous researches have analysed the cognisance of social media on CRM through social media usage to leverage relational information. These studies have either explored the Social CRM use or have examined its critical factors in enterprises (Choudhury & Harrigan, 2014; Harrigan & Miles, 2014; Kubina & Lendel, 2015). Seeking the current challenge of visibility, market coverage and accessibility to the customers in FMCG industry, the FMCG companies emphasize the requirement to purposefully align social media usage with CRM activities. These challenges could be reduced by ensuring social CRM collaboration to track and connect customers. Thus the study attempts to fill the gap by exploring the role of Social CRM with special reference to brand extension strategies influencing consumers' engagement and brand equity with respect to the FMCG sector in India. (Martínez et al., 2009) study has examined the role of advertising in brand extension whereas Völckner & Sattler, 2006 has focused direct and mediating effects of retailer acceptance, Marketing support and History of previous brand extensions, Parent-brand experience as drivers in brand extension. Dens & Pelsmacker, 2010 have used hypothetical brand extensions which lacks presentation of real behaviour of customers. The proposed model attempts to collect the actual behaviour response of FMCG customers. Also, Social CRM approaches have not been explored rigorously in the Indian context. The previous models established for developed markets could not be simulated for developing country like India. Since research has recognized the significance of Social CRM, Brand Equity in the context of Indian FMCG brands and Indian customers. The current study is an attempt to bridge the gap in the existing field of literature. It is a novel attempt to propose a comprehensive model to investigate Social CRM based Brand extension strategies and its associated relationship with customer engagement and brand equity. Construct, Perceived Fit (Buil et al., 2009), Brand Image (Ansary & Nik Hashim, 2018; Martínez & de Chernatony, 2004), Brand Experience (Prentice et al., 2019), Brand Love (Islam & Rahman, 2016; Junaid et al., 2019) have been derived after the review of literature and has been added to further examine the relation of brand extension on customer engagement behaviour and to review the study from multidimensional perspective. Seeking the importance of Branding for business is significant. The model will be able to represent the adoption of Social CRM in the field of brand extension and building brand engagement and equity amongst. The transition from traditional CRM to Social CRM shift is still in the initial phase to unlock the full potential of technology. Thus proposed model will try to relate the importance of embracing the technology to control the relationship. The study also carries newness in form of adding multidimensional perspective in the conceptual model by exploring the importance of Brand love, brand image,

Perceived fit with parent brand and brand experience as relative approach towards reaching to engaged customers and increasing brand equity formation which will help to assess the use of Social CRM in type of consumers to be engaged in value creation and seeking new ways to increase brand equity. Consequently, the paper is planned in the following manner. Firstly, the theoretical background is introduced by analysing literature on Social CRM, Perceived Fit, Brand Image, Brand Experience, Brand Love, CEB and BE. The constructs of brand image, brand equity, and drivers of brand equity are then defined. On the basis of which the model is proposed and leads us to hypothesize the relationships, succeeded by the discussion on research methodology and results. Lastly the paper is concluded with managerial implications and future research directions.

THEORETICAL BACKGROUND AND PROPOSED FRAMEWORK

Brand Extension through Social CRM Techniques

Disruptive technologies have acquired most of the advertisement; Interaction and relationship through the use of latest digital technologies. These technologies have enabled the companies to reach each and every customer. Initially CRM platform was used to interact with customers which were typically one sided communication by the companies. The new ways of relationship marketing and building brand image and equity by social CRM have been recently analysed in engaging customers. The Social CRM is the business strategy where advanced technology is used to involve the customers in collaborative ways for delivering constructive value in a reliable business environment (Greenberg, 2010). Twitter, Instagram, Facebook, Pinterest, YouTube, LinkedIn are the recent social media platforms prevalent amongst customers. Conversation being the centre part of Social CRM therefore almost all company's websites is allowing interaction (Chau and Xu, 2012). Due to large no. of active customers on social media, companies like Flipkart, Tripadvisor, Amazon, Myntra, Bigbasket are letting customers to post their reviews, comments and ratings with this the companies Social CRM are able to solve problem and answer queries instantly. Social CRM dynamic capabilities provide opportunity to interact with customers in real time and also have ability to collect massive clienteles data (Pagani and Mirabello, 2012; Bijmolt et. Al. 2010). Therefore Social CRM could help in engaging customers and fetch information (O'Cass and Weerawardena, 2009). Brand extension strategies can only be successful when people will be aware about them and can associate with them in the similar way as original brand. Advertising impact on brand extension strategies have widely been studied by authors like Völckner and Sattler, 2006; Aaker and Keller, 1990; van Riel et al. 2001 where feedback and extension acceptance relationships have been established. By means of Social Media enabled CRM a company can easily reach to its existing and prospect customers. Social Media enabled CRM massive information collection has capability to network customers, categorize new market trends and can easily reach to new market (Warfield, 2009). Studies advocate the use of social media based CRM in customer engagement (Lee & Park, 2022). communications and distribution of information (Agnihotri, et. al, 2012; Hennig-Thurau et al., 2010, Schivinski, & Dabrowski, 2014, Choudhury & Harrigan, 2014, Dewnarain et al., 2021). Studies have established a significant positive impact of social media communication on loyalty and brand equity (Masa'deh et. al.,2021; Lohanda & Berto, 2022, Zollo et.al.,2020) Thus it becomes significant to explore the effect of Brand Extension in FMCG sectors through Social Media based CRM whether the Social CRM could lead to engaged behaviour amongst customers and how it will impact the value of brand amongst customers that needs to be explored. Thus, we hypothesize a positive influence of Social Media Enabled CRM on customer engagement behaviour and brand equity.

H1: Social CRM campaign for Brand extension has significant positive impact on Customer engagement.

H2: Social CRM campaign for Brand extension has significant positive impact on Brand Equity.

Perceived Fit

Successful brand extensions depend upon the assessment of consumers of the extended product similarity with the existing original brand. The newly launched product is weighed according to the fitness of its association in a product category having similar identifiable label is termed as perceived fit. Product similarity and concept consistency are the two determining aspects of perceived fit. (Park, Milberg, & Lawson, 1991). The extent to which customers found similarity of the extension with the other product based on its use in particular situation and the need it satisfies among consumers is termed as Product similarity (Smith & Park, 1992, Schlegelmilch, 2022). Whereas the level an extended product could hold the brand identity and concept is termed as Concept consistency (Park, Milberg. and Lawson, 1991). The higher level of congruency between the extended brand with the parent brand will be able to achieve higher Perceived fit (Buil, Chernatony, & Hem, 2009) and strengthens parent brand equity degree like brand image (Zimmer & Bhat, 2004). Hence, it can be assumed that Effect of perceived fit between the parent brand and the extension is the major bases of brand extension achievement (Volckner and Sattler, 2006). If brand extension offers a high fit, with the parent brand the customers may allocate their sensitivities and other connotations to the new extended product (Lee & Yoon, 2022). This way it can contribute in increasing the awareness, image, visibility of parent brand and patronage behaviour, accordingly possibility of buying more products of a brand ((Martinez and de Chernatony, 2004; Aaker, 1991; Swaminathan et al., 2001). In contrary to that the poor perceived fit will lead to loss of trust, credibility and failure risk (Aaker, 1992; Keller, 1993). Due to high perceived fit the old schema remains unaffected and customers will show engaging behaviour due to existing positive association and image towards parent and extended brand (Knoerzer & Millemann, 2021). Thus this study will contribute in exploring the effect of perceived fit with positive customer engagement. Perceived fit direct effect on customer engagement has rarely being explored. Thus it becomes important to study and find out the relationship of perceived fit with customer engagement. Thus, we hypothesize a positive influence of perceived fit on customer engagement:

H3: Perceived fit has significant positive effect on customer engagement behaviour.

BRAND IMAGE

Brand Image (BI) has been an important component of marketing since 1950s (Gardner and Levy 1955). BI can be defined as the combination of customer's discernments and persuasions regarding the brand (Campbell, 1993). BI permits the consumers to identify their pertinent needs and comprehend the effective instrument for accomplishing their requirement through brands (Hossain, 2020). Researchers have considered BI as an important element which influences the customers decision to purchase. A strategy to establish a noble brand image differentiates the company's brand from its contenders, which result into auspicious assessments and connotations in the mind of customers (Kumaravel and Kandasamy 2012). Literature based on Brand-image advocates that customer assign human attributes to their loved brand they use leading them to be attached emotionally with the brands (Fournier, 1998). Recent literature based on empirical analysis has associated the relationship of customer engagement and brand image (Islam & Rahman 2016). Heine, 2010 study evaluated the Gen X preference towards functional characteristics of a Brand and relying more on value derived from a brand. Contrary to this Generation Y associate the Image and symbolic characteristics more while purchasing a brand. Brand image is always linked with the one's own image and identity and customers prefer to use those brands which associate and enhance their self-image. These customers will likely be engaged with the brand for long run (Hansen & Jensen, 2009). Consequently, BI is amongst one of the important elements which construct customer engagement behvaiour. The social media is playing a crucial role in establishment of brands (Phan et al., 2011) which leads to engaging behaviour of customers (Lee & Hsieh,2022; Budiman, 2021). Most of the studies shows that BI has a through impact on brand equity (Jaiprakash 2008; Kim et al. 2003) (Ansary & Nik Hashim, 2018; Martínez & de Chernatony, 2004) but have not shown that how this relationship subsists. The existing literature does not show the prevailing mechanism that explains the pathway of impact from the context of BI to brand equity. Thus it becomes important to study and find out the relationship of brand image with customer engagement. Thus, we hypothesize a significant positive relationship of brand image on customer engagement:

H4: Brand Image has significant positive effect on customer engagement behaviour.

BRAND LOVE

Brand love term has been derived from the subject psychology and related to the feeling of attachment and achieving union with a product, person or place (Carrol & Ahuvia, 2006. Recently "brand love" has grown scholarly attention in the field of branding and marketing (Batra, Ahuvia, & Bagozzi, 2012). The term was first investigated as a variable to study relationship in between "love of consumption" and "interpersonal love" (Shimp & Madden, 1988). The term Brand love encapsulates a consumer's craving and eagerness to have that particular branded product. It is an emotional attachment and passion towards specific product and in absence of that specific object it leads to grief (Thomson et al., 2005). It is having strong positive emotions and affection felt by customers using the brand (Langner et al., 2015). The association amid brand and consumer is comparable to the association between romantic partners (Fournier, 1998). This association fill meaning to the consumer life and matches with the self-concept and identity (Bairrada et al., 2018). After using a brand strong connective experience are developed in form of affection, passion and excitement. The bond has long term association of customer with a brand as an affective component combined by brand identity (Langner et al., 2015). Brand love is defined as the "degree of passionate emotional attachment a satisfied customer has for a particular trade name" by Carroll & Ahuvia, 2006. Even some of the brands have been referred as Love Brand (Roberts, 2005). Qualitative research by Suárez, Benito, & Campo (2016) explored brand love in five dimensions-"compensation (intrinsic vs. extrinsic)", "self-congruence (or self-identification)", "emotional bonding", "brand relationship over time" and "passion". Motive of self-image drive consumers to love brands (Albert, Merunka, & Vallette Florence, 2008). Even the products which require considerable time and energy investments are also loved Ahuvia (2005). Creating a product or brand which will be preferred as love brand by the customers is the basis of a successful brand relationship (Fournier (1998). Bergkvist & Bech-Larsen (2010); Lee & Hsieh (2022) investigation has also confirmed relationship between brand love and customer engagement. Brand love strategy provides opportunity to grow brand-loyal customers and converting them into advocates of the brand (Sohail, 2022). Literatures support that there are possibility to portray customer engagement behaviour with the brands which are loved by customers. Thus to test the effect of Brand love level on Customer engagement behaviour, we hypothesize that:

H5: Brand love positively impacts customer engagement.

BRAND EXPERIENCE

The term Brand experience has been defined as the sensations, cognitions and feelings grown by a customer in response to the stimulus aroused by a brand exhibited in brand identity, packaging, atmospherics and interaction done by the brand (Brakus, Schmitt, & Zarantonello, 2009). The feeling is derived when the product is sensed and felt physically. Sensory experiences, affective experiences, behavioural and intellectual experience emerge in a service encounter (Brakus et al., 2009; (Muthu Lakshmi & Suresh, 2021)). Brand experience plays pivotal role in building a affiliation between the consumers and the brand. Brand experience is saviour in this era of cut throat competition. To withstand in this competitive era, it is vital for a company to increase the experience a brand offer to the customers by their branded products and creating a positive association. Brand experience is vital in forming affirmative experiences, enable deeper acquaintances, encourage customers to repurchase and eventually provide positive outcome (Khan and Rahman, 2015; (Muthu Lakshmi & Suresh, 2021))). An affirmative brand experience often means being preferred over the other competing brand or else losing the deal (Cleff et al., 2014). Reichheld & Schefter, 2000 have investigated the connotation of brand experience with brand familiarity and customer satisfaction. At every phase brand experience should be attached to generate an unforgettable brand with loyal customers. Interestingly today well-known brands are creating memorable experience to stimulate emotional feelings in existing and potential customers (NasarAmini, Aali, Faryabi & Bafandeh 2022). Social network sites, blogs are providing platform to interact with customer communities to increase their engagement with the brand. It ultimately leads to repurchasing behavior and development of loyalty persist due to the favourable brand experiences (Erciş, Ünal, Candan, & Yıldırım, 2012). The brand experience is not only limited to the consumption experience whereas go beyond to inspire non-consumers (Khan and Rahman, 2015; (Prentice et al., 2019). Experiences can be sensed in different dimensions like educational, aesthetic, entertainment or escapism depending on what way the consumer is associated with the brand (Pine and Gilmore, 1998). As soon as customers experience emotionally attached and excited about the brand they will portray engagement behaviour with a brand. Thus to examine the effect of brand experience on customer engagement, we hypothesize that:

H6: Brand experience positively influences customer engagement.

EFFECT OF CUSTOMER ENGAGEMENT ON BRAND EQUITY

"The level of customer's cognitive, emotional and behavioral investment in specific brand interactions" has been defined as Customer engagement by Hollebeek (2011b)). Recently the Customer engagement behaviour has emerged as a new concept and has been examined in different terms in shifting perspective such as "Customer Engagement" by Bolton, 2011; Vivek et al., 2012, 2014; "Consumer Engagement" by Dessart et al., 2015, and "Customer Engagement Behaviour" by Wei, Miao, & Huang, 2013 whereas "Customer Brand Engagement" by Hollebeek, 2011 and "Brand Community Engagement" by Kuo & Feng, 2013 and "Brand Engagement" by Keller, 2013. The past studies have shown customer engagement behaviour as emotional, cognitive and behavioural extents of customers towards a particular object and brand (Hollebeek, 2011; Verhoef, Reinartz, & Kraft, 2010). Brodie et al. (2011) has defined Customer engagement variable as psychological state which take place by interactive customer experiences with a brand. Customer engagement behaviour has capability to have emotional impact on consumer behavior (Gambetti & Graffigna, 2010) and customer loyalty (France, Merrilees, & Miller, 2015; Rasool, Shah & Tanveer, 2021). Engaging customers is critical for retaining valued customers and is an imperative portion of the customer satisfaction; as disengaged customers are more likely to switch brands. Positive Customer engagement behaviour with the brand causes higher emotional and functional value and delighted behaviour of customers. Customer engagement isn't merely about pouring profits or getting engaged database. It's also empowering the customer to interact to have the stronger connection with the brand. Customers Engagement behaviour could be done by adding worth to the brand experience will keep brand equity at the front of customer minds (Lee & Park, 2022). Eventually result in reduced customer churn and new sign up of customers. Optimistic associations created by the brand will create more brand loyal consumers who will demonstrate positive word-of-mouth and transfer the brand experience among other communities consequently growing brand equity. Brand equity is the level a brand is assumed by the customers to be competent to meet consumer expectations in the category the brand competes. Affective, cognitive and behavioural engagement redirects variations in brand equity levels (Kuvykaitea & Piligrimiene 2014; Cristóvão,2022; Corkum et. al.2021). Customer engagement behaviour and customer loyalty will indicate the positive or negative pattern of customer toward a brand over a period of time. If a brand desire to positively impact brand equity in near future, it needs to positively influence engagement behaviour and loyalty. The reverse of the same will cause decrease of brand equity over time. Thus to examine the effect of customer engagement behaviour on brand equity, we hypothesize that:

H7: Customer engagement behaviour has significant positive impact on Brand equity.

PROPOSED MODEL OF THE STUDY

With the help of extensive literature we propose the below mentioned model (Figure 1) to examine the postulated hypothesis.

Figure 1. Proposed model of the study

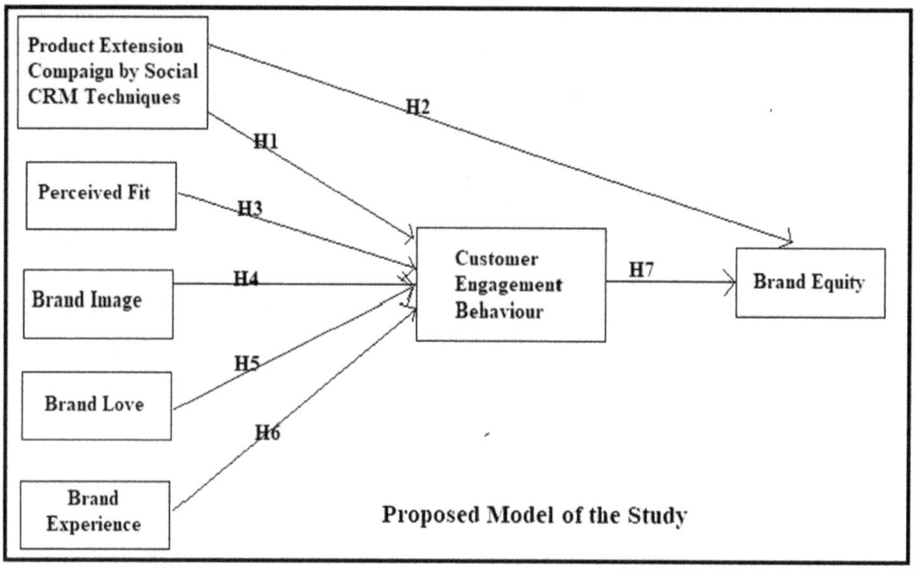

RESEARCH METHODS AND PROCEDURES

Research Design

By using online and offline survey methods a cross sectional research design was used for the study. Hard copies of the questionnaires were filled by the respondents who chose the offline response whereas by means of Google forms the online link of questionnaire was sent to the respondents who were willing to take the online method. Non Random Convenience sampling was use due to unavailability of sampling frame.

DATA COLLECTION PROCESS

India is highly populated and vast country; the data was mainly focused on northern region, Uttar Pradesh, being the highest populated state of the country. With the Indian population growth, the demand for FMCG industries has increased manifold. By using a structured questionnaire as a measurement tool the data was collected in Uttar Pradesh state of India. Uttar Pradesh being the populous state of the country could be true representation of the population. For respondents To be sure of the true demonstration of the population under study, the study was conducted in most of the parts of the Uttar Pradesh and data was availed mainly by customers between age 18 to 60 years and mainly the educated people like teachers and postgraduate students, homemakers in Uttar Pradesh. 10 cities were selected from north, south, east, west and central part of the area for the objective of enhancing customers' representation and generalizability of the findings. These respondents were customers having experience with ITC Aashirwaad brand in last one year and have used product of the brand ITC earlier to complete the survey. Being a user of Brand was decisively used to control and filter questionnaire and was purposely prepared to confirm the survey quality. Agreed participation of respondents in the survey was the last filter question. After explaining the purpose and guaranteeing privacy of respondents through telephonic appointment, the respondents were politely and personally approached. With the help of few assistant scholars who were trained to get responses the data was collected. ITC was selected for studying its brand extension strategies among customers and due to its presence on online platform and their social media based CRM practices. ITC is using social media platform for its organisation to endure competitiveness on the market. ITC presence on Instagram, Facebook, YouTube, Twitter and LinkedIn and has conducted wide-ranging activities on these social media platforms. ITC's has its marketing command points, which are called Sixth Sense, and they specialize in social media discussions to support and create speedy digital promotions and handle customer engagement through social media based CRM practices. The company ITC was selected due to its recent extended product like Lassi, Paneer, ghee, pouch curd and pouch milk in Aashirvaad brand and has successfully launched them in selected markets. The cleaner multi-purpose products surface disinfectant spray, hand sanitizers, soaps and body wash and wipes has now been extended to the brand Savlon. ITC was also chosen for its high customer base and visibility on social media platforms.

QUESTIONNAIRES DESIGN

Keeping in mind the role of demographics a two part/ section questionnaire was framed (Yaya et. al. 2016). The first part of questionnaire consisted demographic information with nominal scale to collect basic information of respondents which include gender of the individual, age, occupation, education, social media usage using frequency questions. The second part of the questionnaire consists of 7 constructs which have been extracted after carrying out the extensive literature review of the previous studies; total 43 questions were proposed to measure Brand equity of Indian customers of ITC FMCG Company. In few constructs, items in the scale were modified on the basis of cultural difference and buying habits of Indian user to make the measurement instrument suitable for Indian context. The response was obtained by using a five-point Likert scale ranging from 1 as "strongly disagree" and 5 as "Strongly Agree". The study was conducted on a total of 462 respondents' sample. As per Jayaram, Kannan, & Tan, 2004 studies the sample size was found to be appropriate since the sample size is 10 times of the numbers of items plus each construct is having at least 3 or more items on which the responses were collected for structural equation modelling . After doing extensive literature review scale has been developed. Total six Items of Brand generated communication were drawn from Schivinski and Dabrowski (2014), in which two items were adopted and modified from Volcker et al. (2008) to measure Brand Extension Advertising impact. Five Items to measure perceived fit was drawn from Hem et al. (2003), Aaker and Keller (1990), Martinez et al. (2009) and Dwivedi et al. (2010). One item is selected each from Aaker and Keller (1990), Martinez et al. (2009) and Dwivedi et al. (2010) and two items were drawn from Hem et al. (2003). Six Items of Brand love was drawn using Carroll and Ahuvia (2006) scale. For brand image the items from Martin and Brown (1990), Aaker (1996), and Weiss et al. (1999) were drawn. The six items encompassed functional, affective and reputation image of brand. The twelve items were selected were adapted from Brakus, Schmitt, and Zarantonello (2009) to measure brand experience. To measure customer engagement behaviour four items were taken from Bergkvist and Bech-Larsen (2010). For overall Brand Equity construct four items have been drawn from Yoo and Donthu (2001). Before distribution of questionnaire, preliminary testing was done in two phases. To check the relevancy of the questionnaire firstly face validity was conducted in two parts. The first focus group comprised of academicians and researchers to review the questions while the second focus group comprised of the FMCG sales managers who judged the relevancy and validity of the questions was asked for the questionnaire. Minor corrections were incorporated after checking validity. The validation score of 3.75 on a scale of 5 was obtained. After validation of the questionnaire by the experts, the pilot study was conducted on the sample size of 35 respondents. Considering the average response rate of 52.7 percent from the respondents in the studies related to data collection and a standard deviation of 20.4% (Baruch & Holtom,2008), 1000 questionnaires were floated for the study and 615 questionnaires were received back with 61.50 percent response rate. After proper scrutiny, 462 of them were considered appropriate for the study. Incomplete questionnaires were considered invalid and removed from the study. Table I depicts demographic characteristics of sample. Females accounted for 53.03% and males 46.97% of the ITC customers.

RESULTS

Confirmatory Factor Analysis

To measure reliability, discriminant validity and convergent validity Confirmatory factor analysis was used. With the help of Cronbach the reliability of the measurement scales was measured. CFA was conducted to explain the pattern of loadings of each measure on a specific factor (Hair et al., 1998; Anderson & Gerbing, 1988; Thompson, 2004; Bryne, 2001; Tatham et al., 2006; Brown and Moore, 2012; Byrne, 2013). Then, squared multiple correlation was performed to judge how well an item measures a construct (Hair et. al,1988; Holmes-Smith, 2001). After checking the squared multiple correlation, 3 items whose R2 values were < 0.5, were deleted. Further CFA was again conducted, and the results indicated that the measurement model is a fit with the sample data. The CFA result (Table II) showed that the goodness of fit was moderately satisfied. As per the results χ^2 is significant (χ^2 =1949.250, χ^2/df ratio = 2.875, ρ = 0.000). Obtained GFI value is 0.957, RMSEA value 0.054, and CFI value is 0.914.

As shown in Table III all variables Cronbach's alpha values are greater than 0.7 which show that all the variables are reliable. With this confirmatory factor analysis also confirm convergent and discriminative validity requirement. The results of this test, as shown in Table II. The results of the confirmatory factor analysis reveal that the data also confirm to the requirements of convergent and discriminative validity. The standardized factor loadings of all the items in a measurement scale are greater than 0.5 (Fornell and Larcker, 1981; Hair et al., 2010).

To check that the measurement scales are separate from other Discriminant validity is utilized in this study. The average variance extracted (AVE) is compared with squared inter-scale correlations for Discriminant validity. To confirm the discriminant validity, the AVE must be greater than the squared inter-scale correlations (Fornell and Larcker, 1981; Hair et al., 2010). Further, for evaluating discriminant validity AVE was calculated for all seven constructs (Hair *et al.*, 2006), and which were found to be ranged from 0.50 to 0.85. As per the Table IV AVE is more than 0.50;

Table 1. Demographic Characteristics of the Sample

Variable	Value label	Number	%
Gender	Male	217	46.97%
	Female	245	53.03%
Age	18-25	105	22.73%
	26-30	121	26.19%
	31-40	201	43.51%
	41-50	23	4.98%
	51 and above	12	2.60%
Education	Diploma	9	1.95%
	Graduate	194	41.99%
	Post graduate	257	55.63%
	Certificate	2	0.43%
Occupation	Government Employee	102	22.08%
	Private Employee.	175	37.88%
	Self-employed / Businessman.	41	8.87%
	Home maker	26	5.63%
	Student	118	25.54%
Internet/Social Media Using Frequency	1 hour below	81	17.53%
	1-3 hours	179	38.74%
	3-5 hours	111	24.03%
	5-7 hours.	59	12.77%
	7 hours above	32	6.93%

Source: Author's Own Contribution

this way convergent validity is confirmed as scores of AVE is > 0.50 beyond the suggested level of Hair et al., 2013. Values of AVE, MSV and ASV are calculated to measure Discriminant validity. As per the Table IV, the scores of AVE is more

Table 2. CFA Result

Variables	GFI	CFI	χ^2/df	RMSEA	Sig
First-order CFA	0.902	0.914	2.875	0.054	0.000

Source: Author's Own Contribution

Table 3. Confirmatory Factor Analysis

Construct	Items	Standardized Factor Loading	Cronbach's Alpha
Social CRM Brand Extension Activities (SCRM)	• I am satisfied with the company's social media communications for ITC Aashirvaad brand. • The company's social media communications for ITC Aashirvaad are very attractive. • This company's social media communications for ITC Aashirvaad brand perform well, when compared with the social media communications of other companies. • Extension product is well supported in advertisements. • Extension product advertisements are memorable. • Frequency of extension product advertisement is 3-4 times a day.	0.76 0.81 0.89 0.79 0.71 0.78	0.78
Perceived Fit (PF)	• The extension of ITC Aashirvaad products makes sense. • ITC Aashirvaad brand has skills to launch the brand extension. • The new product' is similar or dissimilar to the products usually offered by ITC Aashirvaad. • The position of ITC Aashirvaad is similar with extension. • Think about brand ITC Aashirvaad how similar is the competence for making original brand and extension.	0.89 0.87 0.79 0.78 0.73	0.81
Brand Love (BL)	• This is a wonderful brand. • This brand makes me feel good. • This brand is totally awesome. • This brand makes me very happy. • I love this brand. • This brand is a pure delight. • I'm very attached to this brand.	0.81 0.78 0.75 0.81 0.84 0.85 0.81	0.88
Brand Experience (BE)	• This brand makes a strong impression on my visual sense or other senses. . • I find this brand interesting in a sensory way. • This brand does not appeal to my senses. . • This brand induces feelings and sentiments. • I do not have strong emotions for this brand. • This brand is an emotional brand. . • I engage in physical actions and behaviors when I use this brand. • This brand results in bodily experiences. • This brand is not action oriented. • I engage in a lot of thinking when I encounter this brand. . • This brand does not make me think. • This brand stimulates my curiosity and problem solving.	0.84 0.88 0.89 0.89 0.78 0.89 0.77 0.76 0.73 0.87 0.79 0.88	0.81
Brand Image	• This brand has a high quality. • This brand has better characteristics than its competitors. • This brand has a personality that distinguishes itself from competitors. • This brand is a brand that does not disappoint its customers. • This brand is one of the best brands in the sector. • This brand is stable in the market.	0.82 0.86 0.79 0.81 0.79 0.71	0.77
Customer Engagement Behaviour	• I always try to follow the news about the brand. • I frequently talk about the brand to others. • I frequently visit the brand's website. • I am always interested in buying products with this brand name on it.	0.76 0.78 0.82 0.81	0.76
Brand Equity	• It makes sense to buy ITC Aashirvaad brand instead of any other brands. • Even if another brand has the same features as ITC Aashirvaad, I will buy it. • If there is another brand as good as ITC Aashirvaad, I will still buy it. • If another brand is not different from ITC Aashirvaad in any way, it is smarter to purchase it.	0.82 0.91 0.88 0.87	0.78

Source: Author's Own Contribution

Table 4. Reliability and Validity of Constructs

Constructs	CR	AVE	MSV	ASV
SCRM	0.864	0.624	0.314	0.083
PF	0.824	0.513	0.321	0.181
BI	0.912	0.621	0.42	0.23
BL	0.836	0.546	0.342	0.062
BEx	0.842	0.587	0.427	0.263
CEB	0.811	0.518	0.436	0.194
BE	0.881	0.621	0.446	0.251

Notes: Indices: CR-composite reliability; AVE-average variance extracted; MSV-maximum shared variance; ASV-average shared variance; SCRM-Social CRM campaign for Product extension; PF- Perceived Fit, BI-Brand Image, BL-Brand Love, BEx-Brand experience, CEB-Customer Engagement Behaviour, BE-Brand Equity

Source: Author's Own Contribution

Hence, it is confirmed that all the measurement scales used in the study are different from each other, thus data used in our study accomplishes the requirements of convergent, discriminant validity and is appropriate for further analysis.

STRUCTURAL MODEL

Once the measurement model was satisfactory, the structural model was assessed and was well congregated. The Fitness indices of structural models represented an accepted level of model's fitness (GFI=0.854, CFI=0.936; RMSEA=0.58; PCLOSE=0.452, χ^2=872.569; χ^2/df ratio= 1.423, p = 0.001). All the paths are found significant. The Table V shows the structural model and path analysis, which represents that, Social CRM campaign for Product extension is significantly related to Brand Equity, ($\beta = .765$, p =0.001), thus H1 is supported. Social CRM campaign for Product extension is significantly related to Brand Equity ($\beta = 0.676$, p =0.01) supporting H2. H3, which states that Perceived Fit is significantly related to Customer Engagement Behaviour ($\beta = 0.542$, p =0.05) was also supported. Brand Image has significant influence on Customer Engagement Behaviour ($\beta = 0.742$, p =0.01), thus H4 is supported. H5, indicating Brand Love was also found significantly impacting Customer Engagement Behaviour ($\beta = 0.814$, p =0.01). Brand Experience is also significantly related to Customer Engagement Behaviour ($\beta = 0.842$, p =0.01), thus supporting H6. Whereas Customer Engagement Behaviour and Brand Equity are found to be significantly related ($\beta = 0.715$, p =0.01) supporting H7.

Table 5. Structural Results

Factors	Estimate	P	Result
CEB<---SCRM	0.765	0.01	Supported
BE <--- SCRM	0.676	0.01	Supported
CEB <--- PF	0.542	0.05	Supported
CEB <--- BI	0.742	0.01	Supported
CEB <--- BL	0.814	0.01	Supported
CEB <--- BEx	0.842	0.01	Supported
PBE <--- CEB	0.715	0.01	Supported

Notes: χ^2=872.569; χ^2/df ratio= 1.423; GFI=0.854; CFI=0.936; RMSEA=0.58; PCLOSE=0.452; significance at the 0.01 level

Source: Author's Own Contribution

DISCUSSION

The growth and expansion of social media has provided new drifts in thc ficld of online relationship marketing and branding. The social CRM has provided innovative channels in communicating the brand. It can be noticed from the usage of online brand engagement on the social media networking applications. Through the results it is conformed that Social CRM campaign for Product extension is significantly related to Brand Equity, (β = .765, p =0.001). In India companies like ITC, Nestle, Godrej, HUL, Glaxo etc. are focussed towards the preferences and necessities of customers. The social CRM has paved its path in strategically integrating the marketing agenda of the big brands with the customers. Therefore this research study contributes to the knowledge of Social CRM by evaluating its bearing on Customer engagement behaviour and brand equity (β = 0.676, p =0.015). Social Media based CRM can create a company's long standing position. Social Media enabled CRM techniques initiate engagement activities and proccss affirmativc brand equity among customers. These innovative social media expertise will cajole customers in successful implementation of branding strategies. This research has confirmed that brand extension has effect on a brand's image, creating positive association's consumers (Choudhury& Harrigan, 2014). The study provides new dimensions regarding application of social media in creation of brand equity in case of brand extension in the FMCG sector. The study was driven for deeper acumens on the subject and their relationship. The study focuses on how Product Extension Campaign by Social CRM Techniques, Perceived Fit, Brand Image, Brand love and Brand Experience creates Customer Engagement Behaviour which leads to Brand equity.

Firstly, we have explored a positive association amid social media Based CRM techniques for brand extension and customer brand engagement through social media advertisements and search engine effectiveness. This way the research findings support some previous thinking, particularly about customer engagement Yang et.al (2016) and Hollebeek (2011) and Choudhury & Harrigan (2014). Secondly a positive association amid social media based CRM brand extension and brand equity. The result indicates significant positive influence on brand equity. Thus supporting previous studies of Koay et. Al. (2020), Ismail, (2017) and; study of Kim and Ko (2012). Brand extensions strategy empowers firms to influence the parent brand equity reducing the costs and failure of new product. Perceived fit findings (β = 0.542, p =0.005) depict consumer assessments of extensions and outcome of these strategies on brand equity vary according on the basis of fit professed by consumers. Extensions which have high closeness with the original brand create a coherent image consequently rewarding brand with more engaged and loyal customers. This result is contrary to previous studies (Chen and Chen, 2000; Vo¨lckner et al., 2007) where the brand was damaged after the brand extension. The result does support that Perfect perceived fit may facilitate in increasing CBE during brand extension.

The research supports the BL (β = 0.814, p =0.01) and BI (β = 0.742, p =0.01),) may accelerate the development of increased CEB towards a particular FMCG brand. The present research also confirms the effect of brand love and functional, affective and reputation image of brand with customer engagement. Companies who create the culture of Brand love begin to embark same emotions which create a positive attitude toward their preferred FMCG brand and ultimately leading to customer engagement behaviour. The Brand familiarity, knowledge influences the general brand image. Customer usually better appraise those brands and products based on the familiarity with name and image. Prior work of Loureiro et al. (2017), Bergkvist & Bech-Larsen, (2010); Doorn et al., (2010), Junaid et.al., (2019), Islam & Rahman (2016) have also reported the positive effect of BL and BI on CEB.

Consumer experience is how a customer responds while pre-purchase, during consumption and post purchase. Brand creates emotional linkages throughout the process of Customer experience. The study indicates brand experience significant effect on CEB (β = 0.842, p =0.01) which ultimately ropes brand extension strategies and consequently shape brand equity in progressive means. Brand experience has been investigated in different association with the brand in other studies also which confirm its direct, mediating effect on CBE and findings are consistent with Prentice et.al. (2019), Pansari and Kumar (2017), Roberts and Alpert (2010) in diverse industry settings. Such similar finding shows that customer experience is pivotal to engage customers and attain their loyalty behaviours. Brand equity is the worth that is accumulated by a product based on the brand name compared to the other competitive brand (Keller 2003). Higher brand equity represents greater value of the brand owns. Most of the consumers purchase high valued brands owing to its status symbol and social pressure. The study reported the positive and significant effect of customer engagement on Brand equity ($\beta = 0.715$, $p = 0.01$) and results were found to be consistent with Lee and Park (2022), Dwivedi, (2015), Hepola, Karjaluoto & Hintikka (2017). These relationships will cultivate customers' involvement; inspiring customer to take part in new products acceptance, brand communications and buying. This proposed model unlocks opportunities for extended and purposeful reasoning and assessment of the process and the theoretical construct of CEB into BE formation through Social CRM Techniques in Brand extension. On the Basis of present research results, it could be concluded that customers may perhaps enthusiastically participate in brand creation by depicting engagement behaviour and brand extension campaigns of Social CRM.

CONCLUSION AND MANAGERIAL IMPLICATIONS

The study theoretically contribute in the extent literature of Social CRM enabled brand extensions strategies which explores the outcomes of sCRM such as customer engagement and ultimately effecting brand equity. In previous researches Social media, CRM importance in brand extension strategy is emphasized and highlighted (Zubair, Baharun& Kiran, 2022; Choudhury & Harrigan, 2014; Zollo et.al., 2020). The study comprehends that the relationship between engagement and Brand equity will be improved through Social CRM techniques for Low involvement products extension with high brand image and value which provide higher convenience level. Study adds to existing literature by supporting the significances of Perceived Fit, Brand Love, Brand Image, Brand experience in terms of positive outcomes for the customer engagement behaviour towards the company. The results claim that consumers become engaged when the firm shapes its brand image, create positive experience and make it a loving brand among customers to develop emotional relationship which is coherent with the study of Junaid et al., (2019); Islam & Rahman(2016); Buil et al. (2009) & Pansari and Kumar (2017). Brand experience and brand love appeared out to be the significant factors which affect customer engagement. The model discusses the relationship between the brand equity and customer engagement behaviour which are significant for creating acquaintance, relations and brand acceptance. Perceived fit also emerged as one of the factors affecting the consumer behaviour. Consequently high perceived fit reinforces brand engagement thus lowers risk associated with extension (Hem et al., 2003). Good image brands Social CRM campaigns emboldens shopper about the brand association (Martinez et al., 2009) thus reinforces repeat purchase and references. Thus, the study marks the empirical testing of a model which not only displays the

Social CRM Based brand extension aspect also its further impact on brand equity is also verified and the results are significant in context of Indian consumers (Dwivedi & Merrilees, 2013). FMCG products display continuously purchased product so study portrays significant implications for managers who aim to change consumer behaviour and engage consumers in building brand equity. The study belonged to diverse socio-economic status, age group, profile and education hence outcomes have real-world significance.

Ever since the digital innovation like Social CRM has evolved, it has altered the ways of doing business. Operative capabilities of social CRM could improve customer engagement and brand equity that eventually will upsurge the productivity and sale results of an organization towards the high profitability. Through social media interaction with the organization and customers become quickly and easily at their comfort zones improving customer engagement. This way the study confirms and suggests the Brand managers to use digital technology in building brand extension. Brand love, image, cost and worth of possession that customers relate with that brand then customer will not question and will readily buy the product. Realizing the significance of customer experience and emotional relationships brands should provide an ecosystem encompassed of exceptional experiences which should augment smooth flow, new experience, and learning eventually differentiating from competitors. Thus, brand managers should thoughtful to harness touch points to efficiently generate powerful emotions among their customers. The study provides an evidence for the extent customers recognise FMCG brands through social media application and CRM activities. For reaping the benefits of sCRM manager a perfectly calculated and polished Social media based extension campaign on CRM will assuredly be well accepted by customers. Social CRM practices will create more positive impact on customer engagement behaviour and brand equity. As FMCG products are frequently bought thus Social CRM can play a distinctive role in comprehension of brand equity. Managers should give emphasis to the design of positive SCRM strategies and experience content to accentuate love, image and parent brand fit amongst customers.

LIMITATIONS AND FUTURE RESEARCH

The theoretical model of consumer engagement behaviour into brand equity formation, proposed in this article, unveils ways to achieve consumer brand engagement based on the selected constructs and the magnitude of brand engagement consequently affecting brand equity. Like any other research, this study has no exceptions and has certain limitations. Even though the model is tested empirically, it could be further tested for extensively and purposefully, to evaluate consumer engagement behaviour into brand equity creation. The study focuses mainly on urban population, whereas in current scenario FMCG companies are trying to establish their customer base in rural marketing also. Therefore, for further research other regions and sections of society or different sectors like education could be investigated to develop the more effective results and in depth study. The study is cross sectional and deals with ascertaining relationships so further causes of these relationship can be explored. Thus it provides scope to further study Social CRM effects through longitudinal study. The study has examined only five variables as drivers of Customer engagement behaviour so future could address other variables. We have taken only one brand to check its social CRM techniques effect on CEB and BE. Additionally other companies could be taken to compare their results. Model could be extended the model by investigating other possible variables like self-congruence, brand attachment and social CRM interface. Since the emotions like love, virtuous image can frequently change with small variations in the companies' activities; the time-varying influence could be studied further. Given the utmost importance of branding extension in today's competitive era, further research is desirable to facilitate academician, companies and researchers to comprehend more on the ways of enhancing brand equity.

NOTE

This research received no specific grant from any funding agency in the public, commercial, or not-for-profit sectors.

REFERENCES

Aaker, D. A. (1991). *Managing brand equity. Capitalizing on the value of brand name*. The Free Press.

Aaker, D. A. (1992). The value of brand equity. *The Journal of Business Strategy*, *13*(4), 27–32. doi:10.1108/eb039503

Aaker, D. A. (1996). Measuring brand equity across products and markets. *California Management Review*, *38*(3), 102–120. doi:10.2307/41165845

Aaker, D. A., & Keller, K. L. (1990). Consumer evaluations of brand extensions. *Journal of Marketing*, *54*(1), 27–41. doi:10.1177/002224299005400102

Agnihotri, R., Rapp, A., Kothandaraman, P., & Singh, R. (2012). An emotion-based model of salesperson ethical behaviors. *Journal of Business Ethics*, *109*(2), 243–257. doi:10.100710551-011-1123-3

Ahuvia, A. C. (2005). Beyond the extended self: Loved objects and consumers' identity narratives. *The Journal of Consumer Research, 32*(1), 171–184. doi:10.1086/429607

Albert, N., Merunka, D., & Vallette-Florence, P. (2008). When consumers love their brands: Exploring the concept and its dimensions. *Journal of Business Research, 61*, 1062–1075. doi:.jbusres.2007.09.014 doi:10.1016/j

Anderson, J. C., & Gerbing, D. W. (1988). Structural equation modeling in practice: A review and recommended two-step approach. *Psychological Bulletin, 103*(3), 411–423. doi:10.1037/0033-2909.103.3.411

Ansary, A., & Nik Hashim, N. M. H. (2018). Brand image and equity: The mediating role of brand equity drivers and moderating effects of product type and word of mouth. *Review of Managerial Science, 12*(4), 969–1002. doi:10.100711846-017-0235-2

Bairrada, C.M., Coelho, F., & Coelho, A. (2018). Antecedents and outcomes of Brand love: utilitarian and symbolic Brand qualities. *European Journal of Marketing, 52*(3-4), 656-682.

Balachander, S., & Ghose, S. (2003). Reciprocal spillover effects: A strategic benefit of brand extensions. *Journal of Marketing, 67*(1), 4–13. doi:10.1509/jmkg.67.1.4.18594

Baruch, Y., & Holtom, B. C. (2008). Survey response rate levels and trends in organizational research. *Human Relations, 61*(8), 1139–1160. doi:10.1177/0018726708094863

Batra, R., Ahuvia, A., & Bagozzi, R. P. (2012). Brand love. *Journal of Marketing, 76*(2), 1–16. doi:10.1509/jm.09.0339

Bergkvist, L., & Bech-Larsen, T. (2010). Two studies of consequences and actionable antecedents of Brand love. *Journal of Brand Management, 17*(7), 504–518. doi:10.1057/bm.2010.6

Bijmolt, T. H. A., Leeflang, P. S. H., Block, F., Eisenbeiss, M., Hardie, B. G. S., Lemmens, A., & Saffert, P. (2010). Analytics for customer engagement. *Journal of Service Research, 13*(3), 341–356. doi:10.1177/1094670510375603

Bolton, R. N. (2011). Customer engagement: Opportunities and challenges for organizations. *Journal of Service Research, 14*, 272–274. doi:10.1177/1094670511414582

Brakus, J. J., Schmitt, B. H., & Zarantonello, L. (2009). Brand experience: What is it? How is it measured? Does it affect loyalty? *Journal of Marketing, 73*(3), 52–68. doi:10.1509/jmkg.73.3.052

Brodie, R. J., Hollebeek, L. D., Juric, B., & Ilic, A. (2011). Customer engagement: Conceptual domain, fundamental propositions and implications for research in service marketing. *Journal of Service Research*, *14*(3), 352–371. doi:10.1177/1094670511411703

Brown, T. A., & Moore, M. T. (2012). Confirmatory factor analysis. Handbook of structural equation modeling, 361-379.

Budiman, S. (2021). The effect of social media on brand image and brand loyalty in generation Y. The Journal of Asian Finance. *Economics and Business*, *8*(3), 1339–1347.

Buil, I., de Chernatony, L., & Hem, L. E. (2009). Brand extension strategies: Perceived fit, brand type, and culture influences. *European Journal of Marketing*, *43*(11/12), 1300–1324. doi:10.1108/03090560910989902

Byrne, B. M. (2001). *Structural Equation Modeling With AMOS: Basic Concepts, Applications, and Programming*. Taylor & Francis.

Campbell, K. (1993). Researching brands. *Service Industries Journal*, *29*(12), 1687–1706.

Carroll, B. A., & Ahuvia, A. (2006). Some antecedents and outcomes of brand love. *Marketing Letters*, *7*(2), 79–89. doi:10.100711002-006-4219-2

Chahal, H., & Rani, A. (2017). How trust moderates social media engagement and brand equity. *Journal of Research in Interactive Marketing*, *11*(3), 312–335. doi:10.1108/JRIM-10-2016-0104

Chang, Y., Ko, Y. J., Tasci, A., Arai, A., & Kim, T. (2014). Strategic match of athlete endorsement in global markets: An associative learning perspective. *International Journal of Sports Marketing & Sponsorship*, *15*(4), 40–58. doi:10.1108/IJSMS-15-04-2014-B005

Chau, M., & Xu, J. (2012). Business intelligence in blogs: Understanding consumer interactions and communities. *Management Information Systems Quarterly*, *36*(4), 1189–1216. doi:10.2307/41703504

Chen, A. C.-H., & Chen, S. K. (2000). Brand dilution effect of extension failure: A Taiwan study. *Journal of Product and Brand Management*, *9*(4), 243–254. doi:10.1108/10610420010344031

Chen, H., Chiang, R. H. L., & Storey, V. C. (2012). Business intelligence and analytics: From big data to big impact. *Management Information Systems Quarterly*, *36*(4), 1165–1188. doi:10.2307/41703503

Choudhury, M. M., & Harrigan, P. (2014). CRM to social CRM: The integration of new technologies into customer relationship management. *Journal of Strategic Marketing*, *22*(2), 149–176. doi:10.1080/0965254X.2013.876069

Cleff, T., Lin, I. C., & Walter, N. (2014). Can You Feel It? The Effect of Brand Experience on Brand Equity. *IUP Journal of Brand Management, 11*(2).

Corkum, C., Lie, C. X., Crish, J., Jobb, D., & Adreew, J. (2021). Mobile Apps: Customer Engagement, Brand Equity, and Purchase Intention. *Review of Business, Accounting, & Finance*, *1*(2), 215–232.

Cristóvão, F. G. (2022). *Social media practices by human resources companies: how do they impact brand image and customer engagement?* (Doctoral dissertation).

Dens, N., & De Pelsmacker, P. (2010). Consumer response to different advertising appeals for new products: The moderating influence of branding strategy and product category involvement. *Journal of Brand Management*, *18*(1), 50–65. doi:10.1057/bm.2010.22

Dessart, L., Veloutsou, C., & Thomas, A. (2015). Consumer engagement in online brand communities: A social media perspective. *Journal of Product and Brand Management*, *24*(1), 28–42. doi:10.1108/JPBM-06-2014-0635

Dewnarain, S., Ramkissoon, H., & Mavondo, F. (2021). Social customer relationship management: A customer perspective. *Journal of Hospitality Marketing & Management*, *30*(6), 673–698. doi:10.1080/19368623.2021.1884162

Doorn, J. V., Katherine, N. L., Vikas, M., Stephan, N., Doreen, P., Peter, P., & Peter, C. V. (2010). Customer engagement behavior: Theoretical foundations and research directions. *Journal of Service Research*, *13*(3), 253–266. doi:10.1177/1094670510375599

Dwivedi, A. (2015). A higher-order model of consumer brand engagement and its impact on loyalty intentions. *Journal of Retailing and Consumer Services*, *24*, 100–109. doi:10.1016/j.jretconser.2015.02.007

Dwivedi, A., Merrilees, B., & Sweeney, A. (2010). Brand extension feedback effects: A holistic framework. *Journal of Brand Management*, *17*(5), 328–342. doi:10.1057/bm.2009.26

Ebrahim, R. S. (2020). The role of trust in understanding the impact of social media marketing on brand equity and brand loyalty. *Journal of Relationship Marketing*, *19*(4), 287–308. doi:10.1080/15332667.2019.1705742

Erciş, A., Ünal, S., Candan, F. B., & Yıldırım, H. (2012). The effect of brand satisfaction, trust and brand commitment on loyalty and repurchase intentions. *Procedia: Social and Behavioral Sciences*, *58*, 1395–1404. doi:10.1016/j.sbspro.2012.09.1124

Farquhar, P. H. (1989). Managing Brand Equity. *Marketing Research*, *1*(September), 24–33.

Fornell, C., & Larcker, D. G. (1981). Evaluating structural equation models with unobservable variables and measurement error. *JMR, Journal of Marketing Research*, *18*(1), 39–50. doi:10.1177/002224378101800104

Fournier, S. (1998). Consumers and their brands: Developing relationship theory in consumer research. *The Journal of Consumer Research*, *24*(4), 343–373. doi:10.1086/209515

France, C., Merrilees, B., & Miller, D. (2015). Customer brand co-creation: A conceptual model. *Marketing Intelligence & Planning*, *33*(6), 848–864. doi:10.1108/MIP-06-2014-0105

Gambetti, R. C., & Graffigna, G. (2010). The concept of engagement: A systematic analysis of the ongoing marketing debate. *International Journal of Market Research*, *52*(6), 801–826. doi:10.2501/S147078531020166

Gardner, B. B., & Levy, S. J. (1955). The product and the brand. *Harvard Business Review*, *33*(2), 33–39.

Gómez-Suárez, M., Benito, L. E. A., & Campo, S. (2016). Exploring the link between brand love and engagement through a qualitative approach. *International Journal of Business Environment*, *8*(4), 367–384. doi:10.1504/IJBE.2016.080882

Greenberg, P. (2010). The impact of CRM 2.0 on customer insight. *Journal of Business and Industrial Marketing*, *25*(6), 410–419. doi:10.1108/08858621011066008

Hair, J., Tatham, R., Anderson, R., & Black, W. (1998). *Multivariate Data Analysis* (5th ed.). Prentice Hall.

Hair, J.F., Anderson, R.E., Babin, B.J., & Black, W.C. (2010).*Multivariate data analysis: A global perspective* (Vol. 7). Academic Press.

Hair, J. F., Anderson, R. E., Tatham, R. L., & Black, W. C. (2013). *Multivariate data analysis* (9th ed.). Prentice-Hall.

Hansen, N., Kupfer, A. K., & Hennig-Thurau, T. (2018). Brand crises in the digital age: The short-and long-term effects of social media firestorms on consumers and brands. *International Journal of Research in Marketing*, *35*(4), 557–574. doi:10.1016/j.ijresmar.2018.08.001

Harrigan, P., & Miles, M. (2014). From e-CRM to s-CRM. Critical factors underpinning the social CRM activities of SMEs. *Small Enterprise Research*, *21*(1), 99–116. doi:10.1080/13215906.2014.11082079

Heine, K. (2010). The personality of luxury fashion brands. *Journal of Global Fashion Marketing*, *1*(3), 154–163. doi:10.1080/20932685.2010.10593067

Hem, L., Chernatony, L. D., & Iversen, N. M. (2003). Factors influencing successful brand extensions. *Journal of Marketing Management*, *19*(7/8), 781–806. doi:10.1080/0267257X.2003.9728237

Hennig-Thurau, T., Malthouse, E. C., Friege, C., Gensler, S., Lobschat, L., Rangaswamy, A., & Skiera, B. (2010). The impact of new media on customer relationships. *Journal of Service*.

Hepola, J., Karjaluoto, H., & Hintikka, A. (2017). The effect of sensory brand experience and involvement on brand equity directly and indirectly through consumer brand engagement. *Journal of Product and Brand Management*, *26*(3), 282–293. doi:10.1108/JPBM-10-2016-1348

Hollebeek, L. D. (2011a). Demystifying customer brand engagement: Exploring the loyalty nexus. *Journal of Marketing Management*, *27*(7-8), 785–807. doi:10.1080/0267257X.2010.500132

Hollebeek, L. D. (2011b). Exploring customer brand engagement: Definition and themes. *Journal of Strategic Marketing*, *19*(7), 555–573. doi:10.1080/0965254X.2011.599493

Holmes-Smith, P. (2001). Introduction to structural equation modeling using LISREL. ACSPRI-Winter training program, Perth.

Hossain, M. S., Anthony, J. F., Beg, M. N. A., & Zayed, N. M. (2020). Affirmative Strategic Association of Brand Image, Brand Loyalty and Brand Equity: A Conclusive Perceptual Confirmation of the Top Management. Academy of Strategic Management Journal, 19(2).

Islam, J., & Rahman, Z. (2016). The transpiring journey of customer engagement research in marketing: A systematic review of the past decade. *Management Decision*, *54*(8), 2008–2034. doi:10.1108/MD-01-2016-0028

Islam, J. U., & Rahman, Z. (2016). Examining the effects of brand love and brand image on customer engagement: An empirical study of fashion apparel brands. *Journal of Global Fashion Marketing, 7*(1), 45-59. doi:10.1080/20932685.2015.1110041

Ismail, A. R. (2017). The influence of perceived social media marketing activities on brand loyalty. *Asia Pacific Journal of Marketing and Logistics, 29*(1), 129–144. doi:10.1108/APJML-10-2015-0154

Jaiprakash, A. T. (2008). A conceptual research on the association between celebrity endorsement, brand image and brand equity. *Icfai Univ J Mark Manag, 7*(4), 54–64.

Jayaram, J., Kannan, V. R., & Tan, K. C. (2004). Influence of initiators on supply chain value creation. *International Journal of Production Research, 42*(20), 4377–4399. doi:10.1080/00207540410001716516

Jiménez-Castillo, D., & Sánchez-Fernández, R. (2019). The role of digital influencers in brand recommendation: Examining their impact on engagement, expected value and purchase intention. *International Journal of Information Management, 49*, 366–376. doi:10.1016/j.ijinfomgt.2019.07.009

Junaid, M., Hou, F., Hussain, K., & Kirmani, A. A. (2019). Brand love: The emotional bridge between experience and engagement, generation-M perspective. *Journal of Product and Brand Management, 28*(2), 200–215. doi:10.1108/JPBM-04-2018-1852

Ke, X., & Wagner, C. (2022). Global pandemic compels sport to move to esports: Understanding from brand extension perspective. *Managing Sport and Leisure, 27*(1-2), 152–157. doi:10.1080/23750472.2020.1792801

Keller, K. L. (1993). Conceptualizing, measuring, and managing customer-based brand equity. *Journal of Marketing, 57*(1), 1–22. doi:10.1177/002224299305700101

Kenett, Y., & Thompson-Schill, S. L. (2020). *Novel conceptual combination can dynamically reconfigure semantic memory networks*. Academic Press.

Khan, I., & Rahman, Z. (2015). Brand experience anatomy in retailing: An interpretive structural modeling approach. *Journal of Retailing and Consumer Services, 24*, 60–69. doi:10.1016/j.jretconser.2015.02.003

Kim, A. J., & Ko, E. (2012). Do social media marketing activities enhance customer equity? An empirical study of luxury fashion brand. *Journal of Business Research, 65*(10), 1480–1486. doi:10.1016/j.jbusres.2011.10.014

Kim, J. Y. (2003). Communication message strategies for brand extensions. *Journal of Product and Brand Management.*

Knoerzer, K., & Millemann, J. A. (2021). Investigating determinants of brand extension success in a fit and a non-fit scenario. *International Journal of Technology Marketing*, *15*(4), 379–398. doi:10.1504/IJTMKT.2021.119073

Koay, K. Y., Ong, D. L. T., Khoo, K. L., & Yeoh, H. J. (2020). Perceived social media marketing activities and consumer-based brand equity: Testing a moderated mediation model. *Asia Pacific Journal of Marketing and Logistics*, *33*(1), 53–72. doi:10.1108/APJML-07-2019-0453

Kubina, M., & Lendel, V. (2015). Successful Application of Social CRM in The Company. *Procedia Economics and Finance*, *23*, 1190–1194. doi:10.1016/S2212-5671(15)00487-6

Kumaravel, V., & Kandasamy, C. (2012). To what extent the brand image influence consumers' purchase decision on durable products. *Rom J Mark*, *1*, 34–38.

Kuvykaite, R., & Piligrimiene, Z. (2014). Consumer engagement into brand equity creation. *Procedia: Social and Behavioral Sciences*, *156*, 479–483. doi:10.1016/j.sbspro.2014.11.225

Lakshmi, S. M., & Suresh, M. (2021). Modelling of factors influencing brand commitment of FMCG products: A TISM approach. *Materials Today: Proceedings*.

Langner, T., Schmidt, J., & Fischer, A. (2015). Is it really love? A comparative investigation of the emotional nature of Brand and interpersonal love. *Psychology & Marketing, 32*(6), 624-634.

Lee, C. T., & Hsieh, S. H. (2022). Can social media-based brand communities build brand relationships? Examining the effect of community engagement on brand love. *Behaviour & Information Technology*, *41*(6), 1270–1285. doi:10.1080/0144929X.2021.1872704

Lee, J., & Park, C. (2022a). Customer engagement on social media, brand equity and financial performance: A comparison of the US and Korea. *Asia Pacific Journal of Marketing and Logistics*, *34*(3), 454–474. doi:10.1108/APJML-09-2020-0689

Lee, J., & Park, C. (2022b). Social media content, customer engagement and brand equity: US versus Korea. *Management Decision*.

Lee, J., & Yoon, E. (2022). Effects of Parent Brand Equity on Perceived Fit and Customer Behavior of Extended Brand—Focused on MICE Destination. *International Journal of Environmental Research and Public Health*, *19*(8), 4540. doi:10.3390/ijerph19084540 PMID:35457408

Lim, J. S., Pham, P., & Heinrichs, J. H. (2020). Impact of social media activity outcomes on brand equity. *Journal of Product and Brand Management, 29*(7), 927–937. doi:10.1108/JPBM-03-2019-2298

Lohanda, T., & Berto, A. R. (2022). Can Social Customer Relationship Management Activities Evoke Customer Loyalty?. *Jurnal Studi Komunikasi dan Media, 25*(2), 267-276.

Loureiro, S. M. C., Gorgus, T., & Kaufmann, H. R. (2017). Antecedents and outcomes of online Brand engagement. *Online Information Review, 41*(7), 985–1005. doi:10.1108/OIR-08-2016-0236

Martin, G. S., & Brown, T. J. (1990). In search of brand equity: The conceptualization and measurement of the brand impression construct. *Mark Theory Appl, 2*, 431–438.

Martínez, E., & de Chernatony, L. (2004). The effect of brand extension strategies upon brand image. *Journal of Consumer Marketing, 21*(1), 39–50. doi:10.1108/07363760410513950

Martínez, E., Montaner, T., & Pina, J. M. (2009). Brand extension feedback: The role of advertising. *Journal of Business Research, 62*(3), 305–313. doi:10.1016/j.jbusres.2008.05.009

Masa'deh, R. E., AL-Haddad, S., Al Abed, D., Khalil, H., AlMomani, L., & Khirfan, T. (2021). The Impact of Social Media Activities on Brand Equity. *Information (Basel), 12*(11), 477. doi:10.3390/info12110477

Menidjel, C., Benhabib, A., & Bilgihan, A. (2017). Examining the moderating role of personality traits in the relationship between brand trust and brand loyalty. *Journal of Product and Brand Management, 26*(6), 631–649. doi:10.1108/JPBM-05-2016-1163

Milewicz, J., & Herbig, P. (1994). Evaluating the brand extension decision using a model of reputation building. *Journal of Product and Brand Management, 3*(1), 39–47. doi:10.1108/10610429410053077

Moolla, A. I., & Bisschoff, C. A. (2013). An empirical model that measures brand loyalty of fast-moving consumer goods. *Journal of Economics, 4*(1), 1–9. doi:10.1080/09765239.2013.11884959

Muthu Lakshmi, S. T., & Suresh, M. (2021). Modelling of factors influencing brand commitment of FMCG products: A TISM approach. *Materials Today: Proceedings*. Advance online publication. doi:10.1016/j.matpr.2021.01.835

Newberry, C. (2019). *1301 Social media statistics that matter to marketers in 2019*. Available at: https://blog.hootsuite.com/social-media-statistics-for-social-media-managers /#general

Nierobisch, T., Toporowski, W., Dannewald, T., & Jahn, S. (2017). Flagship stores for FMCG national brands: Do they improve brand cognitions and create favorable consumer reactions? *Journal of Retailing and Consumer Services*, *34*, 117–137. doi:10.1016/j.jretconser.2016.09.014

O'Cass, A., & Weerawardena, J. (2009). Examining the role of international entrepreneurship, innovation and international market performance in SME internationalisation. *European Journal of Marketing*, *43*(11/12), 1325–1348. doi:10.1108/03090560910989911

Pagani, M., & Mirabello, A. (2012). The influence of personal and social-interactive engagement in social TV web sites. *International Journal of Electronic Commerce*, *16*(2), 41–67. doi:10.2753/JEC1086-4415160203

Pansari, A., & Kumar, V. (2017). Customer engagement: The construct, antecedents and consequences. *Journal of the Academy of Marketing Science*, *45*(3), 294–311. doi:10.100711747-016-0485-6

Park, C. W., Milberg, S., & Lawson, R. (1991). Evaluation of brand extensions: The role of product feature similarity and brand concept consistency. *The Journal of Consumer Research*, *18*(2), 185–193. doi:10.1086/209251

Phan, M., Thomas, R., & Heine, K. (2011). Social Media and Luxury Brand Management: The Case of Burberry. *Journal of Global Fashion Marketing*, *2*(4), 213–222. doi:10.1080/20932685.2011.10593099

Pine, B. J., & Gilmore, J. H. (1998). *Welcome to the experience economy*. Academic Press.

Prentice, C., Wang, X., & Loureiro, S. M. C. (2019). The influence of brand experience and service quality on customer engagement. *Journal of Retailing and Consumer Services*, *50*, 50–59. doi:10.1016/j.jretconser.2019.04.020

Rasool, A., Shah, F. A., & Tanveer, M. (2021). Relational dynamics between customer engagement, brand experience, and customer loyalty: An empirical investigation. *Journal of Internet Commerce*, *20*(3), 273–292. doi:10.1080/15332861.2021.1889818

Reichheld, F. F., & Schefter, P. (2000). E-loyalty: Your secret weapon on the web. *Harvard Business Review*, *78*(4), 105–113.

Roberts, K. (2005). *Lovemarks: The Future beyond Brands*. Powerhouse Books.

Saqib, N., & Shah, A. M. (2021). Development of empirically-based customer-derived positioning taxonomy for FMCG sector in the Indian emerging market. *Young Consumers*.

Schivinski, B., & Dabrowski, D. (2014). *The consumer-based brand equity inventory: scale construct and validation* (No. 4/2014 (22)). GUT FME Working Paper Series A.

Schlegelmilch, B. B. (2022). Global branding and communication. In *Global Marketing Strategy* (pp. 253–288). Springer.

Seo, E. J., & Park, J. W. (2018). A study on the effects of social media marketing activities on brand equity and customer response in the airline industry. *Journal of Air Transport Management*, *66*, 36–41.

Sharma, R. (2016). Effect of celebrity endorsements on dimensions of customer-based brand equity: Empirical evidence from Indian luxury market. *Journal of Creative Communications*, *11*(3), 264–281.

Shimp, T. A., & Madden, T. J. (1988). Consumer-Object relations: A conceptual framework based analogously on Sternberg's triangular theory of love. *Advances in Consumer Research. Association for Consumer Research (U. S.)*, *15*, 163–168.

Smith, D. C., & Park, C. W. (1992). The effects of brand extensions on market share and advertising efficiency. *JMR, Journal of Marketing Research*, *29*(3), 296–313.

Smith, G. (2004). Brand image transfer through sponsorship: A consumer learning perspective. *Journal of Marketing Management*, *20*(3–4), 457–474.

Sohail, M. S. (2022). Understanding consumer engagement in online brand communities: An application of self-expansion theory. *Journal of Marketing Analytics*, 1-13.

Springen, K., & Miller, A. (1990, July 9). Sequels for the Shelf. *Newsweek*, 42-43.

Srull, T. K., & Wyer, R. S. (1989). Person memory and judgment. *Psychological Review*, *96*(1), 58–83.

Swaminathan, V., Fox, R. J., & Reddy, S. K. (2001). The impact of brand extension introduction on choice. *Journal of Marketing*, *65*(4), 1–15.

Tafesse, W. (2016). An experiential model of consumer engagement in social media. *Journal of Product & Brand Management*, *25*(5), 424-434.

Tanner, J., & Raymond, M. (2015). *Principles of marketing*. University of Minnesota Libraries Publishing. Retrieved from http://lib.hpu.edu.vn/handle/123456789/21516

Tasci, A. D. A., Khalilzadeh, J., & Uysal, M. (2017). Network analysis of the caucasus' image. *Curr. Issues Tour.*, 1–26. doi:10.1080/13683500.2017.1320362

Tatham, R. L., Anderson, R. E., & Black, B. (2006). *Multivariate Data Analysis*. Academic Internet Publisher.

Taylor, V. A., & Bearden, W. O. (2003). Ad spending on brand extensions: Does similarity matter? *Journal of Brand Management, 11*(1), 63–74.

Thompson, B. (2004). Exploratory and confirmatory factor analysis: Understanding concepts and applications. Academic Press.

Thomson, M., MacInnis, D.J., & Whan Park, C. (2005). The ties that bind: Measuring the strength of consumers' emotional attachments to brands. *Journal of Consumer Psychology, 15*(1), 77-91.

Van Riel, A. C., Lemmink, J., & Ouwersloot, H. (2001). Consumer evaluations of service brand extensions. *Journal of Service Research, 3*(3), 220–231.

Venkatesha, G. K. (2021). Trend forming FMCG sector in India-a study. *International Journal of Multidisciplinary Educational Research, 11*(3), 81-87.

Verhoef, P., Reinartz, W., & Krafft, M. (2010). Customer engagement as a new perspective in customer management. *Journal of Service Research, 13*(3), 247–252.

Vivek, S. D., Beatty, S. E., Dalela, V., & Morgan, R. (2014). A generalized multidimensional scale for measuring customer engagement. *Journal of Marketing Theory and Practice, 22*, 401–420. doi:10.2753/MTP1069-6679220404

Vivek, S. D., Beatty, S. E., & Morgan, R. (2012). Customer engagement: Exploring customer relationships beyond purchase. *Journal of Marketing Theory and Practice, 20*, 122–146. doi:10.2753/ MTP1069-6679200201

Volckner, F., & Sattler, H. (2006). Drivers of brand extension success. *Journal of Marketing, 70*(April), 18–34.

Volckner, F., & Sattler, H. (2007). Empirical generalizability of consumer evaluations of brand extensions. *International Journal of Research in Marketing, 24*, 149–162.

Volckner, F., Sattler, H., & Kaufmann, G. (2008). Image feedback effects of brand extensions: Evidence from a longitudinal field study. *Marketing Letters, 19*(2), 109–124.

Wang, H.-J., & Horng, S.-C. (2016). Exploring green brand associations through a network analysis approach. *Psychology and Marketing, 33*(1), 20–35. https://dx.doi.org/10.1002/mar.20854

Warfield, B. (2009). *Webinar conducted by Bob Warfield, CEO of Helpstream A Social CRM Manifesto: How to Succeed with the CRM Virtuous Cycle*. Academic Press.

Weiss, A. M., Anderson, E., & Maclnnis, D. J. (1999). Reputation management as a motivation for sales structure decisions. *Journal of Marketing*, *63*, 74–89.

Yang, S., Lin, S., Carlson, J. R., & Ross, W. T. Jr. (2016). Brand engagement on social media: Will firms' social media efforts influence search engine advertising effectiveness? *Journal of Marketing Management*, *32*(5-6), 526–557.

Yaya, L. H. P., Marimon, F., & Casadesus, M. (2016). Customer Satisfaction and the Role of Demographic Characteristics in Online Banking. In *Web-Based Services: Concepts, Methodologies, Tools and Applications* (pp. 1786–1802). IGI Global.

Yoo, B., & Donthu, N. (2001). Developing and validating a multidimensional consumer-based brand equity scale. *Journal of Business Research*, *52*(1), 1–14.

Zimmer, M. R., & Bhat, S. (2004). The reciprocal effects of extension quality and fit on parent brand attitude. *Journal of Product and Brand Management*, *13*(1), 37–46.

Zollo, L., Filieri, R., Rialti, R., & Yoon, S. (2020). Unpacking the relationship between social media marketing and brand equity: The mediating role of consumers' benefits and experience. *Journal of Business Research*, *117*, 256–267.

ADDITIONAL READING

Choudhury, M. M., & Harrigan, P. (2014). CRM to social CRM: The integration of new technologies into customer relationship management. *Journal of Strategic Marketing*, *22*(2), 149–176. doi:10.1080/0965254X.2013.876069

Choudhury, M. M., & Harrigan, P. (2014). CRM to social CRM: The integration of new technologies into customer relationship management. *Journal of Strategic Marketing*, *22*(2), 149–176. doi:10.1080/0965254X.2013.876069

Islam, J. U., & Rahman, Z. (2016). Examining the effects of brand love and brand image on customer engagement: An empirical study of fashion apparel brands. *Journal of Global Fashion Marketing*, *7*(1), 45–59. doi:10.1080/20932685.2015.1110041

Junaid, M., Hou, F., Hussain, K., & Kirmani, A. A. (2019). Brand love: The emotional bridge between experience and engagement, generation-M perspective. *Journal of Product and Brand Management*, *28*(2), 200–215. doi:10.1108/JPBM-04-2018-1852

Keller, K. L. (2008). *Strategic brand management: Building, measuring, and managing brand equity*. Pearson/Prentice Hall.

Pansari, A., & Kumar, V. (2017). Customer engagement: The construct, antecedents and consequences. *Journal of the Academy of Marketing Science*, *45*(3), 294–311. doi:10.100711747-016-0485-6

KEY TERMS AND DEFINITIONS

Brand Equity: Brand equity is the level a brand is assumed by the customers to be competent to meet consumer expectations in the category the brand competes.

Brand Experience: The term has been defined as the sensations, cognitions and feelings grown by a customer in response to the stimulus aroused by a brand exhibited in brand identity, packaging, atmospherics and interaction done by the brand.

Brand Image: Brand Image can be defined as the combination of customer's discernments and persuasions regarding the brand.

Brand Love: It is customers feeling of attachment and achieving union with a product, person, or place.

Customer Engagement: A customer's Optimistic associations created by the brand in cognitive, emotional, and behavioural ways.

Perceived Fit: The extent to which customers found similarity of the extension with the other product based on its use in particular situation and the need it satisfies among consumers is termed as perceived fit.

Social CRM: Social CRM are dynamic capabilities of digital technologies which provide opportunity to interact with customers in real time and also have ability to collect massive clientele's data.

Chapter 10
Application of MIS in E-CRM:
A Literature Review in FMCG Supply Chain

Aysha Abdulla
Ibn Rushd College for Management Sciences, Saudi Arabia

ABSTRACT

The proliferating demands of consumers today have sparked the need for ECRM, leveraging the technological advancements in MIS and its applications. This chapter elaborates tracking and maintaining ECRM by means of big data analytics tools and artificial intelligence algorithms. It elucidates the predictions and forecasts a business makes based on consumer behaviour. The chapter further delves into the various avenues of artificial intelligence (AI). The taxonomy of AI is explained, and its decision making capability is applied to design and simulate effective SCM systems. Various AI methods are holistically applied to the FMCG supply chain context. In this chapter, the role of big data analytics in aiding the enterprises to maintain ECRM by studying consumer preferences and choices is explored, further advancing into its applications in maintaining FMCG supply chain. This research report provides the various methods of AI used in supply chain and the data analytics tools employed in maintaining ECRM and the FMCG supply chain.

INTRODUCTION

CRM is a widely used acronym that employs long term conducive relations with the customers in order to drive lucrative business value. The avalanche of technological advancement has revolutionized the business models with unprecedented CRM

DOI: 10.4018/978-1-6684-5386-5.ch010

implementations. CRM has thus evolved into ECRM in the recent decades to lure and retain complacent customers through various electronic means. Increased access to customer data via online resources such as social network platforms, various search engines and the creation and storing of cookies facilitate ECRM practices by accumulating swathes of data. Substantial developments in the fields of AI and ML are intricately related to ECRM optimization as they are used to model the various aspects of ECRM. ML models provide a myriad of benefits, by automating the process of purchasing commodities. This means of buying is enhanced further by elucidating the inevitable customer's predisposition into future investments. On the contrary, these models are also effective in avoiding any appalling confrontations the business has to face by predicting the predisposition of a customer to cease to avail its services. An affluent database of customers affirms a thriving business. ECRM paves the path to effective interaction and a better customer experience leading to intelligent ways of developing and sustaining customer ties. Therefore it vividly implies that enterprises with ECRM automation has sustainable customer retention. Several factors like stringent competition in the market, advancements in IT globalization and accelerating customer expectations have revamped the organizations. Thus, there is tremendous competition among enterprises and their supply chains. An agile supply chain requires a mammoth of data to be handled. This explosion in the volume of data has caused the development of various big data analytic technologies that can intelligently analyze large volume of data, which is the dire need of the situation.

This chapter begins with applications of AI in ECRM, the second section discusses Big Data analytics and its alliance to ECRM. It further delves into illustrating the versatility of AI technologies in agile FMCG supply chain. The subsequent section explains the concept of Big Data and its use in defining the current FMCG supply chain trends. Finally, it concludes with recommendations for future research.

LITERATURE REVIEW

AI in ECRM

AI is the technology by which machines can emulate human intelligence and all the endeavours.AI has come a long way evolving through various phases. It has ML models implementing algorithms that learn from diverse sources, take decisions and act beyond human contemplation. It would transform human lives to a degree surpassing technologies in transportation and electricity that have enriched our lives. Braun & Garriga (2018) have proposed that ML models in CRM are beyond statistical computations and implements machine learning. Chen & Popovich

(2003) argue that a large part of contemporary CRM requires the implementation of technology. In addition, Technological revolution has changed the relationships companies have with clients (Winer, 2001). The most significant aspect of this is increased interaction and improved customized experience for the customer, such that companies now have a better ability to establish, nurture, and sustain long-term customer relationships than ever before (Winer 2001; Blázquez, 2014; Parise et al., 2016; Soudagar et al., 2012).

The versatile AI tools in ECRM are deployed in the marketing processes to perform core analysis tasks such as, creating reports and other administrative duties. These tools can harness chatbots to interpret the success factors and guide the sales team to meet sales targets. These chatbots furnish insights that aid in accelerating the sales process. Another significant application of AI is found in sentiment analysis tools that analyze customer emotions during their communication with salespersons. This helps the enterprises build trust with them and avoid any breach of trust as most of the customers hesitate to confide in their vendors. AI tools can analyze customer conversations and examine emotional states using sentiment analysis tools. This in turn helps the vendors respond to the customers in the most convincing way, incrementing their revenue per customer by ten percent.

Natural Language Processing (NLP) is inextricably linked to ECRM tools to automate emails and reports. For instance, Wordsmith developed by automated insights, can be integrated in ECRM tools to automate employee emails.AI enabled ECRM tools also expands its application in sales forecasts. It can study the propensity of a customer in purchasing and allows valuable sales predictions. It also provides insights on customer sales data by analyzing his web activities, geographic and demographic data.

Customer churn is a concrete factor in determining the revenue for a company, a process by which a customer ceases to be with the company.AI tools can significantly aid in analyzing specific patterns in customer data to evaluate the causes for customer churn. Consequently, enterprises can resort to corrective measures to scale down customer churn.

Further to this cause, data in ECRM systems can be used to make effective decisions using AI integrated ECRM systems. These systems can detect potential issues, delete duplicate data, seek incomplete data in other systems and provide suggestions to update old data. AI powered CRM tools yield increased sales. They provide valuable insights for companies to understand their customers and develop new strategies that can increase sales margin. Improved customer satisfaction and loyalty is achieved by analyzing patterns in customer data using ECRM tools that help in understanding customers better. The business, in turn benefits from a higher profit margin. The leading global vendors that are intertwined with AI technologies are Adobe Sense, IBM Watson, Microsoft Cognitive services and dynamics, Oracle

AI, Salesforce Einstein and SAP Leonardo. Thus, AI is effective in automating CRM and raising the value curve for both the business and the customers.

Big Data Analytics And ECRM

Ngai et al. (2009) identify four major CRM dimensions where data analysis is required as follows.

1. Customer Identification: Awareness of the most likely prospective customers
2. Customer attraction: Seek marketing approaches one on one to customers, by sending emails or coupons.
3. Customer retention: Understand user satisfaction by studying online customer behavior and analyzing patterns in customer data.
4. Customer development: Predict future shopping behavior of customers by delving into historical data.

These are the major ECRM dimensions in which Big Data Analytics is leveraged to discover valuable insights about customers. Advancements in ECRM are greatly reliant on the description of the consumer profile, his interest, his prospective purchase and a range of other products and services that can be offered. The analysis of customer data and behaviors allows the discovery of new and valuable information from customers, Braun & Garriga (2018).The CRM database that has been designed since the inception of Banking and telecommunications have evolved with various analytical tools. For instance, Google Analytics according to Dubios (2015) is used by fifty percent of the companies. It analyses online customer behavior by tracking web browsing through storing cookies and other monitoring tools. Thus, businesses have magnanimous amount of customer data that needs to be intelligently extracted using BDA to find patterns in customer behavior that is intended to augment business revenue.

Applications of AI In FMCG Supply Chain

AI offers numerous benefits in business and FMCG supply chain. Time and cost savings targets can easily be met through AI applications. It is expected to scale down the investments in logistics by improving distribution channels and scheduling.

Fast moving consumer goods are commodities that have a high rate of sales and a relatively low price margin. They often refer to perishable goods that have a short shelf like edibles (dairy products, bakery items, fruits and vegetables, over the counter drugs etc.). FMCG are bought frequently and consumed in a short span. It has a huge demand with a very high sales volume. As result the market today, is magnanimous inundated with tough competition. Nestle, Procter and Gamble are some of the largest global FMCG companies. Nestle, for instance manufactures over 2000 products ranging from eatables to over -the- counter drugs. This industry competes hard to obtain a market share. Since the shelf life is short, packaging is an important factor in its production. The logistics and distribution in SCM need to emphasize on its packaging to maximize sales. FMCG results in large sales volume causing influx of revenue to the respective business. Thus, considering the aforementioned FMCG industry and its high volumes of sales, AI technology has a myriad of applications in its rigorous routing; from forecast, logistics, inventory management to the crux of enormous sales. It also aids in acquiring customer satisfaction and loyalty that drives the annual turnover of the business.

Businesses are widely incorporating AI solutions to achieve effective SCM for FMCG market. At its inception, the advent of decision support systems (fuzzy logic, expert systems, multi criteria methods and heuristic optimization) further developed into more sophisticated AI methods such as machine learning, deep learning and image/text processing that have versatile applications in FMCG supply chain industry today. Thus, this chapter paves the path for FMCG supply chain researchers, to gain insight into the scope of research of AI technologies in FMCG SCM. The AI methods used in the various SCM contexts elucidate future research on AI applications in SCM. Furthermore, the use of various AI applications in different SCM contexts is finely elaborated. We begin our journey into AI applications by tracing its classification as explained below.

Definition of AI and its Taxonomy

AI is a vast discipline in computer science that incorporates the development of devices that emulate human cognition to perform tasks. Mckinsey and company have estimated that the monetary gain through AI technologies is expected to reach by $13 trillion by 2030, contributing immensely to global economy. There are diverse views on the definition of AI by different scientists of the world. Since its advent in the early 60's this field has witnessed massive variations, from complete negligence to its acceleration that came to be known as Artificial Intelligence mania. Global leaders like Google, Amazon, IBM and Microsoft have made significant investments that have caused its novel growth.

Based on its application in a system AI can be broadly categorized into three groups, Sensing and interacting, Learning and Decision making. Sensing and interacting is done through text, audio and video (Ramos et al,2008) by means of speech, vision and Natural Language Processing (NLP) that constitute the first category of AI. The second category constitutes the AI methodologies that learn from data, this includes the ML methods such as deep learning (Al Jarrah et al,2015). The third

Table 1. AI Classification and its methods

AI Classification	AI Methods Used
• Sensing and interacting	• NLP: extraction, classification, Translation, Text and Q/A • Speech recognition: Speech to text, Text to speech • Vision: Image recognition and machine vision
• Learning	• Machine Learning: Supervised learning, unsupervised learning and Reinforcement learning
• Decision Making	• Expert Systems: Rule based, fuzzy based, Frame based and hybrid • Planning and scheduling • Optimization: Nature inspired, Knowledge based, market based, Game theory based and decision theory based • Simulation and Modelling

category comprises of applications and methods pertaining to decision making (Duan et al,2019, Pan et al, 2020, Soleimani et al 2018) this includes expert systems, planning, simulation and modelling, scheduling and optimization. This definition given by (Kaplan and Haenlein,2019) is also in consensus with a popular definition of AI as a system's capacity to "correctly interpret external data," "to learn from such data", and "to use those learnings to achieve specific goals and tasks". Table 1 summarizes the widely accepted AI taxonomy.

Sensing and interacting

This area of AI includes various modes of sensing and interacting with the surrounding environment. Natural Language processing (NLP) is a widely used application of AI that builds sophisticated AI systems. It executes tasks under the supervision of human instructions. The main features of NLP operations are text extraction, classification, translation, text generation and answering questions (Collabert et al., 2011; Manning et al., 1999) NLP has resulted in effective human system interactions (Zanon et al., 2020). According to Wichmann et al (2020), it can be used to create supply chain maps for improving supply chain structures resulting from unstructured data. This has a significant impact on FMCG supply chain agility. Cognitive defects are corrected using speech recognition methods and voice based applications (de Barcelos Slva et al., 2020; Graves et al., 2013) Speech recognition is the study of familiarizing words extracted from speech for translating into text and vice versa (Lu et al,2018; Ramos et al., 2008). Though speech recognition software was flawed at the beginning (Ricketts and Hornsby, 2005; Yang et al., 2018), it has witnessed significant improvements in the past decade (Ogawa and Hori, 2017). Exemplary flawless software like Google home, Amazon's transcribe, Microsoft's Alexa and Siri from Apple have recently emerged.

Image and video analytics is the predominant area of Artificial Intelligence, wherein computers can do the analysis and interpretation of data stored in visual sensors (Zhang et al., 2020).AI visuals are categorized into computer vision and image recognition. Image recognition is the process of finding and isolating an object or a feature in a digital image whereas, computer vision comprises the intelligent operations that enable a machine to capture, process and comprehend images to tackle a task. Recently, computer vision has found wide applications in the field of autonomous vehicles, interacting with the surrounding environment (Das et al., 2020).

Learning

Machine Learning (ML) is the development of algorithms that train from data obtained from solving previous problems (Priore et al., 2019).ML can be broadly classified into three main categories of supervised learning, unsupervised learning and reinforcement learning (Overgoor et al., 2019).Supervised learning is associated with algorithms that learn from a known dataset to get an output .Supervised learning models range from decision tree models, linear regression, support vector machines and neural networks (Cui et al,2018;Friedman et al, 2001).The machine determines patterns without any predefined data in unsupervised learning. Unsupervised learning is commonly used to identify similarities in clusters (Sharma et al., 2020). In reinforcement learning, the machine receives a feedback, after completing the task. The feedback process facilitates the process of performance improvement by undergoing several trial and attempts (Mnih et al., 2015). Classification and regression problems are the prime area of supervised learning, whereas clustering and reward based problems are related to unsupervised learning (Guillaumin et al., 2010; Ponulak and Kasinski, 2010).Other ML methods such as deep learning method embodies the features of all the three types of ML methods (LeCun et al., 2015). Since Big Data forms the integral part of business processes today, the application of ML has gained tremendous popularity (Hazen et al., 2014).The mammoth of data received via the supply chain networks can be efficiently processed with the application of various ML models.

Decision making

Supply chain decision making implements AI applications that are broadly categorized into optimization, expert systems, planning and scheduling and simulation and modelling. The application of optimization methods to solve problems had its inception in the early 60's. However, these methods addressed sophisticated and complex problems in this century employing gigantic data sets (Abbasi et al., 2020; Allam and Dhunny,2019; Dey et al., 2018; Fischetti and Fraccaro, 2019; Jiang et al.,2016). Optimization techniques are categorized into nature inspired (ant colony optimization), game theory based (cooperative models), market based (negotiation and auction algorithms), decision based (Bayesian methods) and knowledge based methods. These varied techniques have proved its implications in solving a range of problems related to supply chain optimization and operations. (Diabat and Deskoores, 2016; Melo et al., 2009; Saghei et al., 2020)

Another popular domain of AI is Expert systems which is also known as Knowledge based systems. It constitutes a variety of methods and approaches designed to achieve human excellence in systems (Giarratano and Riley, 1998 & Tecuci, 2012). The units of operations of Expert systems (Kusiak and Chen, 2008) are outlined as,

1. **Knowledge acquisition:** It is the process by which a system acquires knowledge to solve a problem.
2. **Interface engine:** It is used for control strategy
3. **Knowledge reorientation:** It is used to organize knowledge in data frames. Examples include rule based, fuzzy, frame based and hybrid frames that is a combination of more than one type (Zarbakshnia et al., 2018)

Expert System is effectively implemented in areas where human intelligence can be structured formally finding its way to solve cognitive issues (Jakupovic et al., 2014). Recently, AI methods for simulation and modelling have been widely deployed (Chen et al 2008). It aids in rigorous scenario_analysis facilitating decision making by effectively analyzing the behavior of the system (Bennett and Hauser, 2013 & Moayedikia et al., 2020). A commonly used modelling method is agent based computing technique that is widely used to model the dependencies between system components that match real world scenarios (Abar et al., 2017; Rolon and Martinez, 2012).

Planning and scheduling executed using AI methods help in making smart decisions conforming to a set of conditions (Bartak et al., 2010). Planning implies the decisions taken pertaining to the optimal flow of the sequence of activities, whereas scheduling relates to the allocation of tasks to resources (Kreipl and Pinedo, 2004). The recent developments in AI technologies have enabled the managers to take informed decisions based on predictions about any disruption in the normal functioning of a system. Various articles in Scopus have been explored, to study the application of certain AI techniques in various supply chain concepts and also related to particular supply chain fields where various Artificial techniques were implemented.

Simulation and System Dynamics

Simulation methods are used to seek solutions to issues concerned with supply chain design, planning and scheduling. Supply chain network is simulated using an object oriented framework by researchers (Van Der Zee and Van Der Vorst,2005) This framework provides improved decision making thus designing an improved supply chain network. Another researcher Holweg et al. (2005) simulates a multitier supply chain model by changing the key factors in scheduling to compute the improvement in supply chain effectiveness. According to a recent research, Der Zee (2011) concluded that certain vision based simulation models like Petri Nets are not easily comprehensible, hence proposing a structured model that is easily perceptible. This model is simulated according to a domain related reference architecture.

System dynamics models are integrated with discrete event simulator in order to study the impact of customer centricity on improved supply chain networks (Reiner, 2005). The delivery of the business can be improved tremendously by integrating discrete event simulation, that yields a vivid picture of supply chain performance. System dynamics gives a human interface to discrete event simulator (Greasley, 2005). Simulation and system dynamics model the systems differences. Discrete event simulation processes pertain to model coding, verification and validation. However, system dynamics modelers relate to conceptual models. Both, together, aid in better decision making in supply chain models.

Genetic algorithm and agent- based modelling are the major concepts applied in supply chain forecasting and optimizing issues. A combination of GA and a program is used to solve a problem of reverse logistics with product returns (Min et al, 2006). This model is applied to a problem that resulted in products for validity and feasibility testing. There is a 2 tier supply chain model developed using economic order quantity (EOQ)-in which the supplier delivers the order according to (R, Q) rule (Pasandideh et al., 2011). It is a non-linear program framework.GA is computed to find the maximum orders to minimize the total inventory costs.

Agent based modelling is another field of research for supply chain optimization and forecasting. An agent based model is designed for improved routing in the supply chain, that combines a construction and a multi attribute negotiation model into a multi agent model (Xue et al., 2005; Liang and Huang., 2006). A supply chain is simulated using a multi agent system with 3 types of demand inventory systems (periodic review, continuous review and optimal systems) in order to mitigate the total costs to a minimum. Agent based systems reduce the total supply chain cost and uniform ordering curves.

Stochastic programming

A stochastic non- linear programming model minimizes cost of production, inventory and labor in a FMCG supply chain model production planning problems at multiple sites. Leung et al. (2007) and You et al. (2009) investigates risk management for production planning of a multinational and supply chain. It uses a two step stochastic linear program to design a planning model considering customer service, production, inventory, transportation modes and schedules of shipments. After comparing it with a deterministic model, it is concluded that it yields 5% more saving. Furthermore, ROI is calculated on a supply chain network and the problems related to it are addressed. It is formulated as a multi-stage stochastic programming model, considering demand and interest rates as uncertain and scenario trees are built for the planning aspect to obtain maximum gain (Nickel et al., 2012). This fortifies the entire FMCG supply chain model from its inception to the end.

Learning

Using Time series analysis, an adaptive method is explored to determine reliable accuracy in forecast compared to fixed parameter (Gardner, 2006).By examining 60,000 forecast data collected from four supply chain companies, it has been found that larger adjustments in forecasts results in greater accuracy, while smaller adjustments hamper accuracy (Fildes et al, 2009).It was also revealed that there was no significant impact on accuracy via positive adjustments compared to negative adjustments. This primarily benefits the demand forecasting aspect of a business supply chain model thus accelerating FMCG to global market.

Table 2. Summarizes the frequency of AI methods deployed in various supply chain contexts.

Big Data in FMCG Supply Chain

Big data are complex and huge datasets that has a size extending exabyte. The field of Big Data is vast and its characteristics include the **"5 Vs"** variety, verification, velocity, volume and value. BDA has a deep impact on organizational performance. With the advancing literature of BDA, companies can analyze their customer needs better and accordingly serve the customers, eventually driving a higher sales and income. This helps the businesses effectively expand their markets. Several industries implement Big Data applications effectively such as financial services, banking, insurance, marketing, logistics and manufacturing. This section discusses the key concepts of BDA. Statistical analysis, simulation and optimization in supply chain analytics is further discussed and its applications in SCM areas are also explored.

Table 2. AI methods used in Supply chain context

Supply chain context	*AI Methods*				
	Decision Making	*Decision making/ learning*	*Learning*	*Sensing/Interacting*	*Total*
Auction			1		1
Capacity management	2				2
Configuration			1		1
Decision making	2		2		4
Finance	2		2		4
Forecasting	5		13		18
Inventory management	6	1	7		14
Logistics	10		3		13
Manufacturring	10				10
Performance Measurement	4				4
Planning	5				5
Procurement			1		1
Quality management			1		1
Risk management	5		3		8
Social media				1	1
Supplier selection	11		3		14
Supply network design	12		5		17
Sustainability	10		2		12
Technology			2		2
Total	86	1	46	1	132

BDA Potential

Big data points to data that is so huge that can't be accommodated into traditional databases. This data can be captured, stored, aggregated and analyzed. With growth in the volume of data, the tools used for analysis has also become sophisticated. This data is unorganized unlike the traditional data sets. They comprise all kinds of data, structured, semi-structured and unstructured from various sources. It can have an image, numerical, voice and text content. It can range from RFID, global positioning (GPS), point of sale (POS) or in blogs and feeds featuring in Facebook, Instagram,

Twitter etc. BDA employs analytics, which includes statistics and math to analyze Big Data. Big data alone, without the application of analytics is in vain and analytics without being applied to big data is a mere set of statistical and mathematical tools. However, together it aids decision makers acquire valuable insights through effective tools, thus turning patterns in data into Business Intelligence.

FMCG Supply Chain Analytics

The various business sectors that are chained together from raw materials to producers, wholesalers, retailers and customers define supply chain. The flow in Supply chain is not only in terms of material goods but also finances. Supply chain analytics refers to application of BDA techniques that extract valuable information from supply chain (Wang G et al., 2016). Analytics can be broadly classified into descriptive, predictive and Prescriptive analytics (Souza GC, 2014). This helps in effective decision making that lowers overall costs. Hence the implementation of BDA tools has a substantial improvement in supply chain performance. Until the stellar breakthroughs in BDA, researchers and managers have greatly relied on

Figure 1. Relationship between Descriptive, Predictive and Prescriptive Analytics to make decisions and take actions

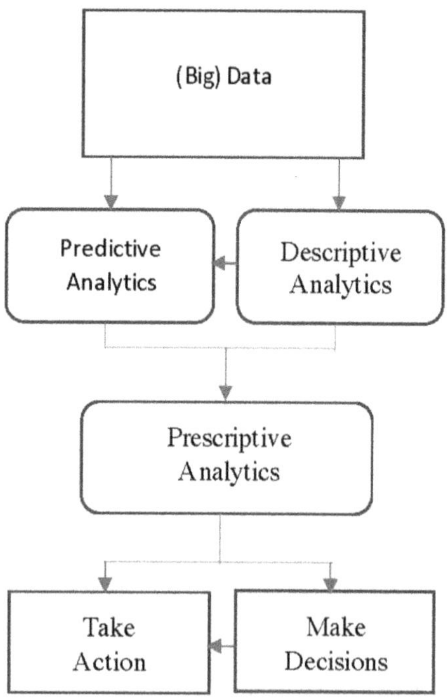

statistical and operational research techniques to balance supply and demand in market (Trkman P et al., 2010). However, the recent advancements in the field of analytics have opened new avenues for managers and researchers. The relationships among descriptive, predictive and prescriptive analytics to make decisions is shown in Figure 1.

The various benefits posed by data supported decision making have forced academicians and researchers integrate big data analysis in Supply chain management.

Statistical Analysis

This is divided into two types, Descriptive and Inferential. In descriptive statistics, past data are used to summarize the future, with the help of graphs or tables or numerical calculation. Inferential statistics is used to deduce the probability of occurrence of a phenomenon and predict their behavior based on a sample of past data. Both, quantitative and qualitative methods can be used simultaneously to make the right decisions. In order to ease uncertainty, statistical analysis is used, such as in distribution, inventory and risk analysis. Statistical multi-variates are also used to manage the supply of materials by mitigating the unwanted risks (Mele FD et al., 2005). Considering the size of big data, supply chain requires strong, convenient techniques for analysis. Regular statistical methods are futile since the gigantic data leads to distortion. Therefore, novel statistical methods have been developed recently. A recent research has developed a statistical algorithm that does a sophisticated analysis of data by deploying specific functions such as Conjugate gradient, Mann Whitney U-testing and ordinary least squares to model and compare the densities and Big data distribution squares (Fan Y et al., 2015). Table 3 differentiates between Descriptive statistics and Inferential statistics.

Table 3. Comparison between Descriptive statistics and Inferential statistics

Comparison metric	*Descriptive statistics*	*Inferential statistics*
What it does?	Organizing, analyzing and presenting data in a meaningful way.	Comparing, testing and predicting data.
Form of final result	Charts, graphs and tables	Probability
Why it is used?	To describe the current situation	To explain the chances of occurrence of an event
Function	Expalins the data that are already known	It attempts to reach to the conclusion that extends beyond data availability.

Simulation

Manufacturers used simulation tools to develop creative products, increase the time to market products and reduce the production costs. Simulation technique is versatile for product design and manufacturing process. Simulation and modelling techniques should be availed to apply large data. Manufacturing of innovative products by means of simulation is challenging since the manufacturers have to constantly operate efficiently, make the investments, adhere to the time constraints in order to launch products in the market and also predict customer preferences (Kambatla et al., 2014). It also helps managers do "what if" analysis under different system configuration (Ranjan R, 2014).A simulator was developed to collect and analyze data that was gathered from the shop floor environment of a smart manufacturing system (Shao G, 2014).Thus decision making was improved in the production system. Simulators can help forecast equipment needed by the manufacturers based on customer order and past data such as throughput, cycle time and delivery. The supply chain simulation can be used for predicting service, testing inventory requirements and analyzing production capacity (LLamasoft, 2016).Several simulation software can evaluate the performance of a system before its development. Enterprise dynamics is the most robust and widely used software to alleviate Supply chain management issues. Thus simulation tools significantly impact the functioning of FMCG supply chains.

Optimization

Optimization methods are powerful ways of supply chain data analytics (Balaraj S, 2013). They are used to extract meaningful information from huge data sets that are generated by complex systems. It encompasses various factors such as capacity and route that can analyze several goals such as demand fulfillment and cost mitigation. Availing supply chain optimization techniques with other techniques such as scenario management, multi user collaboration and performance tracker enables companies to accomplish their objectives. Further to the cause, it supports accurate planning of supply chain, but poses large scale optimization challenge (Wang G, 2016). Based on Scor supply chain simulator model, Souza GC (2014) applied BDA to SCM. It is imperative at all levels of supply chain-operational, tactical and strategic levels. At the tactical and operational levels, Supply chain analytics is used for procurement, demand planning, logistics and inventory. At the strategic level, Supply chain analytics is used for product design, network design and sourcing. Therefore, the effectiveness of optimization techniques is evident from the various levels of supply chain analytics at which it is deployed.

Applications of BDA in Supply Chain Management

The production environment deals with a large amount of data generated by internal and external networks that contains various production equipment on the manufacturing floors. Big data Analytics can yield improved sales and distribution. Thus, the manufacturing industry needs to avail big data analytics to expand their industry. The selection of vendors comprises various factors such as their large number, evaluation metrics, therefore it is a tedious process to select the right vendor. According to research, BDA finds its application in several areas of Supply chain management. The following topics explores the application of BDA in various areas of supply chain (Duan Y, 2019).

BDA in Supplier Relationship Management

Supplier relationship management deals with developing effective communication and interaction with all the suppliers of a company that will aid in strategic planning. Strategic resources and SRM are the driving forces of an organization. BDA can furnish intelligent information on organizational investments, in order to optimize supplier relationships (Jin Y,Jin S, 2013) .It provides an analysis of supplier data and also helps with precise calculation on return on investment (ROI). According to a study, fuzzy synthetic evaluation and analytical hierarchy process were deployed for supplier evaluation and selection that uses Big Data effectively (Wang G, 2018). The aim is to select a supply partner that can adapt to future challenges resulting from Big Data.

BDA in Supply Chain Network Design

It is a strategic design that involves the selection of all supply chain partners through effective decisions in order to accomplish long term business objectives. The network design includes the physical configuration that impact most of the functional units of business. Customer satisfaction and supply chain efficiency are two most important factors in developing supply chain network. It should be able to accomplish long term goals of a business.

With an optimal supply chain design, the company can achieve a competitive edge. (Wang et al., 2016b) A mixed integer non - linear model for locating various distribution sites was developed that uses big data sets for warehouse management, customer demand and transportation. These data sets were analyzed in marketing intelligence tools. Thus, it is well suited for various supply chain network design (Afshari H & Peng Q, 2015).

BDA in Product Design

The main focus of product manufacturers is to develop products that conform to customer preferences. Since customer preferences vary throughout the product development life cycle, designers need effective tools to predict the changes in expectations. The major challenge in product development process is lack of enough information about customer's preferences. The product design process, manufacturing and study of customer purchasing behavior generated surplus data termed as Big Data. Gathering and managing huge data and leveraging analytical techniques to acquire insights and taking decisions based on these insights can reduce the challenges in product design (Suh NP, 2001). Big data influences several sectors and product design is no exception. Engineers integrate sensors and novel technology into their products. Thus while designing the supply chain network, the product features must be considered and all supply chain partners must thus be combined at the design stage (Khan O et al., 2012) .This leads to a flexible supply chain design conforming to the product design (Jin J et al., 2016).Applying BDA techniques to product design leads to the production of new commodities at par with customer requirements and preferences (Suh NP, 2001).Designers can harness customer online behavior and customer purchase data to predict customer needs (Johanson M et al., 2014).This helps in identifying product features and predict future product trends. The major concern of FMCG companies is to sustain their market share for a long time. The application of data analytics tools facilitates product enhancement. Although the application of data analytic tools to extract intelligent data pertaining to products is prevalent, using it for product improvement is still naive. Thus, BDA helps in better informed product development.

BDA in Production Planning and Demand Forecast

Improving demand forecast and production planning with big data are predominant areas alluring great interest to business professionals (Feng Q & Shanthikumar JG, 2018).Precise demand forecast has always been challenging in FMCG supply chain management (Hassani H & Silva ES, 2015).BDA can create innovative services by predicting customers preferences and needs (Arias MB & Bae S, 2016).Thus Big data analytics has proved beneficial in demand forecast followed leading to effective production planning.

BDA in Procurement Management

Logistic organizations considering the gigantic data produced require sophisticated system to manage these data as well as professionals with expertise who can analyze these data and derive valuable insights from them that is then applied to planning and decision making. The diverse data generated from various internal and external automated sources are provided to these organizations at a very rapid pace. Supply chain analytics can be used to manage supplier's performance and supply chain risk (Wang G et al.,2016). Schlegel GL (2014) presented a big data predictive analytic framework to identify, evaluate, reduce and control the supply chain risk.Thus, BDA plays a key role in the procurement by logistic organisations.

BDA in Customized Production

BDA aids manufacturers to increase supply chain efficiency and understand factors that affect production. In today's global milieu, the manufacturing processes incorporate long and complex processes. All the units of each process should be examined. The optimization of supply chain should be achieved by linking supply chain partners intricately to ease the process. Data analytics allows manufacturers to determine all the tasks by analyzing each unit of production process in the supply chain. This facilitates manufacturers to detect vows if any and divulge poor functioning processes. Centralized production, was related to a small group of customers, however BDA has facilitated the prediction of customer preferences to produce customized producers. A recent study has examined the application of BDA in the field of production. Zhong et al (2014) designed RFID enabled big data applied to support shop floor logistics planning and scheduling. In another study he implemented physical internal concept by using IOT, wireless technology and BDA to create an RFID enabled intelligent shop floor. Stich V (2015) presented BDA techniques to forecast demand and production levels in manufacturing companies. Hence, the application of BDA is imperative in achieving customized production according to customer preferences.

BDA in Inventory Management

It is the process that includes order placement, inventory control and procurement. BDA in the supply of nonperishable products increase business efficiency significantly, thus making it lucrative. Big data manages inventory by providing maximum operational efficiency, increased sales and profits, improved customer satisfaction and cost mitigation by migration to cloud.

Big Data creates significant competition by linking the route from suppliers to production system and customers (Cohen MA, 2015). BDA aids in automating inventory control (Sharma M, Garg N, 2016). Data analysis can be implemented to analyze data, draw insights and predict the optimal level of inventory (LLamasoft, 2016).Thus effective inventory management is a result of BDA.

BDA in Logistics

The logistic industry has revolutionized tremendously with the advancement of technology. This sector improves collaboration between various sectors, like supply, manufacturing, distribution and retailers through establishing structural standardization and content of data interchanges. Mitigating costs by scaling down inventory both stocked and in transit has become crucial in today's supply chain environment.

Due to the explosive rise in customer orders, data is generated profusely, thus effective methods are needed to analyze it. As the daily shipments reach a high score, a mammoth of data pertaining to it is produced such as size, weight, origin and destination. Consequently, operational efficiency needs to improve and hence the customer experience. Organizations require data analytic processes and platforms to present their valuable insights to the company.

There is a lot of research prevalent in the area of logistics. BDA is used to provide service in logistics (Ayed AB et al., 2015). Maritime companies also deploy BDA to do effective planning (Brouer BD, 2016). Thus, it is evident that BDA can create agile logistics.

BDA in Agile FMCG Supply Chain

Agile supply chains respond to dynamic changes in the market (Lee Hl, 2004).Choi TM et al (2018) has proposed that Big Data has significant impact on management .Gunesekaran et al (2017) presented that supply chain vows can decelerate supply chain, therefore movement through supply chain was expedited by the implementation of supply chain enablers that employed BDA to achieve better results Gunesekaran et al (2017, 2018).He further stated that BDA has positive impact on both, supply chain and organizational performance (Gunesekaran et al, 2018 & Srinivasan R et al., 2018) .Supply chain and BDA are complementary concepts augmenting and propping each other (Gunesekaran et al, 2018 & Srinivasan R et al., 2018).In case of any disruption in the supply chain, it is successfully mitigated (Jüttner U, Maklan S, 2011). Big data help optimize decision making by aligning organization's goals to the sources and driving insights. BDA also helps in making inventory decisions through more informed knowledge about customer demands. By predicting customer preferences based on historical data, real time data and future data, organizations can avail it to become more agile and efficient.

BDA in Sustainable Supply Chain

Implementing sustainability in the supply chain is difficult (Brockhaus S et al., 2013). Sustainability refers to long term investments towards creating strategic resources (McWilliams A & Siegel DS, 2011).Companies are interested in using BDA in their sustainable efforts (Jelinek M & Bergey P, 2013).According to Mckinsey survey report, companies using BDA are able to predict 65% of customers, that make recurring purchases (Manyika J et al.).Several scholars acknowledge sustainability as an evolving area for BDA applications in business(Hazen BT et al., 2016 & Hsu J, 2013).Considering the growing importance of sustainability and BDA, they should be integrated and used by companies to achieve competitive edge. This topic is yet to be explored by researchers. Organizations must deploy effective methods to analyze excessive data and gain insights from it to achieve the three dimensions of environmental, social and economic sustainability.

CONCLUSION

This chapter has provided valuable insights on the different AI methods that are deployed in ECRM in order to sustain long term customer relations thus increasing the business revenue. It also sheds light on how BDA techniques can be leveraged in order to garner intelligent information that reflects customer preferences and behavior, which in turn determines the prosperity of a business.

The AI taxonomy is given with the various aspects of the taxonomy applied to different supply chain units. This chapter shows that learning methods, have been applied to supply chain forecasting and inventory management. However, machine learning for supply chain risk management could be a new caveat of research. It can be further utilized for supply network design in order to build supply chain robustness and responsiveness. There is also a dearth of research on the applications of sensing and interacting methods of AI in SCM. Machine learning can be combined with NLP to provide insights into supply chain operational challenges, sustainability risks, market and competitor performance, customer preferences and demand.

Further, the chapter explains some of the recent applications of BDA in FMCG SCM. This is applied in various areas of SCM including the demand data at the sales department, retailer data, delivery data, manufacturing data, and the supplier data. BDA are also used in various supply chain activities including supplier relationship management, product design, development, demand planning, inventory, network design, production, procurement, logistics and distribution. Supply chain has to establish close and continuous links between data experts and their business function and also apply appropriate BDA techniques. Hence, mutual coordination and cooperation between different supply chain units must be established, use BDA techniques to link these units, and exist an ability to share and access data and information throughout the entire supply chain. However, this chapter confines to the BDA applications in the FMCG industry thus providing a scope of research pertaining to other industries.

REFERENCES

Abar, S., Theodoropoulos, G. K., Lemarinier, P., & O'Hare, G. M. P. (2017). Agent Based Modelling and Simulation tools: A review of the state-of-art software. *Computer Science Review*, *24*, 13–33. doi:10.1016/j.cosrev.2017.03.001

Abbasi, B., Babaei, T., Hosseinifard, Z., Smith-Miles, K., & Dehghani, M. (2020). Predicting solutions of large-scale optimization problems via machine learning: A case study in blood supply chain management. *Computers & Operations Research*, *119*, 104941. doi:10.1016/j.cor.2020.104941

Afshari, H., & Peng, Q. (2015). Using big data to minimize uncertainty effects in adaptable product design. In *ASME 2015 International Design Engineering Technical Conferences and Computers and Information in Engineering Conference*. American Society of Mechanical Engineers. 10.1115/DETC2015-46475

Al-Jarrah, O. Y., Yoo, P. D., Muhaidat, S., Karagiannidis, G. K., & Taha, K. (2015). Efficient machine learning for big data: A review. *Big Data Research*, *2*(3), 87–93. doi:10.1016/j.bdr.2015.04.001

Allam, Z., & Dhunny, Z. A. (2019). On big data, artificial intelligence and smart cities. *Cities (London, England)*, *89*, 80–91. doi:10.1016/j.cities.2019.01.032

Arias, M. B., & Bae, S. (2016). Electric vehicle charging demand forecasting model based on big data technologies. *Applied Energy*, *183*, 327–339. doi:10.1016/j.apenergy.2016.08.080

Ayed, A. B., Halima, M. B., & Alimi, A. M. (2011). Big data analytics for logistics and transportation. *Supply Chain Management*, *16*(4), 246–259.

Balaraj, S. (2013). Optimization model for improving supply chain visibility. *Infosys Labs Briefings.*, *11*(1), 9–19.

Barbosa, M. W., Vicente, A. D., Ladeira, M. B., & Oliveira, M. P. (2018). Managing supply chain resources with big data analytics: A systematic review. *International Journal of Logistics Research and Applications.*, *21*(3), 177–200. doi:10.1080/13675567.2017.1369501

Barták, R., Salido, M. A., & Rossi, F. (2010). Constraint satisfaction techniques in planning and scheduling. *Journal of Intelligent Manufacturing*, *21*(1), 5–15. doi:10.100710845-008-0203-4

Bennett, C. C., & Hauser, K. (2013). Artificial intelligence framework for simulating clinical decision-making: A Markov decision process approach. *Artificial Intelligence in Medicine*, *57*(1), 9–19. doi:10.1016/j.artmed.2012.12.003 PMID:23287490

Blázquez, M. (2014). Fashion shopping in multichannel retail: The role of technology in enhancing the customer experience. *International Journal of Electronic Commerce*, *18*(4), 97–116. doi:10.2753/JEC1086-4415180404

Braun, A., & Garriga, G. (2018). Consumer Journey Analytics in the Context of Data Privacy and Ethics. In *Digital Marketplaces Unleashed* (pp. 663–674). Springer. doi:10.1007/978-3-662-49275-8_59

Brockhaus, S., Kersten, W., & Knemeyer, A. M. (2013). Where do we go from here? Progressing sustainability implementation efforts across supply chains. *Journal of Business Logistics*, *34*(2), 167–182. doi:10.1111/jbl.12017

Brouer, B. D., Karsten, C. V., & Pisinger, D. (2016). Big data optimization in maritime logistics. In *Big Data Optimization: Recent Developments and Challenges* (pp. 319–344). Springer. doi:10.1007/978-3-319-30265-2_14

Chen, I. J., & Popovich, K. (2003). Understanding customer relationship management (CRM) People, process and technology. *Business Process Management Journal*, *9*(5), 672–688. doi:10.1108/14637150310496758

Chen, S. H., Jakeman, A. J., & Norton, J. P. (2008). Artificial Intelligence techniques: An introduction to their use for modelling environmental systems. *Mathematics and Computers in Simulation*, *78*(2-3), 379–400. doi:10.1016/j.matcom.2008.01.028

Choi, T. M., Wallace, S. W., & Wang, Y. (2018). Big data analytics in operations management. *Production and Operations Management*, *27*(10), 1868 1883. doi:10.1111/poms.12838

Cohen, M. A. (2015). Inventory Management in the Age of Big Data. *Harvard Business Review*. Available from: https://hbr.org/2015/06/inventorymanagement-in-the-age-of-bigdata

Collobert, R., Weston, J., Bottou, L., Karlen, M., Kavukcuoglu, K., & Kuksa, P. (2011). Natural language processing (almost) from scratch. *Journal of Machine Learning Research*, *12*, 2493–2537.

Cui, R., Gallino, S., Moreno, A., & Zhang, D. J. (2018). The Operational Value of Social Media Information. *Production and Operations Management, 27*, 1749–1769.

Das, S., Mandal, S., Bhoyar, A., Bharde, M., Ganguly, N., Bhattacharya, S., & Bhattacharya, S. (2020). Multi-criteria online frame-subset selection for autonomous vehicle videos. *Pattern Recognition Letters, 133*, 349–355.

de Barcelos Silva, A., Gomes, M. M., da Costa, C. A., da Rosa Righi, R., Barbosa, J. L. V., Pessin, G., De Doncker, G., & Federizzi, G. (2020). Intelligent personal assistants: A systematic literature review. *Expert Systems with Applications, 147*, 113193.

der Zee, D.-J. v. (2011). Building insightful simulation models using Petri Nets— A structured approach. *Decision Support Systems, 51*, 53–64.

Dey, N., Hassanien, A. E., Bhatt, C., Ashour, A., & Satapathy, S. C. (2018). *Internet of things and big data analytics toward next-generation intelligence*. Springer.

Diabat, A., & Deskoores, R. (2016). A hybrid genetic algorithm based heuristic for an integrated supply chain problem. *Journal of Manufacturing Systems, 38*, 172–180.

Melo, M. T., Nickel, S., & Saldanha-da-Gama, F. (2009). Facility location and supply chain management – A review. *European Journal of Operational Research, 196*, 401–412.

Saghaei, M., Ghaderi, H., & Soleimani, H. (2020). Design and optimization of biomass electricity supply chain with uncertainty in material quality, availability and market demand. *Energy, 197*, 117165.

Duan, Y., Edwards, J. S., & Dwivedi, Y. K. (2019). Artificial intelligence for decision making in the era of Big Data – evolution, challenges and research agenda. *International Journal of Information Management, 48*, 63–71.

Pan, S., Zhang, L., Thompson, R. G., & Ghaderi, H. (2020). A parcel network flow approach for joint delivery networks using parcel lockers. *International Journal of Production Research*, 1–26.

Soleimani, H., Chaharlang, Y., & Ghaderi, H. (2018). Collection and distribution of returned remanufactured products in a vehicle routing problem with pickup and delivery considering sustainable and green criteria. *Journal of Cleaner Production, 172*, 960–970.

Dubois, L. (2015). *11 Best Web Analytic Tools*. Retrieved from: https://www.inc.com/guides/12/2010/11

Fan, Y., Heilig, L., & Voß, S. (2015). Supply chain risk management in the era of big data. In *International Conference of Design, User Experience, and Usability*. Cham: Springer.

Feng, Q., & Shanthikumar, J. G. (2018). How research in production and operations management may evolve in the era of big data. *Production and Operations Management, 27*(9), 1670–1684.

Fildes, R., Goodwin, P., Lawrence, M., & Nikolopoulos, K. (2009). Effective forecasting and judgmental adjustments: An empirical evaluation and strategies for improvement in supply-chain planning. *International Journal of Forecasting, 25*, 3–23.

Fischetti, M., & Fraccaro, M. (2019). Machine learning meets mathematical optimization to predict the optimal production of offshore wind parks. *Computers & Operations Research, 106*, 289–297.

Friedman, J., Hastie, T., & Tibshirani, R. (2001). The elements of statistical learning. Springer.

Giarratano, J. C., & Riley, G. (1998). *Expert systems*. PWS Publishing Co.

Tecuci, G. (2012). Artificial intelligence. *Wiley Interdisciplinary Reviews: Computational Statistics, 4*, 168–180.

Graves, A., Mohamed, A.-R., & Hinton, G. (2013). *Speech recognition with deep recurrent neural networks. In 2013 IEEE international conference on acoustics, speech and signal processing*. IEEE.

Greasley, A. (2005). Using system dynamics in a discrete-event simulation study of a manufacturing plant. *International Journal of Operations & Production Management, 25*, 534–548.

Guillaumin, M., Verbeek, J., & Schmid, C. (2010). *Multimodal semi-supervised learning for image classification. In 2010 IEEE Computer society conference on computer vision and pattern recognition*. IEEE.

Gunasekaran, A., Papadopoulos, T., Dubey, R., Wamba, S. F., Childe, S. J., & Hazen, B. (2017). Big data and predictive analytics for supply chain and organizational performance. *Journal of Business Research, 70*, 308–317.

Gunasekaran, A., Yusuf, Y. Y., Adeleye, E. O., & Papadopoulos, T. (2018). Agile manufacturing practices: The role of big data and business analytics with multiple case studies. *International Journal of Production Research, 56*(1-2), 385–39.

Hassani, H., & Silva, E. S. (2015). Forecasting with big data: A review. *Annals of Data Science.*, *2*(1), 5–19.

Hazen, B. T., Boone, C. A., Ezell, J. D., & Jones-Farmer, L. A. (2014). Data quality for data science, predictive analytics, and big data in supply chain management: An introduction to the problem and suggestions for research and applications. *International Journal of Production Economics*, *154*, 72–80.

Hazen, B. T., Skipper, J. B., Ezell, J. D., & Boone, C. A. (2016). Big data and predictive analytics for supply chain sustainability: A theory-driven research agenda. *Computers & Industrial Engineering*, *101*, 592–598.

Holweg, M., Disney, S. M., Hines, P., & Naim, M. M. (2005). Towards responsive vehicle supply: A simulation-based investigation into automotive scheduling systems. *Journal of Operations Management*, *23*, 507–530.

Hsu, J. (2013). *Big Business, Big Data, Big Sustainability*. Carbontrust.com.

Jakupović, A., Pavlić, M., & Han, Z. D. (2014). Formalisation method for the text expressed knowledge. *Expert Systems with Applications*, *41*, 5308–5322.

Jelinek, M., & Bergey, P. (2013). Innovation as the strategic driver of sustainability: Big data knowledge for profit and survival. *IEEE Engineering Management Review*, *41*(2), 14–22.

Jin, J., Liu, Y., Ji, P., & Liu, H. (2016). Understanding big consumer opinion data for market-driven product design. *International Journal of Production Research*, *54*(10), 3019–3041.

Jin, Y., & Ji, S. (2013). Partner choice of supply chain based on 3d printing and big data. *Information Technology Journal*, *12*(22), 6822.

Johanson, M., Belenki, S., Jalminger, J., Fant, M., & Gjertz, M. (2014). Big automotive data: Leveraging large volumes of data for knowledge-driven product development. In *2014 IEEE International Conference on Big Data (Big Data)*. IEEE.

Jüttner, U., & Maklan, S. (2011). Supply chain resilience in the global financial crisis: An empirical study. *Supply Chain Management*, *16*(4), 246–25.

Kambatla, K., Kollias, G., Kumar, V., & Grama, A. (2014). Trends in big data analytics. *Journal of Parallel and Distributed Computing*, *74*(7), 2561–2573.

Kaplan, A., & Haenlein, M. (2019). Siri, Siri, in my hand: Who's the fairest in the land? On the interpretations, illustrations, and implications of artificial intelligence. *Business Horizons*, *62*, 15–25.

Khan, O., Christopher, M., & Creazza, A. (2012). Aligning product design with the supply chain: A case study. *Supply Chain Management, 17*(3), 323–336.

Kreipl, S., & Pinedo, M. (2004). Planning and scheduling in supply chains: An overview of issues in practice. *Production and Operations Management, 13*, 77–92.

Kusiak, A., & Chen, M. (1988). Expert systems for planning and scheduling manufacturing systems. *European Journal of Operational Research, 34*, 113–130.

LeCun, Y., Bengio, Y., & Hinton, G. (2015). Deep learning. *Nature, 521*, 436–444.

Leung, S. C., Tsang, S. O., Ng, W.-L., & Wu, Y. (2007). A robust optimization model for multi-site production planning problem in an uncertain environment. *European Journal of Operational Research, 181*, 224–238.

Liang, W.-Y., & Huang, C.-C. (2006). Agent-based demand forecast in multi-echelon supply chain. *Decision Support Systems, 42*, 390–407.

LLamasoft. (2016). *Supply chain simulation: why its time has come*. LLamasoft white paper.

Lu, H., Li, Y., Chen, M., Kim, H., & Serikawa, S. (2018). Brain Intelligence: Go beyond Artificial Intelligence. *Mobile Networks and Applications, 23*, 368–375.

Manning, C. D., Manning, C. D., & Schütze, H. (1999). *Foundations of statistical natural language processing*. MIT Press.

Manyika, J., Sinclair, J., Dobbs, R., Strube, G., Rassey, L., & Mischke, J. (n.d.). *Manufacturing the Future: The Next Era of Global Growth and Innovation*. McKinsey Global Institute. https:// www.mckinsey.com/businessfunctions/operations/our-insights/ the-future-of-manufacturing

McWilliams, A., & Siegel, D. S. (2011). Creating and capturing value: Strategic corporate social responsibility, resource-based theory, and sustainable competitive advantage. *Journal of Management, 37*(5), 1480–1495.

Mele, F. D., Musulin, E., & Puigjaner, L. (2005, January 1). Supply chain monitoring: A statistical approach. *Computer-Aided Chemical Engineering, 20*, 1375–1380.

Min, H., Jeung Ko, H., & Seong Ko, C. (2006). A genetic algorithm approach to developing the multi-echelon reverse logistics network for product returns. *Omega, 34*, 56–69.

Mnih, V., Kavukcuoglu, K., Silver, D., Rusu, A. A., Veness, J., Bellemare, M. G., Graves, A., Riedmiller, M., Fidjeland, A. K., & Ostrovski, G. (2015). Human-level control through deep reinforcement learning. *Nature, 518*, 529–533.

Moayedikia, A., Ghaderi, H., & Yeoh, W. (2020). Optimizing microtask assignment on crowdsourcing platforms using Markov chain Monte Carlo. *Decision Support Systems*, *139*, 113404.

Nickel, S., Saldanha-da-Gama, F., & Ziegler, H.-P. (2012). A multi-stage stochastic supply network design problem with financial decisions and risk management. *Omega*, *40*, 511–524.

Ngai, E. W., Xiu, L., & Chau, D. C. (2009). Application of data mining techniques in customer relationship management: A literature review and classification. *Expert Systems with Applications*, *36*(2), 2592–2602.

Ogawa, A., & Hori, T. (2017). Error detection and accuracy estimation in automatic speech recognition using deep bidirectional recurrent neural networks. *Speech Communication*, *89*, 70–83.

Overgoor, G., Chica, M., Rand, W., & Weishampel, A. (2019). Letting the Computers Take Over: Using AI to Solve Marketing Problems. *California Management Review*, *61*, 156–185.

Panchmatia, M. (2015). *Use Big Data to Help Procurement Make a Real Difference*. Academic Press.

Parise, S., Guinan, P. J., & Kafka, R. (2016). Solving the crisis of immediacy: How digital technology can transform the customer experience. *Business Horizons*, *59*, 411–420.

Pasandideh, S. H. R., Niaki, S. T. A., & Nia, A. R. (2011). A genetic algorithm for vendor managed inventory control system of multi-product multi-constraint economic order quantity model. *Expert Systems with Applications*, *38*, 2708–2716.

Priore, P., Ponte, B., Rosillo, R., & de la Fuente, D. (2019). Applying machine learning to the dynamic selection of replenishment policies in fast-changing supply chain environments. *International Journal of Production Research*, *57*, 3663–3677.

Ramos, C., Augusto, J. C., & Shapiro, D. (2008). Ambient intelligence—The next step for artificial intelligence. *IEEE Intelligent Systems*, *23*, 15–18.

Ranjan, R. (2014). Modeling and simulation in performance optimization of big data processing frameworks. *IEEE Cloud Computing.*, *1*(4), 14–19.

Reiner, G. (2005). Customer-oriented improvement and evaluation of supply chain processes supported by simulation models. *International Journal of Production Economics*, *96*, 381–395.

Ricketts, T. A., & Hornsby, B. W. (2005). Sound quality measures for speech in noise through a commercial hearing aid implementing. *Journal of the American Academy of Audiology*, *16*, 270–277.

Rolón, M., & Martínez, E. (2012). Agent-based modeling and simulation of an autonomic manufacturing execution system. *Computers in Industry*, *63*, 53–78.

Schlegel, G. L. (2014). Utilizing big data and predictive analytics to manage supply chain risk. *The Journal of Business Forecasting.*, *33*(4), 11.

Shao, G., Shin, S. J., & Jain, S. (2014). Data analytics using simulation for smart manufacturing. In *Proceedings of the Winter Simulation Conference*. IEEE.

Sharma, M., & Garg, N. (2016). Inventory control and big data. In *Optimal Inventory Control and Management Techniques* (pp. 222–235). IGI Global.

Sharma, R., Kamble, S. S., Gunasekaran, A., Kumar, V., & Kumar, A. (2020). A systematic literature review on machine learning applications for sustainable agriculture supply chain performance. *Computers & Operations Research*, *119*, 104926.

Soudagar, R., Iyer, V., & Hildebrand, V. (2012). *The customer experience edge: Technology and techniques for delivering an enduring, profitable, and positive experience to your customers*. McGraw-Hill.

Souza, G. C. (2014). Supply chain analytics. *Business Horizons*, *57*(5), 595–605.

Srinivasan, R., & Swink, M. (2018). An investigation of visibility and flexibility as complements to supply chain analytics: An organizational information processing theory perspective. *Production and Operations Management*, *27*(10), 1849–1867.

Stich, V., Jordan, F., Birkmeier, M., Oflazgil, K., Reschke, J., & Diews, A. (2015). Big data technology for resilient failure management in production systems. In *IFIP International Conference on Advances in Production Management Systems*. Cham: Springer.

Suh, N. P. (2001). *Axiomatic Design: Advances and Applications*. Oxford University Press.

Trkman, P., McCormack, K., De Oliveira, M. P., & Ladeira, M. B. (2010). The impact of business analytics on supply chain performance. *Decision Support Systems*, *49*(3), 318–327.

Van Der Zee, D. J., & Van Der Vorst, J. G. A. J. (2005). A Modeling Framework for Supply Chain Simulation. *Opportunities for Improved Decision Making*, *36*, 65–95.

Wang, G., Gunasekaran, A., Ngai, E. W., & Papadopoulos, T. (2016). Big data analytics in logistics and supply chain management: Certain investigations for research and applications. *International Journal of Production Economics*, *176*, 98–110.

Wang, G., Gunasekaran, A., & Ngai, E. W. (2018). Distribution network design with big data: Model and analysis. *Annals of Operations Research*, *270*(1-2), 539–551.

Wichmann, P., Brintrup, A., Baker, S., Woodall, P., & McFarlane, D. (2020). Extracting supply chain maps from news articles using deep neural networks. *International Journal of Production Research*, *58*, 5320–5336.

Winer, R. S. (2001). A framework for customer relationship management. *California Management Review, 43*(4), 89-105.

Xue, X., Li, X., Shen, Q., & Wang, Y. (2005). An agent-based framework for supply chain coordination in construction. *Automation in Construction*, *14*, 413–430.

Yang, X., Audhkhasi, K., Rosenberg, A., Thomas, S., Ramabhadran, B., & Hasegawa-Johnson, M. (2018). Joint modeling of accents and acoustics for multi-accent speech recognition. In *2018 IEEE International Conference on Acoustics, Speech and Signal Processing (ICASSP)*. IEEE.

You, F., Wassick, J. M., & Grossmann, I. E. (2009). Risk management for a global supply chain planning under uncertainty: Models and algorithms. *AIChE Journal. American Institute of Chemical Engineers*, *55*, 931–946.

Zarbakhshnia, N., Soleimani, H., & Ghaderi, H. (2018). Sustainable third-party reverse logistics provider evaluation and selection using fuzzy SWARA and developed fuzzy COPRAS in the presence of risk criteria. *Applied Soft Computing*, *65*, 307–319.

Zhang, J., Chen, M., Sun, H., Li, D., & Wang, Z. (2020). Object semantics sentiment correlation analysis enhanced image sentiment classification. *Knowledge-Based Systems*, *191*, 105245.

Zhong, R. Y., Huang, G. Q., & Lan, S. L. (2014). Shopfloor logistics management using rfid-enabled big data under physical internet. *Proceeding of 1st International Physical Internet Conference,* 1-14.

Zhong, R. Y., Huang, G. Q., Lan, S., Dai, Q. Y., Chen, X., & Zhang, T. (2015). A big data approach for logistics trajectory discovery from RFID-enabled production data. *International Journal of Production Economics*, *165*, 260–272.

Chapter 11
Entrepreneurial Marketing of E-CRM in SMEs

Mahjabeena Najar
King Khalid University, Saudi Arabia

Malik Misbah
King Khalid University, Saudi Arabia

Humara Yaqub
King Khalid University, Saudi Arabia

Mehraj Bilfagih
King Khalid University, Saudi Arabia

ABSTRACT

Marketing in medium and small-scale enterprises (SMEs) is altogether very different to marketing as proposed theoretically for large organizations. This chapter is dedicated to the gathered research on the effect and impact of IBTs on the customer relationship management (CRM) activities (i.e., e-CRM) of SMEs in Gurgaon. A cocktail method approach including online in-depth interviews, online questionnaires, and projective techniques was followed. Of 286 respondents, factor analysis was carried out leading to communication with customers and management of customer information being processed as the main area within the e-CRM in SMEs. In order to provide better communication and information management abilities to varying customers, SMEs are following relatively simple IBTs. It is harder to consolidate customer information into decision making than just the communication side of it. In SMEs, e-CRM tries to be adhoc rather than strategic.

DOI: 10.4018/978-1-6684-5386-5.ch011

INTRODUCTION

As the term CRM (customer relationship management) is self-explanatory, it is basically, managing relationships with customers. The main reason behind the managing and maintaining the relationship with the customers is to gain customer loyalty and therefore retention (Gummesson, 1994; Hunt and Morgan, 1994; Reichheld and Sasser, 1990; Webster, 1992). CRM encompasses a wide range of marketing, but the two main components are particularly important. The first one to focus on, is the customer communication that facilitates the relationship building. Secondly by creating the valuable customer insight that drives effective CRM strategies and can be acquired by management and analysis of customer information.

Even if, SMEs being a major contributor to a developed economy, it is not equally represented in academic literature. According to O'Dwyer et al., 2009, SMEs must innovate around their own processes of business to survive. This chapter focuses on how SMEs may use technology to establish their marketing activities. Furthermore, this chapter explores the strategic and tactical issues immanent in electronic -CRM(e-CRM) in SMES.

BACKGROUND

According to Gummesson, 1994; Reinartz et al., 2004; Harker and Egan, 2006; it is asserted that CRM is philosophically in line with relationship marketing, where the only difference lies in its sole focus on the firm -customer dyad.

CRM in SMEs

Carson and Gilmore, 2000; O'Dwyer et al., 2009 says that the approaches taken to marketing by SMEs are pragmatic adaptations of marketing theory in order to render it relevant to the way they do business. Being small in many ways can be an advantage such as employee loyalty, customer interface, flexibility, response speed and ease of access to market information.

E-CRM in SMEs

CRM with the use of technology is e-CRM. In addition technology here is specified as IBTs, where the unique needs of the SMEs are likely not captured by the some more complex software packages. This chapter is focused on the belief that, for SMEs the relationship with their customers is the key competitive advantage against their competitors, the opportunities imparted by using e-CRM is particularly important.

Previous researches failed on the statistical and strategical investigation of the capabilities i.e., customer communication and customer information management.

Customer Communication

Like communication is at the heart of internet, customer is at the heart of marketing in SMEs. Informal, constant and open communication exists between the firm and the customer and the purpose of this communication is to create a mutual value.

E-CRM may facilitate and enhance more interaction between SMEs and their customer communication capabilities. The tools and techniques that are used for the communication activities may include email, social media, websites and chatrooms for their ability to support and facilitate quicker, and more responsive customer communication. It may be possible to personalize and at the same time automate customer communication which may lead to efficiency gains and more targeted marketing, hence better customer service. However, one thing to consider is the balance between face to face (traditional method) of communication with the virtual one.

Customer Information Management

An effective level communication with customers will need an equally effective customer information system. Hence, e-CRM should provide the ability to acquire, manage and analyze the customer information. Furthermore, the information is the basis of marketing decision making, via recording customer information such as customer personal details, unique requirement website activity, history orders, projected future orders and value to the firm. Many organizations by far using the database technology and more advanced e-CRM systems managed to analyze and predict customer behavior. Furthermore, the e-CRM aim is to sell smarter rather than selling more. In addition, e-CRM has the capability to help organizations in sorting their profitable customers from less profitable ones. Furthermore, e-CRM can assist organizations in calculating their customer life time value.

Challenges of SMEs

For SMEs it is difficult to find technological initiatives and implement them to their fullest. The three main challenges to e-CRM implementation are potential of reduced face-to-face communication, strategic integration and resource constraints; based on which previous researchers found that SMEs declared it difficult to perform true relationship marketing via e-CRM.

Provide broad definitions and discussions of the topic and incorporate views of others (literature review) into the discussion to support, refute, or demonstrate your position on the topic.[1]

METHODOLOGY

The methodology aimed to explore and understand the nature of e-CRM in SMEs and a cocktail approach was acquired to deal with this research question.

Quantitative Phase

The quantitative phase constituted the first phase in our methodology, which was a survey questionnaire instrument. This tool provided us with the data at demographic level of SMEs. In addition, in this phase we focused on the collection of data related to the owners, managers, marketing nature of the organizations. IBTs employment in CRM activities. We also come to know the inherit challenges benefits of e-CRM implementation and adaptation.

Qualitative Phase

This phase was focused to get in-depth interview process and application of projective techniques' main aim of these in-depth interview processes was to have a micro level information and explanation of the quantitative data. From phase one respondents a list of 40 SME owner-managers were selected and the face-to-face interview was conducted.

To provide nano-level insight projective techniques were also employed to provide nano-level insight (Rogers and Beal, 1958; Boddy, 2007). Associative projective techniques were used in this study. According this associative approach the respondents are required to read a list of words and are supposed to choose the ones they most associate with the topic at hand (Ramsey et al., 2006).

In addition, in the Completion technique participants were required to complete a story, conversation, sentence. Bubble drawing was used. The researcher is supposed to initiate response by filling one speech bubble and leaving the other speech and thought bubbles blank for the respondent to fill in. According to Ramsey et al. (2006) thought bubbles bypass the conscious defenses of research participants to a larger extent than the speech bubbles.

Lastly, construction techniques resemble the completion techniques but face the lack of initiation by the researchers. In this study, we preferred a cartoon setting with a blank speech and a blank thought bubble. In addition, each of the interviewees was provided with a projective test booklet and 12/40 completed booklets were received by post.

Sample characteristics

Many reasons let us choose the city (Gurgaon for the research locale. Firstly because of its good SME base in India. Secondly, for the reason that it accounts for approximately 80 per cent of employment and 75 per cent of turnover (BERR, 2009).Over 98 percent of companies in Gurgaon employ less than 50 people (SFA,2007).Furthermore, with regard to employment, approximately 60 per cent of the workforce is employed by the SME sector (SFA,2007).SMEs located in Gurgaon are on the economic periphery and their motivation to engage in e-CRM or in may be accentuated information and communication technologies(ICT) (Ritchie and Brindley, 2005).Also taking into account the widespread internet availability in Gurgaon which measure to 90 percent of Gurgaon in 2005 which suggests that macro -infra structure for e-business and e-CRM exists.

The European Commission's (2005) definition stating that any enterprise employing less than 250 employees is classified as an SME, to which this study adheres to it. Furthermore, this definition is also adopted by the sampling frame, and included the criterion "possess a web site valid e-mail address", to screen out those SMEs that do not have at least this minimal infrastructure to implement e-CRM.

Validity and reliability

In order to increase the validity of the questionnaire, measurement of constructs was based on previous relevant research (Stone,1798) Items based on pertinent literature were developed for constructs that were not readily available. Finally we created a self- report survey based on guidelines provided by Saris and Aallhofer(2007) and Dillman(1978).

Items measurement was done using a five-point Likert-type scale. For Survey items and their sources of the measurements refer to the Appendix. Furthermore, the reliability and validity of the qualitative phase was ensured via prolonged engagement with and persistent observation of the sample population, gaining informant feedback, weighting the evidence, peer debriefing, and rich and thick description (Onwuegbuzie and Leech, 2007). In addition, one of the important points to be noted is the triangulation of the methods, subsequent reliability and validity methods.

RESULT AND ANALYSIS

Phase One

To employ the quantitative phase of the study the principal component analysis (PCA) using orthogonal rotation(varimax) and Kaiser normalization to the underlying structure of the data was used. Also, the technologies PASW/SPSS 17 was used. In addition, for the structure of the correlations among a large number of variables based on a common set of underlying dimensions

the is done using PCA method analysis (Hair et al., 1998) which enables the researcher to determine whether a certain set of items do or do not constitute a construct (Straub, 1989). The suitability of the data for factor analysis was tested by employing the Kaiser-Meyer-Olkin (KMO) measure of sampling adequacy. In addition, the Relative scores of 0.867 and 5,001.175(p<0.001) stated that factor analysis can be performed on the data.

The Kaiser criterion applied, led to the components with latent root criterion. The cross-loaded items were also deleted, resulting in 36/59 items being retained. The rotated component matrix is given in Table I. Furthermore, the resultant eight factors explains that the variance of about 69 percent is displayed in the quantitively data, is deemed adequate to represent data. The range of coronach's α in each factor ranged from 0.74(Factor 7) to 0.91(Factor 1). These levels lie within the acceptable limit of 0.7 for internal consistency of scale reliability of the components that compromise the eight factors (Nunnaly,1978). In the interpretation of data, a minimum parameter of 0.55 was components was set, which is higher than generally accepted level of 0.30.

Even if the overall study ought to identify and explain the various factors underpinning the e-CRM in SMEs, this piece of study focuses on two particular aspects of e-CRM in SMEs, specifically the customer information management and the customer communication.

In second phase of methodology qualitative procedures were adopted. The first procedure was interviewing method and the second projective method. The results from both these methods revealed many issues related to customer communication and customer information management (channel conflict issues, traditional customer communication, impacts of e-communication, managing customer information and perceived customer value.

Channel conflict issues: SME's face difficulty to implement e-CRM through blended online and face-to-face channels. Face-to face channel remains preferable for both the customer and the enterprise. The main problem with e-communication seems to be lack of face-to-face interaction which plays an important role in forming relationship.

Table 1. Related component matrix

Items with Questionnaire instrument	F1	F2	F3	F4	F5	F6	F7	F8
Internet -enabled customer relationship facilitate improved market awareness	0.73							
Internet -enabled customer relationship facilitate personalization.	0.631							
Internet -enabled customer relationship facilitate enhanced customer service	0.654							
Internet -enabled customer relationship improve customer loyalty.	0.618							
Internet -enabled customer relationships generate cost savings in marketing	0.700							
Internet -enabled customer relationships open up international markets for us	0.713							
Internet enabled customer relationship generate more sales for us	0.806							
Internet enabled customer relationships improve our overall profitability	0.775							
Information on customers is central to our decision making		0.608						
Having database to store customer information		0.853						
Database is a key business tool		0.885						
Electronic information on customers compliments our other knowledge		0.830						
Electronic information is more easily managed		0.609						
Electronic information on customers compliments our other knowledge		0.830						
Electronic information on customers is central to our decision making		0.760						
We are at the leading edge of technological innovations			0.675					
We can adopt the internet-based business in stages			0.636					
Management seeks to extend individual staff development in the use of ICTs			0.739					
There is clear and well communicated internet enabled business strategy			0.793					
We have followed a formal process in our internet-enabled business strategy			0.747					
Management are highly involved in present and/or future			0.734					
Relationship with customers improve customer loyalty				0.801				
Relationship with customers improve our overall profitability				0.785				
Relationship with customers generates more sales for us.				0.861				
We are more likely to employ internet technology in relationships with our most valuable customers					0.857			
Value of customer dictates whether we will use internet technology in the relationship					0.783			
We are more likely to employ internet technology in relationships with our least valuable customers					0.803			
It remains difficult to develop trust with customers online						0.715		
Different customers have different preferences while they deal with us						0.703		
Face-to-face relationships are preferred by customer						0.714		
Face-to-face relationships are preferred by customer						0.696		
Communication with our customers is regular							0.656	
We take action to encourage a trusting relationship.							0.859	
Customer relations are what marketing is about for our organization.							0.735	
Internet communication is key to our business.								0.767
Internet communication has improved communication as a whole with customer								0.716
We proactively use internet communication to build customer relation.								0.712
Eigenvalue	10.46	3.72	2.97	1.98	1.84	1.56	1.37	1.08
Percentage of variance explained	29.05	10.33	8.24	5.49	5.10	4.32	3.81	3.00
Cronbach's α factor	0.91	0.89	0.88	0.84	0.82	0.75	0.74	0.86

Face to face interaction helps in understanding many things in terms of emotions, gestures, which is not possible in online interaction. Additionally, the customer feels detached in online interaction.

Traditional customer communications: From the findings, it is concluded that traditional, non IBT-based communication plays an important role in building relationship with customers, thus making it important strategy for SME's. The importance of SME's is in maintaining relationship with customers through normal regular communication and building trust. Communication through emails or phone calls are not preferable at new business relationship, so it is concluded that emails are not efficient enough in developmental stage of relationship, rather are useful in maintenance stages.

Face to face communication helps in being casual and relaxed which is difficult to attain through emails and phone calls.

Impacts of e-communication: From the qualitative data, the emails improve the communication with customers by facilitating systematic and personalized exchange in SME's. So, the main aim is to enhance the role of e-communication in customer relationships. The tools provided by the technology like emails are complementary despite of its usage at initial stage of business process is not that clear. The following quotations endorse the quantitative findings and binds the importance of e-communication in the overall communication process of customer relationships:

Email enhances relationships certainly because it allows efficient flow of information, but it is an enhancement rather than a replacement or substitute (Professional Service, NI).

Email is very important support because it lets us "be on" 24 hours a day. There is no hiding place anymore (Professional Service, NI).

It is all down to interacting with the customers, and email allows that (Retail, N).

Email save time as compared to phone calls engaging both parties for longer periods. Furthermore, emails are also kept as records where the receiver performs many activities like replying, acknowledging, flagging etc the work. Emails also works as concise and clear instruction mode of communication.

Managing customer information: Managing customer information in large scale personally is difficult. From the experimentation one respondent came up with definition of marketing as being "about information, getting information to customers and hopefully influencing what the customer does with that information (Service, NI)". The IBTs role in managing the information differs in firm but is supported by the following quote:

When I had 10 customers, I knew each one personally, but when you grow you lose that (Wholesale, NI).

This participant is stating the fact that the business at low scale with small number of customers, it was easy for him to manage personal ties with the customers and serve their need accordingly. As the business expanded, it became difficult to maintain relationships personally and manage the customer information. So, he had to adopt IBTs to manage the whole activities.

Another participant responded as:

It's knowledge, isn't it, it's your database, it's your lifeblood. So, you have got to keep it maintained, if you don't then you are dead in the water (Professional, NI).

There are many stages of involving IBT in managing the information. The firms who have implemented databases to personalize communication are positive about its efficiency. The following participants responded to this point as:

We have customer database maintained which gets updated with every online order. We do mailshots to every entity in database, we also email monthly newsletters (Retail, NI).

We do target marketing. We do send emails to drama audiences, people who have been to drama previously, but rarely the email go out to everyone. The response isn't that good (Service, NI).

However, informality runs through the information management. Despite of advanced application software respondents rely on simple tools. The following participants showed indifferent attitude saying:

I don't do this right, despite knowing the correct way and what should I do. It is like there are lot of things in life to be done but you don't it. I should have information about the customers what they have ordered in past in database. I know I should do that (Service, NI).

We do it roughly. We don't record information in a proper way (Wholesale, NI).

It can be said that this indifferent approach towards using advanced software packages may lie in perceived time resources involved in disseminating, collecting, and maintaining of information. Another important issue is unawareness of importance of customer information.

Perceived Customer value: An e-CRM has a capability of recognizing the behavior, value and trends of different customers. The data in this study displays that some SMEs are using databases to identify trends such as customer profitability automatically, as some of the respondents quoted as:

Now we have created database that help us examining the customers, their orders, when they have ordered and how much they are spending (Retail, NI).

We have a database with some programs that analyses number of customers who are spending less than what they have spent in past three months, so there is something wrong, means they aren't happy, but we haven't spoken to them about it (Retail/Wholesale, NI).

This is an important finding where the power of technology can be used to make marketing effective and efficient.

To conclude, IBTs facilitate the SMEs to manage two CRM process that is communication and information. The integration of IBTs with traditional communication system is challenging.

DISCUSSION AND CONCLUSION

Customer Communication

Besides the lack of face-to-face communication in their customer relationships, there is a struggle of integrating IBT based communication into customer communication by SME's. The research confirms previous research, which warned the role of e-CRM in customer relationships. Specifically, e-CRM is mistaken as an only technological initiative (Chen and Ching; Lawson-Body and O'Keefe, 2006). the result of which will lead an organization technology and production oriented rather customer oriented (Gummesson, 2002).

In conclusion, SMEs are trying to make e-CRM as successful as face-to-face customer relationship. Gummesson (2002) has elaborated how e-CRM can be made more successful in an organization by combining human knowledge, behavior, attitude with ICT. It is important for SME's also where the customers and employees will be assisted by technology. The study concludes that e-CRM should be technology enabled marketing process (Becker et al, 2009; Ortega et al,2008; Peltier et al, 2009).

Considering traditional customer communication, the findings highlight that it is the customer relationship which is elementary in everything a SME does (Carson et al.,1995; Jack et al.,2010; O'Dwyer et al.,2009). In SME marketing, particularly the face to face, personal communication is common and intrinsic which can be a potential challenge in e-CRM. In person relationship with customer helps SMEs to understand the customers well in terms of their personal information, preferences, buying trends and knowledge regarding competition. Establishing key relationships also helps SMEs to come closer to their market, thus enabling SMEs to exhibit a high level of flexibility to the changing demands of market (Doole et al., 2006; Kocak and Abimbola, 2009).

This method of operation (i.e. establishing customer relationships) focuses on the theoretical marketing relationship and principles of CRM. So marketing is not the activity which only larger organizations can implement, evidently SMEs can perform marketing by joining hands with stakeholders, mostly customers (Carson and Gilmore, 2000; Jack et al., 2010; O'Dwyer et al., 2009). SME's marketing is driven by their customers (Moriarty et al., 2009), they depend on repeat business and on the relationships with the existing customers (Peltier et al., 2009) and where they must deal with a range of influential stakeholders (Jocumsen, 2004), networking plays a significant role for SME marketing purposes (Carson and Gilmore, 2000; Zontanos and Anderson, 2004).

Considering the IBT-based communication, the findings depict that it is important in SMEs, where it improves the overall quality of communication and relationship. Specific means of improvement centre on the role of communication through email in enhancing the efficiency and personalisation of communications. This is an interesting and important extension of knowledge relative to the nature of e-CRM in SMEs.

The research done previously distinguished the role of the internet in customer communication, where the concept of community is at the heart of the original internet concept (Chaston and mangles, 2003). Thus, introducing internet into the customer relationship need not to be their drawback, because e-CRM is not a substitute to face to face contact rather it is a complement. E-CRM has the capability to enhance efficiency of communication and free up the time for more face-to-face communication in the form of meetings. E-CRM has a potential to develop bonds and loyalty by improving the interaction between SME and customer in which the customers preferences are encouraged and prioritized (Keh et al., 2007; Rai et al., 2006; Verhoef et al., 2007). For example, website and e-mail technology can involve the customers in providing the design of a new product and services (Nambisan and Baron, 2007; Simmons et al., 2008). E-CRM can be a method to improve the customer relationships by encouraging dialogue, combining different customer communication channels, and by enabling the personalization of communication (Day and Hubbard, 2003). In conclusion, SMEs seems to be aware of capabilities of e-CRM in establishing customer communication and are implementing it for overall effective marketing and efficiency of business.

Customer Information Management

In e-CRM the main objective is to collect and manage the customer information (Jayachandran et al., 2005; Payne and Frow, 2006; Tan et al., 2002). Information management deals with the gathering and collation of customer data from all customer contact points and in combination with other relevant data, extracting the insights of customer (Payne and Frow, 2006). Customer data can be analyzed to create valuable customer information which can be used to classify customers, predict customer behavior, conduct marketing strategies and to make use of cross-selling and up selling opportunities to the existing customers (Ahearne et al., 2007; Baily et al., 2009). Technology can make accurate and relevant customer information accessible to SME owners or managers (Hutchinson and Quintas, 2008; Jayachandran et al., 2005). Research also specifies that in general the customer information is important for decision making in SMEs as compared to the electronic information. Also, the complexities and level of integrating the tools tens to be low, as many SMEs are using stand-alone databases (Hutchinson and Quintas, 2008).

In this area, previous research has supported building strategies around the differing values of customers to the organization (Ryals and Humphries, 2007; Parvatiyar and Sheth, 2001). This method helps the organizations to calculate the value of customers and devote more resources to valuable/ profitable customers. This strategy has showed up proportion of 20 percent of customers are responsible for 80 percent of revenues which is tremendous for majority of firms; the Pareto 80/20 rule (Parvatiyar and Sheth, 2001; Ryals and Humphries, 2007). However, in the current study the SMEs are not following this strategy where the value of customer does not impact their e-CRM practices, because they do not tend to use the customer information to determine the customer profitability.

In conclusion, it although previous research has determined the drawbacks of e-CRM in SMEs are greater than in larger organizations, SMEs perform e-CRM in different way than larger organizations do. There are number of theoretical conclusions derived from the current study. First, SMEs are performing e-CRM through IBTs to manage their customer relationships. E-CRM facilitates two main capabilities which are customer communication and customer information management. SMEs may afford resources and attention to their nearest and dearest customers. The conclusion is drawn that, while it is challenging to integrate e-CRM with existing relationship processes, e-CRM makes customer information management and accessibility easy.

Managerial Implications

SMEs customer centric approach will help them to use e-CRM to improve efficiency and effectiveness of marketing. By following the large organization strategies

SMEs will not succeed at e-CRM. So, to focus on efficiency of marketing SMEs should implement internet technologies. E-CRM has an important role in customer communication, So, managers should focus on implementing e-CRM as it will free up time which can be utilized for more fruitful activities and valuable face to face meetings. Managers should understand the importance of face to face and e-CRM communication and implement the one accordingly, for example for simple issues an email will work better than a face-to-face meeting or telephonic conversation.

Quality customer communication using e-CRM is dependent on quality of information management process. Managers should manage the customer information in the form of simple databases. This information can be collected through web applications, where websites are linked to databases. Managers should be cautious enough to use e-CRM in place of existing practices in order to avoid malfunctioning of SMEs marketing strategies.

LIMITATIONS

The study focuses on two areas (i.e., customer communication and customer information management) of multifaceted implementation. Second the sampling done has a potential to limit generalizability of findings and conclusions.

REFERENCES

Admiraal, W., & Lockhorst, D. (2009). E-learning in small and medium-sized enterprises across Europe: Attitudes towards technology, learning and training. *International Small Business Journal*, *27*(6), 743–767. doi:10.1177/0266242609344244

Ahearne, M., Hughes, D. E., & Schillewaert, N. (2007). Why sales reps should welcome information technology: Measuring the impact of CRM-based IT on sales effectiveness. *International Journal of Research in Marketing*, *24*(4), 336–349. doi:10.1016/j.ijresmar.2007.09.003

Ang, L., & Buttle, F. (2006). Managing for a successful customer acquisition: An exploration. *Journal of Marketing Management*, *22*(3-4), 295–317. doi:10.1362/026725706776861217

Bailey, C., Baines, P. R., Wilson, H., & Clark, M. (2009). Segmentation and customer insight incontemporary services marketing practice: Why grouping customers is no longer enough. *Journal of Marketing Management*, *25*(3/4), 227–252. doi:10.1362/026725709X429737

Becker, J. U., Greve, G., & Albers, S. (2009). The impact of technological and organisational implementation of CRM on customer acquisition, maintenance and retention. *International Journal of Research in Marketing*, *26*(3), 207–215. doi:10.1016/j.ijresmar.2009.03.006

Bernard, H. R. (2000). *Social Research Methods: Qualitative and Quantitative Approaches*. Sage.

BERR. (2009). *Annual Small Business Survey 2007/08*. Department for Business Enterprise and Regulatory Reform. Available at: www.bis.gov.uk/files/file50124.doc

Blili, S., & Raymond, L. (1993). Information technology: Threats and opportunities for SMEs. *International Journal of Information Management*, *13*(6), 439–448. doi:10.1016/0268-4012(93)90060-H

Boddy, C. R. (2007). Projective techniques in Taiwan and Asia-Pacific market research. *Qualitative Market Research*, *10*(1), 48–62. doi:10.1108/13522750710720396

Boyle, A. B. (2001). The internet in industrial channels: Its use in (and effects on) exchange relationships. *Journal of Business and Industrial Marketing*, *16*(6/7), 452–469. doi:10.1108/EUM0000000006020

Bradshaw, D., & Brash, C. (2001). Managing customer relationships in the e-business world: How to personalise computer relationships for increased profitability. *International Journal of Retail & Distribution Management*, *29*(11/12), 520–529. doi:10.1108/09590550110696969

Carson, D., & Gilmore, A. (2000). SME marketing management competencies. *International Business Review*, *9*(3), 363–382. doi:10.1016/S0969-5931(00)00006-8

Carson, D., Cromie, S., McGowan, P., & Hill, J. (1995). *Marketing and Entrepreneurship in SMEs:An Innovative Approach*. Prentice-Hall.

Chaffey, D., Mayer, R., Johnston, K., & Ellis-Chadwick, F. (2003). *Internet Marketing* (2nd ed.). Prentice-Hall.

Chaston, I., & Mangles, T. (2003). Relationship marketing in online business-to-business markets: A pilot investigation of small UK manufacturing firms. *European Journal of Marketing*, *37*(5/6), 753–773. doi:10.1108/03090560310465134

Chen, J., & Ching, R. K. H. (2007). The effects of information and communication technology on customer relationship management and customer lock-in. *International Journal of Electronic Business*, *5*(5), 478–498. doi:10.1504/IJEB.2007.015446

D'Andrade, R. G. (1995). *The Development of Cognitive Anthropology*. Cambridge University Press. doi:10.1017/CBO9781139166645

Day, S. G., & Hubbard, J. K. (2003). Customer relationships go digital. *Business Strategy Review*, *14*(1), 17–26. doi:10.1111/1467-8616.00240

Denzin, N. K. (1978). *The Research Act: A Theoretical Introduction to Sociological Methods*. Praeger.

Dillman, D. A. (1978). *Mail and Telephone Surveys*. Wiley.

Doern, R. (2009). Investigating barriers to SME growth and development in transition environments: A critique and suggestions for developing the methodology. *International Small Business Journal*, *27*(3), 275–305. doi:10.1177/0266242609102275

Doole, I., Grimes, T., & Demack, S. (2006). An exploration of the management practices and processes most closely associated with high levels of export capability in SMEs. *Marketing Intelligence & Planning*, *24*(6), 632–647. doi:10.1108/02634500610701690

Dwyer, F. R., Schurr, P. H., & Oh, S. (1987). Developing buyer-seller relationships. *Journal of Marketing*, *51*(2), 11–27. doi:10.1177/002224298705100202

European Commission. (2005). *SME Definition*. http://eceuropa.eu/enterprise/enterprise_policy/sme_definition/index_en.htm

Geiger, S., & Martin, S. (1999). The internet as a relationship marketing tool-some evidence from Irish companies. *Irish Marketing Review*, *12*(2), 24–36.

Gilman, M. W., & Edwards, P. K. (2008). Testing a framework of the organization of small firms: Fast-growth, high-tech SMEs. *International Small Business Journal*, *26*(5), 531–558. doi:10.1177/0266242608094028

Gummesson, E. (1994). Making relationship marketing operational. *International Journal of Service Industry Management*, *5*(5), 5–20. doi:10.1108/09564239410074349

Gummesson, E. (2002). *Total Relationship Marketing: Marketing Management Relationship Strategy and CRM Approaches to the Network Economy*. Butterworth-Heinemann.

Hair, J. F. J., Anderson, R. E., Tatham, R. L., & Black, W. C. (1998). *Multivariate Data Analysis* (5th ed.). Prentice-Hall.

Harker, M. J., & Egan, J. (2006). The past present and future of relationship marketing. *Journal of Marketing Management*, *22*(1-2), 215–242.

Harrigan, P., Ramsey, E., & Ibbotson, P. (2009). Investigating the e-CRM activities of Irish SMEs. *Journal of Small Business and Enterprise Development*, *16*(3), 443–465. doi:10.1108/14626000910977161

Hennig-Thurau, T., Malthouse, E. C., Friege, C., Gensler, S., Lobschat, L., Rangaswamy, A., & Skiera, B. (2010). The impact of new media on customer relationships. *Journal of Service Research*, *13*(3), 311–330. doi:10.1177/1094670510375460

Hills, G. E., Hultman, C. M., & Miles, M. P. (2008). The evolution and development of entrepreneurial marketing. *Journal of Small Business Management*, *46*(1), 99–112. doi:10.1111/j.1540-627X.2007.00234.x

Hutchinson, V., & Quintas, P. (2008). Do SMEs do knowledge management? Or simply manage what they know? *International Small Business Journal*, *26*(2), 131–154. doi:10.1177/0266242607086571

Jack, S., Moult, S., Anderson, A. R., & Dodd, S. (2010). An entrepreneurial network evolving: Patterns of change. *International Small Business Journal*, *28*(4), 315–337. doi:10.1177/0266242610363525

Jayachandran, S., Sharma, S., Kaufman, P., & Raman, P. (2005). The role of relational information processes and technology use in customer relationship management. *Journal of Marketing*, *69*(4), 177–192. doi:10.1509/jmkg.2005.69.4.177

Jick, T. D. (1979). Mixing qualitative and quantitative methods: Triangulation in action. *Administrative Science Quarterly*, *24*(4), 602–611. doi:10.2307/2392366

Jocumsen, G. (2004). How do small business managers make strategic marketing decisions? A model of process. *European Journal of Marketing*, *38*(5/6), 659–674. doi:10.1108/03090560410529277

Keh, H. T., Nguyen, T. T. M., & Ng, H. P. (2007). The effects of entrepreneurial orientation and marketing information on the performance of SMEs. *Journal of Business Venturing*, *22*(4), 592–611. doi:10.1016/j.jbusvent.2006.05.003

Kim, K. K., Umanath, N. S., & Kim, B. H. (2006). An assessment of electronic information transfer in B2B supply-channel relationships. *Journal of Management Information Systems*, *22*(3), 293–320.

Kocak, A., & Abimbola, T. (2009). The effects of entrepreneurial marketing on born global performance. *International Marketing Review*, *26*(4/5), 439–452. doi:10.1108/02651330910971977

Kumar, V., Aksoy, L., Donkers, B., Venkatesan, R., Wiesel, T., & Tillmanns, S. (2010). Undervalued or overvalued customers: Capturing total customer engagement value. *Journal of Service Research, 13*(3), 297–310. doi:10.1177/1094670510375602

Lawson-Body, A., & O'Keefe, T. P. (2006). Interorganizational relationships in the context of SMEs B2B e-commerce. *Journal of Electronic Commerce in Organizations, 4*(4), 1–28. doi:10.4018/jeco.2006100101

Moriarty, J., Jones, R., Rowley, J., & Kupiec-Teahan, B. (2009). Marketing in small hotels: A qualitative study. *Marketing Intelligence & Planning, 26*(3), 293–315. doi:10.1108/02634500810871348

Nambisan, S., & Baron, R. A. (2007). Interactions in virtual customer environments: Implications for product support and customer relationship management. *Journal of Interactive Marketing, 21*(2), 42–62. doi:10.1002/dir.20077

Nunnaly, J. (1978). *Psychometric Theory*. McGraw-Hill.

O'Dwyer, M., Gilmore, A., & Carson, D. (2009). Innovative marketing in SMEs. *European Journal of Marketing, 43*(1/2), 46–61. doi:10.1108/03090560910923238

Onwuegbuzie, A. J., & Leech, N. L. (2007). Validity and qualitative research: An oxymoron? *Quality & Quantity, 41*(2), 233–250. doi:10.100711135-006-9000-3

Padmanabhan, B., & Tuzhilin, A. (2003). On the use of optimization for data mining: Theoretical interactions and eCRM opportunities. *Management Science, 49*(10), 1327–1343. doi:10.1287/mnsc.49.10.1327.17310

Padmanabhan, B., Zheng, Z., & Kimbrough, S. O. (2006). An empirical analysis of the value of complete information of eCRM models. *Management Information Systems Quarterly, 30*(2), 247–267. doi:10.2307/25148730

Parvatiyar, A., & Sheth, J. N. (2001). Customer relationship management: Emerging practice process and discipline. *Journal of Economic & Social Research, 3*(2), 1–34.

Patton, M. Q. (2002). *Qualitative Research and Evaluation Methods* (3rd ed.). Sage.

Payne, A., & Frow, P. (2006). Customer relationship management: From strategy to implementation. *Journal of Marketing Management, 22*(1-2), 135–168. doi:10.1362/026725706776022272

Peltier, J. W., Schibrowsky, J. A., & Zhao, Y. (2009). Understanding the antecedents to the adoption of CRM technology by small retailers: Entrepreneurs vs owner-managers. *International Small Business Journal, 27*(3), 307–336. doi:10.1177/0266242609102276

Pett, M. A., Lackey, N. R., & Sullivan, J. J. (2003). *Making Sense of Factor Analysis*. Sage. doi:10.4135/9781412984898

Ragins, J. E., & Greco, J. A. (2003). Customer relationship management and e-business: More than a software solution. *Review of Business*, *24*(1), 25–30.

Rai, A., Patnayakuni, R., & Seth, M. (2006). Firm performance impacts of digitally enabled supply chain integration capabilities. *Management Information Systems Quarterly*, *30*(2), 225–246. doi:10.2307/25148729

Ramsey, E., Ibbotson, P., & McCole, P. (2006). Application of projectives techniques in an e-business research context. *International Journal of Market Research*, *48*(5), 551–573. doi:10.1177/147078530604800506

Raubenheimer, J. E. (2004). An item selection procedure to maximize scale reliability and validity. *SA Journal of Industrial Psychology*, *30*(4), 59–64. doi:10.4102ajip.v30i4.168

Reichheld, F. F., & Sasser, J. W. E. (1990). Zero defections: Quality comes to services. *Harvard Business Review*, *68*(5), 105–111. PMID:10107082

Reinartz, W., Krafft, M., & Hoyer, W. D. (2004). The customer relationship management process: Its measurement and impact on performance. *JMR, Journal of Marketing Research*, *41*(3), 293–305. doi:10.1509/jmkr.41.3.293.35991

Richardson, T. (2005). *What do they want? Broadband! When do they want it? Now!* Available at: www.theregister.com

Ritchie, B., & Brindley, C. (2005). ICT adoption by SMEs: Implications for relationships and management. *New Technology, Work and Employment*, *20*(3), 205–217. doi:10.1111/j.1468-005X.2005.00154.x

Rogers, E. M., & Beal, G. M. (1958). Projective techniques in interviewing farmers. *Journal of Marketing*, *23*(2), 177–183. doi:10.1177/002224295802300210

Ryals, L. (2005). Making customer relationship management work: The measurement and profitable management of customer relationships. *Journal of Marketing*, *69*(4), 252–261. doi:10.1509/jmkg.2005.69.4.252

Ryals, L., & Humphries, A. S. (2007). Managing key business-to-business relationships. *Journal of Service Research*, *9*(2), 312–326. doi:10.1177/1094670507299380

Saris, W. E., & Gallhofer, I. N. (2007). *Design Evaluation and Analysis of Questionnaires for Survey Research*. Wiley. doi:10.1002/9780470165195

SFA. (2007). *Small Firms Association (Ireland), CSO Small Business Report*. Available at: www.sfa.ie

Simmons, G., Armstrong, G. A., & Durkin, M. G. (2008). A conceptualization of the determinants of small business website adoption: Setting the research agenda. *International Small Business Journal*, *26*(3), 351–389. doi:10.1177/0266242608088743

Stone, E. (1978). *Research Methods in Organizational Behaviour*. Scott Foresman.

Straub, D. W. (1989). Validating instruments in MIS research. *Management Information Systems Quarterly*, *13*(2), 147–169. doi:10.2307/248922

Street, C. T., & Meister, D. B. (2004). Small business growth and internal transparency: The role of information systems. *Management Information Systems Quarterly*, *28*(3), 473–506. doi:10.2307/25148647

Tan, X., Yen, D. C., & Fang, X. (2002). Internet integrated customer relationship management –a key success factor for companies in the e-commerce arena. *Journal of Computer Information Systems*, *42*(3), 77–86.

Verhoef, P. C., Neslin, S. A., & Vroomen, B. (2007). Multichannel customer management: Understanding the research shopper. *International Journal of Research in Marketing*, *24*(2), 129–148. doi:10.1016/j.ijresmar.2006.11.002

Verhoef, P. C., Reinartz, W. J., & Krafft, M. (2010). Customer engagement as a new perspective in customer management. *Journal of Service Research*, *13*(3), 247–252. doi:10.1177/1094670510375461

Webb, J. R. (1992). *Understanding and Designing Market Research*. Academic Press.

Webster, F. E. Jr. (1992). The changing role of marketing in the corporation. *Journal of Marketing*, *56*(4), 1–17. doi:10.1177/002224299205600402

Zontanos, G., & Anderson, A. R. (2004). Relationships marketing and small business: An exploration of links in theory and practice. *Qualitative Market Research*, *7*(3), 228–236. doi:10.1108/13522750410540236

Hunt, D. S., & Morgan, M. R. (1994). Relationship marketing in the era of network competition. *Marketing Management*, *3*(1), 18–28.

Harrigan, P., Ramsey, E., & Ibbotson, P. (2008). E-CRM in SMEs: An exploratory study in Northern Ireland. *Marketing Intelligence & Planning*, *26*(4), 385–404. doi:10.1108/02634500810879296

ADDITIONAL READING

Ab Hamid, N. R., & Kassim, N. (2004). Internet technology as a tool in customer relationship management. *The Journal of American Academy of Business, Cambridge*, *4*(1/2), 103–108.

Adebanjo, D. (2003). Classifying and selecting e-CRM applications: An analysis-based proposal. *Management Decision*, *41*(6), 570–577. doi:10.1108/00251740310491517

Creswell, J. W., & Plano Clark, V. (2007). *Designing and Conducting Mixed Methods Research*. Sage.

Gro¨nroos, C. (2004). The relationship marketing process: Communication interaction dialogue value. *Journal of Business and Industrial Marketing*, *19*(2), 99–113. doi:10.1108/08858620410523981

Harrison-Walker, L. J., & Neeley, S. E. (2004). Customer relationship building on the internet in B2B marketing: A proposed typology. *Journal of Marketing Theory and Practice*, *12*(1), 19–35. doi:10.1080/10696679.2004.11658510

Johnson, R. B., Onwuegbuzie, A. J., & Turner, L. (2007). Toward a definition of mixed methods research. *Journal of Mixed Methods Research*, *1*(2), 112–133. doi:10.1177/1558689806298224

Lee-Kelley, L., Gilbert, D., & Mannicom, R. (2003). How e-CRM can enhance customer loyalty. *Marketing Intelligence & Planning*, *21*(4/5), 239–248. doi:10.1108/02634500310480121

Letaifa, S. B., & Perrien, J. (2007). The impact of e-CRM on organisational and individual behaviour: The effect of the remuneration and reward system. *International Journal of E-Business Research*, *3*(2), 13–23. doi:10.4018/jebr.2007040102

Morgan, J. (2007). Customer information management (CIM): The key to successful CRM in financial services. *Journal of Performance Management*, *20*(2), 47–65.

Onwuegbuzie, A. J., & Johnson, R. B. (2006). The validity issue in mixed research. *Research in the Schools*, *13*(1), 48–63.

Ramsey, E., Ibbotson, P., Bell, J., & Gray, B. (2004). A projectives perspective of international 'e' services. *Qualitative Market Research*, *7*(1), 34–47. doi:10.1108/13522750410512868

Sale, J. E. M., Lohfeld, L. H., & Brazil, K. (2002). Revisiting the quantitative-qualitative debate: Implications for mixed-methods research. *Quality & Quantity*, *36*(1), 43–54. doi:10.1023/A:1014301607592 PMID:26523073

Schroder, D., & Madeja, N. (2004). Is customer relationship management a success factor in electronic commerce? *Journal of Electronic Commerce Research*, *5*(1), 38–53.

Selm, M., & Jankowski, N. W. (2006). Conducting online surveys. *Quality & Quantity*, *4*(3), 435–457. doi:10.100711135-005-8081-8

Tagliavini, M., Ravarini, A., & Antonelli, A. (2001). An evaluation model for electronic commerce activities within SMEs. *Information Technology and Management*, *2*(2), 211–230. doi:10.1023/A:1011417703063

Tashakkori, A., & Teddlie, C. (2003). *Handbook of Mixed Methods in Social and Behavioral Research*. Sage.

Teddlie, C., & Yu, F. (2007). Mixed methods sampling: A typology with examples. *Journal of Mixed Methods Research*, *1*(1), 77–100. doi:10.1177/1558689806292430

Teng, K. L. L., Soo, G. O., & Poon, W. C. (2007). The use of customer relationship management (CRM) by manufacturing firms in different industries: A Malaysian survey. *International Journal of Management*, *24*(2), 386–397.

Wang, Y., & Yao, Y. (2002). Sources of China's economic growth 1952-1999: Incorporating human capital accumulation. *China Economic Review*, *116*, 32–52.

Xu, M., Rohatgi, R., & Duan, Y. (2007). E-business adoption in SMEs: Some preliminary findings from electronic components industry. *International Journal of E-Business Research*, *3*(1), 74–90. doi:10.4018/jebr.2007010105

Yin, R. (2003). *Case Study Research: Design and Methods*. Sage.

Zhang, M., Sarker, S., & McCullough, J. (2008). Measuring information technology capability of export-focused small or medium sized enterprises in China: Scale development and validation. *Journal of Global Information Management*, *16*(3), 1–25. doi:10.4018/jgim.2008070101

Chapter 12
Alert-Driven Customer Relationship Management in Online Travel Agencies:
Event-Condition-Actions Rules and Key Performance Indicators

Mimi Mei Wa Chan
The University of Hong Kong, Hong Kong

Dickson K. W. Chiu
https://orcid.org/0000-0002-7926-9568
The University of Hong Kong, Hong Kong

ABSTRACT

Currently, online travel agencies (OTA) allow their customers to make timely travel reservations anytime and anywhere through websites and mobile technologies. Customer service is vital to the success of any tourism and hospitality business, including online travel agencies. One major challenge that online travel agencies face is continuously declining customer experience because this may result in a high customer churn rate. Customer relationship management (CRM) is a strategy used by most organizations to increase customer lifetime value by selecting customers and maintaining their relationships. Delivering timely and consistently higher customer service levels are the goal of every OTA, and they need to evolve and implement a new approach to address customer issues proactively to increase customer retention and loyalty. This study analyzes some common CRM workflows of OTAs and proposes an alert-driven approach to CRM to enhance their effectiveness in creating satisfying customer experiences and retaining customers.

DOI: 10.4018/978-1-6684-5386-5.ch012

INTRODUCTION

Due to technological advancement, online travel agencies (OTA) can succeed in today's travel industry with the increase in timely bookings, which is one of the most significant trends for 21st-century travelers (Chiu, Yueh, Leung, & Hung, 2009; Cheung et al., 2022). According to Research and Markets (2019), the global online travel agency market value was USD$258 billion in 2018 and is forecasted to reach USD$372 billion by 2023. The OTA market has matured over years of development, with increasing travel websites (Zhiliang & Lihua, 2015) and mobile technology usage (Gong et al., 2017). There is a trend of online and last-minute booking, even during travelers' trips, and travelers' information-seeking and booking behavior has changed in recent years (Ni et al., 2021), thus significantly affecting how travelers utilize the services provided by traditional travel agencies. Compared to previous travelers, 21st-century travelers are more independent and powerful, as most travelers can handle various bookings even during their trips, such as flight tickets, hotels, transportation, in-destination navigation, and post-vacation reviews (Gong et al., 2017; Ni et al., 2021).

Customer relationship management (CRM) can enhance the overall performance of an organization and is vital to its success (Vogt, 2011), especially upon significant changes in customer behaviors (Chiu et al., 2003). Past studies have reviewed the success and future of CRM and its facilitation with information systems. While some studies focused on the empirical aspects of CRM in hotels and airlines, scant studies focus on CRM implementation for OTA, especially through an alert management system (AMS). This study first analyzes some common workflow on customer relationship management in most online travel agencies and understands user requirements. To improve service delivery to customers and CRM, this study proposes some CRM implementation based on the concept of alert management and event-condition-action (ECA) rules (Chiu et al., 2003).

LITERATURE REVIEW

Customer Relationship Management

CRM is defined as a customer-focused business strategy integrating sales, marketing, and customer services (Chalmeta, 2006). CRM plays a vital role in creating and adding value to the organization and its customers, primarily enhancing the organization's overall performance (Vogt, 2011). To increase customers' lifetime value to the organization, CRM is a strategy commonly used for selecting customers and maintaining relationships with them (Al-Hazmi, 2021). The organization's overall performance can be measured by its profitability, which means higher profit margins, more loyal customers, lower marketing expenses and labor costs, and more technology usage (Chiu et al., 2003). Besides, CRM is considered a customer-centric management mechanism to improve the relationship between the organization and its customers (Zhiliang & Lihua, 2015).

With the advancement in information and communication technologies (ICT), there are huge opportunities and challenges for CRM enhancement (Payne & Frow, 2006; Chiu et al., 2003). Nowadays, CRM focuses on organizing customer information in computer-authorized systems (Vogt, 2011). Customer records stored in computerized CRM systems support analyzing customer needs and past booking behaviors for future marketing and sales (Chiang, 2019).

Zhiliang and Lihua (2015) suggested that the core value of CRM is to advance and govern sales, marketing, the services of customers, reinforcement, and boost the organization's automation level. They further highlight three aspects of CRM: operational, analytic, and customer, aligning with Chiu et al. (2003). Call centers and e-commerce websites commonly use operational CRM to collect customer data, provide Q&A (question and answer), and handle complaints as a key communication tool between operational departments and customers, which works well for marketing, sales, and services (Chiu et al., 2003; Chiu, Yueh, et al., 2009; Tarasova et al., 2020). Analytic CRM can convert customer data obtained by previous transactions and CRM systems into information, guiding marketing activities, management decision, and service directions (Chiu et al., 2003). Collaborative CRM is useful for communication and information exchange within an organization and its customers and business partners through traditional and online tools (Chiu, Kwok, et al., 2009; Alshurideh et al., 2019).

Online Travel Agency

An OTA is an alternative and improved business strategy for traditional travel agencies, allowing the shift from offline to online (Chang et al., 2019). According to Laudon and Laudon (2022), OTAs earn a commission with every successful online order and are thus considered *transaction brokers* or intermediaries between the suppliers (such as hotels, airlines, and ticketing companies) and the customers. Suppliers provide hotel rooms, flight tickets, and other travel-related products for travelers to purchase on the websites or mobile applications of the OTA, which focus on customer-related issues and satisfy customers with excellent CRM (Baloglu et al., 2010; Chiu, Yueh, et al., 2009). For example, focusing on CRM has been the primary strategy of the Expedia Group, one of the largest online travel agencies (Expedia, 2020).

OTAs commonly offer point-based reward systems to create customer loyalty and encourage long-term business, aiming to identify and build loyal customers' databases and thus reward, promote, and provide specialized services for them (Chan, Chiu, & Ho, 2022). Loyalty programs are vital to the long-term success of OTAs since they can encourage customers to return for more business with the incentive of earning and accumulating reward points (Lee et al., 2022). For example, all Expedia Rewards members can save an extra 10% or more on selected hotels, earn Expedia points on every trip, and use their points to save on travel (Expedia, n.d.). The more the customers travel with Expedia, the higher the rewards.

Alert Management System

Alerts mean urgent requests and critical signals, which are special events (Chiu et al., 2003; Capan et al., 2018). AMS helps organizations implement process and data integration under urgent or important situations to reduce delays and provide better customer services by improving communications and coordination among different departments, staff, and external business partners (Chiu, Cheung, et al., 2010). Typical AMS functions include requesting alerts, canceling alerts, checking alert status, listing active alerts, and receiving delayed responses (Chiu, Kwok, et al., 2009).

The event-condition-action (ECA) rule is the primary mechanism of event-driven computing (Chiu et al., 2003), comprising three parts: an event, a condition, and an action, in which events trigger actions by events with the given specific conditions. Significant events to the system, such as user actions, the transmission of sensor data, and a message from other systems, are identified within an event-driven program (Stopford, 2018). The significance of the ECA rule is to specify how events drive the desired program responses (Rouse, 2016). The semantics of an ECA rule is when an event with significance for the system occurs, the conditions are checked for or evaluated; if the conditions exist or meet pre-established criteria, the appropriate action is executed (Chiu, Cheung, et al., 2010).

ONLINE TRAVELLING AGENCY BACKGROUND

Industry References

This study's ECA rules and alerts design is based on Expedia, Priceline, and Ctrip, key leaders of online travel agencies (Wei, 2021). Their key features are summarized below.

1. Expedia is a US market leader, with two-thirds of online travel agencies' market share. It owned USD$61 billion of bookings and acquired Travelocity and Orbitz in 2015. Its subsidiaries include metasearch engines (i.e., Trivago), business travel targeted (i.e., Egencis), and holiday accommodations (i.e., HomeAway) (Rossini, 2016).
2. Priceline is a European market leader with USD$56 billion of bookings in 2015 (Rossini, 2016) and is great in hotel provision. In travel verticals, it contains metasearch engine (i.e. Kayak.com), hotel rentals (i.e. Booking.com), and restaurant reservation (i.e. OpenTable). It also owns a 9% share of Ctrip (Schaal, 2016).
3. Ctrip is a China market leader with a fast and high growth rate (i.e., 57%) with USD$27 billion of bookings in 2015 (Rossini, 2016). 70% of its bookings are through its mobile application, and it has expanded its market in Asia and other websites, including Quanr, eLong, and MakeMyTrip. It always appears in Skyscanner's metasearch engine (Schaal, 2016).

Common Problems of CRM Systems

The main stakeholders in OTA CRM systems include customers, customer service staff, accounting staff, suppliers, and back-office staff. The existing process and management problems on CRM are highlighted below.

Separate Databases for Storing Customer Data - Traditionally, customer data are stored in different databases like membership, transactions, bookings, profiles, etc. Though database integration is possible within organizations, they are often not integrated among business partners like airlines, hotels, and restaurants (Chiu, Kwok, et al., 2009). Thus, customer services staff may often encounter problems accessing and updating customer data in various databases, thus decreasing productivity and customer care. Furthermore, the customer services staff cannot immediately access the complete customer profile or purchase history (Chiu, Kwok, et al., 2009), resulting in delays in customer responses. Such delays may affect customer satisfaction and customer experience, especially because of travel-related products' volatile price and availability (Chiu et al., 2003; Gong et al., 2017). In addition, maintaining the accuracy and consistency of customer data in various databases is difficult and time-consuming (Vo et al., 2021).

Delay in Management Decision - The role of senior management is to establish the organization's vision, goals, objectives, and business tactics. In particular, managers should identify and manage unexpected problems early to prevent situations from worsening. However, they often cannot detect the problems before they become too serious due to incompetent system design or information availability of existing systems, which results in the delay in management decision-making.

Figure 1. User Case Diagram of Customer Relationship Management

Requirements Overview

To meet the requirements of main stakeholders (i.e., customers, customer service staff, accounting staff, suppliers, and back-office staff), the main features of an enhanced CRM system with the alert-driven approach are highlighted in Figure 1 and discussed below.

Enhanced Customer Database - Efficiency, knowledge, and immediacy are essential elements contributing to customer satisfaction (Chiu et al., 2003). The individual databases should be integrated into a centralized data warehouse for data storage to tackle the problem. Integrating data from multiple databases in the organization and business partners enhances data integrity and ensures data quality (Chiu, Kwok, et al., 2009). Furthermore, it provides data availability and reduces the time for accessing and monitoring data from multiple databases, reducing customer service response time for customer experience enhancement (Hoyer et al., 2020).

Effective and Timely Management Decision Making - The alert-driven approach should be used to design the improved CRM system, particularly ECA rules for specifying alerts for senior management actions (Chiu et al., 2003). Detailed examples of these rules are illustrated in the next section. Further, the enhanced CRM system provides information and analytical tools to assist the senior management in developing business tactics and long-term strategies. Compared to other system designs, the alert-driven approach allows senior management and operations supervisors to detect problems and solve them earlier. Customer service staff can also use the CRM system to get more information for follow-up actions for better and more timely customer care (Sharma et al., 2020).

DESIGN AND IMPLEMENTATION

System Architecture

Based on the requirements mentioned above, Figure 3 depicts the overall system architecture for the CRM system for building customer loyalty and improving customer services for OTAs adapted from Chiu et al. (2009). The role of the AMS is to monitor urgent and essential tasks for submitting and receiving alerts. The Incoming Alert Monitor subsystem receives and queuing alerts from customers, back-office staff, customer services staff, and senior management. The incoming alerts trigger the alert handlers through the Process Execution module to involve routines of the Application Logic. The Process and Alert Definition defines the tasks and alerts based on various requirements outlined in the previous section.

The role of the Outgoing Alert Monitor subsystem is to create and submit alerts through Web service requests with response monitoring. The Outgoing Alert Monitor subsystem comprises three modules: the Role Matching, the Urgencies Strategy Definition, and the Service Provider Monitor. The Role Monitoring module first identifies the service providers to which the alerts will be forwarded. The Urgencies Strategy Definition module identifies the handling policies when the alert acknowledgments are late. The Service Provider Monitoring module is responsible for sending alert messages, receiving responses, and maintaining alert statuses.

Alert Driven Approach to CRM

A CRM system usually comprises two subsystems: front-end and back-end (Memon et al., 2018). The front-end subsystem provides interactive applications to the senior management (i.e., managerial application), customer services staff (i.e., call center), and customers (i.e., customer portal). The back-end subsystem supports the front-end subsystem.

Typically, the back-end subsystem contains a data warehouse for storing all the data, such as customer data, transactions, and orders, for both front-end Application Logic and back-end subsystems, for daily operations and managerial decisions. Chiu et al. (2003) suggested that both analytical and active rule engines should be considered in an event-driven CRM approach. The function of the active rule engine coordinates the timely enactment of CRM activities. The analytic engine is

Figure 2. CRM System Architecture highlighting the Alert Management System

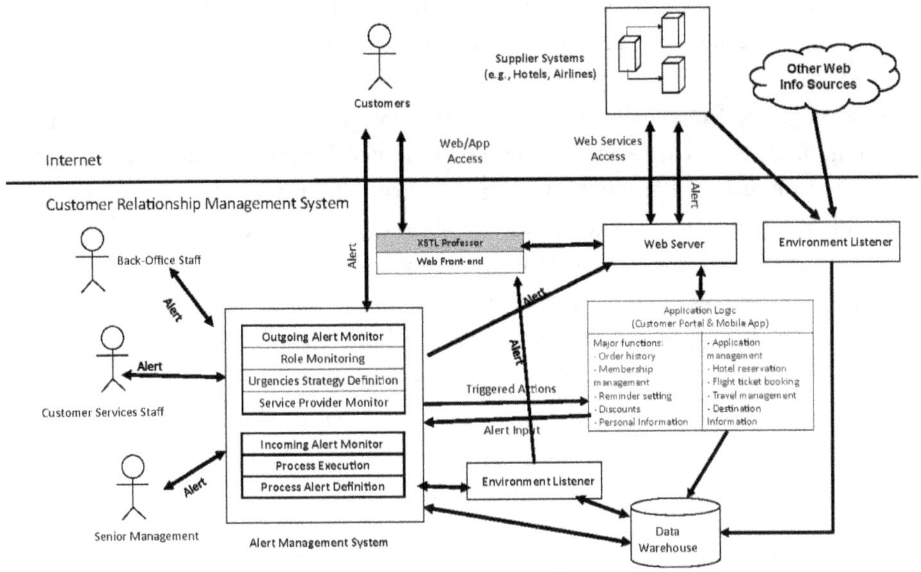

mainly for knowledge discovery, which should be separated from the active rule engine (Renjith et al., 2020).

The rules processed by the Active Rule Engine are defined in the ECA format, as shown in Table 1. In our case, the business events mainly concern customers, the market environment, and the OTA. Rules triggered by events related to customer behaviors include the following exceptional situations that need operational attention for better and more timely handling (Chiu et al., 2003), which include the following (R1 – R5):

- Abnormal order input (from Customer Portal, app, or Call Center)
- Payment due (time event)
- Customer confirms booking (from Customer Portal, app, or Call Center)
- Customer cancel booking (from Customer Portal, app, or Call Center)
- Complaints (from Customer Portal, app, Call Center, or email)

Section (b) of Table 1 illustrates rules triggered by events related to changes in customer profiles, either discovered by the Analytical Engine or actively by customers. These rules push relevant promotion information to customers, and high-tier customers may receive attention from the customer service staff (Chiu, Hung, et al., 2011; Chiu et al., 2003). Typical examples include:

- Customer attrition alert (from Analytical Engine)
- Customer change in segmentation (from Analytical Engine)
- Customer change interest (from Customer Portal)

Section (c) of Table 1 illustrates rules triggered by events related to the market environment directly from the Environment Listener. One type of such event related to information on travel product price changes from Environmental Listener enables the timely relevant price update of individual products, services, or packages (Chiu, Yueh, et al., 2009; Chiu et al., 2003). Other events related to urgent travel alerts, such as airport emergencies, political unrest, and epidemic outburst from the Environmental Listener, can be forwarded immediately to affected customers according to geographic information matching (Chiu, Lin, et al., 2010; Zheng et al., 2019). Section (d) of Table 1 illustrates rules triggered by events related to the OTA releasing important news or changes in its policy (mainly from the Managerial Applications) so that all customers and staff can be timely notified (Chiu et al., 2003).

Managerial Alerts and Key Performance Indicators

Key Performance Indicators (KPIs) are metrics for measuring performance from various dimensions of an organization (Laudon & Laudon, 2022). KPIs provide decision support to senior management by helping them understand the organization's performance along each dimension. Table 2 shows some useful KPIs that can inform the senior OTA management related to CRM (Fedoryshyna et al., 2021). Based on the KPIs mentioned above and other signals from the Analytical Engine, Table 3 shows some ECA rules for senior OTA management, including the following.

- Decrease in advertisement revenue from the booking process
- Decrease in customer retention rate
- Increase in customer turnover rate
- Decrease in customer satisfaction rate
- Increase in customer complaints
- Low conversion rate
- Decrease in new customers
- Long order fulfillment time

Table 1. ECA Rules for CRM

Rule	Event	Condition	Alert Action
(a) Rules Triggered by Events Related to Customer Behavior			
R1	Order input (from customer portal, app, or website)	Abnormal transaction amount	1. Alert customer – cancel or continue 2. Alert customer services staff and accounting staff for attention
R2	Payment due (time event)	Payment unsettled	1. Notify customer for payment or reduce holding 2. Alert customer services staff and accounting staff for attention
R3	Customer confirms booking (from customer portal)	Customer pays for the booking	1. Lightly notify customer services staff with aggregated numbers to keep track of trends 2. Alert also the manager if loyal customers 3. Alert customer that transaction process is completed
R4	Customer cancel booking (from customer portal)	Customer cancels the booking	1. Alert customer services staff about the change
R5	Complaints (from customer portal or email or OTA call center)	Customer sends complaints	1. Record details of customer complaints and resolution in the data warehouse 2. Alert customer services staff to handle complaints to reduce the possibility of customer attrition
(b) Rules Triggered by Events Related to Customer Profile			
R6	Customer attrition alert (from Analytical engine)	i) > 3% ii) Whether valuable high-leveled user	1. Alert customer services staff for the possibility of customer attrition 2. Alert also the manager if loyal customers
R7	Customer change in segmentation (from Analytical Engine)	User-level changes	1. Alert customer services staff if loyal customers 2. Subscribe the customer to new information sources and news 3. Suggest cross-sale
R8	Customer change interest (from customer portal)	User purchase trend changes	1. Alert customer services staff if loyal customers 2. Subscribe the customer to new information sources and news 3. Suggest cross-sale
(c) Rules Triggered by Events Related to Environment			
R9	Information on travel product price changes (from the environmental listener)	Price changes for more than a certain percentage (e.g., 10%)	Send the news to the customers who have subscribed to the information of the destination
R10	Airport emergency/ abnormal situation such as political unrest (from the environmental listener)	Geographical location of customers matched	1. Notify customer for cancellation of the chosen flights 2. Notify senior management and customer services staff for special attention and preparation
R11	Epidemic outburst (from the environmental listener)	Governmental travel alerts on epidemics (such as Covid-19)	1. Notify the customers of potential trip cancellations and modification 2. Notify the suppliers for potential customer reduction
(d) Rules Triggered by Events Related to the Online Travel Agency			
R12	Important news/ changes in the policy of the online travel agency (from managerial applications)	-	Notify all customers and staff

Table 2. Key Performance Indicators for Senior Management

KPI	Example Target	Source	Frequency	Remarks
Customer Retention Rate	70%	CRM	Monthly	The ability to keep a paying customer over a preset period.
Customer Turnover Rate	25%	CRM	Quarterly	The number of customers lost in a given period.
Customer Satisfaction Rate	Above 75%	CRM	Monthly	How satisfied the customers are with the services provided by the online travel agency
Number of customer complaints	Less than 50 cases each month	CRM	Monthly	The number of complaints received through website, app, or email
Conversion Rate	40%	CRM	Monthly	The proportion of visitors to an OTA and purchases at the end
New Customers	30%	CRM	Monthly	The number of new customers
Order Fulfilment Time	Within 3 hours	CRM	Monthly	The average time from order placement to order confirmation

DISCUSSION - BENEFITS OF ENHANCED CRM SYSTEM

In this technological, globalized economy, effective and timely CRM systems are critical for an organization to improve performance, productivity, and profitability. In this section, the applicability of the CRM system to OTA enhanced with alerts and KPI are discussed from the management and operational perspective. Our proposed approach can improve the overall performance and profitability by reducing operational costs and creating positive customer experiences.

Management Level

Cost control (i.e., costs against benefits) is always the main concern of senior management (Chiu, Cheung, et al., 2010; Chiang, 2018; Koçoğlu & Kalem, 2020). Also, simplicity is the key to maximizing performance and accelerating organizational development. Integrating data, including inquiries, bookings, payments, operations, and customer profiles in the data warehouse, is useful for analyzing and identifying performance problems (Chiu et al., 2003). The analytical engine supports knowledge discovery for the AMS to alert appropriate staff at appropriate levels for attention and possible actions (Chiu, Kwok, et al., 2009). Also, with centralized data management, senior management can retrieve and access data and KPIs efficiently, and thus managerial planning process can be facilitated and improved (Fedoryshyna et al., 2021).

Performance measurement through KPI is another advantage of the enhanced CRM system. By using enhanced CRM systems, KPI-driven monitoring can streamline management decision-making processes with timeliness and simplicity. It is useful for timely corrective actions, controlling projects, and overseeing operations, thus

Table 3. ECA Rules of Senior Management

Rule	Event	Example Condition	Action
R13	Decrease in advertisement revenue from the booking process	i) 5% < x =< 10% ii) 10% =< x	1. For i), send more subscribed newsletters and make new own advertisements for our OTA 2. For ii), alert the senior management for strategy changes
R14	Decrease in customer retention rate	Less than 70% in consecutive 3 months	Alert senior management to develop a long-term strategy to increase customer retention
R15	Increase in customer turnover rate	More than 25% in consecutive 3 months	Alert senior management to develop a long-term strategy to reduce customer turnover
R16	Decrease in customer satisfaction rate	Less than 75% in consecutive 3 months	Alert senior management to develop a long-term strategy to increase customer satisfaction
R17	Increase in customer complaints	More than 50 cases each month in consecutive 3 months	Alert senior management to develop a long-term strategy to minimize customer complaints
R18	Low conversion rate	Less than 40% in consecutive 3 months	Alert senior management to develop a long-term strategy and review the organization's direction and existing marketing strategy
R19	Decrease in new customers	Less than 30% in consecutive 3 months	Alert senior management to develop a long-term strategy to increase new customers
R20	Long order fulfillment time	More than 6 hours (the average time for order placement is within 3 hours) in consecutive 3 months	Alert the senior management to develop a long-term strategy and improve manpower planning

helping reduce costs, maintain revenue, and increase efficiency (Laudon & Laudon, 2022).

Operational Level

Customer service is always vital to the success or failure of an OTA. The new CRM system proposed is based on alert management and event-condition-action (ECA) rules, which can help online travel agencies streamline customer services. Our design aim to deliver seamless customer experiences and keep customer information up to date. High-quality data can enhance marketing decisions and achieve effective results. A key benefit of using an enhanced CRM system is saving valuable time accessing and updating customer data and timely alerting customers with useful purchasing and service information. Therefore, the overall performance in various departments, especially in the traditionally expensive call center, can be improved while cutting costs (Chiu et al., 2003). For efficient and effective processing, customer input and signals can be integrated from multiple sources such as the call center, apps, website, and emails. Also, providing personalized recommendations to loyal customers based on their portfolio and recent trends can enhance customer experiences. Timely handling customer complaints and improving services also help reduce attrition and increase customer loyalty (Morgeson III et al., 2020).

CONCLUSION

This study presents an enhanced CRM system architecture based on alert management, event-condition-action (ECA) rules, and KPI-based management, which can facilitate CRM processes under urgent situations and reduce delays to provide quality customer services. The communications and coordination of different departments, staff, and management have been improved. The ECA rules triggered by events related to customer behavior, customer profile, market environment, analytical engine, KPI, and OTA application logic for CRM have been illustrated. In particular, KPI are monitored for the decision support of senior management has also been recommended and with the ECA rules suggested. This alert-based CRM system can improve customer relationships, increase customer loyalty, enhance general staff productivity, facilitate the effectiveness and efficiency of task completion, and improve the management decision-making process. This study serves as a reference to OTA and other service industries for improving their CRM with a contemporary system integration approach.

This chapter only presents some selected processes to facilitate an overview easily understandable by readers without too much tourism or hospitality insider's knowledge. We shall present more in-depth operational design in other publications. Besides, OTAs need to manage their relationships with suppliers, which will be presented in other publications to illustrate service-based value chain issues (Cheung et al., 2021), essential for sharing information about tourism products among suppliers, OTAs, and end-users.

A limitation of this research is mainly due to a conceptual system design, despite careful consideration of various real-life requirements of different system stakeholders. The next phase of our research is to collect feedback from industrial practioners and tourists. Further integration with social network information dissemination and feedback collection is also essential (Chan et al., 2015). We are also interested in empirical studies on the effectiveness of promoting travel products on social media (Ni et al., 2021), user content analysis (Fang, Chiu, and Ho, 2022), and social media user feedback (He, Chiu, & Ho, 2022).

REFERENCES

Al-Hazmi, N. (2021). The impact of customer relationship management on customer retention in travel and tourism organizations. *Management Science Letters*, *11*(1), 247–252. doi:10.5267/j.msl.2020.8.009

Alshurideh, M., Alsharari, N. M., & Al Kurdi, B. (2019). Supply chain integration and customer relationship management in the airline logistics. *Theoretical Economics Letters*, *9*(02), 392–414. doi:10.4236/tel.2019.92028

Baloglu, S., Erdem, M., Brewer, P., Mayer, K., Christodoulidou, N., & Connolly, D. J. (2010). An examination of the transactional relationship between online travel agencies, travel meta sites, and suppliers. *International Journal of Contemporary Hospitality Management*, *22*(7), 1048–1062. doi:10.1108/09596111011066671

Capan, M., Hoover, S., Miller, K. E., Pal, C., Glasgow, J. M., Jackson, E. V., & Arnold, R. C. (2018). Data-driven approach to early warning score-based alert management. *BMJ Open Quality*, *7*(3), e000088. doi:10.1136/bmjoq-2017-000088 PMID:30167470

Chalmeta, R. (2006). Methodology for customer relationship management. *Journal of Systems and Software*, *79*(7), 1015–1024. doi:10.1016/j.jss.2005.10.018

Chan, V. H. Y., Ho, K. K. W., & Chiu, D. K. W. (2022). Mediating effects on the relationship between perceived service quality and public library app loyalty during the COVID-19 era. *Journal of Retailing and Consumer Services*, *67*, 102960. doi:10.1016/j.jretconser.2022.102960

Chang, Y. W., Hsu, P. Y., & Lan, Y. C. (2019). Cooperation and competition between online travel agencies and hotels. *Tourism Management*, *71*, 187–196. doi:10.1016/j.tourman.2018.08.026

Chcung, T. Y., Yc, Z., & Chiu, D. K. W. (2021). Value chain analysis of information services for the visually impaired: A case study of contemporary technological solutions. *Library Hi Tech*, *39*(2), 625–642. doi:10.1108/LHT-08-2020-0185

Cheung, V. S. Y., Lo, J. C. Y., Chiu, D. K. W., & Ho, K. K. W. (2022). (in press). Predicting Facebook's influence on travel products marketing based on the AIDA model. *Information Discovery and Delivery*. Advance online publication. doi:10.1108/IDD-10-2021-0117

Chiang, W. Y. (2018). Establishing high value markets for data-driven customer relationship management systems: An empirical case study. *Kybernetes*, *48*(3), 650–662. doi:10.1108/K-10-2017-0357

Chiu, D. K., Chan, W. C., Lam, G. K., Cheung, S. C., & Luk, F. T. (2003). An event driven approach to customer relationship management in an e-brokerage environment. *36th Hawaii International Conference on System Sciences (HICSS36)*. 10.1109/HICSS.2003.1174392

Chiu, D. K. W., Cheung, S. C., Till, S., Narupiyakul, L., & Hung, P. C. K. (2010). Enhancing E-service Collaboration with Enforcement and Relationship Management: A Methodology from Requirements to Event Driven Realization. *International Journal of Organizational and Collective Intelligence*, *1*(1), 15–43. doi:10.4018/joci.2010100802

Chiu, D. K. W., Hung, P. C. K., & Kwok, K. H. S. (2011). Engineering Financial Enterprise Content Management Services: Integration and Control. *International Journal of Systems and Service-Oriented Engineering*, *1*(2), 86–113. doi:10.4018/jssoe.2010040106

Chiu, D. K. W., Kwok, B. W. C., Wong, R. L. S., Kafeza, M., Cheung, S. C., Kafeza, E., & Hung, P. C. K. (2009). Alerts in Healthcare Applications: Process and Data Integration. *International Journal of Healthcare Information Systems and Informatics*, *4*(2), 36–56. doi:10.4018/jhisi.2009040103

Chiu, D. K. W., Lin, D. T., Kafeza, E., Wang, M., Hu, H., Hu, H., & Zhuang, Y. (2010). Alert based disaster notification and resource allocation. *Information Systems Frontiers*, *12*(1), 29–47. doi:10.100710796-009-9165-0

Chiu, D. K. W., Yueh, Y. T., Leung, H. F., & Hung, P. C. (2009). Towards Ubiquitous Tourist Service Coordination and Process Integration: A Collaborative Travel Agent System with Semantic Web Services. *Information Systems Frontiers*, *11*(3), 241–256. doi:10.100710796-008-9087-2

Expedia. (2020). *Expedia Group reports fourth quarter and full year 2019 results*. Retrieved from https://ir.expediagroup.com/static-files/ac26e4fe-7abc-4349-bba1-547a79d4c3df

Expedia. (n.d.). *Expedia Rewards*. Retrieved from https://www.expedia.com/rewards/howitworks

Fang, J., Chiu, D. K., & Ho, K. K. (2021). Exploring Cryptocurrency Sentiments With Clustering Text Mining on Social Media. In *Intelligent Analytics With Advanced Multi-Industry Applications* (pp. 157–171). IGI Global. doi:10.4018/978-1-7998-4963-6.ch007

Fedoryshyna, L., Halachenko, O., Ohiienko, A., Blyznyuk, A., Znachek, R., & Tsurkan, N. (2021). Digital marketing in strategic management in the field of the tourism. *Journal of Information Technology Management, 13*, 22-41.

Gong, J. Y., Schumann, F., Chiu, D. K. W., & Ho, K. K. W. (2017). Tourists' mobile information seeking behavior: An investigation on China's youth. *International Journal of Systems and Service-Oriented Engineering*, *7*(1), 58–76. doi:10.4018/IJSSOE.2017010104

He, Z., Chiu, D. K. W., & Ho, K. K. W. (2022). Weibo Analysis on Chinese Cultural Knowledge for Gaming. In Z. Sun (Ed.), *Handbook of Research on Foundations and Applications of Intelligent Business Analytics* (pp. 320–349). doi:10.4018/978-1-7998-9016-4.ch015

Hoyer, W. D., Kroschke, M., Schmitt, B., Kraume, K., & Shankar, V. (2020). Transforming the customer experience through new technologies. *Journal of Interactive Marketing*, *51*, 57–71. doi:10.1016/j.intmar.2020.04.001

Koçoğlu, C. M., & Kalem, M. Y. (2020). Electronic Customer Relationship Management in Tourism. In *Handbook of Research on Smart Technology Applications in the Tourism Industry* (pp. 273–294). IGI Global. doi:10.4018/978-1-7998-1989-9.ch013

Lai, W. W., Chiu, D. K., & Feng, Z. (2013). A collaborative food safety service agent architecture with alerts and trust. *Information Systems Frontiers*, *15*(4), 599–612. doi:10.100710796-012-9382-9

Laudon, K., & Laudon, J. P. (2022). *Management information systems: Managing the Digital Firm* (17th ed.). Pearson Education Limited.

Lcc, S. H., Dcalc, C. S., & Lcc, J. (2022). Docs it pay to book direct?: Customers' perceptions of online channel distributors, price, and loyalty membership on brand dimensions. *Journal of Revenue and Pricing Management*, 1–11. doi:10.105741272-022-00382-x

Memon, F. A., Saeed, S., & Shaikh, A. (2018). Systematic Approach of Customer Relationship Management in Much Different Organization. *IBT Journal of Business Studies*, *2*(2), 132 147. doi:10.46745/ilma.jbs.2018.14.02.11

Morgeson, F. V. III, Hult, G. T. M., Mithas, S., Keiningham, T., & Fornell, C. (2020). Turning complaining customers into loyal customers: Moderators of the complaint handling–Customer loyalty relationship. *Journal of Marketing*, *84*(5), 79–99. doi:10.1177/0022242920929029

Ni, J., Chiu, D. K. W., & Ho, K. K. W. (2022). (in press). Exploring Information Search Behavior among Self-Drive Tourists. *Information Discovery and Delivery*. Advance online publication. doi:10.1108/IDD-05-2020-0054

Payne, A., & Frow, P. (2006). Customer relationship management: From strategy to implementation. *Journal of Marketing Management, 22*(2), 135–168. doi:10.1362/026725706776022272

Renjith, S., Sreekumar, A., & Jathavedan, M. (2020). An extensive study on the evolution of context-aware personalized travel recommender systems. *Information Processing & Management, 57*(1), 102078. doi:10.1016/j.ipm.2019.102078

Research and Markets. (2019). *Impact of online travel - Thematic research*. Retrieved from https://www.researchandmarkets.com/reports/4895202/impact-of-online-travel-thematic-research?utm_source=dynamic&utm_medium=GNOM&utm_code=2jsqjr&utm_campaign=1336936+-+Online+Travel+Impact+-+Global+Online+Travel+Market+Forecast+to+Reach+US$372bn+by+2023&utm_exec=cari18gnomd

Rossini, A. (2016). *State of Online Travel Agencies: Ctrip Joins Priceline and Expedia as Global Giant.* Retrieved from https://skift.com/2016/07/07/the-state-of-online-travel-agencies-strong-growth-but-big-challenges-ahead/

Schaal, D. (2016, Nov 28). *Exclusive: Ctrip CEO on Global Ambitions, Skyscanner Buy and the Priceline Relationship*. Retrieved from https://skift.com/2016/11/28/exclusive-ctrip-ceo-on-global-ambitions-skyscanner-buy -and-the-priceline-relationship/

Sharma, A., Sharma, S., & Chaudhary, M. (2020). Are small travel agencies ready for digital marketing? Views of travel agency managers. *Tourism Management, 79*, 104078. doi:10.1016/j.tourman.2020.104078

Stopford, B. (2018). *DesigninFg Event-Driven Systems*. O'Reilly Media, Incorporated.

Tarasova, A., Polukhina, A., & Arnaberdiyev, A. (2020). Information Support for Travel Agency Performance. *International Journal of Recent Contributions from Engineering Science &. IT, 8*(4), 69-76.

Vo, N. N., Liu, S., Li, X., & Xu, G. (2021). Leveraging unstructured call log data for customer churn prediction. *Knowledge-Based Systems, 212*, 106586. doi:10.1016/j.knosys.2020.106586

Vogt, C. A. (2011). Customer relationship management in tourism: Management needs and research applications. *Journal of Travel Research, 50*(4), 356–364. doi:10.1177/0047287510368140

Wei, J. (2021). The impacts of perceived risk and negative emotions on the service recovery effect for online travel agencies: The moderating role of corporate reputation. *Frontiers in Psychology, 12*, 685351. doi:10.3389/fpsyg.2021.685351 PMID:34135837

Zheng, W., Zhou, R., Zhang, Z., Zhong, Y., Wang, S., Wei, Z., & Ji, H. (2019). Understanding the tourist mobility using GPS: How similar are the tourists? *Tourism Management, 71*, 54–66. doi:10.1016/j.tourman.2018.09.019

Zhiliang, D., & Lihua, Y. (2015). Research on CRM system in online travel agent in the context of Internet. *International Journal of Simulation Systems, Science & Technology, 16*(5B), 11.1-11.6.

Compilation of References

Aaker, D. A. (1991). *Managing brand equity. Capitalizing on the value of brand name*. The Free Press.

Aaker, D. A. (1992). The value of brand equity. *The Journal of Business Strategy*, *13*(4), 27–32. doi:10.1108/eb039503

Aaker, D. A. (1996). Measuring brand equity across products and markets. *California Management Review*, *38*(3), 102–120. doi:10.2307/41165845

Aaker, D. A., & Keller, K. L. (1990). Consumer evaluations of brand extensions. *Journal of Marketing*, *54*(1), 27–41. doi:10.1177/002224299005400102

Abar, S., Theodoropoulos, G. K., Lemarinier, P., & O'Hare, G. M. P. (2017). Agent Based Modelling and Simulation tools: A review of the state-of-art software. *Computer Science Review*, *24*, 13–33. doi:10.1016/j.cosrev.2017.03.001

Abbasi, B., Babaei, T., Hosseinifard, Z., Smith-Miles, K., & Dehghani, M. (2020). Predicting solutions of large-scale optimization problems via machine learning: A case study in blood supply chain management. *Computers & Operations Research*, *119*, 104941. doi:10.1016/j.cor.2020.104941

Abu-Shanab, E., & Anagreh, L. (2015). Impact of electronic customer relationship management in banking sector. *International Journal of Electronic Customer Relationship Management*, *9*(4), 254–271. doi:10.1504/IJECRM.2015.074196

Adejumo, A. A. (2019). Integrating Implementation Strategy, Challenges and Success Factors of CRM and e-CRM among Selected FMCG in Nigeria. *International Journal of Business and Risk Management*, *2*(1), 27–35.

Adiyanto, A., & Febrianto, R. (2020). Authentication Of Transaction Process In E-marketplace Based On Blockchain technology. *Aptisi Transactions On Technopreneurship*, *2*(1), 68–74. doi:10.34306/att.v2i1.71

Admiraal, W., & Lockhorst, D. (2009). E-learning in small and medium-sized enterprises across Europe: Attitudes towards technology, learning and training. *International Small Business Journal*, *27*(6), 743–767. doi:10.1177/0266242609344244

Adnan, A. Z., Rahayu, A., Hendrayati, H., & Yusuf, R. (2021). The Role of Electronic Customer Relationship Management (E-CRM) in Improving Service Quality. *Journal of Physics: Conference Series*, *1764*(1), 012051. Advance online publication. doi:10.1088/1742-6596/1764/1/012051

Adu-Asare Idun, A., & Aboagye, Q. A. (2014). Bank competition, financial innovations and economic growth in Ghana. *African Journal of Economic and Management Studies*, *5*(1), 30–51. doi:10.1108/AJEMS-09-2012-0057

Affum, F. (2020). The Unintended Effects of Bank of Ghana's Clean-Up Exercise on Unaffected Financial Institutions: Evidence from Yilo Krobo Municipality, Ghana. *Asian Journal of Economics, Business and Accounting*, 1-12.

Afshari, H., & Peng, Q. (2015). Using big data to minimize uncertainty effects in adaptable product design. In *ASME 2015 International Design Engineering Technical Conferences and Computers and Information in Engineering Conference*. American Society of Mechanical Engineers. 10.1115/DETC2015-46475

Agnihotri, R., Rapp, A., Kothandaraman, P., & Singh, R. (2012). An emotion-based model of salesperson ethical behaviors. *Journal of Business Ethics*, *109*(2), 243–257. doi:10.100710551-011-1123-3

Ahearne, M., Hughes, D. E., & Schillewaert, N. (2007). Why sales reps should welcome information technology: Measuring the impact of CRM-based IT on sales effectiveness. *International Journal of Research in Marketing*, *24*(4), 336–349. doi:10.1016/j.ijresmar.2007.09.003

Ahmed, B. S., Maâti, M. L. B., & Al-Sarem, M. (2020). Predictive Data Mining Model for Electronic Customer Relationship Management Intelligence. *International Journal of Business Intelligence Research*, *11*(2), 1–10. doi:10.4018/IJBIR.2020070101

Ahuja, V., & Medury, Y. (2010). Corporate blogs as e-CRM tools: Building consumer engagement through content management. *Journal of Database Marketing and Customer Strategy Management*, *17*(2), 91–105. doi:10.1057/dbm.2010.8

Ahuvia, A. C. (2005). Beyond the extended self: Loved objects and consumers' identity narratives. *The Journal of Consumer Research*, *32*(1), 171–184. doi:10.1086/429607

Ajzen, I. (1991). The theory of planned behaviour. *Organizational Behavior and Human Decision Processes*, *50*(2), 179–211. doi:10.1016/0749-5978(91)90020-T

Akhlagh, E., Allahyar, D., & Somayeh, Y. (2014). The Impact of Electronic Customer Relationship Management on Improving Marketing Performance of Private Banks. *Interdisciplinary Journal of Contemporary Research in Business*, *6*(6), 134.

Akoka, J., Berti-Équille, L., Boucelma, O., Bouzeghoub, M., Comyn-Wattiau, I., Cosquer, M., Goasdoué-Thion, V., Kedad, Z., Nugier, S., Peralta, V., & Sisaid-Cherfi, S. (2007). A framework for quality evaluation in data integration systems. *ICEIS 2007 - 9th International Conference on Enterprise Information Systems, Proceedings.*

Alba, J., Lynch, J., Weitz, B., Janiszewski, C., Lutz, R., Sawyer, A., & Wood, S. (1997). Interactive home shopping: Consumer, retailer, and manufacturer incentives to participate in electronic marketplaces. *Journal of Marketing*, *61*(3), 38–53. doi:10.1177/002224299706100303

Albert, N., Merunka, D., & Vallette-Florence, P. (2008). When consumers love their brands: Exploring the concept and its dimensions. *Journal of Business Research, 61*, 1062–1075. doi:. jbusres.2007.09.014 doi:10.1016/j

Al-dmour, H. H., Khwaja, R., & Al-dmour, R. (2017). The Impact of Electronic Customer Relationship Management (ECRM) Practices in Business Performance of Jordanian Commercial Banks. *European Journal of Economics. Finance and Administrative Sciences*, *93*, 49–70.

Al-dweeri, R. M., Ruiz Moreno, A., Montes, F. J. L., Obeidat, Z. M., & Al-dwairi, K. M. (2019). The effect of e-service quality on Jordanian student's e-loyalty: An empirical study in online retailing. *Industrial Management & Data Systems*, *119*(4), 902–923. doi:10.1108/IMDS-12-2017-0598

Al-Hawary, S. I. S., & Alhajri, T. M. S. (2020). Effect of Electronic Customer Relationship Management on Customers' Electronic Satisfaction of Communication Companies in Kuwait. *Calitatea*, *21*(175), 97–102.

Al-Hawary, S. I. S., & Al-Smeran, W. F. (2016). Impact of Electronic Service Quality on Customers Satisfaction of Islamic Banks in Jordan. *International Journal of Academic Research in Accounting. Finance and Management Sciences*, *7*(1), 170–188.

Al-Hazmi, N. (2021). The impact of customer relationship management on customer retention in travel and tourism organizations. *Management Science Letters*, *11*(1), 247–252. doi:10.5267/j.msl.2020.8.009

Alim, S., & Ozuem, W. (2014). The Influences of e-CRM on Customer Satisfaction and Loyalty in the UK Mobile Industry. *Journal of Applied Business and Finance Researches*, *3*(2), 47–54.

Alim, S., & Ozuem, W. (2016). The influences of e-CRM on customer satisfaction and loyalty in the UK mobile industry. *Journal of Applied Business and Finance Researches*, *3*(2), 47–54.

Al-Jarrah, O. Y., Yoo, P. D., Muhaidat, S., Karagiannidis, G. K., & Taha, K. (2015). Efficient machine learning for big data: A review. *Big Data Research*, *2*(3), 87–93. doi:10.1016/j.bdr.2015.04.001

Allam, Z., & Dhunny, Z. A. (2019). On big data, artificial intelligence and smart cities. *Cities (London, England)*, *89*, 80–91. doi:10.1016/j.cities.2019.01.032

Alshurideh, M. (2022). Does electronic customer relationship management (E-CRM) affect service quality at private hospitals in Jordan? *Uncertain Supply Chain Management*, *10*(2), 325–332. doi:10.5267/j.uscm.2022.1.006

Alshurideh, M., Alsharari, N. M., & Al Kurdi, B. (2019). Supply chain integration and customer relationship management in the airline logistics. *Theoretical Economics Letters*, *9*(02), 392–414. doi:10.4236/tel.2019.92028

Amazhanova, K., & Huseynov, F. (2018). The impact of electronic customer relationship management on customer satisfaction in Turkey. *Yönetim. Ekonomi ve Pazarlama Araştırmaları Dergisi, 2*(4), 13–26.

Amegavie, L. O., Mensah, N. M. D., & Kwame, A. J. (2019). Consumer Relationship Management and Its Effect on Organizational Performance Within the Telecommunication Industry of Ghana. *European Journal of Business and Management Research, 4*(6). Advance online publication. doi:10.24018/ejbmr.2019.4.6.166

Amiah, G., Martin, M., Minard, M., Smruthi, S. T. S., Alexandrova, Y., Khokhar, A., & Trajcevski, G. (2020). TOSNOS: To Online Shop, or Not-to Online Shop-Enabling Combined Improvements. In *2020 IEEE International Conference on Pervasive Computing and Communications Workshops* (pp. 1-3). IEEE.

Amoako, G. K., Arthur, E., Christiana, B., & Katah, R. K. (2012). The impact of effective customer relationship management (CRM) on repurchases: A case study of Golden Tulip hotel Accra –Ghana. *African Journal of Marketing Management, 4*(1), 17–29.

Anaam, E. A., Abu Bakar, K. A., Mohd Satar, N. S., & Ma'arif, M. Y. (2020). Investigating the Electronic Customer Relationship Management Success Key Factors in the Telecommunication Companies: A Pilot Study. *Journal of Computational and Theoretical Nanoscience, 17*(2-3), 1460–1463. doi:10.1166/jctn.2020.8825

Anaam, E. A., Bakar, K. A. A., & Satar, N. S. M. (2020). A Model of Electronic Customer Relationship Management System Adoption In Telecommunication Companies. *Amazonia Investiga, 9*(35), 61–73. doi:10.34069/AI/2020.35.11.5

Anabila, P., & Awunyo-Vitor, D. (2013). Customer relationship management: A key to organisational survival and customer loyalty in Ghana's banking industry. *International Journal of Marketing Studies, 5*(1).

Andah, B. D. (2020). Penerapan Electronic Customer Relationship Management (E-CRM) dalam Upaya Meningkatkan Pendapatan Penjualan pada PT. Cipta Aneka Buah. *IDEALIS: InDonEsiA JournaL. Information Systems, 3*(1), 20–25.

Anderson, J. C., & Gerbing, D. W. (1988). Structural equation modeling in practice: A review and recommended two-step approach. *Psychological Bulletin, 103*(3), 411–423. doi:10.1037/0033-2909.103.3.411

Anduku, Y. F. (2020). *Analysis Of The Relationship Between Social Bonding Strategies And Customer Loyalty Among Supermarkets In Western Region, Kenya; A Focus On The Role Of Brand Identity* (Doctoral Dissertation). Kisii University.

Ang, L., & Buttle, F. (2006). Managing for a successful customer acquisition: An exploration. *Journal of Marketing Management, 22*(3-4), 295–317. doi:10.1362/026725706776861217

Anim, N. A. H. M., & Omar, N. A. (2021). Does gamification work in a serious context? The influence of gamification, utilitarian, and hedonic features in the community-based crowdfunding platform. *Malaysian Journal of Society and Space*, *17*(2), 79–92.

Ansary, A., & Nik Hashim, N. M. H. (2018). Brand image and equity: The mediating role of brand equity drivers and moderating effects of product type and word of mouth. *Review of Managerial Science*, *12*(4), 969–1002. doi:10.100711846-017-0235-2

Anshari, M., Almunawar, M. N., Lim, S. A., & Al-Mudimigh, A. (2019). Customer relationship management and big data enabled: Personalization & customization of services. *Applied Computing and Informatics*, *15*(2), 94–101. doi:10.1016/j.aci.2018.05.004

Ardyan, E., & Sugiyarti, G. (2018). The influence of e-CRM capability and co-information sharing activity on product competitiveness and marketing performance of small and medium-sized enterprises. *International Journal of Electronic Customer Relationship Management*, *11*(2), 158–178. doi:10.1504/IJECRM.2018.090208

Arias, M. B., & Bae, S. (2016). Electric vehicle charging demand forecasting model based on big data technologies. *Applied Energy*, *183*, 327–339. doi:10.1016/j.apenergy.2016.08.080

Asante, K., & Achiaa, A. (2018). Determinants of consumer adoption of online air ticketing in Ghana. *Management Science Letters*, *8*(11), 1215–1222. doi:10.5267/j.msl.2018.8.003

Ashnai, B., Smirnova, M., Henneberg, S. C., & Naudé, P. (2019). Dyadic Operationalization in Business Relationships: The Empirical Example of Marketing-Purchasing Collaboration. *Journal of Business-To-Business Marketing*, *26*(1), 19–42. Advance online publication. doi:10.1080/1051712X.2019.1565134

Awang, Z. (2014). Research Methodology and Data Analysis (2nd ed.). UiTM Press.

Ayed, A. B., Halima, M. B., & Alimi, A. M. (2011). Big data analytics for logistics and transportation. *Supply Chain Management*, *16*(4), 246–259.

Baashar, Y., Alhussian, H., Patel, A., Alkawsi, G., Alzahrani, A. I., Alfarraj, O., & Hayder, G. (2020). Customer relationship management systems (CRMS) in the healthcare environment: A systematic literature review. *Computer Standards & Interfaces*, *71*, 103442. doi:10.1016/j.csi.2020.103442 PMID:34170994

Bagozzi, R., & Yi, Y. (1988). On the evaluation of structural equation models. *Journal of the Academy of Marketing Science*, *16*(1), 74–94. doi:10.1007/BF02723327

Bailey, C., Baines, P. R., Wilson, H., & Clark, M. (2009). Segmentation and customer insight incontemporary services marketing practice: Why grouping customers is no longer enough. *Journal of Marketing Management*, *25*(3/4), 227–252. doi:10.1362/026725709X429737

Bairrada, C.M., Coelho, F., & Coelho, A. (2018). Antecedents and outcomes of Brand love: utilitarian and symbolic Brand qualities. *European Journal of Marketing, 52*(3-4), 656-682.

Balachander, S., & Ghose, S. (2003). Reciprocal spillover effects: A strategic benefit of brand extensions. *Journal of Marketing*, *67*(1), 4–13. doi:10.1509/jmkg.67.1.4.18594

Balaraj, S. (2013). Optimization model for improving supply chain visibility. *Infosys Labs Briefings.*, *11*(1), 9–19.

Ballou, D. P., & Tayi, G. K. (1999). Enhancing data quality in data warehouse environments. *Communications of the ACM*, *42*(1), 73–78. Advance online publication. doi:10.1145/291469.291471

Baloglu, S., Erdem, M., Brewer, P., Mayer, K., Christodoulidou, N., & Connolly, D. J. (2010). An examination of the transactional relationship between online travel agencies, travel meta sites, and suppliers. *International Journal of Contemporary Hospitality Management*, *22*(7), 1048–1062. doi:10.1108/09596111011066671

Bank of Ghana. (2016). *Banking sector stability report July 2016*. Retrieved from: https://www.bog.gov.gh/ privatecontent/MPC_Press_Releases/Banking%20Sector %20Report%20%20-%20 July%202017.pdf

Bank of Ghana. (2019). *List of banks in Ghana*. available at: https://www.bog.gov.gh/ supervision-regulation/registered-institutions/banks/

Barbosa, M. W., Vicente, A. D., Ladeira, M. B., & Oliveira, M. P. (2018). Managing supply chain resources with big data analytics: A systematic review. *International Journal of Logistics Research and Applications.*, *21*(3), 177–200. doi:10.1080/13675567.2017.1369501

Barrutia, J. M., & Gilsanz, A. (2013). Electronic service quality and value: Do consumer knowledge-related resources matter? *Journal of Service Research*, *16*(2), 231–246. doi:10.1177/1094670512468294

Barták, R., Salido, M. A., & Rossi, F. (2010). Constraint satisfaction techniques in planning and scheduling. *Journal of Intelligent Manufacturing*, *21*(1), 5–15. doi:10.100710845-008-0203-4

Baruch, Y., & Holtom, B. C. (2008). Survey response rate levels and trends in organizational research. *Human Relations*, *61*(8), 1139–1160. doi:10.1177/0018726708094863

Bashir, M. A., & Naim, A. (n.d.). *ICT Adoption Analysis for Innovation in Higher Education Sector*. Academic Press.

Batra, R., Ahuvia, A., & Bagozzi, R. P. (2012). Brand love. *Journal of Marketing*, *76*(2), 1–16. doi:10.1509/jm.09.0339

Becker, J. U., Greve, G., & Albers, S. (2009). The impact of technological and organisational implementation of CRM on customer acquisition, maintenance and retention. *International Journal of Research in Marketing*, *26*(3), 207–215. doi:10.1016/j.ijresmar.2009.03.006

Bennett, C. C., & Hauser, K. (2013). Artificial intelligence framework for simulating clinical decision-making: A Markov decision process approach. *Artificial Intelligence in Medicine*, *57*(1), 9–19. doi:10.1016/j.artmed.2012.12.003 PMID:23287490

Bergkvist, L., & Bech-Larsen, T. (2010). Two studies of consequences and actionable antecedents of Brand love. *Journal of Brand Management, 17*(7), 504–518. doi:10.1057/bm.2010.6

Berkowitz. (2006). Customer Relationship Management. 8 Common goals for a CRM Program. *What are Key Drivers of Customer Satisfaction?* Available at: http://onlinesuccesscentre.com

Bernard, H. R. (2000). *Social Research Methods: Qualitative and Quantitative Approaches*. Sage.

BERR. (2009). *Annual Small Business Survey 2007/08*. Department for Business Enterprise and Regulatory Reform. Available at: www.bis.gov.uk/files/file50124.doc

Berry, L. L. (1995). Relationship marketing. In L. L. Berry, G. L. Shostack, & G. D. Upah (Eds.), *Emerging Perspective on Services Marketing* (pp. 25–38). American Marketing Association.

Bhatnagar, A., & Saxena, R. (2013). CRM vs E-CRM to study and understand the impact of traditional CRM vs technological CRM. *International Conference on Technology and Business Management*, 1–6.

Bhattacherjee, A., & Lin, C. P. (2015). A unified model of IT continuance: Three complementary perspectives and crossover effects. *European Journal of Information Systems, 24*(4), 364–373. doi:10.1057/ejis.2013.36

Bijmolt, T. H. A., Leeflang, P. S. H., Block, F., Eisenbeiss, M., Hardie, B. G. S., Lemmens, A., & Saffert, P. (2010). Analytics for customer engagement. *Journal of Service Research, 13*(3), 341–356. doi:10.1177/1094670510375603

Bilgihan, A., & Bujisic, M. (2015). The effect of website features in online relationship marketing: A case of online hotel booking. *Electronic Commerce Research and Applications, 14*(4), 222–232. doi:10.1016/j.elerap.2014.09.001

Blankson, C., Omar, O. E., & Cheng, J. M. S. (2009). Retail bank selection in developed and developing countries: A cross-national study of students' bank-selection criteria. *Thunderbird International Business Review, 51*(2), 183–198. doi:10.1002/tie.20257

Blázquez, M. (2014). Fashion shopping in multichannel retail: The role of technology in enhancing the customer experience. *International Journal of Electronic Commerce, 18*(4), 97–116. doi:10.2753/JEC1086-4415180404

Blili, S., & Raymond, L. (1993). Information technology: Threats and opportunities for SMEs. *International Journal of Information Management, 13*(6), 439–448. doi:10.1016/0268-4012(93)90060-H

Block, A., & Segev, A. (1996). *Leveraging e-commerce for competitive advantage: A business value framework.* In Anais da 9Th International Conference on EDI-IOS, Bled, Slovenia.

Boddy, C. R. (2007). Projective techniques in Taiwan and Asia-Pacific market research. *Qualitative Market Research, 10*(1), 48–62. doi:10.1108/13522750710720396

Bojei, J., Julian, C. C., Wel, C. A. B. C., & Ahmed, Z. U. (2013). The empirical link between relationship marketing tools and consumer retention in retail marketing. *Journal of Consumer Behaviour, 12*(3), 171–181. doi:10.1002/cb.1408

Bollen, K. A. (1989). *Structural Equations with Latent Variables*. Wiley. doi:10.1002/9781118619179

Bolton, R. N. (2011). Customer engagement: Opportunities and challenges for organizations. *Journal of Service Research, 14*, 272–274. doi:10.1177/1094670511414582

Boshoff, C. (2007). A psychometric assessment of ES-QUAL: A scale to measure electronic service quality. *Journal of Electronic Commerce Research, 8*(1), 101.

Boulding, W., Kalra, A., Staelin, R., & Zeithaml, V. A. (1993). A dynamic process model of service quality: From expectations to behavioral intentions. *JMR, Journal of Marketing Research, 30*(1), 7–27. doi:10.1177/002224379303000102

Boyle, A. B. (2001). The internet in industrial channels: Its use in (and effects on) exchange relationships. *Journal of Business and Industrial Marketing, 16*(6/7), 452–469. doi:10.1108/EUM0000000006020

Bradshaw, D., & Brash, C. (2001). Managing customer relationships in the e-business world: How to personalise computer relationships for increased profitability. *International Journal of Retail & Distribution Management, 29*(11/12), 520–529. doi:10.1108/09590550110696969

Brakus, J. J., Schmitt, B. H., & Zarantonello, L. (2009). Brand experience: What is it? How is it measured? Does it affect loyalty? *Journal of Marketing, 73*(3), 52–68. doi:10.1509/jmkg.73.3.052

Braun, A., & Garriga, G. (2018). Consumer Journey Analytics in the Context of Data Privacy and Ethics. In *Digital Marketplaces Unleashed* (pp. 663–674). Springer. doi:10.1007/978-3-662-49275-8_59

Brockhaus, S., Kersten, W., & Knemeyer, A. M. (2013). Where do we go from here? Progressing sustainability implementation efforts across supply chains. *Journal of Business Logistics, 34*(2), 167–182. doi:10.1111/jbl.12017

Brodie, R. J., Hollebeek, L. D., Juric, B., & Ilic, A. (2011). Customer engagement: Conceptual domain, fundamental propositions and implications for research in service marketing. *Journal of Service Research, 14*(3), 352–371. doi:10.1177/1094670511411703

Brouer, B. D., Karsten, C. V., & Pisinger, D. (2016). Big data optimization in maritime logistics. In *Big Data Optimization: Recent Developments and Challenges* (pp. 319–344). Springer. doi:10.1007/978-3-319-30265-2_14

Brown, T. A., & Moore, M. T. (2012). Confirmatory factor analysis. Handbook of structural equation modeling, 361-379.

Bryman, A., & Bell, E. (2007). *Business Research Methods*. Oxford University Press Inc.

Budiman, S. (2021). The effect of social media on brand image and brand loyalty in generation Y. The Journal of Asian Finance. *Economics and Business*, *8*(3), 1339–1347.

Bugaje, I. B. (2015). Effect of Electronic-Customer Relationship Management (e-CRM) on Business Organisations. *Abuja Journal of Business and Management*, *1*(1), 73–80.

Buil, I., de Chernatony, L., & Hem, L. E. (2009). Brand extension strategies: Perceived fit, brand type, and culture influences. *European Journal of Marketing*, *43*(11/12), 1300–1324. doi:10.1108/03090560910989902

Burbidge, B. (2001). *An Introduction to Support Vector Machines for Data Mining. UCL.* Computer Science Dept.

Byrne, B. M. (2001). *Structural Equation Modeling With AMOS: Basic Concepts, Applications, and Programming*. Taylor & Francis.

Campbell, K. (1993). Researching brands. *Service Industries Journal*, *29*(12), 1687–1706.

Capan, M., Hoover, S., Miller, K. E., Pal, C., Glasgow, J. M., Jackson, E. V., & Arnold, R. C. (2018). Data-driven approach to early warning score-based alert management. *BMJ Open Quality*, *7*(3), e000088. doi:10.1136/bmjoq-2017-000088 PMID:30167470

Carroll, B. A., & Ahuvia, A. (2006). Some antecedents and outcomes of brand love. *Marketing Letters*, *7*(2), 79–89. doi:10.100711002-006-4219-2

Carson, D., Cromie, S., McGowan, P., & Hill, J. (1995). *Marketing and Entrepreneurship in SMEs:An Innovative Approach*. Prentice-Hall.

Carson, D., & Gilmore, A. (2000). SME marketing management competencies. *International Business Review*, *9*(3), 363–382. doi:10.1016/S0969-5931(00)00006-8

CGAP. (2019). *Choosing a Profit Strategy for Merchant Payments*. https://www.cgap.org/research/publication/choosing-profit-strategy-merchant-payments

Chaffey, D., Hemphill, T., & Edmundson-Bird, D. (2019). *Digital business and e-commerce management*. Pearson.

Chaffey, D., Mayer, R., Johnston, K., & Ellis-Chadwick, F. (2003). *Internet Marketing* (2nd ed.). Prentice-Hall.

Chahal, H., & Rani, A. (2017). How trust moderates social media engagement and brand equity. *Journal of Research in Interactive Marketing*, *11*(3), 312–335. doi:10.1108/JRIM-10-2016-0104

Chalmeta, R. (2006). Methodology for customer relationship management. *Journal of Systems and Software*, *79*(7), 1015–1024. doi:10.1016/j.jss.2005.10.018

Chang, Y. W., Hsu, P. Y., & Lan, Y. C. (2019). Cooperation and competition between online travel agencies and hotels. *Tourism Management*, *71*, 187–196. doi:10.1016/j.tourman.2018.08.026

Chang, Y., Ko, Y. J., Tasci, A., Arai, A., & Kim, T. (2014). Strategic match of athlete endorsement in global markets: An associative learning perspective. *International Journal of Sports Marketing & Sponsorship*, *15*(4), 40–58. doi:10.1108/IJSMS-15-04-2014-B005

Chan, V. H. Y., Ho, K. K. W., & Chiu, D. K. W. (2022). Mediating effects on the relationship between perceived service quality and public library app loyalty during the COVID-19 era. *Journal of Retailing and Consumer Services*, *67*, 102960. doi:10.1016/j.jretconser.2022.102960

Chaston, I., & Mangles, T. (2003). Relationship marketing in online business-to-business markets: A pilot investigation of small UK manufacturing firms. *European Journal of Marketing*, *37*(5/6), 753–773. doi:10.1108/03090560310465134

Chatterjee, S., Chaudhuri, R., Vrontis, D., Thrassou, A., Ghosh, S. K., & Chaudhuri, S. (2020). Social customer relationship management factors and business benefits. *The International Journal of Organizational Analysis*.

Chau, M., & Xu, J. (2012). Business intelligence in blogs: Understanding consumer interactions and communities. *Management Information Systems Quarterly*, *36*(4), 1189–1216. doi:10.2307/41703504

Chen, A. C.-H., & Chen, S. K. (2000). Brand dilution effect of extension failure: A Taiwan study. *Journal of Product and Brand Management*, *9*(4), 243–254. doi:10.1108/10610420010344031

Cheng, C. H. (2009). *A study on the applications of data mining techniques to enhance customer lifetime value. WSEAS Transactions on Information Science and Applications*.

Cheng, H. H., & Fu, T. J. (2018). The Determinants of Online Shopping Behavior. In *2018 International Conference on Intelligent Autonomous Systems (ICoIAS)* (pp. 97-100). 10.1109/ICoIAS.2018.8494098

Chen, H., Chiang, R. H. L., & Storey, V. C. (2012). Business intelligence and analytics: From big data to big impact. *Management Information Systems Quarterly*, *36*(4), 1165–1188. doi:10.2307/41703503

Chen, I. J., & Popovich, K. (2003). Understanding customer relationship management (CRM) People, process and technology. *Business Process Management Journal*, *9*(5), 672 688. doi:10.1108/14637150310496758

Chen, J., & Ching, R. K. H. (2007). The effects of information and communication technology on customer relationship management and customer lock-in. *International Journal of Electronic Business*, *5*(5), 478–498. doi:10.1504/IJEB.2007.015446

Chen, Q., & Chen, H. M. (2004). Exploring the success factors of eCRM strategies in practice. *Journal of Database Marketing & Customer Strategy Management*, *11*(4), 333–343. doi:10.1057/palgrave.dbm.3240232

Chen, S. H., Jakeman, A. J., & Norton, J. P. (2008). Artificial Intelligence techniques: An introduction to their use for modelling environmental systems. *Mathematics and Computers in Simulation*, *78*(2-3), 379–400. doi:10.1016/j.matcom.2008.01.028

Cheung, M. L., Pires, G., & Rosenberger, P. J. (2020). The influence of perceived social media marketing elements on consumer–brand engagement and brand knowledge. *Asia Pacific Journal of Marketing and Logistics*, *32*(3), 695–720. doi:10.1108/APJML-04-2019-0262

Cheung, T. Y., Ye, Z., & Chiu, D. K. W. (2021). Value chain analysis of information services for the visually impaired: A case study of contemporary technological solutions. *Library Hi Tech*, *39*(2), 625–642. doi:10.1108/LHT-08-2020-0185

Cheung, V. S. Y., Lo, J. C. Y., Chiu, D. K. W., & Ho, K. K. W. (2022). (in press). Predicting Facebook's influence on travel products marketing based on the AIDA model. *Information Discovery and Delivery*. Advance online publication. doi:10.1108/IDD-10-2021-0117

Chiang, W. Y. (2018). Establishing high value markets for data-driven customer relationship management systems: An empirical case study. *Kybernetes*, *48*(3), 650–662. doi:10.1108/K-10-2017-0357

Chin, W. W. (2010). How to write up and report PLS analyses. In Handbook of Partial Least Squares: Concepts, Methods and Application. Springer. doi:10.1007/978-3-540-32827-8_29

Chiu, D. K. W., Cheung, S. C., Till, S., Narupiyakul, L., & Hung, P. C. K. (2010). Enhancing E-service Collaboration with Enforcement and Relationship Management: A Methodology from Requirements to Event Driven Realization. *International Journal of Organizational and Collective Intelligence*, *1*(1), 15–43. doi:10.4018/joci.2010100802

Chiu, D. K. W., Hung, P. C. K., & Kwok, K. H. S. (2011). Engineering Financial Enterprise Content Management Services: Integration and Control. *International Journal of Systems and Service-Oriented Engineering*, *1*(2), 86–113. doi:10.4018/jssoe.2010040106

Chiu, D. K. W., Kwok, B. W. C., Wong, R. L. S., Kafeza, M., Cheung, S. C., Kafeza, E., & Hung, P. C. K. (2009). Alerts in Healthcare Applications: Process and Data Integration. *International Journal of Healthcare Information Systems and Informatics*, *4*(2), 36–56. doi:10.4018/jhisi.2009040103

Chiu, D. K. W., Lin, D. T., Kafeza, E., Wang, M., Hu, H., Hu, H., & Zhuang, Y. (2010). Alert based disaster notification and resource allocation. *Information Systems Frontiers*, *12*(1), 29–47. doi:10.100710796-009-9165-0

Chiu, D. K. W., Yueh, Y. T., Leung, H. F., & Hung, P. C. (2009). Towards Ubiquitous Tourist Service Coordination and Process Integration: A Collaborative Travel Agent System with Semantic Web Services. *Information Systems Frontiers*, *11*(3), 241–256. doi:10.100710796-008-9087-2

Chiu, D. K., Chan, W. C., Lam, G. K., Cheung, S. C., & Luk, F. T. (2003). An event driven approach to customer relationship management in an e-brokerage environment. *36th Hawaii International Conference on System Sciences (HICSS36)*. 10.1109/HICSS.2003.1174392

Choi, T. M., Wallace, S. W., & Wang, Y. (2018). Big data analytics in operations management. *Production and Operations Management*, *27*(10), 1868–1883. doi:10.1111/poms.12838

Choudhury, M. M., & Harrigan, P. (2014). CRM to social CRM: The integration of new technologies into customer relationship management. *Journal of Strategic Marketing*, *22*(2), 149–176. doi:10.1080/0965254X.2013.876069

Christensen, C., & Raynor, M. (2003). *The Innovator's Solution*. Harvard Business School Press.

Chu, K. M. (2020). The Relationships between Online Customer Engagement Value and Electronic Customer Relationship Management Effectiveness of Mobile Games. *Innovative Journal of Business and Management*, *9*(8), 238–245.

Cleff, T., Lin, I. C., & Walter, N. (2014). Can You Feel It? The Effect of Brand Experience on Brand Equity. *IUP Journal of Brand Management*, *11*(2).

Cohen, M. A. (2015). Inventory Management in the Age of Big Data. *Harvard Business Review*. Available from: https://hbr.org/2015/06/inventorymanagement-in-the-age-of-bigdata

Collobert, R., Weston, J., Bottou, L., Karlen, M., Kavukcuoglu, K., & Kuksa, P. (2011). Natural language processing (almost) from scratch. *Journal of Machine Learning Research*, *12*, 2493–2537.

Cook, T. D., & Campbell, D. T. (1979). *Quasi-Experimentation: Design and Analysis Issues for Field Settings*. Houghton Muffin Company.

Corkum, C., Lie, C. X., Crish, J., Jobb, D., & Adreew, J. (2021). Mobile Apps: Customer Engagement, Brand Equity, and Purchase Intention. *Review of Business, Accounting, & Finance*, *1*(2), 215–232.

Cristóvão, F. G. (2022). *Social media practices by human resources companies: how do they impact brand image and customer engagement?* (Doctoral dissertation).

Cui, R., Gallino, S., Moreno, A., & Zhang, D. J. (2018). The Operational Value of Social Media Information. *Production and Operations Management*, *27*, 1749–1769.

D'Andrade, R. G. (1995). *The Development of Cognitive Anthropology*. Cambridge University Press. doi:10.1017/CBO9781139166645

Danquah, B. A., & lin Dong, C. (2018). Empirical Evidence on Sources of Consumer Trust on E-Commerce of Ghana. In *Third International Conference on Economic and Business Management (FEBM 2018)*. Atlantis Press. 10.2991/febm-18.2018.41

Das, S., Mandal, S., Bhoyar, A., Bharde, M., Ganguly, N., Bhattacharya, S., & Bhattacharya, S. (2020). Multi-criteria online frame-subset selection for autonomous vehicle videos. *Pattern Recognition Letters*, *133*, 349–355.

Davis, F. D., Bagozzi, R. P., & Warshaw, P. R. (1992). Extrinsic and intrinsic motivation to use computers in the workplace. *Journal of Applied Social Psychology*, *22*(14), 1111–1132. doi:10.1111/j.1559-1816.1992.tb00945.x

Davis, J. A. (1971). *Elementary Survey Analysis*. Prentice Hall.

Dawn, S. K., & Chowdhury, R. (2011). Electronic Customer Relationship Management (E-CRM): Conceptual Framework and Developing a Model. *International Journal of Business & Information Technology*, *1*(1), 75–84.

Day, S. G., & Hubbard, J. K. (2003). Customer relationships go digital. *Business Strategy Review*, *14*(1), 17–26. doi:10.1111/1467-8616.00240

de Barcelos Silva, A., Gomes, M. M., da Costa, C. A., da Rosa Righi, R., Barbosa, J. L. V., Pessin, G., De Doncker, G., & Federizzi, G. (2020). Intelligent personal assistants: A systematic literature review. *Expert Systems with Applications*, *147*, 113193.

Dehghanpouri, H., Soltani, Z., & Rostamzadeh, R. (2020). The impact of trust, privacy and quality of service on the success of E-CRM: The mediating role of customer satisfaction. *Journal of Business and Industrial Marketing*, *35*(11), 1831–1847. doi:10.1108/JBIM-07-2019-0325

Dens, N., & De Pelsmacker, P. (2010). Consumer response to different advertising appeals for new products: The moderating influence of branding strategy and product category involvement. *Journal of Brand Management*, *18*(1), 50–65. doi:10.1057/bm.2010.22

Denzin, N. K. (1978). *The Research Act: A Theoretical Introduction to Sociological Methods*. Praeger.

der Zee, D.-J. v. (2011). Building insightful simulation models using Petri Nets— A structured approach. *Decision Support Systems*, *51*, 53–64.

Dessart, L., Veloutsou, C., & Thomas, A. (2015). Consumer engagement in online brand communities: A social media perspective. *Journal of Product and Brand Management*, *24*(1), 28–42. doi:10.1108/JPBM-06-2014-0635

Dewnarain, S., Ramkissoon, H., & Mavondo, F. (2021). Social customer relationship management: A customer perspective. *Journal of Hospitality Marketing & Management*, *30*(6), 673–698. doi:10.1080/19368623.2021.1884162

Dey, N., Hassanien, A. E., Bhatt, C., Ashour, A., & Satapathy, S. C. (2018). *Internet of things and big data analytics toward next-generation intelligence*. Springer.

Dhingra, M., & Dhingra, V. (2013). Determinants of Electronic customer relationship management (e-CRM) for customer satisfaction in banking sector in India. *African Journal of Business Management*, *7*(10), 762–768. doi:10.5897/AJBM11.712

Diabat, A., & Deskoores, R. (2016). A hybrid genetic algorithm based heuristic for an integrated supply chain problem. *Journal of Manufacturing Systems*, *38*, 172–180.

Dibb, S., Simkin, L., Pride, W., & Ferrell, O. (2006). *Marketing: Concepts and Strategies* (5th ed.). Houghton Mifflin.

Dillman, D. A. (1978). *Mail and Telephone Surveys*. Wiley.

Dodds, W. B., & Monroe, K. B. (1985). The effect of brand and price information on subjective product evaluations. *Advances in Consumer Research. Association for Consumer Research (U. S.), 12*(1).

Doe, J. K., Van de Wetering, R., Honyenuga, B., & Versendaal, J. (2017). Toward a firm technology adoption model (F-TAM) in a developing country context. *MCIS 2017 Proceedings, 23.*

Doern, R. (2009). Investigating barriers to SME growth and development in transition environments: A critique and suggestions for developing the methodology. *International Small Business Journal, 27*(3), 275–305. doi:10.1177/0266242609102275

Doole, I., Grimes, T., & Demack, S. (2006). An exploration of the management practices and processes most closely associated with high levels of export capability in SMEs. *Marketing Intelligence & Planning, 24*(6), 632–647. doi:10.1108/02634500610701690

Doorn, J. V., Katherine, N. L., Vikas, M., Stephan, N., Doreen, P., Peter, P., & Peter, C. V. (2010). Customer engagement behavior: Theoretical foundations and research directions. *Journal of Service Research, 13*(3), 253–266. doi:10.1177/1094670510375599

Drost, E. A. (2011). Validity and reliability in social science research. *Education Research and Perspectives, 38*(1), 105.

Duan, Y., Edwards, J. S., & Dwivedi, Y. K. (2019). Artificial intelligence for decision making in the era of Big Data – evolution, challenges and research agenda. *International Journal of Information Management, 48*, 63–71.

Dubois, L. (2015). *11 Best Web Analytic Tools*. Retrieved from: https://www.inc.com/guides/12/2010/11

Dwivedi, A. (2015). A higher-order model of consumer brand engagement and its impact on loyalty intentions. *Journal of Retailing and Consumer Services, 24*, 100–109. doi:10.1016/j.jretconser.2015.02.007

Dwivedi, A., Merrilees, B., & Sweeney, A. (2010). Brand extension feedback effects: A holistic framework. *Journal of Brand Management, 17*(5), 328–342. doi:10.1057/bm.2009.26

Dwyer, F. R., Schurr, P. H., & Oh, S. (1987). Developing buyer-seller relationships. *Journal of Marketing, 51*(2), 11–27. doi:10.1177/002224298705100202

Ebrahim, R. S. (2020). The role of trust in understanding the impact of social media marketing on brand equity and brand loyalty. *Journal of Relationship Marketing, 19*(4), 287–308. doi:10.1080/15332667.2019.1705742

Ebrahim, R., Ghoneim, A., Irani, Z., & Fan, Y. (2016). A brand preference and repurchase intention model: The role of consumer experience. *Journal of Marketing Management, 32*(13-14), 1230–1259. doi:10.1080/0267257X.2016.1150322

Ekanayake, C. S. (2016). *Consumer engagement with social media, brand equity and intention to purchase* (Doctoral dissertation).

Eltahir, A. M., Ahmed, T. M., Ahmed, H., & Abdalfadil, T. A. (2021). Comparative study of customer relationship management (CRM) and electronic customer relationship management (E-CRM). *International Journal of Advanced and Applied Sciences*, *8*(7), 1–6. doi:10.21833/ijaas.2021.07.001

Emergen Research. (2022). *Top 10 Leading Digital Payment Companies in the World.* https://www.emergenresearch.com/blog/top-10-leading-digital-payment-companies-in-the-world

Erciş, A., Ünal, S., Candan, F. B., & Yıldırım, H. (2012). The effect of brand satisfaction, trust and brand commitment on loyalty and repurchase intentions. *Procedia: Social and Behavioral Sciences*, *58*, 1395–1404. doi:10.1016/j.sbspro.2012.09.1124

Ericsson, K. A., & Smith, J. (1991). Prospects and limits of the empirical study of. *Toward a general theory of expertise: Prospects and limits, 1*(1).

European Commission. (2005). *SME Definition.* http://eceuropa.eu/enterprise/enterprise_policy/sme_definition/index_en.htm

Evangelopoulos, N. (2001). Tracing Taylorism's technical and sociotechnical duality through Latent Semantic Analysis. Analysis. *Journal of Business and Management*, 57–74.

Evans, M., Jamal, A., & Foxall, G. (2006). *Consumer Behaviour*. John Wiley & Sons Ltd.

Expedia. (2020). *Expedia Group reports fourth quarter and full year 2019 results*. Retrieved from https://ir.expediagroup.com/static-files/ac26e4fe-7abc-4349-bba1-547a79d4c3df

Expedia. (n.d.). *Expedia Rewards*. Retrieved from https://www.expedia.com/rewards/howitworks

Fang, J., Chiu, D. K., & Ho, K. K. (2021). Exploring Cryptocurrency Sentiments With Clustering Text Mining on Social Media. In *Intelligent Analytics With Advanced Multi-Industry Applications* (pp. 157–171). IGI Global. doi:10.4018/978-1-7998-4963-6.ch007

Fanning, S. (2019). The marketing concept (4th ed.). Academic Press.

Fan, Y., Heilig, L., & Voß, S. (2015). Supply chain risk management in the era of big data. In *International Conference of Design, User Experience, and Usability*. Cham: Springer.

Farmania, A., Elsyah, R. D., & Tuori, M. A. (2021). Transformation of CRM Activities into e-CRM: The Generating e-Loyalty and Open Innovation. *Journal of Open Innovation*, *7*(2), 109. doi:10.3390/joitmc7020109

Farquhar, P. H. (1989). Managing Brand Equity. *Marketing Research*, *1*(September), 24–33.

Fedoryshyna, L., Halachenko, O., Ohiienko, A., Blyznyuk, A., Znachek, R., & Tsurkan, N. (2021). Digital marketing in strategic management in the field of the tourism. *Journal of Information Technology Management, 13*, 22-41.

Feinberg, R. A., Kadam, R., Hokama, L., & Kim, I. (2002). The State of Electronic Customer Relationship Management in Retailing. *International Journal of Retail & Distribution Management*, *30*(10), 470–481. doi:10.1108/09590550210445344

Feng, Q., & Shanthikumar, J. G. (2018). How research in production and operations management may evolve in the era of big data. *Production and Operations Management*, *27*(9), 1670–1684.

Fiansyah, E. (2020, November). Post Implementation Review of Electronic Customer Relationship Management (E-CRM) Implementation in Port Services Company, Indonesia. In *2020 International Conference on Informatics, Multimedia, Cyber and Information System (ICIMCIS)* (pp. 301-306). IEEE. 10.1109/ICIMCIS51567.2020.9354300

Field, A. (2013). *Discovering Statistics using SPSS* (4th ed.). Sage.

Fildes, R., Goodwin, P., Lawrence, M., & Nikolopoulos, K. (2009). Effective forecasting and judgmental adjustments: An empirical evaluation and strategies for improvement in supply-chain planning. *International Journal of Forecasting*, *25*, 3–23.

Fischetti, M., & Fraccaro, M. (2019). Machine learning meets mathematical optimization to predict the optimal production of offshore wind parks. *Computers & Operations Research*, *106*, 289–297.

Fishbein, M., & Ajzen, I. (1975). *Belief, attitude, intention and behavior: An introduction to theory and research reading*. Addison-Wesley.

Fjermestad, J., & Romano, N. C. Jr. (2003). Electronic customer relationship management: Revisiting the general principles of usability and resistance – an integrative implementation framework. *Business Process Management Journal*, *9*(5), 572–591. doi:10.1108/14637150310496695

Fornell, C., & Larcker, D. F. (1981). Evaluating structural equation models with unobservable variables and measurement error. *JMR, Journal of Marketing Research*, *18*(1), 39–50. doi:10.1177/002224378101800104

Fournier, S. (1998). Consumers and their brands: Developing relationship theory in consumer research. *The Journal of Consumer Research*, *24*(4), 343–373. doi:10.1086/209515

France, C., Merrilees, B., & Miller, D. (2015). Customer brand co-creation: A conceptual model. *Marketing Intelligence & Planning*, *33*(6), 848–864. doi:10.1108/MIP-06-2014-0105

Friedman, J., Hastie, T., & Tibshirani, R. (2001). The elements of statistical learning. Springer.

Gambetti, R. C., & Graffigna, G. (2010). The concept of engagement: A systematic analysis of the ongoing marketing debate. *International Journal of Market Research*, *52*(6), 801–826. doi:10.2501/S147078531020166

Gardner, B. B., & Levy, S. J. (1955). The product and the brand. *Harvard Business Review*, *33*(2), 33–39.

Garg, N., & Sharma, K. (2020). Machine Learning in Text Analysis. In Handbook of Research on Emerging Trends and Applications of Machine Learning (pp.383-402). IGI Global. doi:10.4018/978-1-5225-9643-1.ch018

Geiger, S., & Martin, S. (1999). The internet as a relationship marketing tool-some evidence from Irish companies. *Irish Marketing Review*, *12*(2), 24–36.

Giarratano, J. C., & Riley, G. (1998). *Expert systems*. PWS Publishing Co.

Gilman, M. W., & Edwards, P. K. (2008). Testing a framework of the organization of small firms: Fast-growth, high-tech SMEs. *International Small Business Journal, 26*(5), 531–558. doi:10.1177/0266242608094028

Gogtay, N. J., & Thatte, U. M. (2017). Principles of correlation analysis. *The Journal of the Association of Physicians of India, 65*(3), 78–81. PMID:28462548

Gold, A. H., Malhotra, A., & Segars, A. H. (2001). Knowledge management: An organizational capabilities perspective. *Journal of Management Information Systems, 18*(1), 185–214. Advance online publication. doi:10.1080/07421222.2001.11045669

Gómez-Suárez, M., Benito, L. E. A., & Campo, S. (2016). Exploring the link between brand love and engagement through a qualitative approach. *International Journal of Business Environment, 8*(4), 367–384. doi:10.1504/IJBE.2016.080882

Gong, J. Y., Schumann, F., Chiu, D. K. W., & Ho, K. K. W. (2017). Tourists' mobile information seeking behavior: An investigation on China's youth. *International Journal of Systems and Service-Oriented Engineering, 7*(1), 58–76. doi:10.4018/IJSSOE.2017010104

González-Serrano, L., Talón-Ballestero, P., Muñoz-Romero, S., Soguero-Ruiz, C., & Rojo-Álvarez, J. L. (2020). A big data approach to customer relationship management strategy in hospitality using multiple correspondence domain description. *Applied Sciences (Basel, Switzerland), 11*(1), 256. doi:10.3390/app11010256

Gould, J. D., & Lewis, C. (1985). Designing for usability: Key principles and what designers think. *Communications of the ACM, 28*(3), 300–311. Advance online publication. doi:10.1145/3166.3170

Graves, A., Mohamed, A.-R., & Hinton, G. (2013). *Speech recognition with deep recurrent neural networks. In 2013 IEEE international conference on acoustics, speech and signal processing*. IEEE.

Greasley, A. (2005). Using system dynamics in a discrete-event simulation study of a manufacturing plant. *International Journal of Operations & Production Management, 25*, 534–548.

Greenberg, P. (2010). The impact of CRM 2.0 on customer insight. *Journal of Business and Industrial Marketing, 25*(6), 410–419. doi:10.1108/08858621011066008

Grönroos, C. (2007). *In search of a new logic for marketing: Foundations of contemporary theory*. John Wiley and Sons Incorporated.

Guillaumin, M., Verbeek, J., & Schmid, C. (2010). *Multimodal semi-supervised learning for image classification. In 2010 IEEE Computer society conference on computer vision and pattern recognition*. IEEE.

Gummesson, E. (1994). Making relationship marketing operational. *International Journal of Service Industry Management, 5*(5), 5–20. doi:10.1108/09564239410074349

Gummesson, E. (2002). *Total Relationship Marketing: Marketing Management Relationship Strategy and CRM Approaches to the Network Economy*. Butterworth-Heinemann.

Gunasekaran, A., Marri, H. B., McGaughey, R. E., & Nebhwani, M. D. (2002). E-commerce and its impact on operations management. *International Journal of Production Economics*, *75*(1-2), 185–197. doi:10.1016/S0925-5273(01)00191-8

Gunasekaran, A., Papadopoulos, T., Dubey, R., Wamba, S. F., Childe, S. J., & Hazen, B. (2017). Big data and predictive analytics for supply chain and organizational performance. *Journal of Business Research*, *70*, 308–317.

Gunasekaran, A., Yusuf, Y. Y., Adeleye, E. O., & Papadopoulos, T. (2018). Agile manufacturing practices: The role of big data and business analytics with multiple case studies. *International Journal of Production Research*, *56*(1-2), 385–39.

Guttman, R. H., Moukas, A. G., & Maes, P. (1998). Agent-mediated electronic commerce: A survey. *The Knowledge Engineering Review*, *13*(2), 147–159. doi:10.1017/S0269888998002082

Hadiyati, E. (2016). Study of marketing mix and aida model to purchasing on line product in indonesia. *British Journal of Marketing Studies, 4*(7).

Hagberg, J., Sundström, M., & Nicklas, E. Z. (2016). The digitalisation of retailing: An exploratory framework. *International Journal of Retail & Distribution Management*, *44*(7), 694–712. doi:10.1108/IJRDM-09-2015-0140

Hair, J.F., Anderson, R.E., Babin, B.J., & Black, W.C. (2010).*Multivariate data analysis: A global perspective* (Vol. 7). Academic Press.

Hair, J. F. J., Ringle, C. M., & Sarstedt, M. (2011). PLS-SEM: Indeed, a silver bullet. *Journal of Marketing Theory and Practice*, *19*(2), 139–152. doi:10.2753/MTP1069-6679190202

Hair, J. F., Anderson, R. E., Tatham, R. L., & Black, W. C. (1998). *Multivariate data analysis*.

Hair, J. F., Black, W. C., Babin, B. J., & Anderson, R. E. (2010). *Multivariate Data Analysis: A Global Perspective*. Pearson Education Inc.

Hair, J. F., Hult, G. T. M., Ringle, C. M., & Sarstedt, M. (2017). *A primer on partial least squares structural equation modeling (PLS-SEM)* (2nd ed.). Sage.

Hair, J., Tatham, R., Anderson, R., & Black, W. (1998). *Multivariate Data Analysis* (5th ed.). Prentice Hall.

Halstead, D., Hartman, D., & Schmidt, S. L. (1994). Multisource effects on the satisfaction formation process. *Journal of the Academy of Marketing Science*, *22*(2), 114–129. doi:10.1177/0092070394222002

Han, H., Nguyen, H. N., Song, H. J., Chua, B. L., Lee, S., & Kim, W. (2019). Role of social network services (SNS) sales promotions in generating brand loyalty for chain steakhouses. *Journal of Quality Assurance in Hospitality & Tourism*, *20*(5), 617–645. doi:10.1080/1528008X.2019.1579078

Hanif, M. I., Ahsan, M., Bhatti, M. K., & Loghari, M. S. (2020). The Effect of Electronic Customer Relationship Management on Organizational Performance with Mediating Role of Customer Satisfaction. *International Review of Management and Marketing*, *10*(5), 138–147. doi:10.32479/irmm.9934

Hansen, N., Kupfer, A. K., & Hennig-Thurau, T. (2018). Brand crises in the digital age: The short-and long-term effects of social media firestorms on consumers and brands. *International Journal of Research in Marketing*, *35*(4), 557–574. doi:10.1016/j.ijresmar.2018.08.001

Hardjono, B., & Tan, B. Y. (2017). Brand Extension of Fast Moving Consumer Goods To Customers' Perception. *Trikonomika*, *16*(2), 51–62. doi:10.23969/trikonomika.v16i2.714

Hardoon, D. R., Szedmak, S., & Shawe-Taylor, J. (2004). Canonical correlation analysis: An overview with application to learning methods. *Neural Computation*, *16*(12), 2639–2664. doi:10.1162/0899766042321814 PMID:15516276

Harker, M. J., & Egan, J. (2006). The past present and future of relationship marketing. *Journal of Marketing Management*, *22*(1-2), 215–242.

Harrigan, P., & Miles, M. (2014). From e-CRM to s-CRM. Critical factors underpinning the social CRM activities of SMEs. *Small Enterprise Research*, *21*(1), 99–116. doi:10.1080/13215906.2014.11082079

Harrigan, P., Ramsey, E., & Ibbotson, P. (2008). E-CRM in SMEs: An exploratory study in Northern Ireland. *Marketing Intelligence & Planning*, *26*(4), 385–404. doi:10.1108/02634500810879296

Harrigan, P., Ramsey, E., & Ibbotson, P. (2009). Investigating the e-CRM activities of Irish SMEs. *Journal of Small Business and Enterprise Development*, *16*(3), 443–465. doi:10.1108/14626000910977161

Hassani, H., & Silva, E. S. (2015). Forecasting with big data: A review. *Annals of Data Science.*, *2*(1), 5–19.

Hassan, R. S., Nawaz, A., Lashari, M. N., & Zafar, F. (2015). Effect of customer relationship management on customer satisfaction. *Procedia Economics and Finance*, *23*, 563–567. doi:10.1016/S2212-5671(15)00513-4

Hassan, S., Nadzim, S. Z. A., & Shiratuddin, N. (2015). Strategic Use of Social Media for Small Business Based on the AIDA Model. *Procedia: Social and Behavioral Sciences*, *172*, 262–269. Advance online publication. doi:10.1016/j.sbspro.2015.01.363

Haudi, H., Handayani, W., Musnaini, M., Suyoto, Y., Prasetio, T., Pitaloka, E., & Cahyon, Y. (2022). The effect of social media marketing on brand trust, brand equity and brand loyalty. *International Journal of Data and Network Science*, *6*(3), 961–972. doi:10.5267/j.ijdns.2022.1.015

Hazen, B. T., Boone, C. A., Ezell, J. D., & Jones-Farmer, L. A. (2014). Data quality for data science, predictive analytics, and big data in supply chain management: An introduction to the problem and suggestions for research and applications. *International Journal of Production Economics, 154*, 72–80.

Hazen, B. T., Skipper, J. B., Ezell, J. D., & Boone, C. A. (2016). Big data and predictive analytics for supply chain sustainability: A theory-driven research agenda. *Computers & Industrial Engineering, 101*, 592–598.

Heine, K. (2010). The personality of luxury fashion brands. *Journal of Global Fashion Marketing, 1*(3), 154–163. doi:10.1080/20932685.2010.10593067

Helkkula, A., & Kelleher, C. (2010). Circularity of customer service experience and customer perceived value. *Journal of Customer Behaviour, 9*(1), 37–53. doi:10.1362/147539210X497611

Hellier, P. K., Geursen, G. M., Carr, R. A., & Rickard, J. A. (2003). Customer repurchase intention: A general structural equation model. *European Journal of Marketing, 37*(11), 1762–1800. doi:10.1108/03090560310495456

Hem, L., Chernatony, L. D., & Iversen, N. M. (2003). Factors influencing successful brand extensions. *Journal of Marketing Management, 19*(7/8), 781–806. doi:10.1080/0267257X.2003.9728237

Hendriyani, C., & Auliana, L. (2018). Transformation from Relationship Marketing to Electronic Customer Relationship Management: A Literature Study. *Review of Integrative Business and Economics Research, 7*(2), 116–124.

Hendriyani, C., & Auliana, L. (2018). Transformation from relationship marketing to electronic customer relationship management: A literature study. *Review of Integrative Business and Economics Research, 7*, 116–124.

Hennig-Thurau, T., Malthouse, E. C., Friege, C., Gensler, S., Lobschat, L., Rangaswamy, A., & Skiera, B. (2010). The impact of new media on customer relationships. *Journal of Service.*

Hennig-Thurau, T., Malthouse, E. C., Friege, C., Gensler, S., Lobschat, L., Rangaswamy, A., & Skiera, B. (2010). The impact of new media on customer relationships. *Journal of Service Research, 13*(3), 311–330. doi:10.1177/1094670510375460

Hepola, J., Karjaluoto, H., & Hintikka, A. (2017). The effect of sensory brand experience and involvement on brand equity directly and indirectly through consumer brand engagement. *Journal of Product and Brand Management, 26*(3), 282–293. doi:10.1108/JPBM-10-2016-1348

Herman, L. E., Sulhaini, S., & Farida, N. (2021). Electronic customer relationship management and company performance: Exploring the product innovativeness development. *Journal of Relationship Marketing, 20*(1), 1–19. doi:10.1080/15332667.2019.1688600

He, Z., Chiu, D. K. W., & Ho, K. K. W. (2022). Weibo Analysis on Chinese Cultural Knowledge for Gaming. In Z. Sun (Ed.), *Handbook of Research on Foundations and Applications of Intelligent Business Analytics* (pp. 320–349). doi:10.4018/978-1-7998-9016-4.ch015

Hilal, M. I. M. (2019). *The effects of services marketing mix elements on brand equity and customer response to tourist's hotels in the east coast of Sri Lanka*. Academic Press.

Hills, G. E., Hultman, C. M., & Miles, M. P. (2008). The evolution and development of entrepreneurial marketing. *Journal of Small Business Management*, *46*(1), 99–112. doi:10.1111/j.1540-627X.2007.00234.x

Hirschmann, R. (2021, April 9). *FMCG market in Malaysia - statistics & facts*. https://www.statista.com/topics/7617/fmcg-market-in-malaysia/

HodaN. (2010). *CRM Implementation: Critical Success Factors*. doi:10.2139/ssrn.2406488

Hollebeek, L. D. (2011a). Demystifying customer brand engagement: Exploring the loyalty nexus. *Journal of Marketing Management*, *27*(7-8), 785–807. doi:10.1080/0267257X.2010.500132

Hollebeek, L. D. (2011b). Exploring customer brand engagement: Definition and themes. *Journal of Strategic Marketing*, *19*(7), 555–573. doi:10.1080/0965254X.2011.599493

Holmes-Smith, P. (2001). Introduction to structural equation modeling using LISREL. ACSPRI-Winter training program, Perth.

Holweg, M., Disney, S. M., Hines, P., & Naim, M. M. (2005). Towards responsive vehicle supply: A simulation-based investigation into automotive scheduling systems. *Journal of Operations Management*, *23*, 507–530.

Homans, G. C. (1958). Social behavior as exchange. *American Journal of Sociology*, *63*(6), 597–606. doi:10.1086/222355

Hooper, D., Coughlan, J., & Mullen, M. R. (2008). Structural equation modelling: Guidelines for determining model fit. *Electronic Journal of Business Research Methods*, *6*(1), 53–60.

Hossain, M. S., Anthony, J. F., Beg, M. N. A., & Zayed, N. M. (2020). Affirmative Strategic Association of Brand Image, Brand Loyalty and Brand Equity: A Conclusive Perceptual Confirmation of the Top Management. Academy of Strategic Management Journal, 19(2).

Hoyer, W. D., Kroschke, M., Schmitt, B., Kraume, K., & Shankar, V. (2020). Transforming the customer experience through new technologies. *Journal of Interactive Marketing*, *51*, 57–71. doi:10.1016/j.intmar.2020.04.001

Hsu, J. (2013). *Big Business, Big Data, Big Sustainability*. Carbontrust.com.

Huang, Y., Chai, Y., Liu, Y., & Shen, J. (2018). 'Architecture of next-generation e-commerce platform. *Tsinghua Science and Technology*, *24*(1), 18–29. doi:10.26599/TST.2018.9010067

Hunt, D. S., & Morgan, M. R. (1994). Relationship marketing in the era of network competition. *Marketing Management*, *3*(1), 18–28.

Hutagalung, B., & Situmorang, S. H. (2018, January). The Effect Of Social Media Marketing On Value Equity, Brand Equity And Relationship Equity On Young Entrepreneurs In Medan City. In *1st Economics and Business International Conference 2017 (EBIC 2017)* (pp. 534-540). Atlantis Press. 10.2991/ebic-17.2018.84

Hutchinson, V., & Quintas, P. (2008). Do SMEs do knowledge management? Or simply manage what they know? *International Small Business Journal*, *26*(2), 131–154. doi:10.1177/0266242607086571

Ibrahim, Y., Abbas, T. M., & Kamal, M. (2021). The Use of Electronic Customer Relationship Management (E-CRM) Features through Hotel' Website to Enhance Customer Loyalty and Brand Image. *Journal of Association of Arab Universities for Tourism and Hospitality*, *21*(7), 103–125. doi:10.21608/jaauth.2021.79828.1190

Ibrahim, Y., Abbas, T. M., & Kamal, M. A. (2021). The Impact of Online Communities-based Social Customer Relationship Management (S-CRM) on Customer Loyalty and Brand Image on Hotels. *Journal of Association of Arab Universities for Tourism and Hospitality*, *21*(2), 206–232. doi:10.21608/jaauth.2021.84867.1202

Ibrahim, Y., Abbas, T., & Kamal, M. (2021). The Use of Electronic Customer Relationship Management (E-CRM) Features through Hotel' Website to Enhance Customer Loyalty and Brand Image. *Journal of Association of Arab Universities for Tourism and Hospitality*, *21*(1), 106–128.

Insider Intelligence. (2021). *Digital Payment Industry in 2021 : Payment methods, trends, and tech processing payments electronically.* https://www.insiderintelligence.com/insights/digital-payment-services/

Islam, J. U., & Rahman, Z. (2016). Examining the effects of brand love and brand image on customer engagement: An empirical study of fashion apparel brands. *Journal of Global Fashion Marketing*, *7*(1), 45-59. doi:10.1080/20932685.2015.1110041

Islam, J., & Rahman, Z. (2016). The transpiring journey of customer engagement research in marketing: A systematic review of the past decade. *Management Decision*, *54*(8), 2008–2034. doi:10.1108/MD-01-2016-0028

Ismail, A. R. (2017). The influence of perceived social media marketing activities on brand loyalty. *Asia Pacific Journal of Marketing and Logistics*, *29*(1), 129–144. doi:10.1108/APJML-10-2015-0154

Ismail, N. A., & Hussin, H. (2015). Perception on E-CRM features for Airline Websites in Malaysia: Some Empirical Evidence. In *Proceedings of the International Conference of E-Commerce*. UUM.

Jack, S., Moult, S., Anderson, A. R., & Dodd, S. (2010). An entrepreneurial network evolving: Patterns of change. *International Small Business Journal*, *28*(4), 315–337. doi:10.1177/0266242610363525

Jacoby, J. (2002). Stimulus-organism-response reconsidered: An evolutionary step in modeling (consumer) behaviour. *Journal of Consumer Psychology*, *12*(1), 51–57. doi:10.1207/S15327663JCP1201_05

Jaiprakash, A. T. (2008). A conceptual research on the association between celebrity endorsement, brand image and brand equity. *Icfai Univ J Mark Manag*, *7*(4), 54–64.

Jakupović, A., Pavlić, M., & Han, Z. D. (2014). Formalisation method for the text expressed knowledge. *Expert Systems with Applications*, *41*, 5308–5322.

Jayachandran, S., Sharma, S., Kaufman, P., & Raman, P. (2005). The role of relational information processes and technology use in customer relationship management. *Journal of Marketing*, *69*(4), 177–192. doi:10.1509/jmkg.2005.69.4.177

Jayaram, J., Kannan, V. R., & Tan, K. C. (2004). Influence of initiators on supply chain value creation. *International Journal of Production Research*, *42*(20), 4377–4399. doi:10.1080/00207540410001716516

Jelinek, M., & Bergey, P. (2013). Innovation as the strategic driver of sustainability: Big data knowledge for profit and survival. *IEEE Engineering Management Review*, *41*(2), 14–22.

Jeon, H. G., Kim, C., Lee, J., & Lee, K. C. (2021). Understanding E-Commerce Consumers' Repeat Purchase Intention: The Role of Trust Transfer and the Moderating Effect of Neuroticism. *Frontiers in Psychology*, *12*, 690039. doi:10.3389/fpsyg.2021.690039 PMID:34140923

Jick, T. D. (1979). Mixing qualitative and quantitative methods: Triangulation in action. *Administrative Science Quarterly*, *24*(4), 602–611. doi:10.2307/2392366

Jiménez-Castillo, D., & Sánchez-Fernández, R. (2019). The role of digital influencers in brand recommendation: Examining their impact on engagement, expected value and purchase intention. *International Journal of Information Management*, *49*, 366–376. doi:10.1016/j.ijinfomgt.2019.07.009

Jin, J., Liu, Y., Ji, P., & Liu, H. (2016). Understanding big consumer opinion data for market-driven product design. *International Journal of Production Research*, *54*(10), 3019–3041.

Jin, Y., & Ji, S. (2013). Partner choice of supply chain based on 3d printing and big data. *Information Technology Journal*, *12*(22), 6822.

Jocumsen, G. (2004). How do small business managers make strategic marketing decisions? A model of process. *European Journal of Marketing*, *38*(5/6), 659–674. doi:10.1108/03090560410529277

Johan, K., Samantha, W., Tandean, M. J., & Sihombing, S. O. (2020). *The Relationships between Web Design, Reliability, Privacy, Service Quality, and Purchase Intention of Customers at E-commerce Business: An Empirical Study*. Academic Press.

Johanson, M., Belenki, S., Jalminger, J., Fant, M., & Gjertz, M. (2014). Big automotive data: Leveraging large volumes of data for knowledge-driven product development. In *2014 IEEE International Conference on Big Data (Big Data)*. IEEE.

Junaid, M., Hou, F., Hussain, K., & Kirmani, A. A. (2019). Brand love: The emotional bridge between experience and engagement, generation-M perspective. *Journal of Product and Brand Management*, *28*(2), 200–215. doi:10.1108/JPBM-04-2018-1852

Jüttner, U., & Maklan, S. (2011). Supply chain resilience in the global financial crisis: An empirical study. *Supply Chain Management, 16*(4), 246–25.

Kakeesh, D., Al-Weshah, G., & Al-Ma'aitah, N. (2021). Maintaining Customer Loyalty Using Electronic Customer Relationship Management (E-CRM): Qualitative Evidence from Small Food Businesses in Jordan. *Impact of Current Trends in Social Commerce, Economics, and Business Analytics, 39*(7), 1–18. doi:10.25115/eea.v39i7.4810

Kaldeen, M., & Thowfeek, M. H. (2020). *Factors favoring electronic customer relationship management.* E-CRM.

Kambatla, K., Kollias, G., Kumar, V., & Grama, A. (2014). Trends in big data analytics. *Journal of Parallel and Distributed Computing, 74*(7), 2561–2573.

Kampani, N., & Jhamb, D. (2020). Analyzing the Role of E-CRM in Managing Customer Relations: A Critical Review of the Literature. *Journal of Critical Review, 7*(4), 221–226.

Kaplan, A., & Haenlein, M. (2019). Siri, Siri, in my hand: Who's the fairest in the land? On the interpretations, illustrations, and implications of artificial intelligence. *Business Horizons, 62*, 15–25.

Keh, H. T., Nguyen, T. T. M., & Ng, H. P. (2007). The effects of entrepreneurial orientation and marketing information on the performance of SMEs. *Journal of Business Venturing, 22*(4), 592–611. doi:10.1016/j.jbusvent.2006.05.003

Keller, K. L. (1993). Conceptualizing, measuring, and managing customer-based brand equity. *Journal of Marketing, 57*(1), 1–22. doi:10.1177/002224299305700101

Kenett, Y., & Thompson-Schill, S. L. (2020). *Novel conceptual combination can dynamically reconfigure semantic memory networks*. Academic Press.

Ke, X., & Wagner, C. (2022). Global pandemic compels sport to move to esports: Understanding from brand extension perspective. *Managing Sport and Leisure, 27*(1-2), 152–157. doi:10.1080/23750472.2020.1792801

Khalifa, M., & Shen, N. (2005). Effects of electronic customer relationship management on customer satisfaction: a temporal model. In *Proceedings of the 38th Hawaii International Conference on System Sciences*. IEEE Computer Society. 10.1109/HICSS.2005.224

Khalifa, M., & Liu, V. (2007). Online consumer retention: Contingent effects of online shopping habit and online shopping experience. *European Journal of Information Systems, 16*(6), 780–792. doi:10.1057/palgrave.ejis.3000711

Khalifa, M., & Shen, N. (2009). Modeling electronic customer relationship management success: Functional and temporal considerations. *Journal of Behaviour and Information Technology, 28*(4), 373–387. doi:10.1080/01449290802030373

Khan, A., Baharudin, B., & Lee. (2010). A review of machine learning algorithms for text-documents classification. *Journal of Advances in Information Technology, 1*(1), 4-20.

Khanh, C. N. T., Phong, L. T., & Cao, K. D. (2021). The impact of organizational factors on E-CRM success implementation. *VINE Journal of Information and Knowledge Management Systems*. Advance online publication. doi:10.1108/VJIKMS-05-2020-0096

Khan, I., & Rahman, Z. (2015). Brand experience anatomy in retailing: An interpretive structural modeling approach. *Journal of Retailing and Consumer Services*, *24*, 60–69. doi:10.1016/j.jretconser.2015.02.003

Khanlari, A. (Ed.). (2015). *Strategic customer relationship management in the age of social media*. IGI Global. doi:10.4018/978-1-4666-8586-4

Khan, N., Naim, A., Hussain, M. R., Naveed, Q. N., Ahmad, N., & Qamar, S. (2019, May). The 51 v's of big data: survey, technologies, characteristics, opportunities, issues and challenges. In *Proceedings of the international conference on omni-layer intelligent systems* (pp. 19-24). 10.1145/3312614.3312623

Khan, O., Christopher, M., & Creazza, A. (2012). Aligning product design with the supply chain: A case study. *Supply Chain Management*, *17*(3), 323–336.

Khan, S. A., & Magd, H. (2021). Empirical Examination of Ms Teams in Conducting Webinar: Evidence from International Online Program Conducted in Oman. *Journal Of Content Community And Communication*, *14*(8), 159–175. doi:10.31620/JCCC.12.21/13

Khan, S. A., Thoudam, P. D., Ligori, A. A., & Saleem, M. (2020). Customer Satisfaction and Customer Loyalty in Online Shopping A Study on University Students of Bhutan. *Delhi Business Review*, *21*(2), 11–22. doi:10.51768/dbr.v21i2.212202002

Kherwa, P., & Bansal, P. (2017). Latent Semantic Analysis: An approach to understand semantic of text. In *2017 International Conference on Current Trends in Computer, Electrical, Electronics and Communication (CTCEEC)* (pp. 870-874). IEEE. 10.1109/CTCEEC.2017.8455018

Khoa, B. T. (2022). Dataset for the electronic customer relationship management based on S-O-R model in electronic commerce. *Data in Brief*, *42*, 108039. doi:10.1016/j.dib.2022.108039 PMID:35313498

Khodakarami, F., & Chan, Y. (2011). Evaluating the Success of Customer Relationship Management (CRM) Systems. *Proceedings of the European Conference on Information Management & Evaluation.*

Kim, A. J., & Ko, E. (2012). Do social media marketing activities enhance customer equity? An empirical study of luxury fashion brand. *Journal of Business Research*, *65*(10), 1480–1486. doi:10.1016/j.jbusres.2011.10.014

Kim, C., Zhao, W., & Yang, K. H. (2008). An Empirical Study on the Integrated Framework of e-CRM in Online Shopping: Evaluating the Relationships Among Perceived Value, Satisfaction, and Trust Based on Customers' Perspectives. *Journal of Electronic Commerce in Organizations*, *6*(3), 1–19. doi:10.4018/jeco.2008070101

Kim, J. Y. (2003). Communication message strategies for brand extensions. *Journal of Product and Brand Management*.

Kim, K. K., Umanath, N. S., & Kim, B. H. (2006). An assessment of electronic information transfer in B2B supply-channel relationships. *Journal of Management Information Systems*, *22*(3), 293–320.

Kim, M. J., Lee, C. K., & Jung, T. (2020). Exploring Consumer Behavior in Virtual Reality Tourism Using an Extended Stimulus-Organism-Response Model. *Journal of Travel Research*, *59*(1), 69–89. doi:10.1177/0047287518818915

Klutse, C. M. (2016). Relationship Management in Hospitality Industry: The case of Hotels in Ghana. *Global Journal of Commerce and Management Perspective*, *5*(1), 12–15.

Knoerzer, K., & Millemann, J. A. (2021). Investigating determinants of brand extension success in a fit and a non-fit scenario. *International Journal of Technology Marketing*, *15*(4), 379–398. doi:10.1504/IJTMKT.2021.119073

Koay, K. Y., Ong, D. L. T., Khoo, K. L., & Yeoh, H. J. (2020). Perceived social media marketing activities and consumer-based brand equity: Testing a moderated mediation model. *Asia Pacific Journal of Marketing and Logistics*, *33*(1), 53–72. doi:10.1108/APJML-07-2019-0453

Kocak, A., & Abimbola, T. (2009). The effects of entrepreneurial marketing on born global performance. *International Marketing Review*, *26*(4/5), 439–452. doi:10.1108/02651330910971977

Koçoğlu, C. M., & Kalem, M. Y. (2020). Electronic Customer Relationship Management in Tourism. In Handbook of Research on Smart Technology Applications in the Tourism Industry (pp. 273-294). IGI Global.

Koçoğlu, C. M., & Kalem, M. Y. (2020). Electronic Customer Relationship Management in Tourism. In *Handbook of Research on Smart Technology Applications in the Tourism Industry* (pp. 273–294). IGI Global. doi:10.4018/978-1-7998-1989-9.ch013

Kotler, P., & Keller, K. L. (2006). *Marketing management* (12th ed.). Academic Press.

Kreipl, S., & Pinedo, M. (2004). Planning and scheduling in supply chains: An overview of issues in practice. *Production and Operations Management*, *13*, 77–92.

Krueger, L. J., Gaeddert, M., Koeppel, L., Brümmer, L. E., Gottschalk, C., Miranda, I. B., . . . Denkinger, C. M. (2020). Evaluation of the accuracy, ease of use and limit of detection of novel, rapid, antigen-detecting point-of-care diagnostics for SARS-CoV-2. medRxiv. doi:10.1101/2020.10.01.20203836

Kubina, M., & Lendel, V. (2015). Successful Application of Social CRM in The Company. *Procedia Economics and Finance*, *23*, 1190–1194. doi:10.1016/S2212-5671(15)00487-6

Kumar, A., Sikdar, P., Gupta, M., Singh, P., & Sinha, N. (2022). Drivers of satisfaction and usage continuance in e-grocery retailing: a collaborative design supported perspective. *Journal of Research in Interactive Marketing*. https://doi-org.ezproxy.um.edu.my/10.1108/JRIM-02-2020-0035

Kumaravel, V., & Kandasamy, C. (2012). To what extent the brand image influence consumers' purchase decision on durable products. *Rom J Mark, 1*, 34–38.

Kumar, M. (2020). Effective Usage of E-CRM and Social Media Tools by Akshay Kumar: Most Prolific Bollywood Actor of Last Decade. *International Journal of Management, 11*(2).

Kumar, M. P., & Kumar, T. S. (2014). E-business: Pros and cons in Customer Relationship Management. *International Journal of Management and International Business Studies, 4*(3), 349–356.

Kumar, P., & Mokha, A. K. (2021). Relationship between E-CRM, Customer Experience, Customer Satisfaction and Customer Loyalty in Banking Industry: A Review of Literature. *International Journal of Multidisciplinary, 6*(2), 127–137.

Kumar, P., & Mokha, A. K. (2022). Electronic Customer Relationship Management (E-CRM) and Customer Loyalty: The Mediating Role of Customer Satisfaction in the Banking Industry. *International Journal of E-Business Research, 18*(1), 1–22. doi:10.4018/IJEBR.293292

Kumar, P., Mokha, A. K., & Pattnaik, S. C. (2022). Electronic customer relationship management (E-CRM), customer experience and customer satisfaction: Evidence from the banking industry. *Benchmarking, 29*(2), 551–572. doi:10.1108/BIJ-10-2020-0528

Kumar, V., Aksoy, L., Donkers, B., Venkatesan, R., Wiesel, T., & Tillmanns, S. (2010). Undervalued or overvalued customers: Capturing total customer engagement value. *Journal of Service Research, 13*(3), 297–310. doi:10.1177/1094670510375602

Kusiak, A., & Chen, M. (1988). Expert systems for planning and scheduling manufacturing systems. *European Journal of Operational Research, 34*, 113–130.

Kütz. (2016). Introduction to E-commerce. Academic Press.

Kuvykaite, R., & Piligrimiene, Z. (2014). Consumer engagement into brand equity creation. *Procedia: Social and Behavioral Sciences, 156*, 479–483. doi:10.1016/j.sbspro.2014.11.225

Lai, W. W., Chiu, D. K., & Feng, Z. (2013). A collaborative food safety service agent architecture with alerts and trust. *Information Systems Frontiers, 15*(4), 599–612. doi:10.100710796-012-9382-9

Lakshmi, S. M., & Suresh, M. (2021). Modelling of factors influencing brand commitment of FMCG products: A TISM approach. *Materials Today: Proceedings*.

Lam, A. Y., Cheung, R., & Lau, M. M. (2013). The influence of internet-based customer relationship management on customer loyalty. *Contemporary Management Research, 9*(4), 419–440. doi:10.7903/cmr.11095

Langner, T., Schmidt, J., & Fischer, A. (2015). Is it really love? A comparative investigation of the emotional nature of Brand and interpersonal love. *Psychology & Marketing, 32*(6), 624-634.

Laudon, K., & Laudon, J. P. (2022). *Management information systems: Managing the Digital Firm* (17th ed.). Pearson Education Limited.

Lawson-Body, A., & O'Keefe, T. P. (2006). Interorganizational relationships in the context of SMEs B2B e-commerce. *Journal of Electronic Commerce in Organizations*, *4*(4), 1–28. doi:10.4018/jeco.2006100101

LeCun, Y., Bengio, Y., & Hinton, G. (2015). Deep learning. *Nature*, *521*, 436–444.

Lee, J., & Park, C. (2022b). Social media content, customer engagement and brand equity: US versus Korea. *Management Decision*.

Lee, C. T., & Hsieh, S. H. (2022). Can social media-based brand communities build brand relationships? Examining the effect of community engagement on brand love. *Behaviour & Information Technology*, *41*(6), 1270–1285. doi:10.1080/0144929X.2021.1872704

Lee, J., & Park, C. (2022a). Customer engagement on social media, brand equity and financial performance: A comparison of the US and Korea. *Asia Pacific Journal of Marketing and Logistics*, *34*(3), 454–474. doi:10.1108/APJML-09-2020-0689

Lee, J., & Yoon, E. (2022). Effects of Parent Brand Equity on Perceived Fit and Customer Behavior of Extended Brand—Focused on MICE Destination. *International Journal of Environmental Research and Public Health*, *19*(8), 4540. doi:10.3390/ijerph19084540 PMID:35457408

Lee, S. H., Deale, C. S., & Lee, J. (2022). Does it pay to book direct?: Customers' perceptions of online channel distributors, price, and loyalty membership on brand dimensions. *Journal of Revenue and Pricing Management*, •••, 1–11. doi:10.105741272-022-00382-x

Lemon, K. N., Rust, R. T., & Zeithaml, V. A. (2001). What drives customer equity? *Marketing Management, 10*(1), 20-25.

Leung, S. C., Tsang, S. O., Ng, W.-L., & Wu, Y. (2007). A robust optimization model for multi-site production planning problem in an uncertain environment. *European Journal of Operational Research*, *181*, 224–238.

Lewis, B. R., & Mitchell, V. W. (1990). Defining and Measuring the Quality of Customer Service. *Marketing Intelligence & Planning*, *8*(6), 11–17. doi:10.1108/EUM0000000001086

Liang, W.-Y., & Huang, C.-C. (2006). Agent-based demand forecast in multi-echelon supply chain. *Decision Support Systems*, *42*, 390–407.

Lim, J. S., Pham, P., & Heinrichs, J. H. (2020). Impact of social media activity outcomes on brand equity. *Journal of Product and Brand Management*, *29*(7), 927–937. doi:10.1108/JPBM-03-2019-2298

Lin, T. C., Wu, S., Hsu, J. S. C., & Chou, Y. C. (2012). The integration of value-based adoption and expectation–confirmation models: An example of IPTV continuance intention. *Decision Support Systems*, *54*(1), 63–75. doi:10.1016/j.dss.2012.04.004

Lin, W., Dongying, L., Haizhang, S., & Shengbao, D. (2017). Research on the evolution law of the semantic web structure of online shopping reviews. *2nd Advanced Information Technology, Electronic and Automation Control Conference (IAEAC)*, 395-398.

Liu, W., Wang, Z., & Zhao, H. (2020). Comparative study of customer relationship management research from East Asia, North America and Europe: A bibliometric overview. *Electronic Markets, 30*(4), 735–757. doi:10.100712525-020-00395-7

Li, X., Zhou, Y., Wong, Y. D., Wang, X., & Yuen, K. F. (2021). What influences panic buying behaviour? A model based on dual-system theory and stimulus-organism-response framework. *International Journal of Disaster Risk Reduction, 64*, 102484. doi:10.1016/j.ijdrr.2021.102484

LLamasoft. (2016). *Supply chain simulation: why its time has come*. LLamasoft white paper.

Lohanda, T., & Berto, A. R. (2022). Can Social Customer Relationship Management Activities Evoke Customer Loyalty?. *Jurnal Studi Komunikasi dan Media, 25*(2), 267-276.

Loureiro, S. M. C., Gorgus, T., & Kaufmann, H. R. (2017). Antecedents and outcomes of online Brand engagement. *Online Information Review, 41*(7), 985–1005. doi:10.1108/OIR-08-2016-0236

Lubis, A., Dalimunthe, R., Absah, Y., & Fawzeea, B. K. (2020). The influence of customer relationship management (CRM) indicators on customer loyalty of sharia based banking system. *Lubis, A*, 84-92.

Lu, H., Li, Y., Chen, M., Kim, H., & Serikawa, S. (2018). Brain Intelligence: Go beyond Artificial Intelligence. *Mobile Networks and Applications, 23*, 368–375.

Lyytinen, K., & Rose, G. M. (2003). The disruptive nature of information technology innovations: The case of internet computing in systems development organisations. *Management Information Systems Quarterly, 27*(4), 557–596. doi:10.2307/30036549

Maecker, O., Barrot, C., & Becker, J. U. (2016). The Effect of Social Media Interactions on Customer Relationship Management. *Business Research, 9*(1), 133–155. doi:10.100740685-016-0027-6

Mahafzah, A. G., Aljawarneh, N. M., Alomari, K. A. K., Altahat, S., & Alomari, Z. S. (2020). Impact of customer relationship management on food and beverage service quality: The mediating role of employees satisfaction. *Humanities & Social Sciences Reviews, 8*(2), 222–230. doi:10.18510/hssr.2020.8226

Majeed, M., Asare, C., Fatawu, A., & Abubakari, A. (2022). An analysis of the effects of customer satisfaction and engagement on social media on repurchase intention in the hospitality industry. *Cogent Business & Management, 9*(1), 2028331. doi:10.1080/23311975.2022.2028331

Mang'unyi, E. E., Khabala, O. T., & Govender, K. K. (2018). Bank customer loyalty and satisfaction: The influence of virtual e-CRM. *African Journal of Economic and Management Studies, 9*(2), 250–265. doi:10.1108/AJEMS-08-2017-0183

Manning, C. D., Manning, C. D., & Schütze, H. (1999). *Foundations of statistical natural language processing*. MIT Press.

Manyika, J., Sinclair, J., Dobbs, R., Strube, G., Rassey, L., & Mischke, J. (n.d.). *Manufacturing the Future: The Next Era of Global Growth and Innovation*. McKinsey Global Institute. https://www.mckinsey.com/businessfunctions/operations/our-insights/ the-future-of-manufacturing

Markets and Markets. (2021). *Digital payment market: Global forecast to 2026.* https://www.marketsandmarkets.com/Market-Reports/digital-payment-market-209834053.html?gclid=CjwKCAjw0a-SBhBkEiwApljU0lvGFZsDX_qj-wwVttzaS-UUgwvRYObnSOrK6IcJWbTkAekxDdfn5BoC2MMQAvD_BwE

Markus, M. L. (1983). Power, Politics, and MIS Implementation. *Communications of the ACM, 26*(6), 430–444. Advance online publication. doi:10.1145/358141.358148

Maroofi, F., Darabi, A., & Torabi, J. (2012). Effects of e-CRM on Customer-Bank Relationship Quality and Results. *International Journal of Academic Research in Accounting.*

Martínez, E., & de Chernatony, L. (2004). The effect of brand extension strategies upon brand image. *Journal of Consumer Marketing, 21*(1), 39–50. doi:10.1108/07363760410513950

Martínez, E., Montaner, T., & Pina, J. M. (2009). Brand extension feedback: The role of advertising. *Journal of Business Research, 62*(3), 305–313. doi:10.1016/j.jbusres.2008.05.009

Martin, G. S., & Brown, T. J. (1990). In search of brand equity: The conceptualization and measurement of the brand impression construct. *Mark Theory Appl, 2*, 431–438.

Masa'deh, R. E., AL-Haddad, S., Al Abed, D., Khalil, H., AlMomani, L., & Khirfan, T. (2021). The Impact of Social Media Activities on Brand Equity. *Information (Basel), 12*(11), 477. doi:10.3390/info12110477

Maskuroh, N., Fahlevi, M., Irma, D., Rita, R., & Rabiah, A. (2022). Social media as a bridge to e-commerce adoption in Indonesia: A research framework for repurchase intention. *International Journal of Data and Network Science, 6*(1), 107–114. doi:10.5267/j.ijdns.2021.9.017

McGoldrick, P. J. (2012). Retailing. In The Marketing Book (pp. 806-835). Routledge.

McWilliams, A., & Siegel, D. S. (2011). Creating and capturing value: Strategic corporate social responsibility, resource-based theory, and sustainable competitive advantage. *Journal of Management, 37*(5), 1480–1495.

Mele, F. D., Musulin, E., & Puigjaner, L. (2005, January 1). Supply chain monitoring: A statistical approach. *Computer-Aided Chemical Engineering, 20*, 1375–1380.

Melo, M. T., Nickel, S., & Saldanha-da-Gama, F. (2009). Facility location and supply chain management – A review. *European Journal of Operational Research, 196*, 401–412.

Melovic, B., Rondovic, B., Mitrovic-Veljkovic, S., Ocovaj, S. B., & Dabic, M. (2020). Electronic Customer Relationship Management Assimilation in Southeastern European Companies—Cluster Analysis. *IEEE Transactions on Engineering Management.*

Memon, F. A., Saeed, S., & Shaikh, A. (2018). Systematic Approach of Customer Relationship Management in Much Different Organization. *IBT Journal of Business Studies, 2*(2), 132–147. doi:10.46745/ilma.jbs.2018.14.02.11

Menidjel, C., Benhabib, A., & Bilgihan, A. (2017). Examining the moderating role of personality traits in the relationship between brand trust and brand loyalty. *Journal of Product and Brand Management, 26*(6), 631–649. doi:10.1108/JPBM-05-2016-1163

Meuter, M. L., Ostrom, A. L., Roundtree, R. I., & Bitner, M. J. (2000). Self-service technologies: Understanding customer satisfaction with technology-based service encounters. *Journal of Marketing, 64*(3), 50–64. doi:10.1509/jmkg.64.3.50.18024

Milewicz, J., & Herbig, P. (1994). Evaluating the brand extension decision using a model of reputation building. *Journal of Product and Brand Management, 3*(1), 39–47. doi:10.1108/10610429410053077

Milović, B. (2012). *Social media and eCRM as a prerequisite for hotel success*. Academic Press.

Min, H., Jeung Ko, H., & Seong Ko, C. (2006). A genetic algorithm approach to developing the multi-echelon reverse logistics network for product returns. *Omega, 34*, 56–69.

Miralam, M. S., Junnaidi, M. H., & Moizuddin, S. (2019). A Study on Customer Satisfaction in FMCG Sector with Select Hypermarkets in Riyadh City Kingdom of Saudi Arabia. *International Review of Management and Business Research, 8*(2), 170–178.

Miremadi, A. R., Ghalamakri, S., & Ramezani, A. A. (2012). Challenges in trust and security by implementation of E-CRM among banks and financial institution: A case study of e-banking in iran". *International Journal of Information Science and Management, 10*, 99–118.

Miremadi, A., & Ghanadiof, O. (2021). The Ultimate Influences of Brand Equity Dimensions on Consumer Decision in Hi-Tech Market. *Academic Journal of Research and Scientific Publishing.* doi. org/. e doi:10.52132/Ajrsp

Misy, P. (2015). *The Influence of e-CRM (Electronic Customer Relationship Management) on Customer Loyalty Case Study: Customers of The Body Shop* (Doctoral dissertation). Universitas Andalas.

Mitchell, A., & Education, A. E. (2018). A review of mixed methods, pragmatism and abduction techniques. In *ECRM 2018 17th European Conference on Research Methods in Business and Management* (p. 269). Academic Conferences and Publishing Limited.

Mnih, V., Kavukcuoglu, K., Silver, D., Rusu, A. A., Veness, J., Bellemare, M. G., Graves, A., Riedmiller, M., Fidjeland, A. K., & Ostrovski, G. (2015). Human-level control through deep reinforcement learning. *Nature, 518*, 529–533.

Moayedikia, A., Ghaderi, H., & Yeoh, W. (2020). Optimizing microtask assignment on crowdsourcing platforms using Markov chain Monte Carlo. *Decision Support Systems, 139*, 113404.

Mohammad Shafiee, M., Seify, M., & Yazdi, A. (2020). Antecedents and Consequences of Implementing Electronic Customer Relationship Management in Small and Medium Enterprises. *New Marketing Research Journal, 10*(1), 129–146.

Mohammed, B., & Mouhoub, M. (2014). Evaluation of an Online Shopping System under Preferences and Constraints. In *Canadian Conference on Electrical and Computer Engineering* (pp. 1-8), IEEE. 10.1109/CCECE.2014.6900974

Mohan, B. C., & Sequeira, A. H. (2016). The impact of customer-based brand equity on the operational performance of FMCG companies in India. *IIMB Management Review*, *28*(1), 13–19. doi:10.1016/j.iimb.2015.11.002

Mohan, G., Sivakumaran, B., & Sharma, P. (2013). Impact of store environment on impulse buying behavior. *European Journal of Marketing*, *47*(10), 1711–1732. doi:10.1108/EJM-03-2011-0110

Moolla, A. I., & Bisschoff, C. A. (2013). An empirical model that measures brand loyalty of fast-moving consumer goods. *Journal of Economics*, *4*(1), 1–9. doi:10.1080/09765239.2013.11884959

Moore, K. (2020). *Ecommerce 101 + The History of Online Shopping: What The Past Says About Tomorrow's Retail Challenges*. Retrieved from big commerce: https://www.bigcommerce.com/blog/ecommerce/#faqs-about-ecommerce

Morgan, R. M., & Hunt, S. (1994). The Commitment-Trust Theory of Relationship Marketing. *Journal of Marketing*, *58*(07), 20–38. doi:10.1177/002224299405800302

Morgeson, F. V. III, Hult, G. T. M., Mithas, S., Keiningham, T., & Fornell, C. (2020). Turning complaining customers into loyal customers: Moderators of the complaint handling–Customer loyalty relationship. *Journal of Marketing*, *84*(5), 79–99. doi:10.1177/0022242920929029

Moriarty, J., Jones, R., Rowley, J., & Kupiec-Teahan, B. (2009). Marketing in small hotels: A qualitative study. *Marketing Intelligence & Planning*, *26*(3), 293–315. doi:10.1108/02634500810871348

Mourya, A. K., & Kaur, H. (2020). Performance and Evaluation of Different Kernels in Support Vector Machine for Text Mining. In *Advances in Intelligent Computing and Communication* (pp. 264–271). Springer. doi:10.1007/978-981-15-2774-6_33

Mumtaz, R. (2019). Awareness and perspectives social media as new strategic marketing approach in minor industries; notion grounded on AIDA model. *Journal of Content. Community and Communication*, *10*(5). Advance online publication. doi:10.31620/JCCC.12.19/22

Mustikasari, A., Krisnawati, M., & Sutrisno, E. (2021). Customer Experience and Repurchase Intention in Multi-Channel: Customer Satisfaction as Mediating Variable. *Journal of Industrial Distribution & Business*, *12*(3), 7–19.

Naim, A. (2022). Factors of Consumer Behaviour of youth from Middle East when purchasing Organic Food. *Global Scientific Review, 3*, 1–7. Retrieved from http://www.scienticreview.com/index.php/gsr/article/view/13

Naim, A., & Khan, M. F. (2021). Measuring the Psychological Behavior of Consumers for Medical Services. *Zien Journal of Social Sciences and Humanities, 2*, 119–131. Retrieved from https://zienjournals.com/index.php/zjssh/article/view/316

Naim, A., Alahmari, F., & Rahim, A. (2021). Role of Artificial Intelligence in Market Development and Vehicular communication. *Smart Antennas: Recent Trends in Design and Applications, 2*(28).

Naim, A. (2021). Applications of E-Learning tools for Achieving Students Learning Outcomes. *Journal of Pedagogical Inventions and Practices, 2*(2), 75–82. https://zienjournals.com/index.php/jpip/article/view/320

Naim, A. (2021). Applications of Marketing Framework in Business Practices. *Journal of Marketing and Emerging Economics, 1*(6), 55–70.

Naim, A. (2021). Applications of MIS in building Electronic Relationship with customers: A case-based study. *Periodica Journal of Modern Philosophy. Social Sciences and Humanities, 1*, 1–8.

Naim, A. (2021). Green Business Process Management. *International Journal of Innovative Analyses and Emerging Technology, 1*(6), 125–134. http://openaccessjournals.eu/index.php/ijiaet/article/view/651

Naim, A. (2021). Green Information Technologies in Business Operations. *Periodica Journal of Modern Philosophy. Social Sciences and Humanities, 1*, 36–49.

Naim, A. (2021). New Trends in Business Process Management: Applications of Green Information Technologies. *British Journal of Environmental Studies, 1*(1), 12–23.

Naim, A. (2022). Economies of Scale for Antenna's Applications in Interior Regions. *International Journal of Innovative Analyses and Emerging Technology, 2*(2), 77–82. http://openaccessjournals.eu/index.php/ijiaet/article/view/1058

Naim, A. (2022). Mapping of social customer relationship management with electronic customer relationship management. *European Journal of Interdisciplinary Research and Development, 2*, 14–25. https://ejird.journalspark.org/index.php/ejird/article/view/10

Naim, A. (2022). Neuro- Marketing Techniques for Proposing Information Driven Framework for Decision Making. *International Journal of Innovative Analyses and Emerging Technology, 2*(2), 87–94. http://openaccessjournals.eu/index.php/ijiaet/article/view/1060

Naim, A. (2022). Neuro-Marketing Techniques for Proposing Information Driven Framework for Decision Making. *International Journal of Innovative Analyses and Emerging Technology, 2*(2), 87–94. http://openaccessjournals.eu/index.php/ijiaet/article/view/1060

Naim, A. (2022). Understanding the customer centric approach to add value to social ECRM (SECRM). *British Journal of Global Ecology and Sustainable Development, 4*, 1–17. https://journalzone.org/index.php/bjgesd/article/view/45

Naim, A. (2022a). Measurement Consumer Mood and Emotions for Fast Moving Consumer Goods. *International Journal of Innovative Analyses and Emerging Technology, 2*(2), 83–86.

Naim, A., & Alqahtani, K. (2021). Role of Information Systems in Customer Relationship Management. *Pulse, 2*(2).

Naim, A., Hussain, M. R., Naveed, Q. N., Ahmad, N., Qamar, S., Khan, N., & Hweij, T. A. (2019, April). Ensuring interoperability of e-learning and quality development in education. In *2019 IEEE Jordan International Joint Conference on Electrical Engineering and Information Technology (JEEIT)* (pp. 736-741). IEEE 10.1109/JEEIT.2019.8717431

Naim, A., Khan, M. F., Hussain, M. R., & Khan, N. (2019). "Virtual Doctor" Management Technique in the Diagnosis of ENT Diseases. *JOE, 15*(9), 88. doi:10.3991/ijoe.v15i09.10665

Naim, A., Muniasamy, A., Clementking, A., & Rajkumar, R. (2022). Relevance of Green Manufacturing and IoT in Industrial Transformation and Marketing Management. In M. Lahby, A. Al-Fuqaha, & Y. Maleh (Eds.), *Computational Intelligence Techniques for Green Smart Cities. Green Energy and Technology*. Springer. doi:10.1007/978-3-030-96429-0_19

Nair, R. D., & Prabhu, P. (2018). *Payments in the Digital Age*. https://dokumen.tips/documents/payments-models-for-the-digital-age-accenture-transforming-the-payments-landscape.html

Nambisan, S., & Baron, R. A. (2007). Interactions in virtual customer environments: Implications for product support and customer relationship management. *Journal of Interactive Marketing, 21*(2), 42–62. doi:10.1002/dir.20077

Namini, N. S. (2016). *Effective Factors on Customer Satisfaction and Customer Loyalty in FMCGs*. https://www.proquest.com/openview/c7530b55b5166341bdebf8e192013648/1?pq-origsite=gscholar&cbl=2026366&diss=y

Nandya, T., & Permana, D. (2021). Analysis of the effect of electronic customer relationship management (E-CRM) and brand trust on customer satisfaction and loyalty in pixy cosmetic products. *Dinasti International Journal of Management Science, 2*(3), 467–483. doi:10.31933/dijms.v2i3.708

Nanji, A. (2013). *Online shopping trends 2013: Most popular categories, top purchase drivers*. Academic Press.

Napitupulu, N. A., & Hidayat, Z. (2020). The Influence of Online Shopping Applications, Strategic Promotions, and Hedonist Habits on e-Shopaholic Behavior. In *2020 International Conference on Information Management and Technology (ICIMTech)* (pp. 922-927). IEEE 10.1109/ICIMTech50083.2020.9211181

Narayanaswamy, R., & Heiens, R. A. (2021). The impact of digital sales channels on web sales: Evidence from the USA's largest online retailers. *Int. J. Electronic Marketing and Retailing, 12*(3), 306–322. doi:10.1504/IJEMR.2021.116505

Nawi, N. B. C., Mamun, A. A., Nasir, N. A. M., & Hamsani, N. H. B. (2021). Examining the risk factors affecting the image of online stores in Malaysia. *International Journal of Electronic Marketing and Retailing, 12*(2), 156–170. doi:10.1504/IJEMR.2021.114244

Nderitu, S. W. (2018). *Influence Of E-Marketing Strategies On Brand Equity Of Parastatals In Kenya* (Doctoral dissertation). University of Nairobi.

Newberry, C. (2019). *1301 Social media statistics that matter to marketers in 2019*. Available at: https://blog.hootsuite.com/social-media-statistics-for-social-media-managers /#general

Ngai, E. W., Xiu, L., & Chau, D. C. (2009). Application of data mining techniques in customer relationship management: A literature review and classification. *Expert Systems with Applications*, *36*(2), 2592–2602.

Nguyen, D. H., de Leeuw, S., & Dullaert, W. E. (2018). Consumer behaviour and order fulfilment in online retailing: A systematic review. *International Journal of Management Reviews*, *20*(2), 255–276. doi:10.1111/ijmr.12129

Nicapotato. (2018). *Women's E-Commerce Clothing Reviews* [Dataset]. https://www.kaggle.com/nicapotato/womens-ecommerce-clothing-reviews

Nickel, S., Saldanha-da-Gama, F., & Ziegler, H.-P. (2012). A multi-stage stochastic supply network design problem with financial decisions and risk management. *Omega*, *40*, 511–524.

Nierobisch, T., Toporowski, W., Dannewald, T., & Jahn, S. (2017). Flagship stores for FMCG national brands: Do they improve brand cognitions and create favorable consumer reactions? *Journal of Retailing and Consumer Services*, *34*, 117–137. doi:10.1016/j.jretconser.2016.09.014

Ni, J., Chiu, D. K. W., & Ho, K. K. W. (2022). (in press). Exploring Information Search Behavior among Self-Drive Tourists. *Information Discovery and Delivery*. Advance online publication. doi:10.1108/IDD-05-2020-0054

Nikou, S. H., Selamat, H. B., Yusoff, R. C. M., & Khiabani, M. M. (2016). Electronic Customer Relationship Management, Customer Satisfaction, and Customer Loyalty: A Comprehensive Review Study. *International Journal of Management and Economics Invention*, *2*(12), 1133–1144. doi:10.18535/ijmei/v2i12.02

Noviana, G. (2021, September). An Analysis of the Implementation of Electronic Customer Relationship Management (E-CRM) Towards Customer Loyalty. In *5th Global Conference on Business, Management and Entrepreneurship (GCBME 2020)* (pp. 434-438). Atlantis Press. 10.2991/aebmr.k.210831.086

Nunnally, J. C. (1978). *Psychometric theory* (2nd ed.). McGraw-Hill.

Nunnaly, J. (1978). *Psychometric Theory*. McGraw-Hill.

O'Cass, A., & Weerawardena, J. (2009). Examining the role of international entrepreneurship, innovation and international market performance in SME internationalisation. *European Journal of Marketing*, *43*(11/12), 1325–1348. doi:10.1108/03090560910989911

O'Dwyer, M., Gilmore, A., & Carson, D. (2009). Innovative marketing in SMEs. *European Journal of Marketing*, *43*(1/2), 46–61. doi:10.1108/03090560910923238

O'Reilly, K., & Paper, D. (2012). CRM and retail service quality: Front-line employee perspectives. *International Journal of Retail & Distribution Management*, *40*(11), 865–881. doi:10.1108/09590551211267610

Oanh, N. (n.d.). *ECRM Meaning, a useful tool for your electroniccustomer relationship management*. Retrieved February 9, 2022, from https://www.appvizer.com/magazine/customer/client-relationship-mgt/ecrm-meaning

OECD. (2005). Guidelines for Collecting and Interpreting Innovation Data. In *The Oslo Manual* (3rd ed.). OECD.

Ogawa, A., & Hori, T. (2017). Error detection and accuracy estimation in automatic speech recognition using deep bidirectional recurrent neural networks. *Speech Communication*, *89*, 70–83.

Oliva, T. A., Oliver, R. L., & MacMillan, I. C. (1992). A catastrophe model for developing service satisfaction strategies. *Journal of Marketing*, *56*(3), 83–95.

Oliver, R. L. (1999). Whence consumer loyalty? *Journal of Marketing*, *63*(4_suppl1), 33–44. doi:10.1177/00222429990634s105

Onwuegbuzie, A. J., & Leech, N. L. (2007). Validity and qualitative research: An oxymoron? *Quality & Quantity*, *41*(2), 233–250. doi:10.100711135-006-9000-3

Oumar, T. K., Mang'unyi, E. E., Govender, K. K., & Rajkaran, S. (2017). Exploring the e-CRM – e-customer- e-loyalty nexus: A Kenyan commercial bank case study. *Management & Marketing. Challenges for the Knowledge Society*, *12*(4), 674–696. doi:10.1515/mmcks-2017-0039

Overgoor, G., Chica, M., Rand, W., & Weishampel, A. (2019). Letting the Computers Take Over: Using AI to Solve Marketing Problems. *California Management Review*, *61*, 156–185.

Owusu-Frimpong, N. (2008). An evaluation of customers' perception and usage of rural community banks (RCBs) in Ghana. *Journal of Emerging Markets*, *3*(2), 181–196. doi:10.1108/17468800810862632

Padmanabhan, B., & Tuzhilin, A. (2003). On the use of optimization for data mining: Theoretical interactions and eCRM opportunities. *Management Science*, *49*(10), 1327–1343. doi:10.1287/mnsc.49.10.1327.17310

Padmanabhan, B., Zheng, Z., & Kimbrough, S. O. (2006). An empirical analysis of the value of complete information of eCRM models. *Management Information Systems Quarterly*, *30*(2), 247–267. doi:10.2307/25148730

Pagani, M., & Mirabello, A. (2012). The influence of personal and social-interactive engagement in social TV web sites. *International Journal of Electronic Commerce*, *16*(2), 41–67. doi:10.2753/JEC1086-4415160203

Palaci, F., Salcedo, A., & Topa, G. (2019). Cognitive and Affective antecedents of Consumers' Satisfaction: A systematic Review of two research approaches. *Sustainability*, *11*(2), 431. doi:10.3390u11020431

Panchmatia, M. (2015). *Use Big Data to Help Procurement Make a Real Difference*. Academic Press.

Pan, S., Zhang, L., Thompson, R. G., & Ghaderi, H. (2020). A parcel network flow approach for joint delivery networks using parcel lockers. *International Journal of Production Research*, 1–26.

Pansari, A., & Kumar, V. (2017). Customer engagement: The construct, antecedents and consequences. *Journal of the Academy of Marketing Science*, *45*(3), 294–311. doi:10.100711747-016-0485-6

Parasuraman, A., Berry, L., & Zeithaml, V. (1988). SERVQUAL: A multiple-item scale for measuring customer perceptions of service quality. *Journal of Retailing*, *64*, 26–43.

Parise, S., Guinan, P. J., & Kafka, R. (2016). Solving the crisis of immediacy: How digital technology can transform the customer experience. *Business Horizons*, *59*, 411–420.

Park, C. W., Milberg, S., & Lawson, R. (1991). Evaluation of brand extensions: The role of product feature similarity and brand concept consistency. *The Journal of Consumer Research*, *18*(2), 185–193. doi:10.1086/209251

Parvatiyar, A., & Sheth, J. N. (2001). Customer relationship management: Emerging practice process and discipline. *Journal of Economic & Social Research*, *3*(2), 1–34.

Pasandideh, S. H. R., Niaki, S. T. A., & Nia, A. R. (2011). A genetic algorithm for vendor managed inventory control system of multi-product multi-constraint economic order quantity model. *Expert Systems with Applications*, *38*, 2708–2716.

Patton, M. Q. (2002). *Qualitative Research and Evaluation Methods* (3rd ed.). Sage.

Payne, A., & Frow, P. (2006). Customer relationship management: From strategy to implementation. *Journal of Marketing Management*, *22*(1-2), 135–168. doi:10.1362/026725706776022272

Peel, J. (2002). *CRM: Redefining Customer Relationship Management* (1st ed.). Digital Press.

Peltier, J. W., Schibrowsky, J. A., & Zhao, Y. (2009). Understanding the antecedents to the adoption of CRM technology by small retailers: Entrepreneurs vs owner-managers. *International Small Business Journal*, *27*(3), 307–336. doi:10.1177/0266242609102276

Pett, M. A., Lackey, N. R., & Sullivan, J. J. (2003). *Making Sense of Factor Analysis*. Sage. doi:10.4135/9781412984898

Pham, T. S. H., & Ahammad, M. F. (2017). Antecedents and consequences of online customer satisfaction: A holistic process perspective. *Technological Forecasting and Social Change*, *124*, 332–342. doi:10.1016/j.techfore.2017.04.003

Phan, M., Thomas, R., & Heine, K. (2011). Social Media and Luxury Brand Management: The Case of Burberry. *Journal of Global Fashion Marketing*, *2*(4), 213–222. doi:10.1080/20932685.2011.10593099

Picton, D., & Broderick, A. (2005). *Integrated Marketing Communications* (2nd ed.). Financial Times.

Pine, B. J., & Gilmore, J. H. (1998). *Welcome to the experience economy*. Academic Press.

PiStrategy. (2016). *Payment ecosystem*. http://pistrategy.org/payment-ecosystem/

Pradana, H. A., Riza, B. S., Naseer, M., Soetarno, D., & Mantoro, T. (2017). The effect of e-CRM towards service quality and net benefits using structure equation modeling. In *Proceedings of the 2017 Second International Conference on Informatics and Computing*. Institute of Electrical and Electronics Engineers. 10.1109/IAC.2017.8280535

Pramudito, D., Mursitama, T. N., Abdinagoro, S. B., & Harischandra, H. (2021). The Moderation Effect of e-Trust and Big Data Quality in e-Grocery: An Empirical Research from Outside of Java Island. *Turkish Journal of Computer and Mathematics Education, 12*(10), 6445–6459.

Prentice, C., Wang, X., & Loureiro, S. M. C. (2019). The influence of brand experience and service quality on customer engagement. *Journal of Retailing and Consumer Services, 50*, 50–59. doi:10.1016/j.jretconser.2019.04.020

Priore, P., Ponte, B., Rosillo, R., & de la Fuente, D. (2019). Applying machine learning to the dynamic selection of replenishment policies in fast-changing supply chain environments. *International Journal of Production Research, 57*, 3663–3677.

Purwanto, A. (2022). How The Role of Digital Marketing and Brand Image on Food Product Purchase Decisions? An Empirical Study on Indonesian SMEs in the Digital Era. *Journal of Industrial Engineering & Management Research, 3*(6), 34–41.

Putra, A. H. P. K., Nurani, N., Ilyas, G. B., Samiha, Y. T., & Lestari, S. D. (2021). Configure the Symmetrical and Asymmetrical Paths of Brand Equity and Relationship of Firm Created Content and User Generated Content as Antecedent. *Jurnal Manajemen Bisnis, 8*(1), 90–103. doi:10.33096/jmb.v1i1.704

Quaye, D. M., Mensah, I., & Amoah-Mensah, A. (2018). Customer relationship management practices affecting customer loyalty supporting small airline carriers in Ghana. *International Journal of Electronic Customer Relationship Management, 11*(4), 411–435. doi:10.1504/IJECRM.2018.096249

Ragins, J. E., & Greco, J. A. (2003). Customer relationship management and e-business: More than a software solution. *Review of Business, 24*(1), 25–30.

Rahimiparvar, N. (2014). eCRM Features that Affect Customer Attitude to Loyalty: A Case Study of a Sample of 402 University Students Enrolled in International Programs in Thailand. *AU-GSB e-Journal, 7*(2).

Rai, A., Patnayakuni, R., & Seth, M. (2006). Firm performance impacts of digitally enabled supply chain integration capabilities. *Management Information Systems Quarterly, 30*(2), 225–246. doi:10.2307/25148729

Ramadhan, W. P., Novianty, S. A., & Setianingsih, S. C. (2017). Sentiment analysis using multinomial logistic regression. In *International Conference on Control, Electronics, Renewable Energy and Communications (ICCREC)* (pp. 46-49). IEEE.

Ramos, C., Augusto, J. C., & Shapiro, D. (2008). Ambient intelligence—The next step for artificial intelligence. *IEEE Intelligent Systems*, *23*, 15–18.

Ramsey, E., Ibbotson, P., & McCole, P. (2006). Application of projectives techniques in an e-business research context. *International Journal of Market Research*, *48*(5), 551–573. doi:10.1177/147078530604800506

Rana, A., Bhat, A., & Rani, L. (2015). A classificatory scheme for antecedents of the sources of "online brand equity". *Journal of Research in Interactive Marketing*, *9*(4), 262–298. doi:10.1108/JRIM-02-2014-0008

Ranjan, R. (2014). Modeling and simulation in performance optimization of big data processing frameworks. *IEEE Cloud Computing.*, *1*(4), 14–19.

Rao, T. (2013). Impact of socio-economic characteristics of the bank customers on CRM. *Tactful Management Research Journal*, *1*, 1–8.

Rashwan, H. H. M., Mansi, A. L. M., & Hassan, H. E. (2019). The impact of the E- CRM (expected security and convenience of website design) on E- loyalty field study on commercial banks. *The Journal of Business and Retail Management Research*, *14*(1), 106–122. doi:10.24052/JBRMR/V14IS01/ART-10

Rashwan, H. H. M., Mansi, A. L., & Hassan, H. E. (2020). Exploring electronic-loyalty antecedents in Egyptian commercial banks; Electronic customer relationship management and banking electronic satisfaction. *The Journal of Business and Retail Management Research*, *14*(2). Advance online publication. doi:10.24052/JBRMR/V14IS02/ART-06

Rasool, A., Shah, F. A., & Tanveer, M. (2021). Relational dynamics between customer engagement, brand experience, and customer loyalty: An empirical investigation. *Journal of Internet Commerce*, *20*(3), 273–292. doi:10.1080/15332861.2021.1889818

Raubenheimer, J. E. (2004). An item selection procedure to maximize scale reliability and validity. *SA Journal of Industrial Psychology*, *30*(4), 59–64. doi:10.4102ajip.v30i4.168

Ravald, A., & Grönroos, C. (1996). The value concept and relationship marketing. *European Journal of Marketing*, *30*(2), 19–30. doi:10.1108/03090569610106626

Reichheld, F. F., & Sasser, J. W. E. (1990). Zero defections: Quality comes to services. *Harvard Business Review*, *68*(5), 105–111. PMID:10107082

Reichheld, F. F., & Schefter, P. (2000). E-loyalty: Your secret weapon on the web. *Harvard Business Review*, *78*(4), 105–113.

Reinartz, W., Krafft, M., & Hoyer, W. D. (2004). The customer relationship management process: Its measurement and impact on performance. *JMR, Journal of Marketing Research*, *41*(3), 293–305. doi:10.1509/jmkr.41.3.293.35991

Reiner, G. (2005). Customer-oriented improvement and evaluation of supply chain processes supported by simulation models. *International Journal of Production Economics*, *96*, 381–395.

Renjith, S., Sreekumar, A., & Jathavedan, M. (2020). An extensive study on the evolution of context-aware personalized travel recommender systems. *Information Processing & Management*, *57*(1), 102078. doi:10.1016/j.ipm.2019.102078

Research and Markets. (2019). *Impact of online travel - Thematic research*. Retrieved from https://www.researchandmarkets.com/reports/4895202/impact-of-online-travel-thematic-research?utm_source=dynamic&utm_medium=GNOM&utm_code=2jsqjr&utm_campaign=1336936+-+Online+Travel+Impact+-+Global+Online+Travel+Market+Forecast+to+Reach+US$372bn+by+2023&utm_exec=cari18gnomd

Rhee, Y. J. (2010). The Effects of e-CRM on Consumer Satisfaction and Repurchase Intention. *Journal of Korean Society of Clothing and Textiles*, *34*(8), 1277–1289. doi:10.5850/JKSCT.2010.34.8.1277

Richardson, T. (2005). *What do they want? Broadband! When do they want it? Now!* Available at: www.theregister.com

Ricketts, T. A., & Hornsby, B. W. (2005). Sound quality measures for speech in noise through a commercial hearing aid implementing. *Journal of the American Academy of Audiology*, *16*, 270–277.

Ringle, C. M., Wende, S., & Becker, J.-M. (2015). *SmartPLS 3*. Boenningstedt: SmartPLS GmbH. http://www.smartpls.com

Ritchie, B., & Brindley, C. (2005). ICT adoption by SMEs: Implications for relationships and management. *New Technology, Work and Employment*, *20*(3), 205–217. doi:10.1111/j.1468-005X.2005.00154.x

Roberts, K. (2005). *Lovemarks: The Future beyond Brands*. Powerhouse Books.

Rogers, E. M., & Beal, G. M. (1958). Projective techniques in interviewing farmers. *Journal of Marketing*, *23*(2), 177–183. doi:10.1177/002224295802300210

Rohm, A., Kaltcheva, V. D., & Milne, G. R. (2013). A mixed-method approach to examining brandconsumer interactions driven by social media. *Journal of Research in Interactive Marketing*, *7*(4), 295–311. doi:10.1108/JRIM-01-2013-0009

Roh, T. H., Ahn, C. K., & Han, I. (2005). The priority factor model for customer relationship management system success. *Expert Systems with Applications*, *28*(4), 641–654. Advance online publication. doi:10.1016/j.eswa.2004.12.021

Rolón, M., & Martínez, E. (2012). Agent-based modeling and simulation of an autonomic manufacturing execution system. *Computers in Industry*, *63*, 53–78.

Rossini, A. (2016). *State of Online Travel Agencies: Ctrip Joins Priceline and Expedia as Global Giant*. Retrieved from https://skift.com/2016/07/07/the-state-of-online-travel-agencies-strong-growth-but-big-challenges-ahead/

Rostami, M., Izadbin, A., Zakipour, M., & Rostami, S. (2016). Assessing electronic customer relationship management (E-CRM) readiness and its impact on banking quality of service (case study: Saderat Bank Branches-West of. *International Journal of Humanities and Cultural Studies*, *2*(4). http://www.ijhcs.com/index.php/ijhcs/article/view/537

Rowley, J. (2008). Understanding digital content marketing. *Journal of Marketing Management*, *24*(5–6), 517–540. Advance online publication. doi:10.1362/026725708X325977

Ryals, L. (2005). Making customer relationship management work: The measurement and profitable management of customer relationships. *Journal of Marketing*, *69*(4), 252–261. doi:10.1509/jmkg.2005.69.4.252

Ryals, L., & Humphries, A. S. (2007). Managing key business-to-business relationships. *Journal of Service Research*, *9*(2), 312–326. doi:10.1177/1094670507299380

Safari, M., & Safahani, N. (2015). An empirical model to explain the effects of electronic customer relationship management on customer e-satisfaction and e-loyalty: Evidence from Iranian service shopping websites. *Journal of Internet Banking and Commerce*.

Saghaei, M., Ghaderi, H., & Soleimani, H. (2020). Design and optimization of biomass electricity supply chain with uncertainty in material quality, availability and market demand. *Energy*, *197*, 117165.

Saleem, Z., & Rashid, K. (2011). Relationship between customer satisfaction and mobile banking adoption in Pakistan. *International Journal of Trade, Economics and Finance*, *2*(6), 537.

Sam, K. M., & Chatwin, C. R. (2015, December). Evaluating the effectiveness of online product planning and layout tools in online apparel shopping. In *IEEE International Conference on Industrial Engineering and Engineering Management (IEEM)* (pp. 635-639). 10.1109/IEEM.2015.7385725

Sánchez-Casado, N., Cegarra-Navarro, J. G., & Tomaseti-Solano, E. (2015, April). The use of Social Networking Sites to create customer knowledge. In *European Conference on Intangibles and Intellectual Capital* (p. 441). Academic Conferences International Limited.

Saqib, N., & Shah, A. M. (2021). Development of empirically-based customer-derived positioning taxonomy for FMCG sector in the Indian emerging market. *Young Consumers*.

Saris, W. E., & Gallhofer, I. N. (2007). *Design Evaluation and Analysis of Questionnaires for Survey Research*. Wiley. doi:10.1002/9780470165195

Sarkis, J., Meade, L. M., & Talluri, S. (2004). E-logistics and the natural environment. *Supply Chain Management*, *9*(4), 303–312. doi:10.1108/13598540410550055

Saunders, M., Lewis, P., & Thornhill, A. (2009). *Research Methods for Business Students* (5th ed.). Prentice Hall.

Savitri, C., Hurriyati, R., Wibowo, L., & Hendrayati, H. (2022). The role of social media marketing and brand image on smartphone purchase intention. *International Journal of Data and Network Science*, *6*(1), 185–192. doi:10.5267/j.ijdns.2021.9.009

Saxena, N., Gera, N., Nagdev, K., & Fatta, D. D. (2021). A conjoint analysis of customers' preferences for e-banking channels. *International Journal of Electronic Marketing and Retailing*, *12*(1), 52–68. doi:10.1504/IJEMR.2021.112254

Schaal, D. (2016, Nov 28). *Exclusive: Ctrip CEO on Global Ambitions, Skyscanner Buy and the Priceline Relationship*. Retrieved from https://skift.com/2016/11/28/exclusive-ctrip-ceo-on-global-ambitions-skyscanner-buy -and-the-priceline-relationship/

Schivinski, B., & Dabrowski, D. (2014). *The consumer-based brand equity inventory: scale construct and validation* (No. 4/2014 (22)). GUT FME Working Paper Series A.

Schlegel, G. L. (2014). Utilizing big data and predictive analytics to manage supply chain risk. *The Journal of Business Forecasting.*, *33*(4), 11.

Schlegelmilch, B. B. (2022). Global branding and communication. In *Global Marketing Strategy* (pp. 253–288). Springer.

Schulze, C., Schöler, L., & Skiera, B. (2015). Customizing social media marketing. *MIT Sloan Management Review*, *56*(2), 8–10.

Seify, M., Tabaeeian, R. A., & Khoshfetrat, A. (2020). Investigating factors in implementation of electronic customer relationship management and its consequences in private hospitals in Isfahan city. *International Journal of Electronic Customer Relationship Management*, *12*(3), 225–245. doi:10.1504/IJECRM.2020.110040

Seo, E. J., & Park, J. W. (2018). A study on the effects of social media marketing activities on brand equity and customer response in the airline industry. *Journal of Air Transport Management*, *66*, 36–41.

Šerić, M., & Gil-Saura, I. (2012). ICT, IMC, and brand equity in high-quality hotels of Dalmatia: An analysis from guest perceptions. *Journal of Hospitality Marketing & Management*, *21*(8), 821–851. doi:10.1080/19368623.2012.633211

SFA. (2007). *Small Firms Association (Ireland), CSO Small Business Report*. Available at: www.sfa.ie

Shahin, A., Gharibpoor, M., Teymouri, S., & Iraj, E. B. (2013). Studying the influence of e-CRM on web-based brand personality–the case of Mellat Bank. *International Journal of Business Information Systems*, *13*(4), 453–470. doi:10.1504/IJBIS.2013.055301

Shahnavazi, A., Nemati Gonbaghi, M., Teymouri, S. F., & Ghasemi Dakdare, B. (2020). Determining the Key Indicators affecting Electronic Customer Relationship Management (e-CRM) Using an integration of balanced scorecard and fuzzy screening techniques (Case Study: Companies Covered by Parsian Data-Processors Group). *Iranian Journal of Optimization*, *12*(1), 21–32.

Shao, G., Shin, S. J., & Jain, S. (2014). Data analytics using simulation for smart manufacturing. In *Proceedings of the Winter Simulation Conference*. IEEE.

Sharma, A., Sharma, S., & Chaudhary, M. (2020). Are small travel agencies ready for digital marketing? Views of travel agency managers. *Tourism Management*, *79*, 104078. doi:10.1016/j.tourman.2020.104078

Sharma, M., & Garg, N. (2016). Inventory control and big data. In *Optimal Inventory Control and Management Techniques* (pp. 222–235). IGI Global.

Sharma, R. (2016). Effect of celebrity endorsements on dimensions of customer-based brand equity: Empirical evidence from Indian luxury market. *Journal of Creative Communications*, *11*(3), 264–281.

Sharma, R., Kamble, S. S., Gunasekaran, A., Kumar, V., & Kumar, A. (2020). A systematic literature review on machine learning applications for sustainable agriculture supply chain performance. *Computers & Operations Research*, *119*, 104926.

Shen, K., & Khalifa, M. (2008). Exploring multidimensional conceptualization of social presence in the context of online communities. *International Journal of Human-Computer Interaction*, *24*(7), 722–748. doi:10.1080/10447310802335789

Shimp, T. A., & Madden, T. J. (1988). Consumer-Object relations: A conceptual framework based analogously on Sternberg's triangular theory of love. *Advances in Consumer Research. Association for Consumer Research (U. S.)*, *15*, 163–168.

Shin, J. K., & Lee, S. Y. (2018). The Effects of the Delivery Service Quality of Online Fresh Food Shopping Malls on E-Satisfaction and Repurchase Intention of Online Customers. *East Asian Journal of Business Economics*, *6*(2), 14–27. doi:10.20498/eajbe.2018.6.2.14

Siaw, G. A., & Gitau, J. K. (2020). *Aspects of Electronic Customer Relationship Management and Guest Satisfaction: A Perspective of 4-Star Hotels in Nairobi County, Kenya*. Academic Press.

Sigala, M. (2011). eCRM 2.0 applications and trends: The use and perceptions of Greek tourism firms of social networks and intelligence. *Computers in Human Behavior*, *27*(2), 655–661. doi:10.1016/j.chb.2010.03.007

Simmons, G., Armstrong, G. A., & Durkin, M. G. (2008). A conceptualization of the determinants of small business website adoption: Setting the research agenda. *International Small Business Journal*, *26*(3), 351–389. doi:10.1177/0266242608088743

Singagerda, F. (2020). How much media marketing and brand image reinforce ecommerce consumer loyalty? *International Journal of Data and Network Science*, *4*(4), 389–396.

Sivaraks, P., Krairit, D., & Tang, J. C. S. (2011). Effects of e-CRM on customer-bank relationship quality and outcomes: The case of Thailand. *The Journal of High Technology Management Research*, *22*(2), 141–157. Advance online publication. doi:10.1016/j.hitech.2011.09.006

Smith, D. C., & Park, C. W. (1992). The effects of brand extensions on market share and advertising efficiency. *JMR, Journal of Marketing Research*, *29*(3), 296–313.

Smith, G. (2004). Brand image transfer through sponsorship: A consumer learning perspective. *Journal of Marketing Management*, *20*(3–4), 457–474.

Sohail, M. S. (2022). Understanding consumer engagement in online brand communities: An application of self-expansion theory. *Journal of Marketing Analytics*, 1-13.

Sohar International School (n.d.a). *Instagram page*. https://www.abq.edu.om/sohar-international-school/

Sohar International School. (n.d.b). *Facebook page*. https://www.facebook.com/abqsohar

Soleimani, H., Chaharlang, Y., & Ghaderi, H. (2018). Collection and distribution of returned remanufactured products in a vehicle routing problem with pickup and delivery considering sustainable and green criteria. *Journal of Cleaner Production*, *172*, 960–970.

Soudagar, R., Iyer, V., & Hildebrand, V. (2012). *The customer experience edge: Technology and techniques for delivering an enduring, profitable, and positive experience to your customers*. McGraw-Hill.

Souza, G. C. (2014). Supply chain analytics. *Business Horizons*, *57*(5), 595–605.

Springen, K., & Miller, A. (1990, July 9). Sequels for the Shelf. *Newsweek*, 42-43.

Srinivasan, R., & Swink, M. (2018). An investigation of visibility and flexibility as complements to supply chain analytics: An organizational information processing theory perspective. *Production and Operations Management*, *27*(10), 1849–1867.

Srull, T. K., & Wyer, R. S. (1989). Person memory and judgment. *Psychological Review*, *96*(1), 58–83.

Stich, V., Jordan, F., Birkmeier, M., Oflazgil, K., Reschke, J., & Diews, A. (2015). Big data technology for resilient failure management in production systems. In *IFIP International Conference on Advances in Production Management Systems*. Cham: Springer.

Stone, E. (1978). *Research Methods in Organizational Behaviour*. Scott Foresman.

Stopford, B. (2018). *DesigninFg Event-Driven Systems*. O'Reilly Media, Incorporated.

Straits, B. C., & Singleton, R. A. (2011). *Social Research: Approaches and fundamentals* (5th ed.). Oxford University Press Inc.

Straub, D. W. (1989). Validating instruments in MIS research. *Management Information Systems Quarterly*, *13*(2), 147–169. doi:10.2307/248922

Street, C. T., & Meister, D. B. (2004). Small business growth and internal transparency: The role of information systems. *Management Information Systems Quarterly*, *28*(3), 473–506. doi:10.2307/25148647

Sturiale, L., & Scuderi, A. (2016). The digital economy: New e-business strategies for food Italian system. *International Journal of Electronic Marketing and Retailing*, *7*(4), 287–310. doi:10.1504/IJEMR.2016.080806

Suh, N. P. (2001). *Axiomatic Design: Advances and Applications*. Oxford University Press.

Swaminathan, V., Fox, R. J., & Reddy, S. K. (2001). The impact of brand extension introduction on choice. *Journal of Marketing*, *65*(4), 1–15.

Swamy, L. N., & Gorabal, J. V. (2020). Logistic regression-based classification for reviews analysis on E-commerce based applications. In *Frontiers in intelligent computing: Theory and applications* (pp. 323–334). Springer. doi:10.1007/978-981-13-9920-6_34

Swift, R. (2001). Accelerating Customer Relationship using CRM and Relationship Technologies. Prentice Hall Inc.

Tadayon, M. A., Ebrahimzade Dastgerdi, R., Gheitani, A., & Sadeghi, M. (2021). Determining the Dimensions of Electronic Customer Relationship Management (E-CRM) in Gharzolhasaneh Mehr Iran Bank. *Journal of System Management*, *7*(4), 93–112.

Tafesse, W. (2016). An experiential model of consumer engagement in social media. *Journal of Product & Brand Management, 25*(5), 424-434.

Tahar, A., Riyadh, H. A., Sofyani, H., & Purnomo, W. E. (2020). Perceived ease of use, perceived usefulness, perceived security and intention to use e-filing: The role of technology readiness. *The Journal of Asian Finance, Economics, and Business*, *7*(9), 537–547. doi:10.13106/jafeb.2020.vol7.no9.537

Tanner, J., & Raymond, M. (2015). *Principles of marketing*. University of Minnesota Libraries Publishing. Retrieved from http://lib.hpu.edu.vn/handle/123456789/21516

Tan, X., Yen, D. C., & Fang, X. (2002). Internet integrated customer relationship management –a key success factor for companies in the e-commerce arena. *Journal of Computer Information Systems*, *42*(3), 77–86.

Tarasova, A., Polukhina, A., & Arnaberdiyev, A. (2020). Information Support for Travel Agency Performance. *International Journal of Recent Contributions from Engineering Science &. IT, 8*(4), 69-76.

Tariq, M., Jamil, A., Ahmad, M. S., & Ramayah, T. (2019). Modeling the effectiveness of electronic customer relationship management (E-CRM) systems: Empirical evidence from Pakistan. *Revista Gestão & Tecnologia, 19*, 77–100. doi:10.20397/2177-6652/0.v0i0.1747

Tasci, A. D. A., Khalilzadeh, J., & Uysal, M. (2017). Network analysis of the caucasus' image. *Curr. Issues Tour.*, 1–26. doi:10.1080/13683500.2017.1320362

Tauber, E. M. (1972). Why do people shop? *Journal of Marketing*, 46–49.

Taylor, S. A., & Hunter, G. L. (2002). The impact of loyalty with e-CRM software and e-services. *International Journal of Service Industry Management, 13*(5), 452–474. doi:10.1108/09564230210447931

Taylor, S., & Todd, P. (1995). Decomposition and crossover effects in the theory of planned behavior: A study of consumer adoption intentions. *International Journal of Research in Marketing, 12*(2), 137–155. doi:10.1016/0167-8116(94)00019-K

Taylor, V. A., & Bearden, W. O. (2003). Ad spending on brand extensions: Does similarity matter? *Journal of Brand Management, 11*(1), 63–74.

Tecuci, G. (2012). Artificial intelligence. *Wiley Interdisciplinary Reviews: Computational Statistics, 4*, 168–180.

Thomas, J. S., & Kumar, R. (2004). Getting the most out of all of your customers. *Harvard Business Review*, 116–123. PMID:15241958

Thompson, B. (2004). Exploratory and confirmatory factor analysis: Understanding concepts and applications. Academic Press.

Thomson, M., MacInnis, D.J., & Whan Park, C. (2005). The ties that bind: Measuring the strength of consumers' emotional attachments to brands. *Journal of Consumer Psychology, 15*(1), 77-91.

Tian, J., & Wang, S. (2017). Signaling Service Quality via Website e-CRM Features: More Gains for Smaller and Lesser Known Hotels. *Journal of Hospitality & Tourism Research (Washington, D.C.), 41*(2), 211–245. doi:10.1177/1096348014525634

Tornatzky, L. G., Fleischer, M., & Chakrabarti, A. K. (1990). *Processes of technological innovation*. Lexington Books.

Tortosa, V., Moliner, M. A., & Sanchez, J. (2009). Internal market orientation and its influence on organisational performance. *European Journal of Marketing, 43*(11/12), 1435–1456. doi:10.1108/03090560910989975

Trkman, P., McCormack, K., De Oliveira, M. P., & Ladeira, M. B. (2010). The impact of business analytics on supply chain performance. *Decision Support Systems, 49*(3), 318–327.

Trochim, W. M. (2006). *Research Methods: Knowledge Base*. http //www. social research methods. Net/kb

Tsou, H. T., & Hsu, H. Y. (2017). Self-Service technology investment, electronic customer relationship management practices, and service innovation capability. In *Marketing at the Confluence between Entertainment and Analytics* (pp. 477–481). Springer. doi:10.1007/978-3-319-47331-4_92

Tusell-Rey, C. C., Nieto, Ó. C., & Padilla, R. T. (2020). Application of data engineering in automatic information analysis for electronic customer relationship management: A survey. *International Journal of Emerging Trends in Engineering Research, 8*(9), 5939–5946. doi:10.30534/ijeter/2020/167892020

Tweneboah-Koduah, E. Y., & Farley, A. Y. D. (2016). Relationship between customer satisfaction and customer loyalty in the retail banking sector of Ghana. *International Journal of Business and Management*, *11*(1), 249. doi:10.5539/ijbm.v11n1p249

Tzavlopoulos, Y. E., Gotzmani, K., Andronikidis, A., & Vassiliadis, C. A. (2019). Determining the impact of e-commerce quality on customers' perceived risk, satisfaction, value and loyalty. *International Journal of Quality and Service Sciences*, *11*(4), 576–587. doi:10.1108/IJQSS-03-2019-0047

Unitt, M., & Jones, I. C. (1999). EDI—The granddaddy of electronic commerce. *BT Technology Journal*, *17*(3), 17–23. doi:10.1023/A:1009664017258

Usman, U., Jalal, A., & Musa, M. (2012). The impact of electronic customer relationship management on consumer's behavior. *International Journal of Advances in Engineering and Technology*, *3*(1), 500–504.

Utomo, S. M., Sandjaja, J. R., Yustiawan, W. S., & Alamsyah, D. P. (2021, September). Consumer Behavior and Sustainable Performance: Perceived of E-Service Quality on Online Shopping. In *2021 9th International Conference on Cyber and IT Service Management (CITSM)* (pp. 1-4). IEEE.

Van Der Zee, D. J., & Van Der Vorst, J. G. A. J. (2005). A Modeling Framework for Supply Chain Simulation. *Opportunities for Improved Decision Making*, *36*, 65–95.

Van Riel, A. C., Lemmink, J., & Ouwersloot, H. (2001). Consumer evaluations of service brand extensions. *Journal of Service Research*, *3*(3), 220–231.

Vasudevan, P., & Arokiasamy, L. (2021). Online Shopping Among Young Generation in Malaysia. *Electronic Journal of Business and Management*, *6*(1), 31–38.

Venkatesha, G. K. (2021). Trend forming FMCG sector in India-a study. *International Journal of Multidisciplinary Educational Research*, *11*(3), 81-87.

Venkatesh, V., & Bala, H. (2008). Technology acceptance model 3 and a research agenda on interventions. *Decision Sciences*, *39*(2), 273–315. doi:10.1111/j.1540-5915.2008.00192.x

Venkatesh, V., Speier, C., & Morris, M. G. (2002). User acceptance enablers in individual decision making about technology: Toward an integrated model. *Decision Sciences*, *33*(2), 297–316. doi:10.1111/j.1540-5915.2002.tb01646.x

Venkatesh, V., Thong, J. Y., & Xu, X. (2012). Consumer acceptance and use of information technology: Extending the unified theory of acceptance and use of technology. *Management Information Systems Quarterly*, *36*(1), 157–178. doi:10.2307/41410412

Verhoef, P. C., Neslin, S. A., & Vroomen, B. (2007). Multichannel customer management: Understanding the research shopper. *International Journal of Research in Marketing*, *24*(2), 129–148. doi:10.1016/j.ijresmar.2006.11.002

Verhoef, P. C., Reinartz, W. J., & Krafft, M. (2010). Customer engagement as a new perspective in customer management. *Journal of Service Research*, *13*(3), 247–252. doi:10.1177/1094670510375461

Verhoef, P., Reinartz, W., & Krafft, M. (2010). Customer engagement as a new perspective in customer management. *Journal of Service Research*, *13*(3), 247–252.

Vila, T. D., & González, E. A. (2022). eCRM. In Encyclopedia of Tourism Management and Marketing. Edward Elgar Publishing.

Vila, T. D., González, E. A., Vila, N. A., & Brea, J. A. F. (2021). Indicators of Website Features in the User Experience of E-Tourism Search and Metasearch Engines. *Journal of Theoretical and Applied Electronic Commerce Research*, *16*(1), 18–36. doi:10.4067/S0718-18762021000100103

Vivek, S. D., Beatty, S. E., Dalela, V., & Morgan, R. (2014). A generalized multidimensional scale for measuring customer engagement. *Journal of Marketing Theory and Practice*, *22*, 401–420. doi:10.2753/MTP1069-6679220404

Vivek, S. D., Beatty, S. E., & Morgan, R. (2012). Customer engagement: Exploring customer relationships beyond purchase. *Journal of Marketing Theory and Practice*, *20*, 122–146. doi:10.2753/ MTP1069-6679200201

Vogt, C. A. (2011). Customer relationship management in tourism: Management needs and research applications. *Journal of Travel Research*, *50*(4), 356–364. doi:10.1177/0047287510368140

Volckner, F., & Sattler, H. (2006). Drivers of brand extension success. *Journal of Marketing*, *70*(April), 18–34.

Volckner, F., & Sattler, H. (2007). Empirical generalizability of consumer evaluations of brand extensions. *International Journal of Research in Marketing*, *24*, 149–162.

Volckner, F., Sattler, H., & Kaufmann, G. (2008). Image feedback effects of brand extensions: Evidence from a longitudinal field study. *Marketing Letters*, *19*(2), 109–124.

Vo, N. N., Liu, S., Li, X., & Xu, G. (2021). Leveraging unstructured call log data for customer churn prediction. *Knowledge-Based Systems*, *212*, 106586. doi:10.1016/j.knosys.2020.106586

Vyas, P. H., & Patel, A. V. (2004). Customising e-CRM Strategy in eMarketing. *Delhi Business Review*, *5*(2), 67–79.

Wang, F., & Head, M. (2007). How can the Web Help Build Customer Relationships? An Empirical Study on E-Tailing. *Information & Management*, *44*(2), 115–129. doi:10.1016/j.im.2006.10.008

Wang, F., Head, M., & Archer, N. (2002). E-tailing: An analysis of web impacts on the retail market. *The Journal of Business Strategy*, *19*(1), 73–93. doi:10.54155/jbs.19.1.73-93

Wang, G., Gunasekaran, A., & Ngai, E. W. (2018). Distribution network design with big data: Model and analysis. *Annals of Operations Research*, *270*(1-2), 539–551.

Wang, G., Gunasekaran, A., Ngai, E. W., & Papadopoulos, T. (2016). Big data analytics in logistics and supply chain management: Certain investigations for research and applications. *International Journal of Production Economics*, *176*, 98–110.

Wang, H.-J., & Horng, S.-C. (2016). Exploring green brand associations through a network analysis approach. *Psychology and Marketing*, *33*(1), 20–35. https://dx.doi.org/10.1002/mar.20854

Wang, R., & Chan-Olmsted, S. (2020). Content marketing strategy of branded YouTube channels. *Journal of Media Business Studies*, *17*(3-4), 294–316. Advance online publication. doi:10.1080/16522354.2020.1783130

Warfield, B. (2009). *Webinar conducted by Bob Warfield, CEO of Helpstream A Social CRM Manifesto: How to Succeed with the CRM Virtuous Cycle*. Academic Press.

Watson, B. C. (2011). Barcode empires: Politics, digital technology, and comparative retail firm strategies. *Journal of Industry, Competition and Trade*, *11*(3), 309–324. doi:10.100710842-011-0109-2

Webb, J. R. (1992). *Understanding and Designing Market Research*. Academic Press.

Webster, F. E. Jr. (1992). The changing role of marketing in the corporation. *Journal of Marketing*, *56*(4), 1–17. doi:10.1177/002224299205600402

Wei, J. (2021). The impacts of perceived risk and negative emotions on the service recovery effect for online travel agencies: The moderating role of corporate reputation. *Frontiers in Psychology*, *12*, 685351. doi:10.3389/fpsyg.2021.685351 PMID:34135837

Weiss, A. M., Anderson, E., & Maclnnis, D. J. (1999). Reputation management as a motivation for sales structure decisions. *Journal of Marketing*, *63*, 74–89.

Wichmann, P., Brintrup, A., Baker, S., Woodall, P., & McFarlane, D. (2020). Extracting supply chain maps from news articles using deep neural networks. *International Journal of Production Research*, *58*, 5320–5336.

Winer, R. S. (2001). A framework for customer relationship management. *California Management Review*, *43*(4), 89-105.

Woodcock, N., & Green, A. (2010). *Social CRM as a business strategy, the customer framework*. Retrieved from http://customerframework.com

Xue, X., Li, X., Shen, Q., & Wang, Y. (2005). An agent-based framework for supply chain coordination in construction. *Automation in Construction*, *14*, 413–430.

Xu, F., Pan, Z., & Xia, R. (2020). E-commerce product review sentiment classification based on a naïve Bayes continuous learning framework. *Information Processing & Management*, *57*(5), 102221. doi:10.1016/j.ipm.2020.102221

Yang, S., Lin, S., Carlson, J. R., & Ross, W. T. Jr. (2016). Brand engagement on social media: Will firms' social media efforts influence search engine advertising effectiveness? *Journal of Marketing Management*, *32*(5-6), 526–557.

Yang, X., Audhkhasi, K., Rosenberg, A., Thomas, S., Ramabhadran, B., & Hasegawa-Johnson, M. (2018). Joint modeling of accents and acoustics for multi-accent speech recognition. In *2018 IEEE International Conference on Acoustics, Speech and Signal Processing (ICASSP)*. IEEE.

Yang, Z., & Babapour, H. (2022). Critical variables for assessing the effectiveness of electronic customer relationship management systems in online shopping. *Kybernetes*. Advance online publication. doi:10.1108/K-10-2021-0952

Yaya, L. H. P., Marimon, F., & Casadesus, M. (2016). Customer Satisfaction and the Role of Demographic Characteristics in Online Banking. In *Web-Based Services: Concepts, Methodologies, Tools and Applications* (pp. 1786–1802). IGI Global.

Yi, Y., & Nataraajan, R. (2018). Customer satisfaction in Asia. *Psychology and Marketing*, *35*(6), 387–391. doi:10.1002/mar.21093

Yoo, B., & Donthu, N. (2001). Developing and validating a multidimensional consumer-based brand equity scale. *Journal of Business Research*, *52*(1), 1–14.

Yoon, J. H., Chung, J. B., & Kim, Y. M. (2008). A Study on the e-CRM, Customer Satisfaction, Repurchase Intention and Word of Mouth Intention in the Internet Shopping Mall. *Journal of Information Systems*, *17*(1), 63–82. doi:10.5859/KAIS.2008.17.1.063

YooY.LyytinenK.BolandR.BerenteN.GaskinJ.SchutzD.SrinivasanN. (2010). The Next Wave of Digital Innovation: Opportunities and Challenges: A Report on the Research Workshop' Digital Challenges in Innovation Research. *Available at* SSRN 1622170. doi:10.2139/ssrn.1622170

You, F., Wassick, J. M., & Grossmann, I. E. (2009). Risk management for a global supply chain planning under uncertainty: Models and algorithms. *AIChE Journal. American Institute of Chemical Engineers*, *55*, 931–946.

Yu, W., Jacobs, M. A., Salisbury, W. D., & Enns, H. (2013). The effects of supply chain integration on customer satisfaction and financial performance: An organisational learning perspective. *International Journal of Production Economics*, *146*(1), 346–358. doi:10.1016/j.ijpe.2013.07.023

Zailskaitė-Jakštė, L. (2018). *Consumer engagement behaviour in social media communication impact on brand equity* (Doctoral dissertation). Kauno Technologijos Universitetas.

Zailskaite-Jakštė, L., Damaševičius, R., Ostreika, A., & Anubhav, K. (2018, July). Consumers Engagement Behaviour in Social Media: Do Different Brand Categories Matter? In *ECRM 2018 17th European Conference on Research Methods in Business and Management* (p. 444). Academic Conferences and Publishing Limited.

Zaim, H., Ramdani, M., & Haddi, A. (2020). E-CRM Success Factors as Determinants of Customer Satisfaction Rate in Retail Website. *International Journal of Computer Information Systems and Industrial Management Applications*, *12*, 82–92.

Zaman, K., Bibi, S., Arshad, A., & Shahzad, A. (2012). Customer Loyalty in FMCG Sector of Pakistan. *Information Management and Business Review*, *4*(1), 41–48. doi:10.22610/imbr.v4i1.962

Zarbakhshnia, N., Soleimani, H., & Ghaderi, H. (2018). Sustainable third-party reverse logistics provider evaluation and selection using fuzzy SWARA and developed fuzzy COPRAS in the presence of risk criteria. *Applied Soft Computing*, *65*, 307–319.

Zatalini, M. A., & Pamungkas, T. N. (2017). Exploring the Success Factors of E-CRM Implementation on B2C E-Commerce: Satisfaction and Loyalty A Conceptual Framework. *Jurnal Ekonomi Bisnis*, *22*(2), 94–106.

Zephaniah, C. O., Ogba, I. E., & Izogo, E. E. (2020). Examining the effect of customers' perception of bank marketing communication on customer loyalty. *Scientific American*, *8*, e00383.

Zhang, J., Chen, M., Sun, H., Li, D., & Wang, Z. (2020). Object semantics sentiment correlation analysis enhanced image sentiment classification. *Knowledge-Based Systems*, *191*, 105245.

Zhang, L., Wang, S., & Liu, B. (2018). Deep learning for sentiment analysis: A survey. *Wiley Interdisciplinary Reviews. Data Mining and Knowledge Discovery*, *8*(4). Advance online publication. doi:10.1002/widm.1253

Zheng, W., Zhou, R., Zhang, Z., Zhong, Y., Wang, S., Wei, Z., & Ji, H. (2019). Understanding the tourist mobility using GPS: How similar are the tourists? *Tourism Management*, *71*, 54–66. doi:10.1016/j.tourman.2018.09.019

Zhiliang, D., & Lihua, Y. (2015). Research on CRM system in online travel agent in the context of Internet. *International Journal of Simulation Systems, Science & Technology*, *16*(5B), 11.1-11.6.

Zhong, R. Y., Huang, G. Q., & Lan, S. L. (2014). Shopfloor logistics management using rfid-enabled big data under physical internet. *Proceeding of 1st International Physical Internet Conference*, 1-14.

Zhong, R. Y., Huang, G. Q., Lan, S., Dai, Q. Y., Chen, X., & Zhang, T. (2015). A big data approach for logistics trajectory discovery from RFID-enabled production data. *International Journal of Production Economics*, *165*, 260–272.

Zimmer, M. R., & Bhat, S. (2004). The reciprocal effects of extension quality and fit on parent brand attitude. *Journal of Product and Brand Management*, *13*(1), 37–46.

Zollo, L., Filieri, R., Rialti, R., & Yoon, S. (2020). Unpacking the relationship between social media marketing and brand equity: The mediating role of consumers' benefits and experience. *Journal of Business Research*, *117*, 256–267.

Zontanos, G., & Anderson, A. R. (2004). Relationships marketing and small business: An exploration of links in theory and practice. *Qualitative Market Research*, *7*(3), 228–236. doi:10.1108/13522750410540236

About the Contributors

George Asamoah is a lecturer in the Ghana Institute of Journalism. He has more than 15 years of solid B2B marketing experience, delivering profitable solutions to drive sales, attract and maintain customers, and building a solid corporate brand. He has special talent for enhancing corporate marketability through electronic and print marketing tools as well as clear, effective corporate messaging. He has gained extensive experience communicating with vendors and event support personnel, and effectively managed overseas marketing team. Dr. Asamoah has had over five years teaching experience and his areas of interest are Entrepreneurship, Social Media Marketing, Principles of Marketing, Marketing Communications, Marketing Management, Strategic Marketing Planning, Business Communications, Marketing Research, Consumer Behaviour, Sales Management and Products/Brands Management.

Mimi Mei Wa Chan received the B.Sc. in Information Management and M.Sc. in Library and Information Management degrees from the University of Hong Kong. She is currently working as a Library Assistant in an academic library in Hong Kong. Her research interests are in Librarianship and Information Science.

Dickson K. W. Chiu received the B.Sc. (Hons.) degree in Computer Studies from the University of Hong Kong in 1987. He received the M.Sc. (1994) and the Ph.D. (2000) degrees in Computer Science from the Hong Kong University of Science and Technology (HKUST). He started his own computer consultant company while studying part-time. He has also taught at several universities in Hong Kong. His teaching and research interest is in Library & Information Management, Service Computing, and E-learning with a cross-disciplinary approach, involving library and information management, e-learning, e-business, service sciences, and databases. The results have been widely published in around 300 international publications (most of them have been indexed by SCI/-E, SSCI, and EI, such as top journals MIS Quarterly, Computer & Education, Government Information Quarterly, Decision Support Systems, Information Sciences, Knowledge-Based Systems, Expert Systems with Application, Information Systems Frontiers, IEEE Transactions, including many taught master and undergraduate project results and around 20 edited books. He received a best paper award in the 37th Hawaii International Conference on System Sciences in 2004. He is an Editor (-in-chief) of Library Hi Tech, a prestigious journal indexed by SSCI (impact factor 2.357). He is the Editor-in-chief Emeritus of the International Journal on Systems and Service-Oriented Engineering (founding) and International Journal of Organizational and Collective Intelligence, and serves in the editorial boards of several international journals. He co-founded several international workshops and co-edited several journal special issues. He also served as a program committee member for around 300 international conferences and workshops. Dr. Chiu is a Senior Member of both the ACM and the IEEE, and a life member of the Hong Kong Computer Society. According to Google Scholar, he has over 5,000 citations, h-index 38, i-10 index 109, ranked worldwide 1st in "LIS," "m-learning," and "e-services."

Joshua Kofi Doe is a lecturer in the Ghana Institute of Journalism and a teacher by profession. Prior to becoming an academic, he worked in the tourism industry and spearheaded the establishment of a virtual office where marketing and transactions could be completed online. His research interest is in the application of technological innovation to marketing activities for institutional growth and efficiency. He has two "best paper" awards from to his credit. One from "the 12th IADIS International Conference Information Systems 2019" and the other from "The 17th International Conference on Web Based Communities and Social Media 2020".

Sadaf Fatima is a research scholar from Department of Business Administration, Faculty of Management Studies and Research, Aligarh Muslim University, Aligarh, India. She has earned MBA degree from the same University. Her specialization is HRM and Finance. She has attended conferences and presented many papers at national and international level. Her areas of interest are Organizational Behavior, Organizational Development, SHRM and HRM.

Najmul Hoda is an Assistant Professor in Department of Business Administration at the College of Business, Umm Al-Qura University. He completed his PhD in Management from Birla Institute of Technology, India in 2013. His dissertation focused on faith-based microfinance institutions. His main research interests are social banking, sustainable finance, entrepreneurial finance, and pedagogy in higher education. He is associated with several WoS/Scopus indexed journals as reviewer/advisor.

Shad Ahmad Khan is working as an Assistant Professor in College of Business, University of Buraimi, Sultanate of Oman.

Manoj Kumar currently working as Associate Professor in the Institute of Management, Commerce and Economics at Shri Ramswaroop Memorial University, having an experience of more than 15 years in the field of accounting and finance. He holds a doctorate degree in Commerce, from the Department of Commerce, University of Lucknow. His area of research includes Mobile Banking, Artificial Intelligence, Insolvency Resolution, Management Accounting. He is having many publications in various Scopus Indexed and national and international journal, presented many papers in national and international conferences and attended large number FDPs and QIP's to update his knowledge.

Hesham Magd has more than twenty-five years of combined experience in traditional and nontraditional higher education teaching, training, consultancy, community development, academic administration, curricula design, organizational change and development, distinguished research and scholarly writing, resulting in Honors, awards and recognition for academic excellence and outstanding achievement. Hesham is currently heavily involved in International accreditation and reshaping the aviation education in Oman and offer strategic direction on the direction of the sector In his previous appointments throughout the world in British, European, and American oriented Curriculum (Middle East, USA, and UK), he has been the driving force behind strategic institutional development during the time of profound change in the Higher Education in the Middle East. Hesham has broad knowledge of the UK, USA, Middle East University Systems, and Quality and accreditation systems (AACSB, AABI, OAAA, NCAAA…).

Muhammad Saleem is working as a lecturer in College of Business, University of Buraimi. He is specialized in the area of marketing.

Rinki Verma currently working as Associate Professor in the School of Management at Babu Banarsi Das University, Lucknow, having an experience of more than 13 years in the area of Marketing and General Management. She holds doctorate degree from MNNIT, Allahabad. Her research area includes Public Private Partnership, Internet Advertising, E- Service Quality, Artificial Intelligence. She is having publications in various Scopus indexed, and reputed national & international journal and presented research papers in national and international conferences organized by reputed institutions and attended many MDPs, QIP's etc. She has been a trainer in the training programs on Conflict Management, Behavioral Change, Change Management, etc for Primary Medical Staff (PMS-DOCTORS) and senior officers (Non-Defense Academy).

Index

D

E

F

I

K

L

M

N

O

P

R

S

T

www.ingramcontent.com/pod-product-compliance
Lightning Source LLC
LaVergne TN
LVHW080602300926
849162LV00005B/1028